The
Religion
That Started
in a Hat

To Scott Preston

Josh Kittler
Rom. 8:28

The Religion That Started in a Hat

A Reference Manual *for* Christians *who* Witness *to* Mormons

Jack Kettler

MCP Books
2301 Lucien Way #415
Maitland, FL 32751
407.339.4217
www.mcpbooks.com

Mr. Kettler has worked in Corporate America for 38 years, served as a Ruling Elder in the Orthodox Presbyterian Church, is a successful Nutraceutical Representative and an active member of the blogosphere. Visit him online at http://www.thereligionthatstartedinahat.com.

ISBN-13: 978-1-63505-016-5
LCCN: 2016910992

Distributed by Itasca Books

Typeset by Anna Kiryanova
Illustrations by Ron Adair

Printed in the United States of America

1

Sola scriptura

(BY SCRIPTURE ALONE),

THE FINAL COURT OF APPEAL

2

Sola fide

(BY FAITH ALONE)

3

Sola gratia

(BY GRACE ALONE)

4

Solo Christo

(CHRIST ALONE)

5

Soli Deo gloria

(GLORY TO GOD ALONE)

CONTENTS

PART II

PRIESTS, PROPHETS AND APOSTLES: A COMPARISON OF THEIR QUALIFICATIONS, ROLES AND RESPONSIBILITIES

Part III

<u>WITNESSING TO MORMONS</u>

PART IV

A HOUSE DIVIDED AND OTHER ABSURDITIES

PART V

<u>A CHALLENGE, A RESPONSE
AND A CONFESSION OF FAITH</u>

APPENDIXES

PREFACE

My reference manual will give Christians a hands-on tool that will help them prepare to witness to Mormons on a variety of important topics. This work is intended to provide the reader with first and foremost, a biblical refutation of Mormonism in the areas of scriptural authority, God's sovereignty, soteriology, the idea of present day apostles, the alleged apostasy of the church and eschatology. There will be a detailed refutation of Mormonism in subsequent chapters ranging from its founding historical problems, false prophecies, internal contradictions and absurdities, its un-biblical view of the God-head, to philosophical worldview absurdities. Many of my arguments in this work are polemical in nature, as is necessitated in contending for the faith.

In addition, I have substantial notes and scriptural references in this work to document my assertions and challenges with regard to Mormon theology's aberrational nature in comparison with historic Christianity. This will give you ample opportunity to double-check the facts and explore my statements further. My goal is to give you a completely transparent look at both theologies – something that Mormonism is reticent to do.

My experience in witnessing to Mormons has ranged from individual meetings with Mormons, to guest presentations in numerous Christian churches. At one time I was president of the Colorado Ex-Mormons for Jesus. The Ex-Mormons for Jesus had wide local support from the Christian clergy. See the letter from the pastor of Shepherd of the Hills Lutheran Church, which had an amazing list of signers giving support to the Ex-Mormon ministry in Appendix Fourteen.

In addition, see my correspondence with Hugh Nibley in Appendix Fourteen who was one of the top scholars in the modern Mormon Church. He graduated summa cum laude from UCLA and completed his PhD as a University Fellow at UC Berkeley. He taught at Claremont College in California before serving in military intelligence in World War II. From 1946 until his death in 2005, he was associated with and taught at Brigham Young University.

I want to express my indebtedness to many un-named Christian anti-cult apologists and Reformed theologians who have made this work possible. I am simply standing on their shoulders, helping carry on their work.

"If after a rigid examination, it [the Book Of Mormon] be found an imposition, it should be extensively published to the world as such; the evidences and arguments upon which the imposture was detected should be clearly and logically stated, that those who have been sincerely yet unfortunately deceived, may perceive the nature of the deception, and be reclaimed, and that those who continue to publish the delusion, may be exposed and silenced, not by physical force, neither by persecutions, bare assertions, nor ridicule, but by strong and powerful arguments — by evidences adduced from scripture and reason." — Orson Pratt's Works, 1899 Ed., p.69.

This work is a thoroughgoing Presbyterian/Reformed refutation of Mormonism,

Jack Kettler

INTRODUCTION

This work is intended to provide the reader with first and foremost, a biblical refutation of Mormonism in the subject of Scriptural authority, God's sovereignty, soteriology, the idea of present day apostles, the alleged apostasy of the church and eschatology. I have provided a detailed refutation of Mormonism in subsequent chapters ranging from its founding historical problems, false prophecies, internal contradictions and absurdities, its un-biblical view of the God-head, to philosophical worldview absurdities. In the area of terminology, a convenient quick reference guide provides help to break through the vast differences in definitions of the language used by Mormons and historical Christianity. Some terminology in this manual may be technical; wherever possible I've tried to provide definitions or explanations. All passages of Scripture will be from the King James Version, unless otherwise noted, since it's the translation often used by Mormons, and therefore the most useful in Mormon refutations.

In this work, I have included my philosophical challenge to the Mormon worldview titled *Pagan Influence upon the Mormon World View*, which I sent to the Mormon prophet and apostles. To date, I have received no response. Also included is my interaction with Brigham Young University professors in a section titled "*The Nonsense Column*," followed by a summary of witnessing methods and my testimony regarding why I am no longer a Mormon. Additionally, there are various appendices with a great deal of useful information.

HOW TO UNDERSTAND
MY ARGUMENTS:

Many of my arguments in this work are polemical in nature. To be blunt, I want to tear down the false truth-claims of Mormonism because they deny the divine attributes of God. Polemical argumentation is seen in 2 Corinthians 10:3-5, "For though we walk in the flesh, we do not war after the flesh (For the weapons of our warfare are not carnal, but mighty through God to the pulling down of strong holds). Casting down imaginations, and every high thing that exalteth itself against the knowledge of God, and bringing into captivity every thought to the obedience of Christ..." As Christians, we are to destroy the false arguments that are raised against the true knowledge of God. We are to bring every thought captive to the obedience of Christ. Pulling or tearing down false knowledge and false arguments is inescapably polemical.

WHY IS THIS RESPONSE TO MORMONISM NECESSARY?

Not only do Mormons claim to be Christian, they claim to be the "Only True Church." A Christian response to the following charges is necessary.

Mormon prophet Joseph Fielding Smith said:

> For hundreds of years the world was wrapped in a veil of spiritual darkness, until there was not one fundamental truth belonging to the place of salvation that was not, in the year 1820, so obscured by false tradition and ceremonies, borrowed from paganism, as to make it unrecognizable, or else it was entirely denied.

> Joseph Fielding Smith, *Doctrines of Salvation* Vol. 3, (Salt Lake City, Utah, Bookcraft, 1989), p.282.

Recent Mormon leader Ezra Taft Benson said:

> This is not just another Church. This is not just one of a family of Christian churches. This is the Church and kingdom of God, the only true Church upon the face of the earth...

> Ezra Taft Benson, *Teachings of Ezra Taft Benson* (Salt Lake City, Utah, Bookcraft, 1988), p.164-165.

Former Mormon apostle McConkie says:

> A perverted Christianity holds sway among the so-called Christians of apostate Christendom.
>
> Bruce R. McConkie, *Mormon Doctrine* (Salt Lake City, Utah, Bookcraft, 1979), p.132.

McConkie's disdain for Christianity is evident when he says:

> Virtually all the millions of apostate Christendom have abased themselves before the mythical throne of a mythical Christ whom they vainly suppose to be a spirit essence who is incorporeal uncreated, immaterial and three-in-one with the Father and Holy Spirit.
>
> McConkie, *Mormon Doctrine* p. 269.

WAYS THIS MANUAL CAN BE USED:

For starters, if you are talking with Mormons about the nature of the Godhead, you can find relevant material in the chapter on *The Trinity* and the chapter on *A Comparison of the Mormon and Christian View of God*. If you are talking with Mormons about the biblical test to determine if someone is a true prophet then it would be helpful to consult the chapter *Beware of False Prophets*. There will be some repeating of biblical passages or overlap cited between chapters for the reader's convenience in order to save time when preparing for a witnessing encounter. In addition, in most cases, I have attached the source material of the quote directly beneath the quote itself for the reader's convenience, rather than using endnotes.

This Reference Manual will provide a hands-on tool that will help readers be informed on the differences between historic Christian beliefs and Mormonism and prepare them to witness to Mormons on a variety of important topics. It has been said that the best defense is a good offense. This is why I have positively stated the Christian position on a number of topics, the most important being the setting forth of a scriptural view of what the Bible says about itself. It is my prayer that this material will find a wide hearing among members of Reformed Churches, which is my targeted audience. The reader is encouraged to use this work in order to document and reference various aspects of Mormon theology and in order to see the vast differences between it and orthodox Christianity.

Sometimes Mormons will not accept your quoting a past leader of their church by saying something like: "That is not the official doctrine of our church." I encourage the reader to not get bogged down in debates with Mormons about the official position of Mormonism when discussing aspects of Mormon theology verses scriptural theology. The reason for this is that it is almost impossible to find out what the official position is. I say this because the official view of Mormonism is seemingly whatever the leaders of Mormonism, at any given moment, say it is.

The Mormons I cite in this manual were or are members of Mormonism in good standing, meaning that they were not under church discipline for the writings that I quote, nor were their particular writings publicly repudiated except Brigham Young's infamous "Adam god" doctrine. This is a fair standard. If the Mormon who is quoted was never disciplined for his writings, then it is fair to cite the individual's writing as representative of the range of beliefs that have been spawned by the theology of Mormonism.

In this work, I make no apologies for my historic Protestant Faith, i.e., Calvinism. As a Christian, I would say that the importance and function of Scripture plays epistemologically is primary or foundational. This view of Scripture can be delineated as: all knowledge must be contained within a system and deduced or inferred from its starting principles, as in the Christian case, the Bible. This is in sharp contrast to Mormon epistemology, which is, at its core, a form of materialistic rationalism with a strong sensory empirical commitment. If the reader is not convinced of my particular convictions in the area of soteriology, this reference material will still be of much use in documenting the radical nature of Mormon theology and more importantly in refuting Mormon theology by way of exposing its numerous contradictions and its failure to meet biblical standards.

> Convince us of our errors of doctrine, if we have any, by reason, by logical arguments, or by the word of God, and we will be ever grateful for the information.
>
> Orson Pratt, *The Seer* (Salt Lake City: Eborn Books, 1990), p. 15.

> I have had many revelations; I have seen and heard
> for myself, and know these things are true, and
> nobody on earth can disprove them. ... I say to
> the whole world, receive the truth, no matter who
> presents it to you. Take up the Bible, compare the
> religion of the Latter-day Saints with it, and see if
> it will stand the test.
>
> Brigham Young, Journal *of Discourses* Vol. 6, (Liver-
> pool, England: Asa Calkin, 1844), p. 46.

In this manual we will take up the Bible, and compare it with the Mormon religion!

SPECIAL DEBTS:

I'm dependent on and indebted to Rev. Dr. Leonard J. Coppes in this work for my understanding of the authority and sufficiency of Scripture, the relationship of Older and New Covenant, covenantal development in redemptive history, continuities and discontinuities between the Covenants, understanding Van Til's presuppositionalism and assistance in correspondence in dealing with BYU professors.

Dr. Leonard J. Coppes is a graduate of Bethel Seminary (B.D.), Princeton Seminary (Th.M.), and Westminster Seminary (Th. D.) and has done extended graduate work at Dropsie University. He has been an Orthodox Presbyterian pastor for over 40 years. He has authored numerous books including *Are Five Points Enough? The Ten Points of Calvinism.* Other works include a biblico-theological critiques of contrary positions from Dispensationalism to Klinianism and a positive presentation of Biblical Theology in *From Adam to Adam: OT Biblical Theology.*

Also, I want to express my dependence and indebtedness to Dr. Greg L. Bahnsen for two lectures that have deeply influenced my thinking in the area of the authority and sufficiency of the Scriptures. These two lectures are titled *Is Sola Scriptura sufficient for today?* And *Is Sola Scriptura a Protestant Concoction?* These lectures can be obtained from the Covenant Tape Ministry. Also, Dr. Bahnsen's article *The Concept and Importance of Canonicity* from September/October 1990 Volume 1, Number 5 issue of ANTITHESIS: A review of Contemporary Thought and Culture.

Greg L. Bahnsen, (1948-1995), was an ordained minister in the Orthodox Presbyterian Church. He received his Ph.D. in philosophy from the University of Southern California, specializing in the theory of knowledge. He previously received the B.A. (magna cum laude, philosophy) from Westmont College, and then simultaneously earned the M.Div. and Th.M. degrees from Westminster Theological Seminary.

In addition, I want to express my indebtedness to Alan Myatt, Ph.D. Adjunct Associate Professor of Theology and Missions at Gordon-Conwell Theological Seminary for teaching me the method of presuppositional questioning of the Mormon worldview found in Chapter Twelve, Eighteen and Nineteen.

Alan Myatt, Ph.D. Degrees: B.A. (Vanderbilt University), M.Div. (Denver Seminary), Ph.D. (Denver University/Iliff School of Theology) Publications: *Teologia Sistemática: uma análise histórica, bíblica e apologética para o contexto atual* (*Systematic Theology: An Historical, Biblical and Apologetic Analysis for Today's Context*, Franklin Ferreira Edições Vida Nova, 2007) Biography: Dr. Myatt served 12 years as a missionary in Brazil with the International Mission Board of the Southern Baptist Convention.

PART I

ESSENTIAL DOCTRINES OF CHRISTIANITY IN OPPOSITION TO MORMONISM

Food for Thought:

"A dog barks when his master is attacked. I would be a coward if I saw that God's truth is attacked and yet would remain silent." - John Calvin

CHAPTER 1

SOLA SCRIPTURA

MORMON BELIEFS
VERSUS THE BIBLE

n this chapter we will look at Mormon beliefs that are in opposition to the Scriptures. In particular, we will look at beliefs that have been held by various Mormons since the beginning relating to the place that Scripture holds in Mormonism. The various Mormon beliefs will then be contrasted with the teachings of Scripture. It will be left to the reader to determine if the beliefs of the Mormons cited are in harmony with what the Bible declares about itself.

A correct view of Scripture is fundamental to any attempt to establish a system of sound doctrine. It is important to have a theory of knowledge based upon a correct view of Scripture. The Christian must build his foundation of knowledge upon the Scriptures of the Old and New Testaments. Many people assume that what they perceive to be truth is evident to all. This is not the case. Evidence is interpreted within the framework of a worldview. Therefore, it is imperative to have a correct scriptural worldview.

The historic Christian worldview accepts the authority of the Old and New Testaments as being God's infallible Word. We do not believe parts of the Bible are missing nor that the text is corrupted as Mormons assert, thus making the understanding of the doctrine of God and salvation impossible to know. What constitutes a biblically coherent approach to life or to a worldview? The Bible must be the bedrock or foundation for all of life and beliefs. P.T. Barnum said, a sucker is born every minute. Many people do not grasp the potential for deception or even self-deception, and without the Scriptures as the sure guide, falling into deception is always a very real danger.

Today in the Post Modern era, experience is set-forth as the ultimate test for truth. Experiential testimonials, secular and religious, are used as recruitment techniques to gain members. The Christian must not succumb to this erroneous approach to truth, namely letting experiences guide us. On the contrary, the Scriptures must always interpret and test experience, as well as tradition, spiritual leaders and even the official theology of the church.

The Reformed faith is unique in that it places the Scripture paramount as the ultimate authority for life and truth. Many competing religious movements have attempted to undermine this teaching. When the Scriptures are acknowledged as the supreme authority, people are less likely to follow deceptive religious con-men. The first chapter of the *Westminster Confession* says the Scriptures are "The whole counsel of God, concerning all things necessary for His own glory, man's salvation, faith, and life..." Similarly, Protestant Reformers use the term *Sola Scriptura*, Scripture alone, to express their belief in the prominence and infallibility of the Bible.

It should be obvious that God's Word is inseparable from His authority. The real issue is one of authority. What role does the Bible have? False religious leaders attack the reliability of the Bible in order to subordinate people to their own authority.

The pattern is always the same; the claim is that the Bible is not sufficient. The attacks upon biblical authority and sufficiency are sometimes very subtle, although at times bold claims are made about alleged missing or corrupted parts of the Scriptures. In the case of false religions, you need their leaders, traditions, books, or special insights to make up for the missing or unclear parts of the Bible. This is one of the claims of Mormonism, and one of the reasons it can never be aligned with true Christianity.

The thesis that will be set forth herein is that since the Bible consisting of the Old and New Testament is the Word of God, the believer can be certain that the Scriptures are authoritative and sufficient. Consequently, the Bible is the final court of appeal when seeking for truth. Neither the church nor the state should bind the consciences of men to non-biblical doctrine.

The Scriptures declare God to be sovereign and the absolute ruler over all. God has either preserved His Word from corruption or He has not. These are the only two choices. It will be seen as self evident from the Scriptures referenced that God has sovereignly preserved His Word from corruption. This means that the believer can have confidence that he has the complete and sufficient Word of God, upon which to rest and base his life. This is the plain teaching of Scripture found throughout its pages.

It is my prayer that what God has revealed in the Bible about his Word will be edifying in the following chapter studies, which serve as the groundwork for this reference manual. The Bible provides a powerful testimony concerning itself. God has clearly spoken in the Bible. We can have the utmost confidence in Scripture.

With that said, let us begin our comparative survey of the beliefs of the Mormon people.

THE MORMON VIEW
OF SCRIPTURE

In the Mormon work titled the *Pearl Of Great Price* we read:

> We believe the Bible to be the word of God as far as
> it is translated correctly; we also believe the Book
> of Mormon to be the word of God.
>
> Joseph Smith, *Pearl Of Great Price* (Salt Lake City:
> The Church of Jesus Christ of Latter-Day Saints,
> 1977), p. 60.

It is important to notice the qualification that is placed only upon the Bible and not the *Book of Mormon* in this quotation. Mormon theology does not believe the Bible to be reliably translated.

An important point of instruction:

When a Christian hears this type of assertion from a Mormon, it is important to respond by asking the Mormon for examples of passages in Scripture that have been mistranslated. Insist that the Mormon provide examples of how a particular Hebrew or Greek word or phrase should be translated correctly and why the current translation is inaccurate. So suggest that at a future meeting they bring examples of where the Hebrew and Greek words or phrases have been mistranslated. Do not let the Mormon get away with false assertions of this nature without a vigorous response. What the Christian will discover is that the Mormon has no credible examples of mistranslated passages in the Bible; they are simply parroting erroneous accusations. You may also at this point ask the Mormon what the normal standards are for evaluating historical documents like the Old and New Testaments. If they cannot answer you, then respond by asking them why they feel qualified to assert that the Bible has been mistranslated.

This opens the door to talk about the reliable Grammatico-Historical-Hermeneutical Method. This method of interpretation focuses attention not only on literary forms but upon grammatical constructions and historical contexts from which the Scriptures were written. It is the literal school of interpretation, which is the hermeneutical methodology embraced by virtually all evangelical Protestant exegetes and scholars. Knowledge of Hebrew and Greek is crucial to this process. In addition, see chapter fourteen on how Bible translation is conducted by the Wycliffe

Translators. This scholarly approach is a sharp contrast to Joseph Smith's magic "seer stone with face in a hat" method.

Early Mormon apostle Orson Pratt in his book *The Seer* gives us his view of the Bible:

> But the Bible has been robbed of its plainness; many sacred books having been lost, others rejected by the Romish Church, and what few we have left, were copied and re-copied so many times, that it is admitted that almost every verse has been corrupted and mutilated to that degree that scarcely any two of them read alike.
>
> Orson Pratt, *The Seer* (Salt Lake City: Eborn Books, 1990), p. 213.

Orson Pratt makes this assertion and significantly does not provide one shred of evidence for this in his work.

Mormon founder Joseph Smith in the work *The Teachings Of The Prophet Joseph Smith* compiled by Joseph Fielding Smith, relates his views concerning the Bible:

> From sundry revelations which had been received, it was apparent that many important points touching the salvation of men, had been taken from the Bible, or lost before it was compiled.
>
> Joseph Smith, *The Teachings of the Prophet Joseph Smith*, Arranged by Joseph F. Smith (Salt Lake City: Deseret Book Company, 1976), p. 9-10.

Smith, like Pratt, is good at making assertions without seeing the need to back up his assertions with evidence.

In this same work in a small section titled *Errors in the Bible* we find more of Joseph Smith's views about the reliability of the Bible:

Ignorant translators, careless transcribers, or designing and corrupt priests have committed many errors.

Joseph Smith, *The Teachings of the Prophet Joseph
Smith* p. 327.

Orson Hyde in the *Journal of Discourses* has this to say about the Bible:

The words contained in this Bible are merely a history of what is gone by; it was never given to guide
the servant of God in the course he should pursue.
The Bible is not a sufficient guide, it is only the
history of the people who lived 1800 years ago.

Orson Hyde, *Journal of Discourses* Vol. 2, (Liverpool, England: Asa Calkin, 1855), p. 75.

All that can be said about Orson Hyde's comments is that they reveal his profound ignorance of
the Scriptures.

**Bruce R. McConkie in his work titled *Mormon Doctrine* sets forth his belief that the Bible has
been perverted by men:**

The great perversion of the Scriptures, in which
many plain and precious truths were deleted by evil-
ly [sic] disposed persons (1 Ne. 13), took place primarily in the early centuries of the Christian Era.

McConkie, *Mormon Doctrine* p. 422.

In the *Book Of Mormon* itself we find in 1 Nephi 13:28-29:

Wherefore, thou seest that after the book [Bible]
hath gone forth through the hands of the great
abominable church, that there are many plain and
precious things taken away from the book of the
Lamb of God.... because of the many plain and

precious things which have been taken out of the book, [Bible] which were plain unto the understanding of the children of men, according to the plainness which is in the Lamb of God because of these things which are taken away out of the gospel of the Lamb, an exceeding great many do stumble, yea, insomuch that Satan hath great power over them.

Joseph Smith, the *Book Of Mormon* (Salt Lake City: The Church of Jesus Christ of Latter-Day Saints, 1977), p. 23.

The extra-biblical revelations of the Mormons serve to attack and undermine confidence in Holy Scripture. As seen, Mormon leaders do not have a high view of Scripture. They believe that the Bible has errors in it, due to intentional deletions of many important truths. The Bible is received as Scripture by Mormons, but with a pronounced reservation, namely "as far as it is translated correctly." A careful study of Mormonism will reveal that whenever the Bible does not agree with other Mormon doctrines, this is where the Bible is believed to be in error.

It is claimed that Joseph Smith's "inspired version" (published by the Reorganized Church of Jesus Christ of Latter Day Saints, now called The Community of Christ) corrects many of the supposed errors in Bible. Since Smith did not read Hebrew or Greek or have extant manuscripts to work with during his supposed translation, one can legitimately question just how Smith's Bible can be called a translation at all. Smith's "inspired version" translation was done in a similar fashion as the *Book Of Mormon*. This unique and unconventional process is not open to investigation, or replication by future scholars; one must simply take Smith at his word.

As in all sub-Christian sects, one finds in Mormonism a depreciation of the Bible. This serves to create a dependence upon their extra-biblical revelation. In Mormonism this takes two forms: Other books, and the pronouncements of the Mormon leaders.

As said earlier, either God lets His Word be corrupted or He doesn't. As Christians, we know He doesn't. But if God allowed the Bible to be corrupted, what does that say about His omnipotence, sovereignty and provision for His people? By doubting the Bible, Mormons have already irrevocably moved away from God.

So we now turn our attention to the Christian view of Scripture. We will do so under the following headings: Scriptural Authority, the Old Testament and Biblical Considerations, New Testament Considerations, God's Word to be Written Down, The Sufficiency of the Scriptures, and The Closing of the Canon of Scripture. This section is lengthy, but absolutely imperative to establish, since it is the bedrock of Christian life and beliefs.

The Authority of Scripture, the Christian View

Scriptural authority, the Old Testament and biblical considerations

As stated, the authority of Scripture flows from the fact that it is God's Word and declares itself to be God's Word. It follows necessarily, that the Scriptures are binding upon the Christian as doctrine and for all of life. We will also see clear biblical evidence that the people of Israel had an objective written scriptural canon as a guard against false prophets and teachers.

The prophet Isaiah declares the power of God's Word when it is sent forth:

> So shall my word be that goeth forth out of my
> mouth: it shall not return unto me void, but it shall
> accomplish that which I please, and it shall prosper
> in the thing whereto I sent it. (Isaiah 55:11)

David in the Psalms further confirms this truth:

> By the word of the LORD were the heavens made;
> and all the host of them by the breath of his mouth.
> And, The counsel of the LORD standeth for ever,
> the thoughts of his heart to all generations. (Psalms
> 33:6, 11)

Not only is God and His Word irresistible when sent forth, it is important to see at the start of this study just how closely God is identified with the Scriptures. Just as the words of God have immense power to create, so too they will last forever. Any words this powerful will also have the force to continue existing unchanged. No generation will be without His words.

Consider this example from the book of Romans:

> For the <u>scripture saith</u>, Whosoever believeth on
> him shall not be ashamed. (Romans 10:11)

The apostle Paul in the book of Romans says, "For the Scripture saith." It is significant to note, when you consult Isaiah 28:16 whom the apostle is quoting, you find that it is God speaking. Scripture references itself to reinforce the continuity and life-generating power of God's words.

To establish this further:

> Therefore <u>thus saith the Lord God</u>, Behold, I lay
> in Zion for a foundation a stone, a tried stone, a
> precious corner stone, a sure foundation: he that
> believeth shall not make haste. (Isaiah 28:16)
>
> (Underlining emphasis is mine throughout
> this study)

And then in Romans we also read:

> For the scripture saith unto Pharaoh, Even for this
> same purpose have I raised thee up, that I might
> show my power in thee, and that my name might be
> declared throughout all the earth. (Romans 9:17)

Was God speaking or the Scriptures? If there is any doubt, we know for sure after reading Exodus 9:16 that it is <u>God speaking</u>, whereas, Romans says, "the Scripture saith." Therefore, it is clear that God and the Scriptures are so closely identified as to be synonymous. In essence, we learn from these examples, "thus saith the Lord God" and the phrase "the Scriptures saith" can be and are used interchangeably.

Again for emphasis, it merits repeating that the Scriptures declare God to be sovereign, or the absolute ruler over all. God has either preserved His Word from corruption or He has not. These are the only two choices. It is evident from the Scriptures that God has the power to preserve His Word from corruption as evidenced by the testimony of the Scriptures themselves.

Since the Christian recognizes the authority of Scripture, we will examine what God has revealed in the Bible about his Word. The Bible provides a powerful testimony concerning itself. God has clearly spoken in the Bible. We can have the utmost confidence in Scripture.

THE BIBLICAL VIEW
OF THE OLD TESTAMENT SCRIPTURES

The scriptural passages in this section of the present study give biblical rationale for putting confidence in the Word of God. The passages cited in this section from the Old Testament clearly teach that the Old Testament itself is the Word of God. The New Testament passages cited in this section clearly refer to the Old Testament as Scripture or the very Word of God. Because of this, there is no reason to doubt that the Old Testament is the Word of God.

The following five passages speak of the Word of God:

> Ye shall not add unto the word which I command you, neither shall ye diminish aught from it, that ye may keep the commandment of the Lord your God which I command you. (Deuteronomy 4:2)

> Thy word is a lamp unto my feet, and a light unto my path. (Psalms 119:105)

> Every word of God is pure: he is a shield unto them that put their trust in him. Add thou not unto his words, lest he reprove thee, and thou be found a liar. (Proverbs 30:5-6)

> Whoso despiseth the word shall be destroyed: but he that feareth the commandment shall be rewarded. (Proverbs 13:13)

> The grass withereth, the flower fadeth: but the word of our God shall stand forever. (Isaiah 40:8)

We see that these five passages set God's Word apart from the writings of men by the fact that God's words are "pure," "a lamp and light," and are "eternal." If you despise the Word by rejecting or altering it you will be destroyed. What man can claim this about his writings? Not one!

Furthermore, when reading the Old Testament there is no mistaking that God is speaking to man beginning in Genesis 1:3 with the phrase "And God said" or the similar phrase "And the Lord said." Exodus 32:9. In addition, you have God speaking using the familiar terminology "Thus saith the Lord" or "saith the Lord" in places such as Genesis 22:16; Exodus 5:1, all the way to Malachi 1:2. In the prophets we read passages like "And say, Here ye the word of the Lord" (Jeremiah 19:3). There are many variations of these above phrases. In fact, there are many hundreds of Old Testament passages like this, which establish the divine authenticity of the Old Testament.

How does the New Testament view the Old? For the remainder of this study we will see a consistent New Testament testimony.

Consider the importance of the following New Testament verse:

> These were more noble minded than those in
> Thessalonica, in that they received the word with
> all readiness of mind, and searched the Scriptures
> daily, whether those things were so. (Acts 17:11)

This should be the practice of all believers. The believers in Berea used the Scriptures as a test for the truth or falsity of a given message and are commended for this practice. In this particular instance, the Bereans were commended for examining even the Apostle Paul's message. Surely, this gives the individual Christian the basis for questioning church doctrine if not established biblically. This verse from Acts 17:11 deals primarily with the Old Testament Scriptures, since at this stage in redemptive history the New Testament was in the process of being given and compiled. Because of this, we can infer that the Old Testament is the Word of God. It was the Old Testament that was searched by the Bereans to see if Paul's message was true.

Consider the words of Christ himself when speaking of the Old Testament Scriptures:

> ...the Scripture cannot be broken. (John 10:35)

This passage speaks directly of the Old Testament but goes beyond it and refers to the New Testament as well. If the Scriptures "cannot be broken," then we are to bind ourselves to its teaching. Unquestionably, according to our Lord here in John's gospel, the Scriptures are set forth as the highest court of appeal.

How did the Old Testament prophecy of Scripture come? The Apostle Peter teaches that the Scriptures came from God as the Spirit of God moved holy men to speak:

> Knowing this first, that no prophecy of the Scripture is of any private interpretation. For the prophecy came not in old time by the will of man: but holy men of God spake as they were moved by the Holy Ghost. (2 Peter 1:20-21)

In this passage, Peter clearly sets the Old Testament apart from human writings. The apostle Paul says the same thing when he tells us that it was the "oracles" or the very Word of God, which was committed to the Jewish people in the Old Testament.

Consider Paul's germane teaching:

> Much in every way: chiefly, because that unto them were committed the oracles of God. (Romans 3:2 NKJ)

We also find that the word translated "oracles" occurs in the New Testament several more times. For example, in Acts 7:38, Hebrews 5:12, and 1 Peter 4:11 we see "oracles" mentioned. These examples are all referring to the Scriptures as being that which was spoken by God.

In the next passage from Luke, Jesus is referring to the Old Testament Scriptures. How did Christ view these Scriptures? To begin with, Jesus establishes His identity from the Scriptures. And secondly, He did not believe any portions of Scripture had disappeared or existed in some separate body of oral traditions as evidenced by the phrase "in all the Scriptures."

Christ appealing to an objective body of writings:

> And beginning at Moses and all the prophets, he expounded unto them in all the Scriptures the things concerning himself. (Luke 24:27)

Along this same line, after Jesus quotes the prophet Isaiah in Luke 4:18-19.

> And he began to say unto them, This day is this Scripture fulfilled in your ears. (Luke 4:21)

Not only does Christ identify Isaiah's writing as Scripture he goes on later in Luke 16:30-31 to show the importance of scriptural testimony as over and against even a miracle such as someone returning from the dead. This is significant because it sets forth the Scriptures as more important than experience.

Consider another important passage from Luke:

> Abraham saith unto him, They have Moses and
> the prophets, let them hear them. (Luke 16:29)

What does the rich man ask for? The visitation of a spirit? But Abraham declines, pointing the rich man back to Scripture.

This passage reinforces the authority of the Old Testament, because Moses and the prophets spoke the Word of God with finality and we are told to "hear them." At this point because of the relevance of the above passage it would be good to note the necessity of using the Scriptures to interpret experience. This is of the utmost importance. Many people use experience and emotions or feelings to interpret the Bible without even realizing it.

The careful reader of God's Word should use the grammatical and historical contexts when interpreting the Scriptures. You should not come to the text with preconceived ideas that may color your interpretation. People who claim to have had spiritual experiences often fall into the trap of allowing those experiences to influence their understanding of a particular text of Scripture. If experience governs the interpretation of Scripture, it inevitably leads to error.

We see more of Christ's view of Scripture in the gospel of John: "Therefore the Jews sought the more to kill him, because he not only had broken the sabbath, but said also that God was his Father, making himself equal with God" (John 5:18). In this passage Jesus responds to the Jew's attempt to kill him because of His claim of Deity by appealing to the Old Testament Scripture again:

> For had ye believed Moses, ye would have believed
> me: for he wrote of me. But if ye believe not his writ-
> ings, how shall ye believe my words? (John 5:46, 47)

The crux of Christ's argument is an admonition to search the Old Testament Scriptures, which further establishes their credibility and authority. Hopefully this important affirmation by the Savior concerning the authority of the Old Testament Scripture is not overlooked.

It is significant to see how Jesus makes this connection:

> Search the Scriptures; for in them ye think ye have
> eternal life: and they are they which testify of me.
> (John 5:39)

In this passage from John, Jesus tells the disciples about one of the most important testimonies of the Scriptures, namely, how His person and work are inseparably connected to the Scriptures.

We should note how God speaking in and through the Scriptures, directs His people to study the Scriptures in order to gain patience, comfort, and hope. The apostle Paul gives the believer assurance by clearly referring to the Old Testament Scriptures as the place to obtain these very things.

Consider this statement of the apostle Paul, which confirms this:

> For whatsoever things were written aforetime were
> written for our learning, that we through patience
> and comfort of the Scriptures might have hope.
> (Romans 15:4)

It should be established beyond any doubt that the New Testament consistently calls the Old Testament the Scriptures or, in other words, the Word of God.

Another issue that needs to be addressed is whether Old Testament people of God had possession of the Scriptures in an identifiable or recognizable form. It should be noted that the Scriptures were read and studied in the synagogues of ancient Israel. The people of Israel were to commit God's Word to memory and teach it to their children and write His Word on the door-posts of their houses. This command of God has tremendous implications in the life of modern believers.

Consider God's Command:

> And these words, which I commanded thee this
> day, shall be in thine heart: And thou shalt teach
> them diligently unto thy children, and shalt talk
> of them when thou sittest in thine house, and
> when thou walkest by the way, and when thou liest
> down, and when thou risest up. And thou shalt

> bind them for a sign upon thine hand, and they
> shall be as frontlets between thine eyes. And thou
> shalt write them upon the posts of thy house, and
> on thy gates. (Deuteronomy 6:6-9)

This verse shows us that there was an ongoing daily reading and teaching of the Scriptures, which created a deep respect in Israel for the Word of God. There was a reverence for God's Word in Israel. In fact, Israel has been known as "people of the book." As God spoke in the Old Testament, these words were recorded and faithfully transcribed to preserve this Word for proceeding generations. This preservation is evidenced by the fact that the Scriptures were read in the synagogues of Israel. Christ himself read and taught the Word in the synagogues (Luke 4:16-21).

The astute reader will notice that Jesus "closed the book, and he gave it again to the minister." Jesus was demonstrating that Israel had the Word of God in written form. Israel did not just have fragments of God's Word; they had a recognizable body of writing. So it is not surprising in Luke's gospel we see clear indication of the Old Testament authoritative books, or the canon of Scripture that existed in Christ's day:

> And he said unto them, These are the words which
> I spake unto you, while I was yet with you, that
> all things must be fulfilled, which were written <u>in
> the law of Moses</u>, and <u>in the prophets</u>, and <u>in the
> psalms</u>, concerning me. (Luke 24:44)

This verse refers to the three sections of the Old Testament canon. The Old Testament canon consisted of the <u>Law</u>, the <u>Prophets</u>, and the <u>Writings</u> in which the <u>Psalms</u> was a part. There was clearly a distinguishable structure and a list of authoritative books in the Old Testament at this point in redemptive history.

In the following passage we find more proof that establishes a distinguishable written canon of Scripture in Christ's day:

> That the blood of all the prophets, which was shed
> from the foundation of the world, may be required
> of this generation. From the blood of Abel unto
> the blood of Zacharias, which perished between the

altar and the temple: verily I say unto you, it shall
be required of this generation. (Luke 11:50-51)

This passage sets the time frame for Old Testament prophetic revelation between the death of Abel in Genesis 4:8 and Zechariah's death. The death of Zechariah is recorded in 2 Chronicles 24:20-21. At first sight this seems to present a problem because of the order of our modern Bibles. It would seem to exclude any Old Testament books following 2 Chronicles. In Christ's day the canon of Scripture included the book of Chronicles, which was not then divided into two volumes, placed out of historical order. It was originally found after Ezra and Nehemiah, thus making it the last book of the Jewish canon. So according to this order, Zecharias was the last sufferer at the hands of the Old Testament religious apostates.

The testimony of the Scriptures stands sure. That testimony is that the Old Testament is the Word of God. It can be said with certainty; there was indeed a distinguishable Old Testament written canon of Scripture in Christ's day. The importance of a recognizable written canon of Scripture possessed by the Old Testament people of God cannot be underestimated in its importance. An objective body of canonical writings is far superior to an undetermined fluctuating oral tradition, or dubious so-called additional books of revelation.

Hopefully, those who have attempted to cast doubt on the scriptural canon and its binding authority in order to establish and validate new revelations will not miss this. There are no missing books, secondary sources of divine revelation, or an alleged body of "sacred tradition." Christ fully accepted the canon as it stood in His day, based on His Words:

The Scripture cannot be broken. (John 10:35)

In conclusion, to doubt the divine authenticity of the Old Testament is to doubt Christ. The Old Testament people of God knew that they possessed the Word of God, and consequently, were careful in handling the texts of Scripture. The New Testament people of God were no less careful. There is no indication that the Word of God referenced in this study was or is anything other than the Scriptures, which are recorded in our Bibles.

This is why we declare:

He that rejecteth me, and receiveth not my words,
hath one that judgeth him: the Word that I have

spoken, the same [Christ's Word] shall judge him
in the last day. (John 12:48)

The scriptural passages that are referenced and commented on in this study provide biblical rationale for having confidence in the Word of God. In addition, these passages also clearly teach that the New Testament is the Word of God. The New Testament writers viewed their own writings as Scripture, and because of what the passages in this study teach, there is no reason to doubt that the New Testament is the Word of God.

The following passage dealing with John the Baptist gives New Testament revelation the same status as Old Testament revelation:

> But what went ye out for to see? A prophet yea, I say
> unto you, and more than a prophet. For this is he,
> of whom it is written, Behold, I send my messenger
> before thy face, which shall prepare thy way before
> thee. Verily I say unto you, Among them that are born
> of women there hath not risen a greater than John the
> Baptist: notwithstanding he that is least in the king-
> dom of heaven is greater than he. (Matthew 11:9-11)

The above verses teach three points that are relevant: 1. John was a prophet and his coming was foretold in the Old Testament Scriptures; 2. "Among them that are born of women there hath not risen a greater than John the Baptist." Thus, John was greater than the Old Testament prophets; 3. And as Jesus said in Matthew, "the least in the kingdom of heaven is greater than he." In which case, the New Testament prophets were greater than he. In light of this verse, the biblical, and indeed, logical conclusion is that the New Testament prophets were also inspired by God just like the Old Testament prophets.

The Old Testament is completed by the revelation of Christ in the New Testament. This is why the apostle Peter says:

> We have also a more <u>sure word</u> of prophecy...
> (2 Peter 1:19).

> We can say, a more "sure word" because: God, who

at sundry times and in divers manners spake in
time past unto the fathers by the prophets, <u>Hath
in these last days spoken unto us by his Son</u>, whom
he hath appointed heir of all things, by whom also
he made the worlds; (Hebrews 1:1-2)

Consider Christ's explicit utterance concerning the importance of His words:

Heaven and earth shall pass away, <u>but my words
shall not pass away</u>. (Matthew 24:35)

Christ identifies his words on the same level as the prophet Isaiah who says:

The word of our God <u>shall stand forever</u>.
(Isaiah 40:8)

The heavens and earth are temporal and "shall pass away," but not Christ's words!

The apostolic teaching was to be received on the same level as Isaiah. The early Christians received the teaching of Christ's apostles as authoritative.

We see proof of this of church view of apostolic authority from the book of Acts:

And <u>they continued steadfastly in the apostle's
doctrine</u> and fellowship, and in breaking of bread,
and in prayers. (Acts 2:42)

The early Christian disciples "continued in the apostle's doctrine" because they viewed it as the authoritative Word of God. "Steadfastly" in this passage means to persevere, to adhere closely and give oneself continually to the apostle's doctrine.

And when they had prayed, the place was shaken
where they were assembled together; and they were
all filled with the Holy Ghost, and they spake the
word of God with boldness. (Acts 4:31)

In this passage, we see how the early disciples saw God confirm, through signs and wonders, that the apostles were preaching the Word of God.

Jesus makes it indisputable; He spoke the Word of God:

> For he whom God hath sent <u>speaketh the words of God</u>: for God giveth not the Spirit by measure unto him. (John 3:34)

> <u>For I have given unto them the words which thou gavest me</u>; and they have received them, and have known surely that I came out from thee, and they have believed that thou didst send me. (John 17:8)

Jesus promised His disciples that the Holy Spirit would provide a true account of things He had taught them:

> But the Comforter, which is the <u>Holy Ghost, whom the Father will send in my name, he shall teach you all things</u>, and bring all things to your remembrance, whatsoever I have said unto you. (John 14:26)

We can have certainty that the Bible is the Word of God. The Holy Ghost, a.k.a. the Holy Spirit controlled and guarded this process of bringing to their remembrance everything He had taught them.

In the following verses the reader should notice how the apostle Paul viewed his own epistles and their origin. Paul clearly viewed his epistles as the Word of God and as commandments that came from God.

Because of Paul's apostolic authority, he is able to say:

> Which things also we speak, <u>not in the words which man's wisdom</u> teacheth, <u>but which the Holy Ghost teacheth</u>; comparing spiritual things with spiritual. (1 Corinthians 2:13)

Paul is therefore affirming that his words were authoritative because they were established not by fallen man, but by the Holy Ghost who is infallible because He is indeed God as the Third Person of the Trinity and it is impossible for God to lie. (Hebrews 6:18)

> If any man think himself to be a prophet, or spiritu-
> al, let him acknowledge that the things that I write
> unto you <u>are the commandments of the Lord</u>. (1
> Corinthians 14:37)

Paul says clearly that the things he wrote to the Corinthian Church are "the commandments of the Lord."

> Paul, An apostle, (not of men, neither by man, <u>but
> by Jesus Christ, and God the Father</u>, who raised
> him from the dead;).... But I certify you, brethren,
> that the gospel which was preached of me is not
> after man. For I neither received it of man, neither
> <u>was I taught it, but by revelation</u> of Jesus Christ.
> (Galatians 1:1, 11-12)

In this passage from Galatians, Paul says he received his teaching by "revelation" from "God the Father."

> For the <u>scripture saith</u>, thou shalt not muzzle the
> ox that treadeth out the corn. And, The labourer is
> worthy of his reward. (1 Timothy 5:18)

This passage from Paul's letter to Timothy is a quote from the words of Jesus in Luke 10:7 in which Jesus is referring to Deuteronomy 25:4 for proof of His words; "for the labourer is worthy of his hire...". Not only he is indicating that this passage from Luke's gospel is Scripture, it is also significant that Paul is connecting an Old Testament reference cited by Jesus in Luke's gospel in the New Testament and labels them equally as Scripture.

> And the <u>things</u> that thou hast heard of me, among
> many witnesses, the same commit thou to faithful
> men, who shall be able to teach others also. (2
> Timothy 2:2)

Paul gave Timothy the "things" or doctrine that he was to teach, and instructs him to "commit" these teachings to "faithful men" in the same way that they were committed to himself, that these truths might be protected and retained in the church. Hence, we can conclude that these teachings of Paul were the Word of God and not the mere words of man. Paul, through the Holy Spirit, was also making provision for the preservation of the Scriptures so that they would not become corrupted or lost.

> For our gospel came not unto you in word only, <u>but also in power, and in the Holy Ghost</u>, and in much assurance; as ye know what manner of men we were among you for your sake. (1 Thessalonians 1:5)

Paul here connects his gospel preaching as the Word of God since it was given to him by the "power" of God, i.e., through the inspiration of the "Holy Ghost."

> For this cause also thank we God without ceasing, because, <u>when ye received the word of God which ye heard of us</u>, ye received it not as the word of men, <u>but as it is in truth, the word of God</u>, which effectually worketh also in you that believe. (2 Thessalonians 2:13)

In this passage from Thessalonians, Paul is referring to his apostolic message, which was heard and received by the disciples as the "Word of God."

> Therefore, brethren, stand fast, and <u>hold the traditions which ye have been taught</u>, whether by word, [teaching, preaching] <u>or our epistle</u> [written letter]. (2 Thessalonians 2:15)

Paul's apostolic teachings are described as "traditions" in this passage. Not always, but in this case the context requires and Paul wants us to understand, that the "traditions" he is mentioning are the Word of God. For an example of traditions that are not Scripture, consider how Jesus mentions the tradition of the elders in Mark 7:3. Christ goes on in the gospel of Mark 7:9 to say that the Pharisees had substituted the commandments of God with the traditions of men.

> <u>All scripture is given by inspiration of God</u>, [Paul most certainly is including the New Testament writings here] and is profitable for doctrine, for

reproof, for correction, for instruction in righteousness. (2 Timothy 3:16)

The word "inspired" comes from a Greek word meaning "God-breathed." Peter uses the same
Greek word for "Scripture" (γραφὴ) to describe the writings of the apostle Paul (γραφὰς plural
form of the same word) in 2 Peter 3:16. Moreover, after looking at the above passages, we can see
that Paul's writings clearly evidence that they are the Word of God. Notice in particular how Peter
views Paul's writings:

Peter places Paul's epistles at the same level as the rest of Scripture:

> ...our beloved brother Paul also according to the
> wisdom given unto him hath written unto you;
> As also in all his epistles...in which are some
> things hard to be understood, which they that are
> unlearned and unstable wrest, as they do also the
> other scriptures, unto their own destruction. (2
> Peter 3:15-16)

Another important passage from Paul will be important to look at:

> And when this epistle is read among you, cause
> that it be read also in the church of the Laodiceans.
> (Colossians 4:16)

Only the Word of God has this type of force attached to it. The church should never relent and
be pressured to have the mere words of man read in the church with equal footing as Scripture. In
addition, there is a pattern described in Colossians 4:16 concerning the reading of Paul's epistle
in the church which should be noted. This is important because it follows the same pattern as
synagogue worship where the Scriptures were read as part of the service.

For biblical evidence in support of this assertion about synagogue practice we read:

> For Moses of old time hath in every city them that
> preach him, being read in the synagogues every
> Sabbath day. (Acts 15:21)

Early Christians followed the pattern of synagogue worship quite closely at points. This reading of an apostolic epistle to the Colossians is a powerful confirmation that the apostolic epistles were viewed as the Word of God in the practice of the Church. The apostolic letters were read and expounded along with the Old Testament Scriptures. Without fear of contradiction, the early Church read the Old Testament Scriptures right along side of the emerging corpus of New Testament writings. And, it should be noted that the first-century church extensively utilized the Old Testament as its most powerful apologetic weapon.

There is further testimony of New Testament revelation that should be considered. Specifically, the reader should survey the numerous occasions where the words read, readest, and reading appear. This is powerful evidence that Israel had the written Scriptures and that they were expected to know them. The astute reader will recall Jesus saying, "Have ye not <u>read</u> what David did" in Matthew 12:3. When Christ says this, it confirms that the Scriptures were widely distributed and known in Israel.

The next passage to be considered declares the gospel message to be Scripture:

> For I delivered unto you first of all that which I also received, how that Christ died for our sins <u>according to the Scriptures</u>; And that he was buried, and that he rose again the third day according to the Scriptures. (1 Corinthians 15:3-4)

In Ephesians, Paul shows us the superiority of New Testament revelation:

> How that by <u>revelation</u> he made known unto me the mystery; (as I wrote afore in few words, Whereby, when ye read, ye may understand my knowledge in the mystery of Christ) Which <u>in other ages was not made known</u> unto the sons of men, <u>as it is now revealed unto his holy apostles and prophets by the Spirit</u>. (Ephesians 3:3-5)

In the Old Testament period, certain things were still a mystery, since they were not "made known unto the sons of men." New Testament revelation now makes "known" the mystery of redemption in Christ.

The New Testament repeatedly cites or quotes the Old Testament for proof of New Testament theology. For this reason and others shown, it should be clear that the New Testament texts are the Word of God. Also it can be said, the New Testament is interlocked and interwoven with the Old Testament, which clearly demonstrates their fundamental unity.

And furthermore, if one considers the numerous mentions of the Old Testament in the New and takes these into consideration there are probably over six-hundred quotations from the Old Testament in the New Testament canon. Moreover, there are numerous times where Christ and the apostles quote the Old Testament directly. For instance, in Matthew 19:4-5, Jesus quotes Genesis 2:24, and in Hebrews 1:5 the writer is mentioning Psalms 2:7. Also, there are many other passages where the Old Testament is referred to but no specific Scripture is quoted. These are known as 'Old Testament allusions' in the New Testament.

To support this assertion, consider when the apostle John says:

> For I testify unto every man that heareth the words of the prophecy of this book, If any man shall add unto these things, God shall add unto him the plagues that are written in this book: And if any man shall take away from the words of the book of this prophecy, God shall take away his part out of the book of life, and out of the holy city, and from the things which are written in this book. (Revelation 22:18-19)

This quote from Revelation is just one example of the many times where the New Testament connects itself to the Old Testament without a direct reference. What passage is Revelation referring to in the Old Testament? The reference is:

> What thing soever I command you, observe to do it: thou shalt not add thereto, nor diminish from it. (Deuteronomy 12:32)

CONCLUDING OBSERVATIONS

The New Testament revelation completes the Old Testament revelation and functions as an inspired commentary on the Old Testament Scriptures. The Old Testament is incomplete without the New, and the New Testament stands upon the foundation of the Old, and presupposes knowledge of the Old. The Old Testament provides indispensable background knowledge at almost every point without which the New Testament would be much weaker and its true meaning would be lost. The Old Testament provides the revelation upon which the New Testament builds. The two form a compete unit, inseparably joined together as a single-minded divine testimony. That testimony is Christ.

With this in mind and in conclusion, consider the Great Commission:

> And Jesus came and spake unto them, saying, <u>All power is given unto me in heaven and earth</u>. Go ye therefore, and teach all nations, baptizing them in the name of the Father, and of the Son, and of the Holy Ghost: Teaching them to observe <u>all things whatsoever I have commanded you</u>: and, lo, <u>I am with you</u> always, even unto the end of the world. Amen. (Matthew 28:18-20)

We can be sure that Christ as the sovereign God guarantees the success of the "Great Commission" by His omnipotent presence. Thus, we have the guarantee of Christ Himself that we have victory because of the power of the Word of God. As stated at the beginning, the New Testament writers viewed their own writings as Scripture. Consequently, because of what the passages referenced in this study teach, there is no reason to doubt that the New Testament is the Word of God.

THE WORD OF GOD:
TO BE WRITTEN DOWN

In this study we will see that God's Word was to be written down and set forth as truth that is superior to the oral traditions and experiences of men. The inscription of God's Word is the *prima facie* blueprint that is set forth in the Scriptures. As will be seen, there are good reasons for the inscription of God's Word. One important reason is that all men have to deal with the question of authority, and having God's Word in written form makes it possible to know the Lord's commands. Along with this is the issue of certainty. Before submitting to commands, we need to have certainty that the authority is grounded in the Word of God and not a nebulous tradition made up by men.

Is ultimate authority found in God, man, or the church? How are questions of absolute truth answered? Do we look to oral traditions for answers? If so, how many traditions are there and do they all agree? Are we guided by subjective feelings? Do we just simply follow the leaders? Or, are the Scriptures reliable as the standard to guide us and settle disputes? This idea of following the leader is the approach used by some religions. The inscription of God's Word gives us an objective divine standard to determine truth. We will see that it is normative and God's design for the inscription of His Word.

Observe the clear commands that are set forth in God's Word about this:

> For whatsoever things were <u>written</u> aforetime were <u>written</u> for our learning... (Romans 15:4)

> And Moses <u>wrote</u> all the words of the Lord... And he [Moses] took the <u>book </u>of the covenant, and <u>read</u> in the audience of the people... (Exodus 24:4, 7)

> Now go, <u>write it</u> before them in a table, and <u>note it in a book</u>, that it may be for the time to come for ever and ever. (Isaiah 30:8)

> Take thee a roll of a <u>book</u>, and <u>write therein all the words</u> that I have spoken unto thee against Israel, and against Judah, and against all the nations, from the day I spake unto thee, from the days of Josiah, even unto this day. (Jeremiah 36:2)

> Only be thou strong and very courageous, that thou mayest observe to do according to all the law, which Moses my servant commanded thee: turn not from it to the right hand or to the left, that thou

mayest prosper whithersover thou goest. This book of the law shall not depart out of thy mouth, but thou shalt meditate therein day and night, that thou mayest observe to do according to all that is written therein: for then thou shalt make thy way prosperous, and then thou have good success. (Joshua 1:7-8)

And the Lord answered me, and said, Write the vision, and make it plain upon tables, that he may run that readeth it. (Habakkuk 2:2)

Saying, I am Alpha and Omega, the first and the last: and, What thou seest, write in a book and send it unto the seven churches... (Revelation 1:11)

God's word was to be written down so that His people could know how to live in a way pleasing to Him and be able to know right from wrong. Apart from the objective written standard of Scripture, man is left with his own subjective opinions. In addition to the scriptural pattern just seen, there are numerous examples, by biblical writers, of the appeal to what had been previously written.

A few examples are:

Then stood up Jeshua the son of Jozadak, and his brethren the priests, and Zerrubbabel the son of Shealtiel, and his brethren, and builded the altar of the God of Israel, to offer burnt offerings thereon, as it is written in the law of Moses the man of God. (Ezra 3:2)

But he answered and said, It is written, Man shall not live by bread alone, but by every word that proceedeth out of the mouth of God. (Matthew 4:4)

And Jesus answered him, saying, It is written, That man shall not live by bread alone, but by every word of God. (Luke 4:4)

> For <u>it is written</u>, I will destroy the wisdom of the wise, and will bring to nothing the understanding of the prudent. (1 Corinthians 1:19)

> <u>Because it is written</u>, Be ye holy; for I am holy. (1 Peter 1:16)

When Jesus says, "because," or "it is written," this was the end of the debate for Him. Christ used this very phrase when He rebuffed Satan during the wilderness temptation. In fact, Jesus used "it is written" to preface His teaching or to end an argument numerous times. Moreover, there is not one example in Scripture where Christ's human opponents questioned the authority of Scripture after Jesus used this argument. Jesus clearly used the Scriptures as the final court of appeal. Christ and the apostle Paul viewed the written Scripture as authoritative and cited them frequently.

Consider the following examples of this normative pattern:

> And beginning at Moses and all the prophets, he expounded unto them <u>in all the scriptures</u> the things concerning himself. (Luke 24:27)

> Search <u>the scriptures</u>; for in them ye think ye have eternal life: <u>and they are they</u> which testify of me. (John 5:39)

> Having therefore obtained help of God, I continue unto this day, witnessing both to small and great, saying none other things than those which the <u>prophets and Moses did say</u> should come. (Acts 26:22)

Where did the prophets and Moses say certain things should come? This passage in Acts 26:22 recounts how the Old Testament prophets and Moses were recorded in Scripture prophesying the coming of Christ and His work of redemption.

> For what saith <u>the scripture</u>? Abraham believed God, and it was counted unto him for righteousness. (Romans 4:3)

It is beyond dispute that God commanded His word to be written to provide His people with directions for life. Not only did Israel have the Scriptures, so did those beyond the borders of Israel. The Ethiopian eunuch in Acts 8:27-39 is a case in point. The Ethiopian was reading from the prophet in (Isaiah 53:7-8) about Christ when Philip meets him. Philip takes over as recorded in verse 35 and starts with the passage from Isaiah that the eunuch was reading and told him about Christ and how to be saved.

What should be done with the written word? Consider Paul's command to Timothy:

> What you heard from me, keep as the pattern of sound teaching, with faith and love in Christ Jesus. Guard the good deposit that was entrusted to you, guard it with the help of the Holy Spirit who lives in us. (2 Timothy 1:13-14 NIV)

What did Paul mean by "sound teaching" (or sound words) in 2 Timothy 1:13?

> Hold fast the form of sound words, which thou hast heard of me, in faith and love which is in Christ Jesus. **By sound words which he had heard from Paul, can be meant nothing but the doctrine of the gospel,** which, as it is itself pure, and consistent with itself, not rotten, one piece of which will not hold with the other, so it tends to make souls sound as to their spiritual health: this doctrine Timothy had been instructed in by Paul; whether he had given him a written form of them or no is not much material, for this (if he did) was not that which he would have him.
>
> Matthew Poole's *Commentary on the Holy Bible* (Peabody, Massachusetts, Hendrickson Publishers, 1985) pp. 791, 792.

"Guard the good deposit." What was this good deposit Paul speaks of in 2 Timothy 1:14?

Parallel with the thought just expressed is that contained in verse 14: That precious (or: excellent) thing which was entrusted to you guard through the Holy Spirit who dwells within us.

The **"precious deposit" is, of course, the gospel,** taken in its widest sense (see on 1 Tim. 6:20). It consists of "the sound words" which Timothy has heard from Paul (see the preceding verse). It is precious or excellent because it belongs to God and results in his glory through the salvation of those who accept it by sovereign grace (see verses 8–10 above). Again (as in 1 Tim. 6:20) Timothy is urged once for all to guard this deposit. He must defend it against every attack and never allow it to be changed or modified in the slightest degree.

But since the enemy is strong and Timothy is weak, Paul very wisely adds the thought that this guarding cannot be done except "through the Holy Spirit who dwells within us," that is, within Paul, Timothy, all believers (Rom. 8:11).

Timothy, then, should hold on to the pure gospel, the sound doctrine, as Paul has always done.

William Hendriksen, *New Testament Commentary: Thessalonians, Timothy and Titus* (Grand Rapids, Michigan, Baker Book House, 1984), p. 237.

Timothy should "guard" God's revelation, namely, the gospel. This is completely reasonable and parallels 1 Timothy 1:11, where Paul told Timothy that the glorious Gospel of the blessed God had been committed to his trust. Likewise, Christian believers are to guard the treasure of God's Word.

"The good deposit" is a collection of writings, namely, portions of the written New Testament. The gospels and letters of Paul in the First Century were being circulated among the churches.

The "good deposit" or the gospel of God, most assuredly included the emerging corpus of the New Testament Canon. Eventually, the supporting oral traditions would be eclipsed and superseded by the completed canon.

After seeing the commentary evidence, we can extrapolate that this "deposit" was a distinguishable collection of writings. This is clearly presupposed from Paul's command to "guard it." You cannot guard a nebulous, indefinable recollection of oral traditions. It should also be noted there is no indication that this "deposit" was inadequate. The apostolic teachings are described as: "traditions" in 2 Thessalonians 2:15, "form of sound words" in 2 Timothy 1:13, "the faith" in Jude 1:3; "that good thing" in 2 Timothy 1:14, "the holy commandment" in 2 Peter 2:21, "the apostle's doctrine" in Acts 2:42, and "the faithful word and sound doctrine" in Titus 1:9. These passages referring to apostolic teaching also demonstrate evidence of the New Testament canon during the apostolic age.

It is important to note how the Apostle used the word "traditions" in 2 Thessalonians:

> In traditions which you were taught there is no suggestion of the Romanist idea of Tradition, conceived as an authority distinct from the written Word of God; for the Apostle continues, whether by word or latter of ours (the pronoun belongs to both nouns). He bids them hold by what he had taught, whether it came through this channel or that, provided it were really from himself (comp. 2 Thessalonians 2:2, and ch. 2 Thessalonians 3:14; 2 Thessalonians 3:17). He is now beginning to communicate with the Churches by letter, and stamps his Epistles with the authority of his spoken word. The sentence asserts the claim of the true Apostolic teaching, as against any who would "beguile" the Church away from it. Comp. 1 Corinthians 11:2: "I praise you that in all things you remember us, and hold fast the traditions, even as I delivered them to you."

The Apostle's "traditions" included, besides doctrine, also the "charges" (or "commands") he gave
on matters of morals and practical life (ch. 2 Thessalonians 3:4; 1 Thessalonians 4:2). The body of
Christian doctrine, brought to its finished form,
he calls in his last letters "the deposit" (1 Timothy
6:20; 2 Timothy 1:12; 2 Timothy 1:14); while his
practical teaching is "the charge" (or "commandment"), 1 Timothy 1:5; 1 Timothy 1:18.

G. G. Findlay, *The Cambridge Bible for Schools and
Colleges: Thessalonians* (Cambridge University Press,
1898), p.157.

We should note John Gill's comments on "traditions" from 2 Thessalonians 2:15:

And hold the traditions which ye have been taught:
meaning the truths of the Gospel, which may be
called traditions, because they are delivered from
one to another; the Gospel was first delivered by
God the Father to Jesus Christ, as Mediator, and
by him to his apostles, and by them to the churches
of Christ; whence it is called the form of doctrine
delivered to them, and the faith once delivered to
the saints: and also the ordinances of the Gospel
which the apostles received from Christ, and as
they received them faithfully delivered them, such
as baptism and the Lord's supper; as well as rules of
conduct and behaviour, both in the church, and in
the world, even all the commandments of Christ,
which he ordered his apostles to teach, and which
they gave by him; see 2 Thessalonians 3:6. And so
the Syriac version here renders it, "the commandments": and these were such as these saints had
been taught by the apostles, under the direction of

Christ, and through the guidance of his Spirit; and were not the traditions of men or the rudiments of the world, but what they had received from Christ, through the hands of the apostles.

John Gill, *Old and New Testaments, 2 Thessalonians* (Grace Works, Multi-Media Labs), 2011, p. 37.

During the lifetime of the apostles their "traditions" or teachings i.e., the revelation of the New Testament was conveyed in two ways: first, orally by their teaching and preaching and second, by their writings, 2 Thessalonians 2:15. It is important to note, there is no evidence that there was any difference between their oral teaching and preaching, and their written epistles. This holds true for God's spokesmen in the Old Testament well. Any oral traditions that were in conflict with the written Scriptures would have been rejected in accordance with Isaiah 8:20, "because there is no light in them." Apostolic teaching was restricted to the Scriptures alone like the prophets of old which were recorded in the Old Testament canon. Surviving oral traditions and non-canonical writings may have value, but only as non-authoritative sources.

It should be self-evident that after the apostles died, their writings were the only means the church had to distribute their teachings or "traditions" with accuracy. "Why is this so," someone might ask? Many may recall classroom exercises where the teacher would give a student a word or sentence and then instruct the student to pass the word or sentence verbally around the class room so that the previous student in the process could not hear. When the last student in the process received the word or sentence he would announce it to the class. The teacher would then make known the original word or sentence. The original word or sentence had changed in this process and was never the same thing as at the beginning. This exercise demonstrates the inferiority of oral or verbal communications.

In spite of the inferiority of verbal or oral communications, some religious practices such as Roman Catholicism and Eastern Orthodoxy make use of oral traditions which have caused much confusion and doctrinal deviation in church history. There are traditions that exist outside of the Bible, some of which are good as well as bad. The elevation of oral traditions to a status of equality with the Scriptures has allowed doctrinal perversions to creep into the church. This is comparable to the experience-dominated hermeneutic that subtly causes biblical misinterpretation.

It is interesting to note that an oral tradition ultimately has to be written down or it will be lost, again proving the superiority of the written Word of God. Once this oral tradition is written down, it then stands alongside Scripture in some religious traditions as an equal authority. There are many religious groups that maintain oral traditions that are now written down. What one finds is that there are many extra-biblical writings that were once oral, now written, that conflict with each other. It seems that ultimately if accepting these traditions, you have to then depend upon what the leaders tell you as to the meaning and validity of this oral-now-written tradition. As will be seen, Christ denounced a number of man-made traditions quite strongly in the Scriptures. Extra-biblical traditions must always be evaluated in light of Scripture.

Did Jesus ever refer to traditions or teaching of the religious leaders of His day? Yes, and these traditions do not command authority in the same way as His appeal to "it is written" in Matthew 4:4; 21:13; Mark 9:12; John 8:17. The phrase "it is written" is a clear reference to the finality of the Word of God. It should be noted that when Jesus says, "it was said by them of old time" he is referring to something other than the Scriptures. Jesus was simply correcting or setting the record straight. These were the traditions of men and not the commandments of God He was speaking against.

An example of this is when Christ was referring to the commentary of the Jewish elders that was in error, not the Old Testament Scriptures themselves:

> Ye have heard that it was said by them of old time,
> Thou shalt not kill; and whosoever shall kill shall
> be in danger of the judgment. (Matthew 5:21)

We find another example in Matthew's gospel where Christ was referring to the traditions or teaching (either in written or oral form) of the Pharisees.

Consider where He says:

> Ye have heard that it hath been said, Thou shalt
> love thy neighbour, and hate thine enemy.
> (Matthew 5:43)

Once again, Christ is referring to the false teaching of the Pharisees, not an error in Scripture. Jesus mentioned the tradition of the elders in Mark 7:3. Christ goes on in Mark 7:9 to say that the Pharisees had substituted the traditions of men for the commandments of God. This was a serious error. We must always be on guard against false traditions being substituted for the Word of God. Hopefully the reader sees how Christ always corrected the false traditions of the Pharisees by citing the written Word of God.

Christ condemned the teaching and tradition of the Pharisees in the strongest terms in Matthew 23. Christ's denunciation of Pharisaical teaching is so strong that it should give any one pause before attempting to elevate their own traditions or revelations to a status of equality with the biblical Scriptures. In addition, Christ places tremendous emphasis on the Scriptures and knowing them correctly.

In fact, Jesus rebuked the religious leaders for not knowing the Scriptures:

> And Jesus answering said unto them, Do ye not
> therefore err, because <u>ye know not the Scriptures</u>,
> neither the power of God? (Mark 12:24)

The religious leaders of Christ's day erred because they did not know the Scriptures. This strongly implies that the Scriptures are reliable and trustworthy as evidenced by Christ's rebuke of the leaders for not knowing them.

If the Scriptures are reliable and trustworthy, it follows that they are sufficient. This rebuke of Christ makes no sense if the Scriptures are incomplete or were unavailable. If the Scriptures were incomplete, then whatever knowledge was possessed would be incomplete and the leaders whom Christ had rebuked could claim justifiable ignorance.

When Jesus quotes the Old Testament or says, "it is written," this should inspire confidence in the Scriptures because Jesus is establishing them as God's highest authority. He obviously knew that the Scriptures were reliable and He quoted them as authoritative. Again, we see that the Scriptures existed and were widely known in Israel.

There are numerous places where Christ and the apostles quote the Old Testament directly. For example, in Matthew 19: 4, 5, Jesus quotes Genesis 2:24. In Hebrews 1:5 the writer is mentioning Psalms 2:7. In Acts 18:24, 28 we learn of Apollos who was "<u>mighty in the Scriptures</u>" and convinced the Jews publicly that Jesus was Christ from the Scriptures. What Scriptures were these? They were the Old Testament Scriptures. This sheds important light on how important the Scriptures are. Apollos did not use testimonials or new revelations to convince the Jews; he used the Scriptures.

Early Christians and Christians today have preached orally and have written sermons and books. Yet there is a major difference between our preaching and writing and that of the apostles. The Word of the apostles was revelatory, while ours is simply repeating the divinely inspired Word of the apostles. The apostle's words were original and authoritative. The Church's and our words are derivative and only authoritative as long as it is completely faithful to the word of the apostle's, i.e., the Word of God.

The astute reader will see the clear pattern in Scripture of appealing to what had been previously written. This establishes a normative pattern of using the Scriptures to determine truth. Therefore, using the Scriptures to interpret the Scriptures and allowing them to be the highest or final court of appeal is biblical and it is the duty of God's people to submit to their authority. This is so because when the Scriptures speak, it is God speaking!

And finally, in light of our Lord's perennial emphatic declaration "it is written," the apostle Paul sets down the rule for the Church of God:

> Now, brothers, I have applied these things to myself and Apollos for your benefit, so that you may learn from us the meaning of the saying, "<u>Do not go beyond what is written</u>." Then you will not take pride in one man over against another. (1 Corinthians 4:6 NIV)

It seems beyond dispute that God's Word written in the Scriptures is the only sure infallible source of truth!

THE SUFFICIENCY OF SCRIPTURES

The self-evident testimony of the Scriptures is that they are sufficient. The Scriptures are completely adequate to meet the needs of the believer. This teaching is all over the face of the Scriptures. The believer can have confidence in the Scriptures. God's Words are described as "pure," "perfect," "a light," and "eternal." This conclusion is one that can be drawn from or deduced from the Scriptures by good and necessary consequence.

For example, consider the testimony from the following passages:

> The words of the LORD are pure words: as silver
> tried in a furnace of earth, purified seven times.
> Thou shalt keep them, O LORD, thou shalt preserve
> them from this generation for ever. (Psalms 12:6-7)

> For ever, O LORD, thy word is settled in heaven.
> (Psalms 119:89)

> Thy word is a lamp unto my feet, and a light unto
> my path. (Psalms 119:105)

> The law of the Lord is perfect, converting the soul:
> the testimony of the Lord is sure, making wise the
> simple. The statutes of the Lord are right, rejoicing
> the heart: the commandment of the Lord is pure,
> enlightening the eyes. The fear of the Lord is clean,
> enduring for ever: the judgments of the Lord are
> true and righteous altogether. (Psalms 19:7-9)

Because the Scriptures are true, they are "righteous altogether." Moreover, if the law of God were incomplete, the conversion of the soul would be tenuous at best. The necessary biblical conclusion is that the Scriptures are complete. And, as will be seen, Mormonism teaches that believers can become unconverted.

The Scriptures have more to say along this line of reasoning:

> But the Comforter, which is the Holy Ghost, whom
> the Father will send in my name, he shall teach you
> all things, and bring to your remembrance, whatso-
> ever I have said unto you. (John 14:26)

This promise of Christ to his apostles tells us that the Holy Spirit will teach them "all things," and bring to their remembrance all things that he said unto them. This is a promise by God to the apostles that important information (i.e., revelation) would be given to them. It is a justifiable biblical conclusion that this revelation would be complete and sufficient because Jesus said "all things." The wording "all things" is used in a qualified sense, but admitting this in no way contradicts the conclusion that this apostolic revelation (now Scripture) would be anything less than complete and sufficient. The "all things" pertain to whatsoever God intended to reveal, including His revelation necessary for salvation.

Along this same line of thinking, consider Paul's ministry to the church. Did Paul leave anything out of his words to the church?

Absolutely not, listen to the apostle:

> And how I kept back nothing that was profitable
> unto you, but have shown you, and have taught
> you publicly, from house to house... For I have
> not shunned to declare to declare unto you <u>all the</u>
> <u>counsel of God</u>. (Acts 20:20, 27)

Paul did not believe that God's Word was insufficient. This is proved by his use of the phrase "all the counsel of God." Paul believed that he had this counsel for the Church. This whole "counsel of God" was the same message that Moses and the prophets spoke. See Acts 26:22 for proof of this; "Having therefore obtained help of God, I continue unto this day, witnessing both to small and great, saying none other things than those which the prophets and Moses did say should come..." The Scripture tells us that what is written will lead us to God that we might have life. This would again be tenuous at best if parts of Scripture have been lost, corrupted, or were insufficient.

Consider the further testimony of Scripture:

> But these <u>are written</u>, that ye might believe that
> Jesus is the Christ, the Son of God, and believing
> ye might have life through his name. (John 20:31)

> But the <u>word of the Lord endureth for ever</u>. And
> this is the word which by the gospel is preached
> unto you. (1 Peter 1:25)

It is clear that Peter had confidence in God's Word. The Scriptures were given so that we might obtain life, and they endure forever. The believer does not need anything more than the written Word of God. In the next verse notice how God says, "All Scripture is given that the man of God may be perfect, thoroughly furnished unto all good works."

The implications of this for the doctrine of the sufficiency of the Scriptures are enormous:

> All Scripture is given by inspiration of God, and is
> profitable for doctrine, for reproof, for correction,
> for instruction in righteousness: That the man of
> God may be perfect, thoroughly furnished unto all
> good works. (2 Timothy 3:16-17)

The Greek word translated "inspiration" means "God-breathed," or that God is the source of the Scriptures. God's inspiration of the Scriptures sets them apart from all other writings of men. They came from him. God used men to write His Word in the Bible. He did it in such a way as to make sure that what was written was exactly what He intended or designed. This means the Scriptures are divinely inspired.

What if the Scriptures were incomplete? If the Scriptures were incomplete, the "man of God" would never be able to "be perfect, thoroughly furnished unto all good works." Paul's instruction here would not be true if portions of the Scriptures were lost or some other standard needed. That is because the Scriptures are connected to this process of the perfecting of the man of God.

In a similar fashion, the next verse clearly sets forth the sufficiency of Scripture:

> Think not that I am come to destroy the law, or
> the prophets: I am not come to destroy, but to ful-
> fil. For verily I say unto you, Till heaven and earth
> pass, one jot or one tittle shall in no wise pass from
> the law, till all be fulfilled. (Matthew 5:17)

Jesus said that the least part of the law would not pass away. One implication is that nothing would be lost. If the least is to be preserved, then surely, the weightier things will not be lost. Consequently, we can have confidence that God's Word is complete. There are not books missing from the Bible nor do we need some kind of nebulous oral tradition interpreted exclusively by church leaders.

The next passage from Isaiah warns us about those who will go beyond Scripture:

> To the law and to the testimony: if they speak not
> according to this word, it is because there is no
> light in them. (Isaiah 8:20)

Isaiah sets God's word forth as the standard. In preparation for the close of the apostolic era, like Isaiah, Paul sets forth the Scriptures as the objective source that must be the final court of appeal.

By apostolic command believers are bound to the written word:

> Now brothers, I have applied these things to myself
> and Apollos for your benefit, so that you may learn
> from us the meaning of the saying, <u>Do not go beyond
> what is written</u>.... (1 Corinthians 4:6) (NIV)

In the Tyndale *New Testament Commentary on First Corinthians*, Leon Morris makes the following comment about the above verse:

> "not beyond what is written" was a catch-cry famil-
> iar to Paul and his readers, directing attention to
> the need for conformity to Scripture.
>
> Leon Morris, *The Tyndale New Testament Com-
> mentary 1 Corinthians* (Grand Rapids, Michigan,
> Inter-Varsity Press, and Eerdmans, 1983), p. 78.

The above passage in First Corinthians clearly condemns all forms of extra-biblical revelation including an oral tradition that is allegedly on par with the written Word of God. There is no need to go beyond Scripture. Why? Because it is complete.

The biblical tests of a prophet found in Deuteronomy 12:32 - 13:4; Deuteronomy 18:20-22; and Isaiah 8:20 clearly set forth Scripture as the standard and a sufficient guide. Remember, Jesus used this standard to stop the mouths of His adversaries when He said, "Have ye never read" in Mark 2:25 regarding David's actions. What did the Pharisees say in response to this? Nothing! Some religions teach that you are supposed to pray about the purported prophet and his message, then see if it rings true by getting a confirming sensation after prayer. The Old Testament believer in contrast was to compare the purported prophet and his message with what had been revealed and written by God in His Word.

In the book of Galatians, Paul continues this same pattern for testing purported revelation:

> But though we, or an angel from heaven, preach
> any other gospel unto you than that which we have
> preached unto you, let him be accursed. As we said
> before, so say I now again, If any man preach any
> other gospel unto you that that ye have received, let
> him be accursed. (Galatians 1:8-9)

Hopefully the reader has discerned the clear pattern in Scripture. This pattern is appealing to what has been written. As mentioned previously, when Christ said, "It is written," this denotes finality and certainty because there was nothing more authoritative than God's Word. It should be noted that Christ's commentary on the Scriptures is infallible; ours is not.

The Apostle Paul follows this same pattern of appealing to Scripture:

> And that from a child thou hast known the holy
> scriptures, which are able to make thee wise unto
> salvation through faith which is in Christ Jesus. (2
> Timothy 3:15)

The written word is the standard and it has not changed. Consider the importance of the following verse:

> Which is the church of the living God, the pillar
> and foundation of the truth. (1 Timothy 3:15 NIV)

Hopefully, nothing said by this writer in this study on the authority and sufficiency of the Scriptures would cause anyone to think that the church is unimportant. The church is very important. How is this so? The church today, like a pillar or foundation, defends and supports the gospel. How does the church do this? (1) By "Holding forth the word of life..." Philippians 2:16; (2) by "... rightly dividing the word of truth" 2 Timothy 2:15; (3) by "teaching all nations..." Matthew 28:19; (4) and by "guarding the good deposit" 2 Timothy 1:13-14 (NIV).

The church should do these things with all the resources in its power. These tasks would be impossible if Scripture were incomplete or corrupted. Why? Because you could not know if you were "holding forth the word of life" or the word of men. God commands us to "rightly divide the word of life." God would not command us to rightly divide something which we did not possess. Why? If we did not possess the Scriptures it would be an impossibility to rightly divide them. The biblical conclusion is that Scripture has been preserved. Listen to the apostle Peter:

> By the word of God, which liveth and abideth for
> ever. (1 Peter 1:23)

Can anything be clearer? Peter is not talking about anything other than the written Scriptures.

Peter goes on to say:

> According as his divine power hath given unto
> us all things that pertain unto life and godliness,
> through the knowledge of him that hath called us
> to glory and virtue. (2 Peter 1:3)

As Peter instructs us, there are a great number of spiritual blessings that God has given us. We can have confidence that "all things" would have to include Scripture as one of those things. There is not any limitation expressed here because the passage is dealing with what God has given us for salvation. Consequently, we have confidence in the sufficiency of Scripture.

Consider the following examples on Jesus' view of the accuracy of the Old Testament Scriptures and their prophetic fulfillment concerning himself: Matthew 26:31; Matthew 26:54; Mark 9:12, 13; John 13:18; John 17:12. Jesus referred to Old Testament individuals in the following verses: John 8:56 (Abraham); Luke 17:26-32 (Noah and Lot); Matthew 3:3 (Isaiah); and in Luke 4:24-27 (Elijah and Elisha). The case is irrefutable: Jesus believed in the reliability of the written Word of God. Consequently, the believer can have confidence in the reliability and trustworthiness of Scripture. Reliability and sufficiency go hand in hand. An insufficient or incomplete document is not reliable.

There is no evidence that Jesus believed the Scriptures to be anything less than complete. The tremendous spiritual corruption of Israel in Christ's day, which culminated in the destruction of the Jewish nation in 70 A. D. (Matthew 23:34-36), did not affect the Old Testament canon. The canon was intact in Christ's day, and the discovery of the Dead Sea Scrolls confirms the accuracy of the Hebrew Masoretic Text used by the King James translators many centuries later. In fact, there is virtually no difference between the First Century copies of Old Testament Dead Sea copies and the Masoretic text that is one thousand years older.

The New Testament books were brought into the canon of Scripture as the church bore testimony to the fact that our present New Testament books claimed to be by their very nature the Word of God. This was a process in which the testimony of the Holy Spirit bore witness by and with the Scriptures in the hearts of men. This was not a process where the church, as a divinely inspired entity, determined what the canon of Scripture would be. The Scriptures themselves bore this testimony of their inspiration.

Some teach that the church in and of itself made this decision. But the Word of God does not depend upon man or the church. The Scriptures do not come from the church. They come from God. The Scriptures do not need our confirmation to be true. Their truthfulness is independent of man and even the church. There is more manuscript evidence for New Testament revelation than any other writing from antiquity. Therefore, we can have the same confidence that alleged corruption during the New Testament Church Age did not alter the New Testament canon of Scripture in any way. God is LORD of heaven and earth. He is Sovereign and "none can stay his hand..." (Daniel 4:35). Preserving His Word is a small matter for Him.

In conclusion, we can say, the Scriptures of the Old and New Testaments are the infallible Word of God and a sure rule of faith. In addition, they are the final court of appeal to settle religious disputes, and the Bible includes everything we need to know to receive salvation and to live a godly life.

> You have Scripture for a master instead of me; from
> there you can learn whatever you would know.
> John Chrysostom

In summary thus far, *The Westminster Confession* "Chapter 1, Of the Holy Scripture" says:

> I. Although the light of nature, and the works of
> creation and providence, do so far manifest the
> goodness, wisdom, and power of God, as to leave
> men inexcusable; yet are they not sufficient to give
> that knowledge of God, and of his will, which is
> necessary unto salvation; therefore it pleased the
> Lord, at sundry times, and in divers manners, to

reveal himself, and to declare that his will unto his Church; and afterwards for the better preserving and propagating of the truth, and for the more sure establishment and comfort of the Church against the corruption of the flesh, and the malice of Satan and of the world, to commit the same wholly unto writing; which maketh the holy Scripture to be most necessary; those former ways of God's revealing his will unto his people being now ceased.

The Sufficiency of Holy Scripture

We believe that this Holy Scripture fully contains the will of God and that all that man must believe in order to be saved is sufficiently taught therein.[1] The whole manner of worship which God requires of us is written in it at length. It is therefore unlawful for any one, even for an apostle, to teach otherwise than we are now taught in Holy Scripture:[2] yes, even if it be an angel from heaven, as the apostle Paul says (Galatians 1:8). Since it is forbidden to add to or take away anything from the Word of God (Deuteronomy 12:32),[3] it is evident that the doctrine thereof is most perfect and complete in all respects.[4]

We may not consider any writings of men, however holy these men may have been, of equal value with the divine Scriptures; nor ought we to consider custom, or the great multitude, or antiquity, or succession of times and persons, or councils, decrees or statutes, as of equal value with the truth of God, since the truth is above all;[5] for all men are of themselves liars, and lighter than a breath. (Psalm 62:9)

Notes to quote for the confession:

[1] 2 Timothy 3:16, 17; 1 Peter 1:10-12.

[2] 1 Corinthians 15:2; 1 Timothy 1:3.

[3] Deuteronomy 4:2; Proverbs 30:6; Acts 26:22; 1 Corinthians 4:6; Revelation 22:18, 19.

[4] Psalm 19:7; John 15:15; Acts 18:28; Acts 20:27; Romans 15:4.

[5] Mark 7:7-9; Acts 4:19; Colossians 2:8; 1 John 2:19. 6 Deuteronomy 4:5, 6; Is 8:20; 1 Corinthians 3:11; Ephesians 4:4-6; 2 Thessalonians 2:2; 2 Timothy 3:14, 15.

Likewise:

> We therefore reject with all our heart whatever does not agree with this infallible rule, 6 as the apostles have taught us: Test the spirits to see whether they are of God. (1 John 4:1)

> If any one comes to you and does not bring this doctrine, do not receive him into your house or give him any greeting. (2 John 1:10)

THE CLOSING
OF THE CANON OF SCRIPTURE

The Scriptures are complete, and divine revelation has ceased. In fact, the ceasing of divine revelation is seen right in the texts of Scripture. This is what is meant when theologians talk about "the closing of the canon."

Consider the biblical evidence for this:

> Beloved, when I gave all diligence to write unto you of the common salvation, it was needful for me to write unto you, and exhort you that ye should earnestly contend for the faith which was once delivered unto the saints. (Jude 3:3)

Also, it should be noted how the *New King James Version* renders the last part of this verse:

Which was once for all delivered to the saints.
(Jude 3:3 NKJV)

This verse in Jude clearly anticipates the closing of the New Testament Canon. What does Jude mean by the phrase "the faith"?

Simon J. Kistemaker in the *New Testament Commentary* of the book of Jude says the following:

> What is this faith Jude mentions? In view of the context, we understand the word faith to mean the body of Christian beliefs. It is the gospel the apostles proclaimed and therefore is equivalent to the apostles teaching. (Acts 2:42)
>
> Simon J. Kistemaker, *New Testament Commentary Jude*
> (Grand Rapids: Baker Book House, 1987), p. 371.

The phrase once [*hapax*] delivered is important. *Hapax* means once for all.

In *Vine's Expository Dictionary of New Testament Words* we find this comment concerning *hapax*:

> Once for all, of what is perpetual validity, not requiring repetition.
>
> W. E. Vine, *Vine's Expository Dictionary Of New Testament Words* (Iowa Falls: Riverside, 1952), p. 809.

The following verse provides more important information concerning the completion of Scripture:

> And are built upon the foundation of the apostles
> and prophets, Jesus Christ himself being the chief
> corner stone. (Ephesians 2:20)

This verse in Ephesians tells us that the apostles are part of the foundation of the church. There is only one foundation that the church has. The Scripture in John 14:26 teaches that the apostles were taught "all things." Paul commanded Timothy to "guard the good deposit" of truth in 2 Timothy 1:14. Clearly this "deposit" was identifiable or else Paul's command to Timothy would not make sense. Furthermore, in order to guard it, this deposit could not have been a nebulous association of oral traditions. Written documents can be compared to forgeries, whereas oral traditions by their very nature are open to endlessly differing accounts and interpretations.

Since the apostles were taught all things, there would be no need for further revelation. What can you add to "all things"? The "good deposit" or the "all things" was tied to the apostolic period at the foundation of the church. The authoritative apostolic writings became part of the New Testament canon. The biblical conclusion is that, after their death, apostolic revelation ceased. Why? On account of the fact that after the death of the apostles their special office in the church ceased. The church has only one foundation, not layers of foundations on top of each other, as the "ongoing-apostolic-office" view would require. In light of this, the ongoing Mormon apostolic offices cannot be true.

The next verse from Daniel cannot be disregarded in its importance for the subject of the closing of the canon:

> Seventy weeks are determined upon thy people and
> upon thy holy city, to finish the transgression, and
> to make an end of sins, and to make reconciliation
> for iniquity, and to bring in everlasting righteous-
> ness, and to seal up the vision and prophecy, and
> to anoint the most Holy. (Daniel 9:24)

The terminus or completion of this prophecy is clearly in the First Century. Verses in Daniel 9:25-27 make it clear that when the seventy-week period begins, this week will continue uninterrupted until the seventy week period is over or complete. Christ's death and resurrection made an end of the sins of His people. He accomplished reconciliation for His people. Christ's people have experienced everlasting righteousness because of the fact that we are clothed in Christ's righteousness, which is everlasting. The phrase "and to seal up the vision and prophecy" clearly sets forth the closing of the canon of Scripture.

E. J. Young in *The Geneva Daniel Commentary* makes the following observations concerning "vision" and prophecy" in the Old Testament:

> Vision was a technical name for revelation given to the

OT prophets (cf. Isaiah 1:1, Amos 1:1, etc.) The prophet was the one through whom this vision was revealed to the people. The two words, vision and prophet, therefore, serve to designate the prophetic revelation of the OT period.... When Christ came, there was no further need of prophetic revelation in the OT sense. E. J. Young, *Daniel* (Oxford: The Banner Of Truth Trust, 1988), p. 200.

Ellicott's *Commentary for English Readers* is in agreement with E. J. Young on Daniel 9:24:

To Seal Up.—σφραγίσαι, Theod.; συντελεσθῆναι, LXX.; impleatur, Jer.; the impression of the translators being that all visions and prophecies were to receive their complete fulfilment in the course of these seventy weeks. It appears, however, to be more agreeable to the context to suppose that the prophet is speaking of the absolute cessation of all prophecy. (Comp. 1Corinthians 13:8.)

Charles John Ellicot, *A Bible Commentary for English Readers* Vol. 5, (London: Cassell, 1882), p. 387

Since there is no fundamental difference between Old and New Testament revelation, and the source of the revelation is identical, there is no reason to doubt that all giving of new revelation ceased in the First Century.

In a similar fashion, in Adam Clarke's commentary concerning this same phrase we read:

...to put an end to the necessity of any farther revelations, by completing the canon of Scriptures, and fulfilling the prophecies which related to his person, sacrifice and the glory that should follow.

Adam Clarke, *Clarke's Commentary* Vol. 4, (Nashville: Abingdom Press, 1956), p. 602.

A passage in 1 Corinthians sheds even more light on the completion of Scripture:

> For we know in part, and we prophesy in part.
> But when that which is perfect is come, then that
> which is in part shall be done away.
> (1 Corinthians 13:9-10)

The passage says that something that is "in part" will be done away with when "that which is perfect is come." What is the apostle referring to when he says that something perfect is coming?

Theologian Gordon H. Clark comments on this:

> There is one phase, not so far mentioned: "When the completion comes," or "when that which is perfect comes." This raises the question: Completion of what? It could be the completion of the canon. Miracles and tongues were for the purpose of guaranteeing the divine origin of apostolic doctrine. They cease when the revelation was completed. Even the word knowledge is better understood this way. Instead of comparing present-day extensive study of the New Testament with Justin's [Martyr] painfully inadequate understanding of the Atonement, it would be better to take knowledge as the apostolic process of revealing new knowledge. This was completed when revelation ceased.
>
> Gordon H. Clark, *First Corinthians* (Jefferson, Maryland: The Trinity Foundation, 1991), pp. 212-213.

Clark is right on track when connecting the coming perfection with the completion of the Scriptures. The tongues and prophecy of the apostolic era confirmed and bore witness to the truthfulness of that message. But tongues, prophecy, and revelatory knowledge were lacking when compared with the written Scripture. The written Scriptures are far superior to spoken words.

Dr. Leonard Coppes also has relevant comments regarding this section of Scripture:

This is a clear statement that when the knowledge being given through the apostles and prophets is complete, tongues and prophecy shall cease. Tongues, prophecy, and knowledge (*gnosis*) constitute partial, incomplete stages. Some may stumble over the idea that "knowledge" represents a partial and incomplete (revelational) stage. But is rightly remarked that Paul distinguishes between *sophia* and *gnosis* in I Cor. 12:8 All three terms (tongues, prophecy, knowledge) involve divine disclosure of verbal revelation and all three on that basis alone ceased when the foundation (i.e., the perfect) came (10). Verse 11 speaks of the partial as childlike (cf., 14:20) and the perfect as manly (the apostolic is "manly," too, cf., 14:20). Paul reflecting on those who are limited to these childlike things describes this limitation as seeing in a mirror darkly (12). When the perfect (the apostolic *depositum*) is come, full knowledge is present.

Leonard J. Coppes, *Whatever Happened to Biblical Tongues?* (Chattanooga, Tennessee: Pilgrim Publishing Company, 1977), pp. 59-60.

Coppes, like Clark, connects the perfection with the completion of the canon. The next passage of Scripture cited contains a strong warning not to tamper with God's Word.

This verse is particularly relevant for the closing of canon during the First Century at this point in redemptive history:

For I testify unto every man that heareth the words of the prophecy of this book, If any man shall add unto these things, God shall add unto him the plagues that are written in this book: And if any man shall take away from the words of the book of this prophecy, God shall take away his part out

of the book of life, and out of the holy city, and
from the things which are written in this book.
(Revelation 22:18-19)

The book of Revelation, for good reasons, is believed to be the last book written. It was completed prior to 70 A.D. The passages in Revelation 1:3 and 22:6, 12 are time indicators that point to an early date to this book. Why someone may ask. The wording in these texts such as "for the time is at hand" and "which must shortly be done" provide convincing evidence for an early date prior to 70 A.D. for John's revelation. This is because, the First Century fulfillment of the prophecies within the book are relevant to dating of Revelation prior to 70 A.D. So the time-sensitive texts previously mentioned become important indicators pointing towards dating the book in the First Century.

In addition, the temple in chapter eleven is shown to still be in existence, also supporting this early date prior to 70 A.D. If an early date for the book of Revelation is accurate, then it allows the book to fit into the time frame of Daniel's prophecy. Accordingly, the book of Revelation fits into the time frame and purview of Daniel's "seventy weeks." Therefore, those who argue for continued revelation do so at the peril of their souls since they are urging men to violate this scriptural warning recorded in the last book of the canon.

Another passage that sheds important light on the penalty for giving false revelation is in Zechariah thirteen. The context of this section of Zechariah places it in the First Century. See Zechariah 11:13; 12:10; 13:1; 13:7 for proof of this First Century setting.

Consider this warning not to add to God's word:

It shall come to pass that if anyone still prophesies,
then his father and mother who begot him will say
to him, You shall not live, because you have spoken
lies in the name of the Lord. And his father and
mother who begot him shall thrust him through
when he prophesies. (Zechariah 13:3 NKJ)

This passage supports the view that prophecy has ended in light of the fact that the death penalty is still to be carried out for false prophetic utterances and is in harmony with Daniel 9:24. The phrase "If anyone still prophesies" makes it clear that prophecy has ended. The death penalty is required for those who give new revelation. Why? Because it is false revelation since God has ceased giving revelation. This is the consistent theme of Scripture. Again, see Revelation 22:18-19; Galatians 1:8, 9; Deuteronomy 13:5 for the penalties and curses associated with violating this prohibition.

Consider the important fact that Jesus is the incarnate word of God:

> And the Word was made flesh, and dwelt among us, (and we beheld his glory, the glory as of the only begotten of the Father,) full of grace and truth. (John 1:14)

Because of the incarnation, the next passage may be the most important verse in our study regarding the completion of the Scriptures:

> God, Who at sundry times and in divers manners spake in times past unto the fathers by the prophets, Hath in these last days spoken unto us by his Son, whom he hath appointed heir of all things, by whom he also made the worlds. (Hebrews 1:1-2)

This passage in Hebrews makes it clear that Christ Jesus is the final and complete revelation of God. God in times past spoke through the prophets. Now, He speaks through Christ. God speaks to us in and through the Scriptures which Jesus said "testify of me" (John 5:39). Jesus also admonished his disciples saying "And beginning at Moses and all the prophets, he expounded unto them in all the Scriptures the things concerning himself" (Luke 24:27). Christ is the head cornerstone of the Church's foundation. He is the head of His Church.

Jesus as the head of the Church commissioned the twelve apostles to speak in His name with His authority and power:

> And when he had called unto him his twelve disciples, he gave them power against unclean spirits, to cast them out, and to heal all manner of sickness and all manner of disease.... These twelve Jesus sent forth... (Matthew 10:1-5)

These apostles whom Jesus commissioned spoke in His name (2 Peter 3:2) and they wrote in His name (1 Corinthians 14:37).

God confirmed the words of the apostles with power:

> Truly the signs of an apostle were wrought among
> you in all patience, in signs, and wonders, and
> mighty deeds. (2 Corinthians 12:12)

The words of the apostles were essentially the words of Christ, and as was shown earlier, the words of the apostles that God intended to preserve for His Church were committed to writing. Beyond the words of Christ and His apostles, new alleged revelations are nothing more than an attempt to rebuild or add to the foundation of the church. Any attempt to add to Scripture is a direct attack upon the person and work of Christ. How is this so? The Scriptures are so connected to Christ e.g., Luke 24:27, and John 5:39, that any attempt to undermine them is an attack upon Christ himself. In the book of Colossians we see Christ's preeminence over all of creation:

> Who is the image of the invisible God, the first-
> born of every creature: For by him were all things
> created, that are in heaven, and that are in earth,
> visible and invisible, whether they be thrones,
> or dominions, or principalities, or powers: all
> things were created by him and for him: And he
> is before all things, and by him all things consist.
> (Colossians 1:15-17)

The Father declared concerning Jesus in Matthew 17:5: "…This is my beloved Son, in whom I am well pleased; hear ye him." Where do we hear the words of Christ? It has been abundantly demonstrated that we hear Christ speaking in the Scriptures of the Old and New Testaments. In addition, when we read "the Scriptures hath said" and "God hath said" we see how the Scriptures and God speaking are equated in such a way as to be identical. Therefore, the testimony of Christ is so connected with and interwoven into the very fabric of Scripture that to deny the authority of Scripture in any fashion is to deny Christ Himself.

In conclusion it can be said: the voice of Scripture is assuredly the word of God. The testimony from Scripture itself leads to the realization that the Scriptures are sufficient and the final court of appeal or "*Sola Scriptura*" as the men of the reformation put it. This should be the testimony of the church and all of God's people. The word of God does depend upon man or the church. The Scriptures do not need our confirmation to be true. Their truthfulness is independent of man and even the church. For those who go beyond Scripture to differing authorities such as "sacred traditions," new revelations, or spiritual experiences, it must be said that this is nothing more or less than setting yourself or some alleged authority above the Scriptures.

When Jesus said, "it is written," He established beyond all doubt that the Scriptures are the only and authoritative, cohesive, incorruptible Word of God. A pattern has been seen where the writers of Scripture appeal to other Scriptures establishing two important principles of Protestantism. They are, first, that the Scripture is the best interpreter of Scripture, and second, that since the Scriptures are identical with God speaking they must be the highest court of appeal for the Christian.

Consequently, because of the declaration "It is written," the Scriptures are authoritative and sufficient. In light of this and the closing of the canon, new revelations (no matter who gives them) are false revelations. The Scriptures came from God, not the church. God is the author of the Scriptures. Therefore, the Scriptures are the highest authority. Alleged spiritual experiences, new revelations and traditions must not guide man, only the Scriptures where God has spoken. For those who disagree with this conclusion, the burden of proof is upon them.

For a presuppositional defense of Scripture, see *The Importance and Necessity of Special Revelation*, appendix one.

CHAPTER 2

PRIMACY OF SCRIPTURES

n this chapter, which concludes my studies on the reliability of the Scriptures, it is necessary to comment on several objections that have been raised against the historic Protestant view of Scripture. My comments are against objections that have been made in public forums and advanced by various organized religious groups. I have encountered these arguments when discussing the Protestant view of Scripture with the followers of Joseph Smith Jr., Roman Catholics, Eastern Orthodox and those in the Charismatic movement. I, in turn, will raise a number of questions that the opponents of *Sola Scriptura* should consider. It is not my intention to engage in an extensive interaction with the opponents of *Sola Scriptura*, since Protestant theologians have done so on many occasions. A number of different "straw man" arguments could be raised against the historic view of Scripture covered in my previous articles. But these fallacious arguments collapse when they misstate their opponent's position, since attacking a misstated position does nothing to refute the actual position under consideration.

First, someone may cite a passage like "Ye shall not add unto the word which I command you, neither shall ye diminish ought from it, that ye may keep the commandments of the Lord your God which I command you" (Deuteronomy 4:2), which forbids the adding to or the diminishing of Scripture, and claim that this verse teaches the closing of the canon at that point in redemptive history. This is a specious attempt to demonstrate that the Protestant view of Scripture "just does not work". Passages of this nature simply refer to prohibiting man from adding to Scripture rather than demanding a closing of the canon. The passage from Deuteronomy cannot demand a closed canon at that point, since previous Scripture had set forth predictive events that had not been fulfilled at that point in history.

Another may cite a passage like, "And there are also many other things which Jesus did, the which, if they should be written every one, I suppose that even the world itself could not contain the books that should be written. Amen..." (John 21:25), which refers to the potential of Christ's teaching filling the whole world with books, in an attempt to distort the meaning of a passage like,

"But the Comforter, which is the Holy Ghost, whom the Father will send in my name, he shall teach you all things, and bring all things to your remembrance, whatsoever I have said unto you..." (John 14:26), which deals with Christ's message to the apostles. Yet, hyperbole is being used as a rhetorical device in John 21:25. Hence it is a fallacious interpretation that seeks to open the door for continued revelation by leading people to believe that there is still more to the "all things."

John 14:26 certainly does not mean that Jesus taught his apostles all about the occult and deviant sexual practices. Jesus said many words that are not recorded in Scripture. Jesus probably talked about the weather and thanked his mother for a good meal and these instances are not recorded. There is clearly a limitation in the "all things" of the passage. John 14:26 is understood in relation to passages like; "According as his divine power hath given unto us all things that pertain unto life and godliness, through the knowledge of him that hath called us to glory and virtue" (2 Peter 1:3) and "All Scripture is given by inspiration of God, and is profitable for doctrine, for reproof, for correction, for instruction in righteousness: That the man of God may be perfect, thoroughly furnished unto all good works" (2 Timothy 3:16-17).

Is it true that not every word of Christ and the apostles is recorded in the Bible? Yes, and John even says this "And many other signs truly did Jesus in the presence of his disciples, which are not written in this book" (John 20:30). John follows up this statement in verse 20:30 with an important conclusion that: "But these are written, that ye might believe that Jesus is the Christ, the Son of God, and that believing ye might have life through his name" (John 20:3, 12). The phrase in the first part of the verse "are written" is expressing the same truth as "it is written." If "it is written," it is Scripture and has been canonized. If it is not recorded in the Bible it is not Scripture. That is the implicit conclusion that cannot be overlooked.

Second, it may be objected that passages like, "If he called them gods, unto whom the word of God came, and the Scripture cannot be broken" (John 10:35) and 2 Timothy 3:16-17 refer only to the Old Testament and cannot be used to prove the completion of New Testament Scripture.

It is admitted that these passages do primarily refer to the Old Testament. But the New Testament is also established as Scripture, so the passages in question by definition must include the New Testament within their scope. And these passages are not the only ones used to support the completion of the Scriptures.

There are several different manifestations of theological systems that contend for authorities that are opposed to the Bible alone as being the infallible final court of appeal for life and truth. I will touch upon some of them briefly. The following three categories are examples of this pattern, but by no means exhaust the number of examples of aberrations that could be cited.

1. GROUPS THAT FOLLOW JOSEPH SMITH JR.

The various expressions of the followers of Joseph Smith Jr. have a vested interest in undermining the authority of Scripture. If the Bible's authority is called into question, then the case is made for dependence upon an additional authority structure. In the case of Joseph Smith's followers, their authority is to be found in the hierarchy and doctrines of the Mormon church. Their authority is primarily derived from three additional books, namely, the *Book of Mormon, Doctrine and Covenants,* and the *Pearl of Great Price,* that they call "Scripture" in the pronouncements of their leaders and in official church publications and general conference meetings. This means that there are many, many volumes of Mormon "authoritative" writings.

There are two main groups that are adherents to Joseph Smith and a number of smaller groups. These groups all believe in continued, ongoing revelations which add to the Bible. It is a fact that Utah followers of Joseph Smith and the followers of the Reorganized Church (now officially called the Community of Christ) disagree with each other as to exactly what the new revelations are. The latter group believes that some of the former group's revelations are false. The Utah followers of Joseph Smith are polytheistic, whereas the Reorganized Church, now the Community of Christ is not (this is no small difference.)

All of these groups that adhere to the theology of Joseph Smith have more than one man claiming to be the only prophet on earth. This is somewhat reminiscent of a period in church history where more than one individual at the same time claimed to be the Pope. In addition, these followers of Joseph Smith or "Smithite groups" have among themselves more than twelve men who claim to be apostles. Obviously, something is wrong. Both the Utah followers of Joseph Smith and their separate Reorganized brethren assert that historical Christian believers need their revelations. How do we know if the new revelations are accurate? How can the contradictory revelations given by the various Joseph Smith styled prophets be explained? Are these new alleged revelations being properly interpreted? How do we know? In the case of all Smithite groups, they consistently claim the Bible is insufficient, so you have to take someone's (their leaders') word for it. Supposedly their leaders, who interpret the new revelations, are infallible and sufficient. This particular claim is not only unacceptable; it is ludicrous and fails to overthrow the infallibility of the Christian Scriptures.

INTRODUCTION TO
THE NEXT TWO SECTIONS:

The next two sections deal with objections to the view of Scripture set forth above. For example, some groups raise oral traditions and experiences to the level of the sacred writings of Scripture. While these next two sections do not deal directly with Mormonism, an educated Mormon may utilize them in trying to question the completeness, sufficiency and the closing of the canon of Scripture. Additionally, the Reformed reader will be able to gain some practical knowledge on how to respond to other blatant and subtle attacks upon the reliability of Scripture.

2. ORAL SACRED TRADITION GROUPS

In particular, it has been alleged by some Roman Catholics that the Bible does not teach *Sola Scriptura*. Some former Protestants, now Roman Catholic apologists, have said that Sola Scriptura means "the Bible plus nothing else." This is a straw-man argument, and is false. *Sola Scriptura* means that the Bible is the <u>final court of appeal</u>, not the only court of appeal. To the Roman Catholic we ask, "Where does the Bible direct God's people to an outside authority structure such as an oral sacred tradition?" The force of this question should not be dismissed. As demonstrated in my preceding articles on Scripture, we see that *Sola Scriptura* is taught all over the face of Scripture and that the traditions of men are condemned by Christ repeatedly. In essence, the critics of *Sola Scriptura* are saying that the Protestant must accept, as the final authority, whatever is stated by the Roman or Eastern Orthodox Church.

But if the church is always correct, why did Christ attack the religious authorities of the Old Testament Church? Christ did this using the strongest terminology, such as hypocrites and vipers. The fact is that sometimes even the church will err in its doctrine. If the Old Testament Church erred, why should anyone deny or be surprised at the fact that the church in the gospel age can and has fallen into error as well? What happens when the church misinterprets the Bible? Can the believer challenge the misinterpretation? As Protestants we say yes to the last question, but this does not mean by doing so we are disregarding or repudiating the church. It means that we have to test all things in light of Scripture. This includes even the rulings and doctrine of the church. If this is necessary, it should be done in humility. The faithful church sees that the Scriptures always stand as the final infallible authority above it. Christ is the head of the church. He speaks through the Scriptures. The faithful church should always be reforming and checking itself in light of Scripture.

How can error creep into the church? The leaders in the Old Testament covenant nation did not want the people to misinterpret and break God's law. This sounds like a worthy goal. Who would want that to happen? To prevent this, the elders of Israel built walls and fences created with man-made regulations to go around God's law. These man-made laws are found in the Talmud. These additional laws would allegedly keep the people from even getting close to actually breaking one of God's laws. Did this work? What were the consequences of this? These man-made laws actually produced ignorance in Israel regarding God's law. The traditions of the elders became confused with the word of God. They, in fact, became a great burden for God's people. Not only were these traditions of men a burden, they also made the commandments of God of no effect (Mark 7:13).

Likewise, the Roman Church did not want people to misinterpret Scripture because it is God's Word. This ostensibly sounds good, since it is wrong and sinful to misinterpret God's Word, and it would bring judgment upon those who did so. What was the Roman Church's attempted solution to this possibility of misinterpretation? The Roman Church placed the Bible on its list of forbidden books! If the people did not have the Bible to read, then they would not be able to misinterpret it. The logic may be correct, but it is perverse. Eventually, the people in the Roman Churches were not able to recognize the difference between the church's laws, traditions, superstitions, and heresies, and the true Word of God. In fact, these strategies by ancient Jewish leaders and Romanists produced a greater ignorance of the law of God and the Scriptures. These strategies to keep the people of God from breaking God's law or misinterpreting the Bible were noble on the surface, but in reality are evil, since they produce ignorance among the people of God.

Does the theory of "oral sacred tradition" invalidate the Protestant doctrine of *Sola Scriptura*? How do we know if sacred traditions are true? Is it because the church says so? How do we know the word of the church regarding a particular sacred tradition is true? Is it because it is in agreement with sacred tradition? If this is the case, then we would seem to be going in a circle.

In Eastern Orthodoxy and Romanism, tradition is elevated on a par equal with Scripture. So it needs to be asked: Has God revealed all his revelation now? Or is the body of revelation, i.e., "sacred tradition" still expanding? If it's still expanding, how long will these alleged traditions continue to expand or grow? If the sacred oral traditions are written down, what becomes of them? Are they now considered to be equivalent to the Old and New Testament writings? If so, why not revise the Scriptures by adding them to the Bible? Is there a sacred book of traditions? Are there commentaries that explain these "sacred traditions"? If so, are these commentaries inspired? Can every-day men read them? Or, do we need a special leader to decipher the meaning?

Does this expanding body of revelations or traditions ever contradict each other? It should be noted that Roman Catholic theology is still evolving because of the influence of these traditions. The development of Mariology is an example of this. One would have to be dishonest to deny that there are contradictions between the different traditions. For example, Eastern Orthodoxy and Roman Catholics have traditions that contradict each other at various points. The role of "feasts," "fasts," "festivals," the "*filoque*," "papal claims," "original sin," "purgatory," the "immaculate conception" and the use of "icons" are examples of divergent, contradictory traditions. And furthermore, there is much debate and disagreement upon exactly what some traditions mean in the first place.

It should be noted that the Eastern Orthodox Church first acted on a basic principle of Protestantism by breaking with the Roman Church in 1054 over the *filoque* controversy. The *filoque* controversy erupted when a Roman Catholic Pope, outside of a church council, changed the Nicene Creed. The fact is, there are serious theological differences between Roman Catholicism and Eastern Orthodoxy, which include divisions or factions among themselves, as well as with new age mysticism, liberalism, and outright humanism, manifesting themselves in a variety of ways.

In defense of Protestantism, it needs to be explained how someone may look at the Reformation doctrine of *Sola fide* (by faith alone) and say this is not what the Bible teaches. They might say, "The Bible says we are saved by grace." Yet the Latin phrase that highlights this Protestant doctrine does not even mention grace, it only speaks of faith. Such statements would reveal an appalling amount of ignorance. Sola Fide, or "by faith alone" must be understood in its historical context. The debate that was raging at the time concerned faith as the means through which a person was saved or justified. Both positions had the doctrine of salvation by grace in their formulas.

Although the Roman Church uses the word "grace" in its formulation of justification, their sacramental system has subverted the biblical doctrine of grace and turned it into a system of works.

The Protestant battle cry was "by faith alone" in contrast to the Roman Church, which was essentially saying "faith plus works." Understanding the historical circumstances of the debate clears up any misconception about the Protestant use of the formula "by faith alone", which did not leave out grace at all. *Sola gratia* or "by grace alone" went right along with *Sola fide*.

In fact, there were five "solas" that the Protestants used and in Latin the phrases are:

1. *Sola scriptura* (by Scripture alone)

2. *Sola fide* (by faith alone)

3. *Sola gratia* (by grace alone)

4. *Solo Christo* (Christ alone)

5. *Soli Deo gloria* (glory to God alone)

The Romanist position essentially said that faith plus works produced justification, which placed man in a tenuous state of grace. In the Romanist view, man could fall from this state of grace. The Protestant position in contrast to this said that it was "faith alone" (the result of God's imputing grace) that produced justification, thus saving man. If *Sola fide* is taken out of its historical context it can be made to appear to be in conflict with Scripture. The Latin formula is a phrase drawing attention to the difference between the Protestant and Romanist positions on justification. The Protestant position did not reduce it to "faith only," minus grace, as the surface meaning of the Latin might appear. It should be noted that an objection like this is only a clever 'straw-man' fallacy that capitalizes on the ignorance of modern readers.

Likewise, the Protestant doctrine of *Sola Scriptura*, if taken out of its historical context, can be made to appear to be unconvincing. The debate surrounding *Sola Scriptura* was a debate over ultimate authority. The Roman Church claims that it, the church, was the infallible final court of appeal. If time is taken to study the debate during the Reformation, it is clearly seen that the Protestants were claiming that the Bible the only infallible rule of faith and is the final court of appeal. They were not saying, "the Bible plus nothing else." An ignorant person in the twentieth century looking at the Latin formula just on the surface may get this impression. If they believe this is the Protestant position, it is the result of their own ignorance. To properly understand the Latin formula used by the men of the reformation, you must understand the context of the debate at the time.

The Protestants were not claiming that a person was forbidden to use commentaries or to refer to church history, or to have church synods and assemblies to help settle disputes. To illustrate, John Calvin produced a commentary set on the Bible that is still the standard against which all others are measured. Philip Schaff, a noteworthy Protestant historian, wrote a valuable eight-volume church history, a three-volume work on the creeds of Christendom, and edited the thirty-eight-volume church fathers set.

It is beyond dispute that Protestantism has produced a rich tradition of scholarship. Does this violate its own stated position? Of course not! The Protestant position is not some kind of simplistic "the Bible plus nothing" theory. Those who allege this are dishonest or ignorant. Since the Scriptures are the Word of God, Protestants have always maintained that there could be no other authority to which they may appeal. It should be noted that Protestants are not against traditions. Reformation Protestants are simply against traditions that are contrary to Scripture. Protestants believe strongly in the church's role in the interpretation of Scripture. The *Regula Fidei* or what is known as the 'Rule of Faith', guards against the danger of the individual setting himself up as the ultimate interpreter of Scripture.

Radical individualism in the area of interpretation of Scripture is akin to anarchy. It should be noted that the Reformation Protestants strongly condemned the radical individualism of the Anabaptists of their day, which sought to overthrow all authority. The Ecumenical Creeds serve an important role in understanding the Rule of Faith. In Protestantism, debates on the meaning of Scripture take place in the church. In Reformed Churches in particular, there are courts of appeal to guard against the possibility of error at any level of the debate. Protestants claim that the Bible is the infallible final court of appeal in settling debates. This is the meaning of *Sola Scriptura*.

It is important to note that the Roman Church had placed the Bible on their list of forbidden books. The Roman Church during that time, and even today, does not allow their people to be like the Berean Church in the book of Acts (17:11). It should be remembered that this church was commended for searching the Scriptures. How can you search the Bible if it is forbidden? In reality, the reason for this ban on the Scriptures was that the Roman Church did not want any challenges to its authority. Thus, the Roman Church had set itself up as the infallible final court of appeal. It tolerated and perpetuated spiritual abuse and corruption, which led up to the events surrounding the Protestant Reformation. Is the church the infallible final court of appeal, or the Scriptures? Again, the question is one of authority. What is the ultimate authority? Since the church is made up of fallible men, we must answer the question in favor of the God-inspired Scriptures as the final authority.

In another line of attack, some Roman Catholics have said that the Protestant doctrine of *Sola Scriptura* is responsible for all the numerous denominations that interpret the Bible differently. It is true that a number of Protestants interpret the Bible differently. Sin in the human condition, not Protestant theology, is responsible for this problem. Some Roman Catholics believe that factions or divisions within Protestantism are evidence of the correctness of their view. This is a fallacious assumption. Falsities in your opponent's position does not necessarily guarantee the correctness of your own position. For Roman Catholics and the Eastern Orthodox to pretend that their theologians and church members are in agreement on everything is grossly dishonest. As already mentioned, it should be again noted that there are numerous factions within both of these groups. Unless your own house is free from different interpretations and factions, it is patently hypocritical to raise an objection like this.

Roman Catholics believe that men cannot understand and interpret the Bible properly on their own. That is why you need the church. This is an epistemological objection. Does looking to the church rather than the Scriptures solve this alleged problem? If we cannot understand the Word of God written down and preserved in the Scriptures of the Old and New Testaments, how can there be certainty that the word of the church will be any clearer? If the individual cannot understand properly the Word of God in the Scriptures, then surely, the individual will not be able to understand the word of the church either. If this epistemological objection were valid, it would undercut anyone's understanding of the word of the church as well, and therefore is of no help to Catholics arguing against the Protestant view. It is an epistemological objection that proves to be a double-edged sword turning against the Roman Catholic view.

3. CHARISMATIC, EXPERIENCE ORIENTED GROUPS

The modern day charismatic movement is notorious for allowing experiences to influence their interpretation of Scripture. Adherents of the charismatic movement believe that God still speaks through the continued presence of revelatory gifts such as tongues, prophecy and words of knowledge in the church. Do the Charismatic revelatory gifts convey authoritative knowledge? If so, how is this revelatory knowledge fundamentally different from revelation given by the followers of Joseph Smith, which also claims to be authoritative? If they are not authoritative, what is the purpose of these "revelations," since these same revelations in substance may already be in the Scriptures? Revelation, if real, is authoritative. Non-authoritative revelation is a contradiction of terms. God's revelation cannot be separated from His authority. In fairness, charismatic followers usually do not believe that modern day revelatory knowledge contradicts the Bible. It is interesting to note that the Smithites also believe that their revelations do not contradict the Bible. Simply believing something is no guarantee of the truth or reality of the belief.

If the charismatic revelatory gifts are imparting new revelation, then this is a dangerous movement away from the authority of Scripture. In many cases, the charismatic is unwittingly accepting an authority other than the Bible, namely the new revelation. In addition, rather than *Sola Scriptura* being the guiding principle of the charismatic movement, many adherents of this movement have adopted a "just let the spirit lead or move" approach to arriving at truth for life decisions. In fact, this "just letting the spirit lead or move" seems to be the *modus operandi* of much of the charismatic movement.

Sometimes this claim of "letting the spirit lead or move" has been used as a pretext leading to doctrinal abuse or public sins, such as a man running off with the wife of another man. This writer personally knows cases where people, believing that they received words of prophetic knowledge, actually sold their homes and moved away at great financial loss, only to find out later that such a move accomplished nothing at all beneficial. Despite claims to the contrary, this movement has spawned abuses in practice and doctrine, which is the very fruit of a non-biblical system of authority.

Many followers of the charismatic movement pay lip service to the principle of *Sola Scriptura*. This is undermined, however, when so-called spiritual experiences actually influence the interpretation of the Scriptures. In light of this flawed hermeneutic, namely, letting the alleged spiritual experience (tongues speaking, words of knowledge, and prophecy) influence an understanding of the Scripture, it is not surprising that sound doctrine gives way to interpretations of Scripture that are influenced by these self-same experiences. The astute reader sees the circular reasoning that plagues this approach. Since the charismatic has either allegedly witnessed or spoken in tongues, the Bible is interpreted in such a fashion as to support the charismatic interpretations of the Bible. Thus, the charismatic assumes this must be what the Bible teaches, since they have witnessed or experienced it. This is nothing more than a dangerous subjectivist circle of interpretation. The role of Scripture and experience are reversed, experience gaining the upper hand in this system. As already mentioned, the fruit of this, in addition to producing faulty theology, has led to practices contrary to the Bible.

In fact, it is not too strong to say that many of the modern-day charismatic abuses rival the abuses that were produced by the medieval Roman Church. When experience is lifted up as the guiding interpretive principle, objectivity is lost. Experience is in the realm of subjectivity. In essence, the theology of the charismatic movement subverts in principle the doctrine of *Sola Scriptura* and can end up supporting something other than the Scriptures as being the infallible final court of appeal. Does the charismatic believer want to establish alleged revelatory gifts as an additional source of authority? If so, how is this fundamentally different than Rome's "sacred tradition"? Both are sources of authority that stand outside of Scripture. This analysis may be painful for the charismatic to accept, but it is true.

CONCLUSION

In conclusion, Roman Catholicism and Eastern Orthodoxy reject *Sola Scriptura* in favor of "sacred tradition." It should be remembered that both of these religious bodies disagree strongly on a number of traditions, and Eastern Orthodoxy in particular has numerous factions. Various followers of Joseph Smith reject it in favor of continued on-going revelations which come from their apostles and prophets. The charismatic churches in principle subvert *Sola Scriptura* because of their belief that modern revelation found in tongues and prophecy provides authoritative knowledge. If authoritative revelatory knowledge is ongoing, whatever the form (sacred tradition or new revelation) then the authority of Scripture would now have an equal. The fact is, the Scriptures of the Old and New Testaments have no equal. Furthermore, these other sources end up resulting in sectarianism and outright false interpretations of Scripture.

Whose authority or word do I have to accept if the Scriptures are unreliable? Why should I believe one claim over against another? Do the new revelations in the charismatic movement or the "sacred traditions" of Roman Catholicism result in unique interpretations of the Bible? These non-biblical sources actually influence the interpretation of God's Word. The biblical pattern for interpreting Scripture which is seen in the New Testament is to always refer to the Old Testament or other New Testament writers. This establishes the norm for using the Scripture to interpret other Scriptures. This was the practice of the Berean believers in the book of Acts. In addition, and as a safe guard, we need to be careful not to cut ourselves off from the past *Regula Fidei*, or Rule of Faith. We should find out how other believers in church history interpreted the Scriptures and why. It is possible that believers in times past may have insights into the grammar or historical setting that have been lost to modern interpreters. This is one reason why the church is important because of the preservation of the history of interpretation in commentaries.

In contrast, it should be noted that the majority of the church fathers were in agreement with the Protestant position on *Sola Scriptura*. Out of many things said on the Scriptures, I will reference four quotes by three church fathers:

> For example, "For doctrine." For thence we shall know, whether we ought to learn or to be ignorant of anything. And thence we may disprove what is false, thence we may be corrected and brought to a right mind, may be comforted and consoled, and if anything is deficient, we may have it added to us. "That the man of God may be perfect." <u>For this is the exhortation of the Scripture given, that the man of God may be rendered perfect by it; without this therefore he cannot be perfect. Thou hast the Scriptures, he says, in place of me. If thou wouldest learn anything, thou mayest learn it from them.</u> And if he thus wrote to Timothy, who was filled with the Spirit, how much more to us! Thoroughly furnished unto all good works; not merely taking part in them, he means, but "thoroughly furnished."

> John Chrysostom, (Homily 9, commentary on 2 Timothy 3:16-17)

> Knowledge of the Bible protects us and ignorance of it results in a multitude of evils. "<u>This is the cause of all evils, the not knowing the Scriptures.</u> We go into battle without arms, and how are we to come off safe?" (Hom. IX On Colossians) "<u>But if we bid you believe the Scriptures, and these are simple and true, the decision is easy for you. If any agree with the Scriptures, he is the Christian; if any fight against them, he is far from this rule.</u>"

> John Chrysostom, (Homily 33 in Acts of the Apostles)

What then? After all these efforts were they tired? Did they leave off? Not at all. They are charging me with innovation, and base their charge on my confession of three *hypostases*, and blame me for asserting one Goodness, one Power, one Godhead. In this they are not wide of the truth, for I do so assert. Their complaint is that their custom does not accept this, and that Scripture does not agree. What is my reply? I do not consider it fair that the custom which obtains among them should be regarded as a law and rule of orthodoxy. If custom is to be taken in proof of what is right, then it is certainly competent for me to put forward on my side the custom which obtains here. If they reject this, we are clearly not bound to follow them. <u>Therefore let God-inspired Scripture decide between us; and on whichever side be found doctrines in harmony with the word of God, in favour of that side will be cast the vote of truth</u>. Basil, (Letter 189, 3)

This is no unsupported statement of his own, which might lead to error, but a warning to us to confess that Christ died and rose after a real manner, not a nominal, since the tact <u>is certified by the full weight of Scripture authority;</u> and that we must understand His death <u>in that exact sense in which Scripture declares it</u>. In his regard for the perplexities and scruples of the weak and sensitive believer, he adds these solemn concluding words, <u>according to the Scriptures,</u> to his proclamation of the death and the resurrection. He would not have us grow weaker, driven about by every wind of vain doctrine, or vexed by empty subtleties and false doubts: he would summon faith to return, before it were shipwrecked, to the haven of piety, believing and confessing the death and resurrection of Jesus Christ, Son of Man and Son of God, <u>according to the Scriptures,</u> this being the safeguard of reverence against the attack of the adversary, so to understand the death and resurrection of Jesus Christ, as it was written of Him. There is no danger in faith: the reverent confession of the hidden mystery of God is always safe. Christ was born of the Virgin, but conceived of the Holy Ghost <u>according to the Scriptures</u>. Christ wept, but <u>according to the Scriptures:</u> that which made Him weep was also a cause of joy. Christ hungered; but <u>according to the Scriptures,</u> He used His power as God against the tree which bore no fruit, when He had no loath Christ suffered: but <u>according to the Scriptures,</u> He was about to sit at the right hand of Power. He complained that He was abandoned to die: but <u>according to the Scriptures,</u> at the same moment He received in His kingdom in Paradise the thief who confessed Him. He died: but <u>according to the Scriptures,</u> He rose again and sits at the right hand of God. In the belief of this mystery there is life: this confession resists all attack.

Hilary of Poitiers, (On the Trinity, Book 10, 67)

In summary, if the Scriptures are unreliable how could any other source be reliable? Discrediting the Bible would prove more than the critics of the Bible intend. It would in essence prove too much, namely, that no knowledge is possible. If God is incapable of preserving His Word you certainly cannot have confidence in the word of men. If God has not spoken reliably in history, then mankind is left in the quicksand of subjectivity. If God has not spoken reliably in history, it is preposterous for a church to claim to speak infallibly. The Smithites and Charismatics may claim that their revelations are reliable today, but their constant contradictions prove that this *simply cannot be true. If God has not spoken reliably in the past, He certainly cannot speak* reliably in the present.

Who has more authority on earth, God or the church? The answer is obvious. The Scriptures declare God to be sovereign and the absolute ruler over all. As stated in a previous chapter, God has either preserved His Word from corruption or He has not. These are the only two choices. It is self-evident from the Scriptures that God has sovereignly preserved His Word from corruption as evidenced by the testimony of the Scriptures themselves. As shown, the believer can have confidence that he has the complete and sufficient Word of God to rest and base his life upon. The followers of Joseph Smith have their new revelations, and the charismatics indulge in their experiences, all of which cause misinterpretations of the Scriptures and doctrinal perversions. "Sacred tradition," new revelations, and revelatory gifts all take away from the written Scriptures of the Old and New Testaments, which Jesus said testify of Him.

As my previous sections have shown, the Scriptures declare themselves to be the Word of God in no uncertain terms. Their authority and sufficiency is seen throughout the whole of Scripture. God ceased giving divine revelation and closed the canon of Scripture in the First Century. The canon of Scripture is what God has preserved for His Church. Providentially, God did not preserve every last word Jesus uttered. Why? That is a question that rests with the secret counsel of God (Deuteronomy 29:29). We can be sure that with God's perfect control of all things, we can know that we have "all things" (2 Peter 1:3) that God has commanded us for life and doctrine. The view of Scripture outlined in this article does not invalidate the use of historical information, tradition, commentaries, confessions, creeds and teachers. Scripture, however, is the infallible final court of appeal, and Scripture should test all things. If we are obedient to Christ, we likewise will appeal to what "is written."

Note: I want to express my dependence and indebtedness to Dr. Greg L. Bahnsen for two lectures that have deeply influenced my thinking in the area of the authority and sufficiency of the Scriptures. These two lectures are entitled *Is Sola Scriptura sufficient for today?* And *Is Sola Scriptura a Protestant Concoction?* These lectures can be obtained from the Covenant Tape Ministry. Also, Dr. Bahnsen's article *The Concept and Importance of Canonicity* from September/October 1990 Volume 1, Number 5 issue of ANTITHESIS: A review of Contemporary Thought and Culture.

CHAPTER 3

THE SOVEREIGNTY OF GOD

THE BIBLE VERSUS
MORMON THEOLOGY
ON GOD'S SOVEREIGNTY

overeignty means that God, as the ruler of the Universe, has the right to do whatever He wants. And it means that he is in complete control over everything that happens. For an in-depth study of God's sovereignty, systematic theologies cover this subject under the section dealing with God's attributes.

Francis Turretin, when discussing the topics of God's dominion and sovereignty, says:

The proof of both occurs in Predestination.

Francis Turretin, *Institutes of Elenctic Theology* (Phillisburg, Presbyterian and Reformed, 1992), p. 251.

Turretin is correct in seeing the relationship between sovereignty and soteriology. If God is absolutely sovereign, our salvation is dependent upon Him. In Exodus 3:14 God declares Himself to be the "I AM that I AM" or the great "I AM," the self-existent one. From this revelation of God's self-existence flows His sovereignty. We understand sovereignty as the doctrine that God is the Supreme King and Ruler of the Universe. His will causes all things to happen and by virtue of the fact that God is the creator, He is the owner of all things. Everything is dependent upon Him.

By definition there can be only one Sovereign God. Therefore, that one Sovereign God is absolutely unique. In other words, God is transcendent. By this we mean that God is above and beyond all of His creative works. God is not to be confused with anything that is created. When God is confused or identified with His creation this is the grossest form of idolatry. See Romans 1:22-23 for scriptural proof of this.

We will begin by looking at some Mormon writers who will demonstrate that the god of Mormonism is not unique and is not sovereign. In fact, some of the writers will openly reject some of God's attributes which are related to His sovereignty. There are a number of modern Mormon writers who freely use such words as sovereignty, omniscience, omnipresence, and omnipotence. It should be noted that these writers have radically redefined these words. Some of the Mormons that will be quoted openly worship a finite non-sovereign god. The Mormon god is clearly not sovereign in the traditional understanding.

The Mormon view of sovereignty has tremendous implications for soteriology. A finite, non-sovereign god cannot save anyone. At best, this type of god could only function as some kind of celestial cosmic cheerleader. This type of finite god may try to show his followers the way to salvation, but in reality would not be able to offer any effective assistance.

THE SOVEREIGNTY OF GOD, IN THE MORMON VIEW

Do Mormons believe in a unique, transcendent, sovereign God?

The early Mormon, Orson Pratt, has some interesting comments about God. We need to first see Pratt's ideas about man, and his eternal progress eventually culminating in godhood. This view of Pratt's could be described as a type of celestial, evolutionary reincarnation. The end product is millions of gods, which are made up of eternal matter. This eternal matter has intelligence and has taken various forms in its upward evolutionary progress towards godhood.

Since there can be only one Sovereign God by definition, it follows that Pratt's millions of Mormon gods are not gods at all. No doubt, many Christians will be shocked at the following quotations, which represent his view of historical Christianity:

Let us see what Orson Pratt has to say about man and God:

> Admitting the eternity of the capacities, then the materials of which our spirits are composed, must have been capable of thinking, moving, willing, before they were organized in the womb of the celestial female. Proceeding that period there was an endless duration, and each particle of our spirits had an eternal existence, and was in possession of eternal

capacities. Now can it be supposed, for one moment, that these particles were inactive and dormant from all eternity until they received their organization in the form of the infant spirit? Can we suppose that particles, possessed of the power to move themselves, would not have exerted that power, during the endless duration preceding their organization? If they were once organized in the vegetable kingdom, and then disorganized by becoming the food of celestial animals, and then again re-organized in the form of the spirits of animals, which is a higher sphere of being, then, is it unreasonable to suppose that the same particles have, from all eternity, been passing through an endless chain of unions and disunions, organizations and disorganizations, until at length they are permitted to enter into the highest and most exalted sphere of organization in the image and likeness of God? A transmigration of the same particles of spirits from a lower to a higher organization, is demonstrated from the fact that the same particles exist in a diffused scattered state, mingled with other matter; next, they exist in a united form, growing out of the earth in the shape of grass, herbs, and trees; and after this, these vegetables become food for celestial animals, and these same particles are organized into their offspring, and thus form the spirits of animals. Here, then, is apparently a transmigration of the same particles of spirit from an inferior to a superior organization, wherein their condition is improved, and their sphere of action enlarged. Who shall set any bounds to this upward tendency of spirit? Who shall prescribe limits to its progression? If it abide the laws and conditions of its several states of existence, who shall say that it will not progress until

> it shall gain the very summit of perfection, and exist
> in all the glorious beauty of the image of God?
>
> Orson Pratt, *The Seer* (Salt Lake City, Eborn Books,
> 1990), p. 102, 103.

It is quite clear from the above quotation that Pratt believed in some type of evolutionary rein-carnation. The intent of this quotation is to demonstrate that the Mormon god is not unique. In Mormonism, man can become god. The Mormon god is the product of forces that exist inde-pendently from him. Everything is moving upward towards godhood. What is this driving force? Is this force ultimately more important than the Mormon god? Does this force control the Mormon god, or does the Mormon god control the force? Or, is this force some other type of god?

Let us consider more of Pratt's Mormon theology:

> It has been most generally believed that the Saints
> will progress in knowledge to all eternity: But when
> they become one with the Father and Son, and
> receive a fullness of their glory, that will be the end
> of all progression in knowledge, because there will
> be nothing more to be learned. The Father and
> the Son do not progress in knowledge and wisdom,
> because they already know all things past, present,
> and to come. All that become like the Father and
> Son will know as much as they do, and consequent-
> ly will learn no more. The Father and Son, and all
> who are like them and one with them, already know
> as much as any Beings in existence know, or ever
> can know. In the twenty-second paragraph of this
> article we showed that there could not possibly be
> but one God, so far as the attributes are concerned,
> but so far as it regards persons, that there were an
> immense number of Gods. Now we wish to be dis-
> tinctly understood that each of these personal Gods
> has equal knowledge with all the rest; there are none

among them that are in advance of the others in knowledge; though some may have been Gods as many millions of years, as there are particles of dust in all the universe, yet there is not one truth that such are in possession of but what every other God knows. They are all equal in knowledge, and in wisdom, and in the possession of all truth.

Orson Pratt, *The Seer* p. 117.

Some of these gods that Pratt refers to have apparently been god longer than the Mormon Father-god has been. Pratt, in the above quotation, refers to the twenty-second paragraph of his lengthy article in which he further confuses the reader as to who God is.

Pratt has this to say:

It is truth, light, and love that we worship and adore; these are the same in all worlds; and as these constitute God...Wherever you find a fullness of wisdom, knowledge, truth, goodness, love, and such like qualities, there you find God in all His glory, power, and majesty, therefore, if you worship these adorable perfections you worship God.

Orson Pratt, *The Seer* p. 24.

Ultimately, the god in Pratt's Mormon theology is not even personal. For Pratt, "truth, light, and love" are god. When considering the totality of Scripture, this theory of Pratt's makes no sense at all. All of the gods in Pratt's Mormon universe are the same. They all share the same amount of knowledge and power. This concept of God is meaningless. For example, isn't the "point" of believing in God to acknowledge someone higher than yourself? This is defeated if you can become equal to God. As will be seen, the Bible, God's revelation to man, sets forth a much different view. Pratt's Mormon god is clearly not sovereign or unique. Instead, his god is finite!

What did Mormon founder Joseph Smith have to say that is relevant to this subject?

Let us consider some of Smith's thoughts on this:

> The intelligence of spirits had no beginning, neither will it have an end. That which has a beginning may have an end. There never was a time when there were not spirits: for they are coequal with our Father in heaven.
>
> Joseph Smith, *Journal of Discourses* Vol. 6, (Liverpool, England: Asa Calkin, 1844), p. 6.

Mormon leader Wilford Woodruff said this:

> God himself is increasing and progressing in knowledge, power, and dominion, and will do so, worlds without end.
>
> Wilford Woodruff, *Journal of Discourses* Vol. 6, p.120.

Smith's god seems to be remarkably different from Pratt's Mormon god. Who is right, Smith or Pratt?

Are both men wrong? Smith's god is co-equal with these so-called intelligences and is increasing in "power and dominion." This is clearly not the Sovereign God of Holy Scripture. If Smith's god is gaining in "power and dominion" divine attributes such as omniscience, omnipotence, and omnipresence should not be applied to a deity of this nature.

Bruce R. McConkie, a fairly recent modern Mormon writer, has this to say about God's ability to rule:

> It is only because of apostasy and rebellion that he is kept from ruling in the hearts of men in the present state of things.
>
> McConkie, *Mormon Doctrine* p. 657.

McConkie, probably more than most Mormon writers, utilizes words such as sovereignty, omniscience, omnipresence, and omnipotence. Mormon philosophy professor Kent E. Robson takes McConkie to task for using these terms in such a way as to bring Mormonism perilously close to a form of absolutism that would destroy its:

> unique finitistic theology.
>
> Gary James Bergera, ed., *"Ominpotence, Omnipresence, and Omniscience in Mormon Theology"*, in *Line Upon Line* (Salt Lake City, Signature Books 1989), p. 69.

It should be noted, however, that McConkie redefines these terms in such a way as to place them clearly outside of historic Christian thought. What should be noted in the above quotation from McConkie is how he limits God's rule. God, according to McConkie, is limited in His rule as a result of some action on the part of man. As will be seen, the Scriptures declare that God is sovereign and nothing can stay his hand. Even the will of man is unable to do so.

The next quotation will come from one of Mormonism's "Standard Works."

We will look at the Book of Abraham in the Pearl of Great Price:

> And thus there shall be the reckoning of the time of one planet above another, until thou come nigh unto Kolob, which Kolob is after the reckoning of the Lord's time; which Kolob is set nigh unto the throne of God, to govern all those planets which belong to the same order as that upon which thou standest.
>
> Joseph Smith, *Pearl Of Great Price* p. 36.

Here we have the Kolob governing other planets. It is possible Smith understood this as some kind of gravitational force, which he understood as a type of governing. At any rate, in Mormon Scripture the idea of natural law is present. If God is sovereign there is no such thing as a sovereign natural law, unless of course one wants to defend a form of Deism. God does not govern the universe according to natural law. He governs the universe by his powerful Word.

Note: It is ill-defined if Kolob is a star or planet in Mormon theology. One reference to Kolob is in the Book of Abraham. According to this work translated from the Egyptian by Smith, Kolob is the heavenly body nearest to the throne or residence of God. While the Book of Abraham refers to Kolob as a star, it also refers to planets as stars, and this is why some Mormon writers consider Kolob to be a planet.

The next Mormon writer we will consider is W. Cleon Skousen.

He has some very revealing things to say about the Mormon god's lack of sovereignty:

> God is omnipotent, but only within the circumscribed boundaries of law, truth, and justice...But who is it that occupies a position great enough in the universe to require of the exalted Elohim his Godhood in case He should violate any of the principles of truth and justice...In other words, as God extended His power and influence throughout His great kingdom, He did so by obtaining the voluntary cooperation and support of vast concourses of intelligences.
>
> W. Cleon Skousen, *The First 2000 Years* (Salt Lake City, Bookcraft, 41st Printing, 1991), p. 354-355.

Skousen asks the question, "who is it that occupies a position great enough in the universe to require of the exalted Elohim?" That is a good question. Mormons may want to ask themselves who the real God is. Are the eternal laws, principles and intelligences in reality the god of the Mormon universe? The Mormon god cannot govern unless he meets the requirements of many outside forces. In other words, Skousen seems to be saying that there are abstract forces by which god is ruled. It is quite clear that the Mormon god is not sovereign.

Kent E. Robson, a Mormon philosophy professor at the University of Utah, has an interesting essay in the book *Line Upon Line* which promotes a belief in a finite god. He is concerned about Mormonism's drift towards absolutism.

Mr. Robson explains an essential element of the Mormon position as follows:

> For Mormons, God "organized" previously existing elements according to certain principles or laws which are themselves independent of him and are to some extent out of his control.

> Gary James Bergera, ed., *Line Upon Line* p. 69-70.

It is clear according to Mr. Robson that the god of the Mormons is finite and certainly not sovereign in the traditional sense of the term. If God does not control these so-called principles or laws, who does? Are these principles and laws in reality God? Do they control God? Where did these principles and laws come from?

Kent E. Robson closes his essay, which promotes the glories of believing in a finite god with these words:

> Mormons who are attracted to terms of absolutism should carefully consider what else they may unintentionally be embracing. They should consistently renounce such attributes [omnipotence, omnipresence, and omniscience] or clearly distinguish between Mormon usage and traditional Christian usage. Unless this is done, I fear that absolutism may yet invade and perhaps change the uniqueness and very appeal of Mormon theology.

> Gary James Bergera, ed., *Line Upon Line* p. 74.

Mr. Robson can surely be commended for his honesty in this essay concerning his Mormon beliefs. It would probably be more than could be hoped for if Mormon writers took Mr. Robson's admonition to heart and did distinguish for their readers the different way in which they use traditional Christian terminology. If all Mormons were as forthright with their beliefs as Mr. Robson, the ongoing debate between Mormons and Christians would surely lose much its animosity over the confusion of terms.

Blake T. Ostler is another Mormon writer who is honest and forthright with his beliefs. It is enjoyable to read his essay in the book *Line Upon Line*.

In the following comments by Mr. Ostler we can see that the Mormon god is dependent upon things outside of himself and consequently, not sovereign:

> The contemporary Mormon concept of a finite God is an adequate object of faith because all individuals, indeed all aspects of reality, look to him for the realization of all that matters most ultimately. The Mormon God is thus the Optimal Actualizer. God makes all things possible, but he can make all things actual only by working in conjunction with free individuals and actual entities. Hence, Mormonism does not shy away from recognizing humans as co-creators in God's purposes. God needs us and we need him for the realization of all that matters most.
>
> *Line Upon Line*, "*The Concept of a Finite God as an Adequate Object of Worship*" p. 79.

It is refreshing to see Mr. Ostler's openness in setting his beliefs apart from historic Christianity. Mr. Ostler's Mormon god is clearly limited by man's so-called "free will." Since Mr. Ostler proceeds logically from a position assuming human autonomy, he cannot accept the truth of both man's responsibility and God's sovereignty. The Mormon god is again seen as a dependent being, who is clearly not the Sovereign God of Scripture.

The final writer we will consider is Peter C. Appleby a philosophy professor at the University of Utah. Free will is an unworkable idea that Mr. Appleby needs to purge from his theological system. At least free will, as he understands it.

Let us see where this concept of free will has led him:

> First, we must deny that God is solely or primarily responsible for the design and creation of our world, since that world is so unjust and unmerciful to many, if not most, of its inhabitants....The second finitist requirement involves the curtailment

of traditional claims about divine power, denying omnipotence and insisting that God has none of the miraculous powers attributed to him in Christian literature....But we deny that God has infallible knowledge of every future occurrence, because this conflicts with the view that moral agents are free in their decisions....These revisions, [in traditional Christian doctrine] of course, would affect some familiar religious discourse. They would deny the orthodox Christian doctrine of the Creation and Fall in order to avoid the charge that God deliberately condemned half of humanity as a means of teaching moral lessons to the other half....

Peter C. Appleby *Line Upon Line, "Finitist Theology and the Problem of Evil"* p. 86-88.

Appleby is not unique in the view he promotes. Once someone accepts, as he does, an un-biblical view of free will, he uses this to eliminate God's sovereignty and God's attributes one by one. Mr. Appleby should know, given his philosophical training that the free will argument will not save his god from being charged with sin. Antony Flew's *God and Philosophy* effectively destroys the notion that the free will of man can save his god from being responsible for the evil in the world.

The real problem with Mr. Appleby's argument is that he employs the standard of human reason to which he holds God accountable. This standard of human reason is a form of rationalism, and is an idol. Mormonism needs to purge itself from the un-biblical rationalism that drives it to reject the God of the Bible.

We will close this survey of various Mormon writers on the subject of God's sovereignty with a relevant quote from the Christian philosopher Gordon H. Clark:

God is sovereign. Whatever he does is just, for this very reason, because he does it. If he punishes a man, the man is justly punished, and hence the man is responsible. This answers the form of argument which runs: Whatever God does is just; eternal punishment is not just; therefore God does not so punish. If the one who argues thus means that he has received a special revelation that there is not eternal punishment, we cannot deal with him here. If, however, he is not laying claim to a special revelation of future history but to some philosophic principle which is intended to show that eternal punishment is unjust, the distinction between our positions becomes immediately obvious. Calvin has rejected the view of the universe which makes a law, whether of justice or of evolution, instead of the law-giver, supreme. Such a view is similar to Platonic dualism which posited a world of Ideas superior to the divine Artificer. God in such a system is finite or limited, bound to follow or obey the independent pattern. But those who hold to the sovereignty of God determine what justice is by observing what God actually does. Whatever God does is just. What he commands men to do or not to do is similarly just or unjust.

Gordon H. Clark, *Religion, Reason, and Revelation* (Jefferson, Maryland, Trinity, 1986), p. 232-233.

Many Mormon writers make much of the supposed influence of Greek philosophy upon Christianity. In reality it is Mormonism that has been influenced by Greek philosophy. For evidence of this, see Chapter Eighteen, entitled, *"Pagan Influence upon the Mormon World View."* This work shows a number of areas in which there exists an essential agreement of thought between Mormonism and ancient pagan philosophy.

There is no standard higher than God. He is holy and just. Mormonism, by postulating a structure of law above God, makes God accountable to something outside of Himself. Attempting to place laws above God to which He is accountable, is nothing more than a bold attempt to de-throne God. As clearly seen in Mr. Appleby's essay, this leads to a continual downgrading or rejection of biblical revelation. By holding to an erroneous concept of free will, and a law structure above God, Mormonism has to reject God's sovereignty, omnipotence, omnipresence, and omniscience. I hope that in the next section on the Christian view of sovereignty, Mormons will be called back to a biblical view of God.

THE SOVEREIGNTY OF GOD, IN THE CHRISTIAN VIEW

The Scriptures speak on the sovereignty of God:

The sovereignty of God teaches that all things are under His absolute rule and control. Without fear of contradiction, it can be said that God works all things according to the counsel of His own will. His plans and purpose are never frustrated. The sovereignty of God may be defined as the exercising of His absolute control and the outworking of both His revealed and hidden will. God's sovereignty means that He is the ultimate Ruler who governs all the affairs of the universe both great and small.

The subject of God's sovereignty is a doctrine that should humble all men. No doctrine of Scripture exalts or glorifies the LORD as does the teaching of His Sovereignty.

Under various headings, we will see Scriptures that establish God's sovereignty. His sovereignty extends to every conceivable area of life and governance of the universe, such as the sovereign will of God over His creation.

We can see God's sovereignty over creation:

> Now therefore, if ye will obey my voice indeed, and keep my covenant, then ye shall be a peculiar treasure unto me above all people: <u>for all the earth is mine.</u> (Exodus 19:5)

> Whatsoever <u>the Lord pleased, that did he in heaven, and in earth; in the seas, and all deep places.</u> (Psalms 135:6)

> O house of Israel, <u>cannot I do with you as this</u>

potter? saith the LORD. Behold, as the clay is in the potter's hand, so are ye in my hand, O house of Israel. (Jeremiah 18:6)

John answered and said, A man can receive nothing, except it be given him from heaven. (John 3:27)

Thou art worthy, O Lord, to receive glory and honor and power: for thou hast created all things, and for thy pleasure they are and were created. (Revelation 4:11)

God is the ruler of every nation:

For the kingdom is the LORD's: and he is the governor among the nations. (Psalms 22:28)

He shall judge among the nations, and shall rebuke many people. (Isaiah 2:4)

For promotion cometh neither from the east, nor from the west, nor from the south. But God is the judge: he putteth down, and setteth up another. (Psalms 75:6-7)

The King's heart is in the hand of the LORD, as the rivers of water he turneth it whitheroever he will. (Proverbs 21:1)

We see God's sovereign will in election and regeneration:

For he saith to Moses, I will have mercy on whom I will have mercy, and I will have compassion on whom I will have compassion. So then it is not of him that willeth, nor him that runneth, but God that showeth mercy. (Romans 9:15-16)

John answered and said, <u>A man can receive nothing, except it be given him from heaven</u>. (John 3:27)

<u>Of his own will begat he us</u> with the word of truth, that we should be a kind of first fruits of his creatures. (James 1:18)

God's sovereign will is seen in personal sanctification:

<u>For it is God which worketh in you both to will and to do of his good pleasure</u>. (Philippians 2:13)

God's will in the suffering of believers:

For it is better, <u>if the will of God be so</u>, that ye suffer for well doing, than for evil doing. (1 Peter 3:17)

God's will in the suffering of Christ:

Saying, <u>Father, if thou be willing</u>, remove this cup from me: nevertheless not will, but thine, be done. (Luke 22:42)

<u>Him being delivered by the determinate counsel and foreknowledge of God</u>, ye have taken, and by wicked hands have crucified and slain. (Acts 2:23)

God's control over man's life and circumstances:

But bade them farewell, saying, I must by all means keep this feast that cometh in Jerusalem: <u>but I will return again unto you, if God will</u>. And he sailed from Ephesus. (Acts 18:21)

That I may come unto you with joy <u>by the will of God</u>, and may with you be refreshed. (Romans 5:32)

For that ye ought to say, <u>If the Lord will, we shall live, and do this, or that</u>. (James 4:15)

The absolute freedom of God's will:

If he cut off, and shut up, or gather together, then <u>who can hinder him</u>? (Job 11:10)

Why dost thou strive against him? <u>for he giveth not account of any of his matters</u>. (Job 33:13)

But our God is in the heavens: he hath done whatsoever he hath pleased. (Psalms 115:3)

A man's heart deviseth his way: <u>but the Lord directeth his steps</u>. (Proverbs 16:9)

There are many devices in a man's heart; <u>nevertheless the counsel of the LORD, that shall stand</u>. (Proverbs 19:21)

<u>Shall the axe boast itself against him that heweth therewith?</u> or shall the saw magnify itself against them that lift it up, or as if the staff should lift up itself, as if it were no wood. (Isaiah 10:15)

Surely your turning of things upside down shall be esteemed as the potter's clay: <u>for shall the work say of him that made it, He made me not?</u> or shall the thing framed say of him that framed it, He had no understanding? (Isaiah 29:16)

Woe unto him that striveth with his Maker! Let the potshered strive with the potsherds of the earth. <u>Shall the clay say to him that fashioneth it, What makest thou?</u> or thy work, He hath no hands? (Isaiah 45:9)

<u>Is it not lawful for me to do what I will with mine own?</u> Is thine eye evil, because I am good? (Matthew 20:15)

For he saith to Moses, <u>I will have mercy on whom
I will have mercy, and I will have compassion on
whom I will have compassion</u>. So then it is not of
him that willeth, nor of him that runneth, but of
God that showeth mercy....Nay but, O man, who
art thou that repliest against God? Shall the thing
formed say to him that formed it, Why hast thou
made thus? <u>Hath not the potter power over the
clay, of the same lump to make one vessel unto
honor, and another unto dishonor</u>. (Romans 9:15,
16, 20-21)

But all these worketh that one and the selfsame
Spirit, <u>dividing to every man severally as he will</u>. (1
Corinthians 12:11)

God's prescriptive revealed will or what He commands in Scripture:

And the LORD said unto Moses, When thou goest
to return into Egypt, see that thou do all those
wonders before Pharaoh, which I have put in thine
hand: <u>but I will harden his heart</u>, that he shall not
let the people go. And thou shalt say to Pharaoh,
Thus saith the LORD, Israel is my son, even my
firstborn: And I say unto thee, Let my son go, that
he may serve me: and if thou refuse to let him go,
behold, I will slay thy son, even thy firstborn. (Exodus 4:18-23)

Turn again, and tell Hezekiah the captain of my
people. Thus saith the LORD, the God of David
thy father, I have heard thy prayer, I have seen thy
tears: behold, <u>I will heal thee</u>: on the third day
thou shalt go up unto the house of the LORD.
And <u>I will add unto thy days fifteen years; and I</u>

will deliver thee and this city out of the hand of the king of Assyria; and I will defend this city for mine own sake, and for my servant David's sake. (2 Kings 20:5, 6)

Not every one that saith unto me, Lord, Lord shall enter into the kingdom of heaven; but he that doeth the will of my Father which is in heaven. (Matthew 7:21)

For whosoever shall do the will of my Father which is in heaven, the same is my brother, and sister, and mother. (Matthew 12:50)

Jesus saith unto them, My meat is to do the will of him that sent me, and to finish his work. (John 4:34)

If any man will do his will, he shall know of the doctrine, whether it be of God, or whether I speak of myself. (John 7:17)

Him, being delivered by the determinate counsel and foreknowledge of God, ye have, and by wicked hands have crucified and slain. (Acts 2:23)

And be not conformed to this world: but be ye transformed by the renewing of your mind, that ye may prove what is that good, and acceptable, and perfect, will of God. (Romans 12:2)

The decretive or concealed will of God:

God's purposes are not always revealed. The secret will of God sometimes appears to contradict the revealed will. And yet – this is only how it appears to us humans, since we are not omniscient and cannot know the scope of God's plan. If we could see all of history, like God does, then all the purposes of His secret and revealed will would make sense.

> But as for you, ye thought evil against me; but God meant it unto good, to bring to pass, as it is this day, to save much people alive. (Genesis 50:20)

> Then God sent an evil spirit between Abimelech and the men of Shechem; and the men of Shechem dealt treacherously with Abimelech. (Judges 9:23)

> And the LORD said, Who shall persuade Ahab, that he may go up and fall at Ramoth-gilead? And one said on this manner, and another said on that manner. And there came forth a spirit, and stood before the LORD, and said, I will persuade him. And the LORD said unto him, Wherewith? And he said, I will go forth, and I will be a lying spirit in the mouth of all his prophets. And he said, Thou shalt persuade him, and prevail also: go forth, and do so. Now therefore, behold, the LORD hath put a lying spirit in the mouth of all these thy prophets, and the LORD hath spoken evil concerning thee. (1 Kings 22:20-23)

> Surely the wrath of man shall praise thee: the remainder of wrath shalt thou restrain. (Psalms 76:10)

> I form the light, and create darkness: I make peace, and create evil: I the LORD do all these things. (Isaiah 45:7)

> Shall a trumpet be blown in the city, and the people not be afraid? shall there be evil in a city, and the LORD hath not done it? (Amos 3:6)

> Him, being delivered by the determinate counsel

and foreknowledge of God, ye have taken, and by wicked hands have crucified and slain. (Acts 2:23)

God's sovereignty is seen in seemingly chance events:

And a certain man drew a bow at a venture, and smote the king of Israel between the joints of the harness: wherefore he said unto the driver of his chariot, Turn thine hand and carry me out of the host; for I am wounded. (1 Kings 22:34)

Wash thyself therefore, and anoint thee, and put thy raiment upon thee, and get thee down to the floor: but make not thyself known unto the man, until he have done eating and drinking. (Ruth 3:3)

By lot was their inheritance, as the LORD commanded by the hand of Moses, for the nine tribes, and for the half tribe. (Joshua 14:2)

Ye shall therefore describe the land unto seven parts and bring the description hither to me, that I may cast lots for you here before the LORD our God. (Joshua 18:6)

The lot is cast into the lap; but the whole disposing thereof is of the LORD. (Proverbs 16:33)

God's sovereign power is beyond that which is accomplished:

Is any thing too hard for the LORD? At the time appointed I will return unto thee, according to the time of life, and Sarah shall have a son. (Genesis 18:14)

Ah LORD God! behold, thou hast made the heaven and the earth by thy great power and stretched out arm, and <u>there in nothing too hard for thee</u>. (Jeremiah 32:17)

Thus saith the LORD of hosts; Behold, I will save my people from the east country, and from the west country; And I will bring them, and they shall dwell in the midst of Jerusalem: and they shall be my people, and I will be their God, in truth and in righteousness. (Zechariah 8:7-8)

And think not to say within yourselves, We have Abraham to our father: for I say unto you, that <u>God is able of these stones to raise up children unto Abraham</u>. (Matthew 3:9)

Thinkest thou that <u>I cannot now pray to my Father, and he shall presently give me more than twelve legions of angels</u>? (Matthew 26:53)

God's sovereign power or His omnipotence:

And he blessed him, and said, Blessed be Abram <u>of the most high God, possessor of heaven and earth</u>. (Genesis 14:19)

Now therefore, if ye will obey my voice indeed, and keep my covenant, then ye shall be a peculiar treasure unto me above all people: <u>for all the earth is mine</u>. (Exodus 19:5)

Thine, O LORD, is the greatness, and the power, and the glory, and the victory, and the magesty: <u>for all that is in the heaven and in the earth is thine</u>; thine is the kingdom, O LORD, and thou art exalted as head above all. (1 Chronicles 29:11)

Thou, even thou, art LORD alone; <u>thou hast made heaven, the heaven of heavens</u>, with all their host, the earth, and all things that are therein, the seas, and all that is therein, and <u>thou preservest them all</u>; and the host of heaven worshippeth thee. (Nehemiah 9:6)

Behold, he taketh away, <u>who can hinder him?</u> who will say unto him, what doest thou? (Job 9:12)

Seeing his days are determined, the number of his months are with thee, <u>thou hast appointed his bounds</u> that he cannot pass. (Job 14:5)

<u>Or who shut up the sea with doors, when it brake forth, as it it had issued out of the womb?</u> When I made the cloud the garment thereof, and thick darkness a swaddlingband for it, And brake up for it my decreed place, and set bars and doors, And said, Hitherto shalt thou come, but no further: and here shall thy proud waves be stayed? (Job 38:8-11)

<u>The heavens are thine, the earth alas is thine</u>: as for the world and the fullness thereof, <u>thou hast founded them</u>. (Psalms 89:11)

Of old hast thou laid the foundation of the earth: and <u>the heavens are the work of thy hand</u>. (Psalms 102:25)

<u>Thou hast set a bound that they may not pass over</u>; that they turn not again to cover the earth. (Psalms 104:9)

Thy kingdom is an everlasting kingdom, <u>and thy dominion endureth throughout all generations</u>. (Psalms 145:13)

Praise ye him, sun and moon: praise him, all ye stars of light. Praise him, ye heaven of heavens, and ye waters that be above the heavens. Let them praise the name of the LORD: <u>for he command- ed, and they were created. He hath also stablished them for ever and ever; he hath made a decree which shall not pass.</u> (Psalms 148:3-6)

<u>When he prepared the heavens, I was there</u>: when he set a compass upon the face of the depth. (Proverbs 8:27)

<u>I know that, whatsoever God doeth, it shall be for ever</u>: nothing can be put to it, nor anything taken from it and God doeth it, that men should fear before him. (Ecclesiastes 3:14)

Consider the work of God: <u>for who can make that straight, which he hath made crooked?</u> (Ecclesiastes 7:13)

Who hath measured the waters in the hollow of his hand, and meted out heaven with the span, and comprehended the dust of the earth in a measure, and weighed the mountains in scales, and the hills in a balance?... Hast thou not known? Hast thou not heard that the everlasting God, the LORD, the Creator of the ends of the earth, fainteth not, nei- ther is weary? <u>There is no searching of his under- standing</u>. (Isaiah 40:12, 26)

Thus saith God the LORD, <u>he that created the heavens, and stretched them out</u>; he that spread forth the earth, and that which cometh out of it; he that giveth breath unto the people upon it, and spirit to them that walk therein. (Isaiah 42:5)

Yea, before the day was <u>I am he; and there is none that can deliver out of my hand</u>: I will work, and who shall let it? (Isaiah 43:13)

Fear ye not me? saith the LORD: <u>will ye not tremble at my presence, which have placed the sand for the bound of the sea by a perpetual decree, that it cannot pass it</u>: and though the waves thereof toss themselves, yet can they not prevail; though they roar, yet can they not pass over it? (Jeremiah 5:22)

Ah LORD God! <u>behold, thou hast made the heaven and the earth by thy great power and stretched out arm</u>, and there is nothing too hard for thee. (Jeremiah 32:17)

Then was the secret revealed unto Daniel in a night vision. Then Daniel blessed the God of heaven. Daniel answered and said, <u>Blessed be the name of God for ever and ever: for wisdom and might are his: And he changeth the times and the seasons: he removeth kings, and setteth up kings: he giveth wisdom unto the wise, and knowledge to them that know understanding</u>: He revealeth the deep and secret things: he knoweth what is in the darkness, and the light dwelleth with him. (Daniel 2:19-22)

How great are his signs! And how mighty are his wonders! <u>His kingdom is an everlasting kingdom, and his dominion is from generation to generation</u>. (Daniel 4:3)

<u>Now the LORD had prepared a great fish to swallow up Jonah</u>. And Jonah was in the belly of the

fish three days and three nights. (Jonah 1:17)

And the LORD God prepared a gourd, and made it to come up over Jonah, that it be a shadow over his head, to deliver him from his grief. So Jonah was exceeding glad of the gourd. (Jonah 4:6)

But Jesus beheld them, and said unto them, With men this is impossible; but with God all things are possible. (Matthew 19:26)

For with God nothing shall be impossible. (Luke 1:37)

For the invisible things of him from the creation of the world are clearly seen, being understood by the things that are made, even his eternal power and Godhead; so that they are without excuse. (Romans 1:20)

And what is the exceeding greatness of his power to us-ward who believe, according to the working of his mighty power. (Ephesians 1:19)

God's sovereign creative power:

Thus saith the LORD, thy redeemer, and he that formed thee from the womb, I am the LORD that maketh all things; that stretcheth forth the heavens alone; that spreadeth abroad the earth by myself. (Isaiah 44:24)

As it is written, I have made thee a father of many nations,) before him whom he believed, even God, who quickeneth the dead, and calleth those things which be not as though they were. (Romans 4:17)

God's sovereign providential control:

<u>Thou didst blow with thy wind, the sea covered them</u>: they sank as lead in the mighty waters. (Exodus 15:10)

<u>The LORD hath prepared his throne in the heavens; and his kingdom ruleth over all</u>. (Psalms 103:19)

Behold, <u>I have created the smith that bloweth the coals in the fire</u>, and that bringeth forth an instrument for his work; and <u>I have created the waster to destroy</u>. (Isaiah 54:16)

<u>Who is he that saith, and it cometh to pass, when the Lord commandeth it not?</u> (Lamentations 3:37)

Are not two sparrows sold for a farthing? and one of them shall not fall on the ground without your Father. But <u>the very hairs of your head are all numbered</u>. (Matthew 10:29-30)

For <u>by him were all things created</u>, that are in heaven, and that are in earth, visible and invisible, whether they be thrones, or dominions, or principalities, or powers: all things were created by him, and for him: And he is before all things, and by him all things consist. (Colossians 1:16-17)

God, who at sundry times and in divers manners spake in time past unto the fathers by the prophets, Hath in these last days spoken unto us by his Son, whom he hath appointed heir of all things, <u>by whom also he made the worlds</u>; Who being the brightness of his glory, and the exceeding image of his person, and upholding all things by the word of his power, when he had by himself purged our sins, sat down on the right hand of the Majesty on high. (Hebrews 1:1-3)

God's sovereign power in redemption:

> Behold, the days come, saith the LORD, that I will make a new covenant with the house of Israel, and with the house of Judah: Not according to the covenant that I made with their fathers in the day that I took them by the hand to bring them out of the land of Egypt; which my covenant they brake, although I was an husband unto them, saith the LORD. But this shall be the covenant that I will make with the house of Israel; After those days, saith the LORD, I will put my laws in their inward parts, and write it in their hearts; and will be their God, and they shall be my people. And they shall teach no more every man his neighbour, and every man his brother, saying, Know the LORD: for they shall all know me, from the least of them unto the greatest of them, saith the LORD: for I will forgive their iniquity, and I will remember their sin no more. (Jeremiah 31:31-33)

> And I will betroth thee unto me for ever; yea, I will betroth thee unto me in righteousness, and in judgment, and in loving kindness, and in mercies. (Hosea 2:19)

> When Israel was a child, then I loved him, and called my son out of Egypt. (Hosea 11:1)

> For I am not ashamed of the gospel of Christ: for it is the power of God unto salvation to every one that believeth; to the Jew first, and also to the Greek. For therein is the righteousness of God revealed from faith to faith: as it is written, The just shall live by faith. For the wrath of God is

revealed from heaven against all ungodliness and unrighteousness of men, who hold the truth in unrighteousness; (Romans 1:16-18)

But unto them which are called, both Jews and Greeks, Christ the power of God, and the wisdom of God. (1 Corinthians 1:24)

God is the sovereign ruler over the nations:

Now in the first year of Cyrus king of Persia, that the word of the LORD by the mouth of Jeremiah might be fulfilled, the LORD stirred up the spirit of Cyrus king of Persia, that he made a proclamation throughout all his kingdom, and put it also in writing, saying. (Ezra 1:1)

God reigneth over the heathen: God sitteth upon the throne of his holiness. (Psalms 47:8)

God hath spoken in his holiness; I will rejoice, I will divide Shechem, and mete out the valley of Succoth. Gilead is mine, and Manasseh is mine; Ephraim also is the strength of mine head; Judah is my lawgiver; Moab is my washpot; over Edom will I cast out my shoe: Philistia, triumph thou because of me. (Psalms 60:6-8)

Arise, O God, judge the earth: for thou shalt inherit all nations. (Psalms 82:8)

The LORD of hosts hath sworn, saying, Surely as I have thought, so shall it come to pass; and as I have purposed, so shall it stand: that I will break the Assyrian in my land, and upon my mountains tread him under foot: then shall his yoke depart from off them, and his burden depart from off their shoulders. This is the purpose that is purposed upon the whole earth: and this is the hand that is stretched out upon all the nations. <u>For the LORD of hosts hath purposed, and who shall disannul it?</u> And his hand is stretched out, and who shall turn it back. (Isaiah 14:24-27)

Israel's enemies are raised up and used by God to accomplish His sovereign will:

And the LORD said unto him, Go, return on thy way to the wilderness of Damascus: <u>and when thou comest, anoint Hazael to be king over Syria: And Jehu the son of Nimshi shalt thou anoint to be king over Israel: and Elisha the son of Shaphat of abelmeholah shalt thou anoint to be prophet in thy room.</u> And it shall come to pass, that him that escapeth the sword of Hazael shall Jehu slay: and him that escapeth from the sword of Jehu shall Elisha slay. (1 Kings 19:15-19)

In those days <u>the LORD began to send against Judah Rezin the king of Syria, and Pekah the son of Remaliah</u>. (2 Kings 15:37)

Therefore <u>the LORD shall set up the adversaries of Rezin against him</u>, and join his enemies together; the Syrians before, and the Philistines behind; and they shall devour Israel with open mouth. For all this his anger is not turned away, but his hand is stretched out still. (Isaiah 9:11-12)

<u>O Assyrian, the rod of mine anger, and the staff in their hand is mine indignation</u>. (Isaiah 10:5)

> And now have I given all these lands into the hand
> of Nebuchadnezzar the king of Babylon, my ser-
> vant; and the beasts of the field have I given him
> also to serve him. (Jeremiah 27:6)

> Yet destroyed I the Amorite before them, whose
> height was like the height of the cedars, and he was
> strong as the oaks; yet I destroyed his fruit from
> above, and his roots from beneath. (Amos 2:9)

For those who honor Scripture, the above passages establish God's sovereign control over man and everything in the created realm. As was seen, God controls even seemingly chance events. God's sovereign
control even extends to man's heart. God not only knows the future, He controls the future. "There is a
vast difference between the teaching of Scripture and the beliefs of prideful people who exalt man-made
teachings in its place." This is especially true as the Scriptures speak of the sovereignty of God.

The biblical Christian will be able to rejoice with the Psalmist by saying: "Thy word is a lamp unto
my feet, and a light unto my path." It is exceedingly sinful to bring God's Word before, and hold
it accountable to, the judgment seat of human reason. As we learn from man's fall in the Garden
of Eden, human autonomy or personal self-rule is idolatry. As the Scriptures have declared, God
is sovereign and in control of everything. Therefore, we can say in harmony with the above Scriptures, He must ultimately be the primary cause of all things.

The Westminster Confession of Faith declares:

> God from all eternity, did, by the most wise and
> holy counsel of His own will, freely, and unchange-
> ably ordain whatsoever comes to pass. (See Appen-
> dix Four - WCF Sections III, I)

FOOD FOR THOUGHT:

"Suppose the word mountain meant metaphor, and dog, and Bible, and the United States. Clearly,
if a word meant everything, it would mean nothing. If, now, the law of contradiction is [only] an
arbitrary convention [as some say], and if [these] 'linguistic theorists' choose some other conven-

tion, I challenge them to write a book in conformity with their principles. As a matter of fact it will not be hard for them to do so. Nothing more is necessary than to write the word metaphor sixty thousand times: Metaphor metaphor metaphor metaphor.... This means the dog ran up the mountain, for the word metaphor means dog, ran, and mountain. Unfortunately, the sentence "metaphor metaphor metaphor" also means, Next Christmas is Thanksgiving, for the word metaphor has these meanings as well." - Gordon H. Clark, God's Hammer: The Bible and Its Critics

"If God did not arrange [the world] this way, then there must be an independent factor in the universe. And if there is such, one consequence and perhaps two follow. First, the doctrine of creation must be abandoned. A creation ex nihilo would be completely in God's control. Independent forces cannot be created forces, and created forces cannot be independent.

Then, second, if the universe is not God's creation, his knowledge of it—past and future—cannot depend on what he intends to do, but on his observation of how it works. In such a case, how could we be sure that God's observations are accurate? How could we be sure that these independent forces will not later show an unsuspected twist that will falsify God's predictions?

And, finally, on this view God's knowledge would be empirical, rather than an integral part of his essence, and thus he would be a dependent knower. These objections are insurmountable. We can consistently believe in creation, omnipotence, omniscience, and the divine decree. But we cannot retain sanity and combine any one of these with free will." - Gordon H. Clark, Religion, Reason & Revelation

CHAPTER 4

SOTERIOLOGY: THE DOCTRINES OF GRACE

he term "soteriology" comes from two Greek terms, *soter* meaning "savior" and *logos* meaning "word." In Christian systematic theologies, the word is used to refer to the study of the biblical doctrine of salvation. It covers topics such as the nature and extent of the atonement, as well as the process of salvation, formed as an eternal divine plan fashioned to bring sinners back into fellowship with God.

In contrast, what exists in Mormonism is a collection of seemingly disconnected statements on various points of soteriology. Mormonism tends to reach doctrinal positions without clear grammatical or historical study of the Bible. Without this objective foundation, further exegetical work is nearly impossible. In this chapter, we will look at the Mormon concepts of the fall, sin, election, the atonement and its extent, grace, and finally the perseverance or eternal security of the believer. These various Mormon doctrines will be set against the vast wealth of scriptural evidence, which clearly refutes Mormon soteriology.

MAN'S DEPRAVITY: THE MORMON VIEW

Man's depravity or "total depravity" is a scriptural doctrine connected to the doctrine of original sin and the fall of man seen in Genesis chapter three. This doctrine interprets the Bible to teach that as a result of man's fall, every person born into this world is morally and ethically corrupt, slaves to sin, and without God's grace, absolutely unable to love God or choose to turn to Christ in faith for salvation.

How does Mormonism view the fall of man and sin? Former Mormon president Joseph Fielding Smith, in his work *Doctrines of Salvation,* Vol. 1, makes a number of comments concerning this subject that is representative of most Mormons.

Let us survey some of his ideas on this important subject:

> How did Adam and Eve sin? Did they come out in direct opposition to God and his government? No.... When Adam was driven out of the Garden of Eden, the Lord passed a sentence upon him. Some people have looked upon that sentence as being a dreadful thing. It was not; it was a blessing. I do not know that it can truthfully be considered even as a punishment in disguise.... "Transgression" Not "Sin" of Adam. I never speak of the part Eve took in this fall as a sin, nor do I accuse Adam of a sin.
>
> Joseph F. Smith, *Doctrines of Salvation* Vol. 1, p. 112, 113, 114.
>
> Any man who believes that little children are born in sin and are tainted by original sin, or the sin of somebody else, has failed to comprehend the nature of the atonement of Jesus Christ.... Every child-I don't care where it is born; I don't care what its color-that is born into this world comes into it innocent in its infant state.... Why, when you look into the face of a little babe and he looks up and smiles at you, can you believe that that little child is tainted with any kind of sin that will deprive it of the presence of God should it die?
>
> Joseph F. Smith, *Doctrines of Salvation* Vol. 2, p. 50-51.

Sadly, the above quotations by Joseph F. Smith are completely at odds with Scripture. His method of looking into little children's faces and determining that they are not sinners is nothing more than wishful humanistic thinking.

James E. Talmage, a Mormon apostle, has something more to say on this topic that is relevant:

> The present fallen status of mankind, as expressed in our mortal condition, was inaugurated by Adam and Eve; but divine justice forbids that we be accounted sinners solely because our parents transgressed. Though the privations, the vicissitudes, and the unrelenting toil enforced by the state of mortal existence be part of our heritage from Adam, we are enriched thereby; for in just such conditions do we find opportunity to develop the powers of soul that shall enable us to overcome evil, to choose the good, and to win salvation and exaltation in the mansions of our Father.
>
> James E. Talmage, *Articles Of Faith* (Salt Lake City, Deseret Book Company 1988), p. 428.

Talmage denies that we should be accounted sinners because of Adam's sin. What Talmage overlooks is the fact that Adam is the federal head of the human race. Adam acted as the representative of the human race and as a result his sin becomes, in a very real way, our sin. A president of a country acts as a representative of his particular nation. His actions may very well cause another nation to invade his nation, thus all of his subjects would experience the results of their president's decisions. The doctrine of federal or covenantal headship is taught throughout Scripture. By rejecting Adam's federal headship over the human race, Talmage and Mormonism also reject Christ's federal headship, since Christ is the second Adam.

We know from Scripture that a husband is the head of his wife. A husband's actions or decisions always affect his wife and children. This is how federal headship functions. In contrast, Talmage believes that we are enriched as a result of Adam's sin. In this regard, Talmage holds to a deficient view of sin. God's people historically have always prayed for deliverance from this old sinful world. Our prayers should be that we would be delivered from personal sins, which bring us much grief and godly sorrow.

What exactly are the effects of sin in the human race? How does sin affect us?

Joseph F. Smith gives some more information on this subject:

> Let us illustrate: A man walking along the road happens to fall into a pit so deep and dark that he cannot climb to the surface and regain his freedom. How can he save himself from his predicament? Not by any exertions on his part, for there is no means of escape in the pit. He calls for help and some kindly disposed soul, hearing his cries for relief, hastens to his assistance and by lowering a ladder, give to him the means by which he may climb again to the surface of the earth. This was precisely the condition that Adam placed himself and his posterity in.
>
> Joseph F. Smith, *Doctrines of Salvation* Vol. 1, p. 126-127.

Adam, according to Mormonism, is aware of his condition, and is able to cry for help. When the ladder is lowered down to him, he is able to climb out of the pit. Is this the condition of man that is set forth in Scripture? Of course not. This is simply a form of humanism or works for salvation. This view of man's condition was also known as Pelagianism (the British monk Pelagius believed that Adam's sin did not affect future generations of humanity. Man in this system essentially saves himself by following the example of Christ). In the early church, Pelagianism was condemned as heresy during the fourth century.

Former Mormon apostle LeGrand Richards explains his understanding of human free will:

> Thus all nations and people have free agency and, according to their choice, the Lord will do unto them.... If all men are not saved, it will be because they, in the exercise of their free will, do not accept his gift of grace.
>
> LeGrand Richards, *A Marvelous Work And A Wonder* (Salt Lake City, Deseret Book Co. 1978), p. 345, 347.

Richards believes that man, though unsaved, has the power within himself to exercise his free will. If man does not do this then he will not be saved. It seems that man, according to Richards, is saved as a result of exercising his own will. Man in his fallen state still has much to contribute towards his salvation according to this Mormon leader. You see this works-for-salvation scheme in all non-Christian religions.

Let us consider another bit of information from Talmage concerning man's state after the fall.

Talmage tells us that man can be sincere and of a humble disposition before being in a state of grace:

> Although faith is called the first principle of the Gospel of Christ, though it be in fact the foundation of religious life, yet even faith is preceded by sincerity of disposition and humility of soul, whereby the word of God may make an impression upon the heart. No compulsion is used in bringing men to a knowledge of God; yet as fast as we open our hearts to the influences of righteousness, the faith that leads to life eternal will be given us of our Father.

> Talmage, *Articles of Faith* p. 97.

Talmage says in the above quote that man must do something. God does not first act upon man to open his heart. Rather, according to Talmage, we must open our hearts to God. How can a man open his heart to God? Why would man want to do this? Man, according to Mormonism, is able to make quite a significant contribution to his own salvation. Mormonism, while not using the term, holds to a form of what is known in Arminian theology as prevenient grace. In this scheme Christ's death overcomes original sin and ensures that man will get out of the grave in the resurrection.

Mormonism clearly holds to a un-biblical view of man and sin. Sin, while being an obstacle in Mormonism, does not prevent man from seeing a need to have faith and call for help. When help comes, then man climbs out of the pit through his own effort. It also should be noted, that unlike Arminians who attempt to exegetically establish similar soteriological interpretations of Scripture, Mormonism is guided in its understanding of Scripture by the pronouncements of the leaders.

MAN'S DEPRAVITY:
THE CHRISTIAN VIEW

ALL OF MANKIND:
DEAD IN SIN!

It can be seen from a cursory reading of the Scriptures that man is fallen in sin. Because of the fall, man is more than just injured, he is dead. If man is dead in sin, how did he get this way? Bible commentators have used the theological term "Original Sin" to explain what happened to man in the beginning. What is the basis for this doctrine? The primary text is found in Romans 5:12-19. What does this passage say? This passage speaks about the fall and of man's guilt in this event.

> Wherefore, as by one man sin entered into the world, and death by sin; and so death passed upon all men, for that all have sinned. (For until the law sin was in the world: but sin is not imputed when there is no law. Nevertheless death reigned from Adam to Moses, even over them that had not sinned after the similitude of Adam's transgression, who is the figure of him that was to come. But not as the offense, so also is the free gift. For if through the offense of one many be dead, much more the grace of God, and the gift by grace, which is by one man, Jesus Christ, hath abounded unto many. And not as it was by one that sinned, so is the gift: for the judgment was by one to condemnation, but the free gift is of many offenses unto justification. For if by one man's offense death reigned by one; much more they which receive abundance of grace and of the gift of righteousness shall reign in life by one, Jesus Christ.) Therefore as by the offense of one judgment came upon all men to condemna-tion; even so by the righteousness of one the free gift came upon all men unto justification of life. For as by one man's disobedience many were made

sinners, so by the obedience of one shall many be

made righteous. (Romans 5:12-19)

This passage clearly teaches the connection between Adam's sin and the human race. Adam as the covenantal or federal head of the human family brought sin to his descendants. This is proved from the fact that death now reigns in the world. The apostle teaches that "all sinned," or all were made or constituted sinners because of their real shared guilt in Adam's sin. This teaching is what is known as "original sin."

As a result of Adam's sin we all come into the world with a fallen nature. Because of our sinful natures we make sinful choices. This original sin, with which we are all born, manifests itself throughout our lives in actual sins which violate God's law, both in sins of commission (active transgression of God's law) and omission (lack of conformity to God's law). In other words we can say, in Adam all have sinned and as a result, in Adam all have died.

IS MAN REALLY DEAD IN SIN?

In the view of some, man is not dead. Man, according to popular belief, just needs an opportunity and a little help. He is able to recognize his condition and call for help. When help comes and assistance is provided, man is able to climb up a ladder out of the problem that faces him. In contrast, the Reformed view teaches that man is dead and unable to call for help or even recognize his condition.

We will now survey a number of passages from Scripture along with comments to prove that the idea that man in his fallen condition can respond to the gospel is in complete opposition with the teaching of Scripture concerning man and sin. The Scriptures declare that man is indeed dead and that he has a heart of stone.

But of the tree of the knowledge of good and evil,

thou shalt not eat of it: for in the day that thou

eatest thereof <u>thou shalt surely die</u>. (Genesis 2:17)

The Hebrew word that is used in this passage twice is *muwth*, which uses two different verb tenses, which translate to "dying" and "die," and is for doctrinal emphasis. The last part of verse 2:17 can be translated literally as "dying you shall die." Adam and Eve's relationship with God was now severed. They died an immediate spiritual death and later physical death, which was passed on to all of their posterity.

> And God saw that the wickedness of man was
> great in the earth, and that every imagination of
> the thoughts of his heart was only evil continually.
> (Genesis 6:5)

God sees and declares that the thoughts of man are nothing but evil, or continually and totally evil. We, as Adam's posterity, have inherited his sinful nature and the sentence of death through our covenantal and organic union with him as our representative head and prime progenitor. Yet it is mankind's individual ownership of our sinful natures that gives rise to the sinful thoughts and deeds that produce personal guilt and assures personal judgment.

> Behold, he putteth no trust in his saints; yea, the
> heavens are not clean in his sight. How much more
> abominable and filthy is man which drinketh iniq-
> uity like water? (Job 15:15-16)

Man in his corrupt and unregenerate state is much filthier than the heavens, and is said to lust or crave wickedness just as he would drink water when thirsty.

> The LORD looked down from heaven upon the
> children of men, to see if there were any that did
> understand, and seek God. They are all gone aside,
> they are all together become filthy: there is none
> that doeth good, no, not one. (Psalms 14:2-3)

Here we see God speaking through David, and the description of the degeneracy of man's nature, along with the reprehensible debasement of all mankind. This verse is echoed in Romans 3:10-12.

> Behold, I was shapen in iniquity; and in sin did my
> mother conceive me. (Psalms 51:5)

David is speaking here of what was mentioned at the outset, namely, "original sin." This inherited sin is the stem or root of his existent sin that permeates his whole being.

> Because sentence against an evil work is not execut-
> ed speedily, therefore the heart of the <u>sons of men</u>
> <u>is fully set in them to do evil</u>. (Ecclesiastes 8:11)

When justice is delayed, man's sin is unrestrained. He becomes brazen-faced and audacious to sin all the more.

> <u>All we like sheep have gone astray</u>; we have turned
> every one to his own way; and the LORD hath laid
> on him the iniquity of us all. (Isaiah 53:6)

Every one of us has turned to evil ways in varying degrees. We have all gone astray and the Lord has assigned or imputed to Christ the sin of all who take refuge in His substitutionary atonement on the Cross.

> But we are as an unclean thing, and <u>all our righ-</u>
> <u>teousness are as filthy rags</u>; and we all do fade as a
> leaf; and our iniquities, like the wind, have taken
> us away. (Isaiah 64:6)

Our so-called righteous acts are nothing more than filthy rags, or quite literally, "menstruation rags" and because of our sins, the wind sweeps us away.

> <u>Can the Ethiopian change his skin, or the leopard</u>
> <u>his spots</u>? Then may ye also do good, that are accus-
> tomed to do evil. (Jeremiah 13:23)

In this passage the prophet speaks clearly of man's inability to change himself by pointing out two impossible things that parallel man's condition. If your nature is evil you cannot change.

> <u>The heart is deceitful above all things, and desper-</u>
> <u>ately wicked: who can know it</u>? (Jeremiah 17:9)

Man's heart is desperately wicked or it can be said, incurable, and even man does not comprehend the magnitude of his own deceitfulness and depravity.

> The good man is perished out of the earth: and there is none upright among men: they all lie in wait for blood; they hunt every man his brother with a net. That they may do evil with both hands earnestly, the prince asketh, and the judge asketh for a reward; and the great man, he uttereth his mischievous desire: so they wrap it up. The best of them is as a brier: the most upright is sharper than a thorn hedge: the day of thy watchmen and thy visitation cometh; now shall be their perplexity. (Micah 7:2-4)

This statement by Micah applies beyond the people of his day and is a general declaration that is in harmony with the apostle Paul when he says that "there is none righteous, no, not one." (Romans 3:10-12)

> And this is the condemnation, that light is come into the world, and men loved darkness rather than light, because their deeds were evil. (John 3:19)

Men loving darkness is the cause of the condemnation, or it can be said to be the reason why men are going to be punished. Man desires sin rather than the holiness of God. Men try to hide in the darkness because their deeds are evil.

> Then Jesus said unto them, Verily, verily, I say unto you, except ye eat the flesh of the Son of man, and drink his blood, ye have no life in you. (John 6:53)

Outside of Christ, there is no life in man. All mankind, like our father Adam, is spiritually dead.

> As it is written, There is none righteous, no, not one: There is none that understandeth, there in none that seeketh after God. They are all gone out of the way, they are together become unprofitable; there is none that doeth good, no, not one. (Romans 3:10-12)

This is undoubtedly a most emphatic portion of Scripture when the apostle Paul here declares man's depravity. All mankind is indicted by the apostle without exception.

> But <u>we had the sentence of death in ourselves</u>, that
> we should not trust in ourselves, but in God which
> raiseth the dead. (2 Corinthians 1:9)

Here the apostle says, "we had the sentence of death in ourselves." The word rendered "sentence" means a judicial ruling, outcome, or verdict. It not only means that Paul knew that he was condemned to die, it also has broader implications for the rest of mankind; the condemnation awaiting them is just, short of participating in the resurrection to life in Christ.

> And you hath he quickened, <u>who were dead in tres-</u>
> <u>passes and sins</u>; Wherein in time past ye walked
> according to the course of this world, according
> to the prince of the power of the air, the spirit
> that now worketh in the children of disobedience:
> Among whom also we all had our conversation in
> times past in the lusts of our flesh, fulfilling the
> desires of the flesh and of the mind; and were
> by nature the children of wrath, even as others.
> (Ephesians 2:1-3)

The apostle says that God made us alive or brought us to life after being dead in sins. This quickening is a spiritual resurrection to life.

THEOLOGICAL IMPLICATIONS AND SCRIPTURAL CONCLUSIONS

We have seen in this survey of Scripture and the corresponding comments that man is dead spiritually. He does not desire the things of God.

Fallen man can lay no claim on God's favor. Man's wickedness is often manifested as religious works see (Genesis 4:3). Cain offered a religious work, the fruit of his own hands. Adam and Eve tried to cover their nakedness with the works of their own hands. God did not accept Adam and Eve's hand-made coverings or Cain's offering of self effort. Many man-made religions will dress themselves up, such as Adam and Eve tried, with outward religious trappings. These types of human works are filthy rags in God's eyes. Fallen man hates God and the things of God. Many fallen men will offend God by throwing humanistic religious works in God's face.

Man's nature is corrupted and he makes all decisions based upon his corrupted or fallen nature. In the view of some, man has a total and complete free will. Unfortunately, many never define what they mean by the term free will, and this problem is further complicated by certain advocates not proving this belief in their particular notion of free will from Scripture. This belief in total free will may be popular and emotionally pleasing, but is it biblical? Many simply assume that there is something called free will and that it is taught in the Bible, or they misinterpret passages to fit the conclusion they want to draw. Contrary to the belief that God is all powerful, in the "free will" view, God cannot even save man unless man first says "yes."

It is clear from the Scriptures that fallen man is spiritually dead, and consequently cannot be really free not to sin. The problem arises for many people because they know that they make choices or decisions. Man most certainly does make choices. The question needs to be asked, why does man choose one thing over another? The solution is found in man's nature. Fallen man makes decisions that are the result of the desires of his nature. Why does man reject the biblical God? Because it is in his rebelliously independent nature to do so. Man's will chooses in harmony with his nature. Romans tells us the following:

> Know ye not, that to whom ye yield yourselves ser-
> vants to obey, his servants ye are to whom ye obey;
> whether of sin unto death, or of obedience unto
> righteousness? (Romans 6:16)

Verse fourteen of this chapter says of those in Christ that we are no longer under the dominion of sin. We were the servant or slaves of sin. We yielded ourselves to sin because this was the inclination of our fallen nature. We are now the servants of righteousness and no longer the slaves of sin. Our innate, sinful natures have been supernaturally changed. The apostle Peter confirms this when he says: "ye might be partakers of the divine nature..." (2 Peter 1:4) The believer now has a new nature. We still make choices or decisions. Since we have a new nature, our desires have been changed. We are now slaves of righteousness.

Both the non-believer and the believer make choices, but they are determined by either a corrupt nature or a changed, divinely regenerated nature. Man's will can only be said to be free if it is understood that this freedom is always in accord with the desires of man's nature. The believer is now a new creation in Christ. We follow Christ because we love Him and want to please Him. The Holy Spirit lives in the believer and guides us and convicts us to do what is right according to the Scriptures.

When a person chooses Christ, one must ask, why did the person do this? Was it his decision on his own, apart from God's action? Or, does man act or choose for Christ as a result of God changing his heart by the power of Holy Spirit? The Scripture declares that unbelievers are spiritually dead (not just sick) and have hearts of stone. Christ, through the work of the Holy Spirit, changes our heart of stone into a heart of flesh. As was said, unbelievers are spiritually dead before Christ quickens us or makes us alive. We are raised from the dead when Christ regenerates us. Regeneration enables saving faith, and happens before we can exercise saving faith.

Therefore, Christ gets the credit for our decision to believe in Him. Unbelievers do not first choose Christ, because they in their fallen state hate Him and are spiritually dead. And furthermore, it should be noted that fallen man's nature is corrupt and fallen man freely chooses in harmony with his fallen nature to reject Christ. So then, when a fallen man is regenerated and exercises faith in the Lord Jesus Christ's atoning work at Calvary, what credit does God get for this decision? "All" is the only possible correct answer. Salvation is all of grace.

Remember, we were the servants or slaves of sin. We yielded ourselves to sin because this was the inclination of our fallen nature. We are now the servants of righteousness and no longer the slaves of sin. Our sin natures have been changed. As the apostle Peter tells us that "ye might be partakers of the divine nature..." (2 Peter 1:4). The believer now has a new nature. We still make choices or decisions. But since we have a new nature, our desires have been changed through the inward work of the Holy Spirit. We are now slaves of righteousness (though not yet perfectly) by His grace.

In conclusion, both the non-believer and the believer make choices, but those choices are determined by either a corrupt nature or a changed, regenerated nature. The will can only be said to be free if it is understood that this freedom is always in accord with the desires of man's nature. It can be said that the will is bound in its original sin nature, yet free through the redeeming power of Jesus. The believer is now a new creation in Christ. We follow Christ because we love Him and want to please Him. The Holy Spirit lives in the believer and guides us and convicts us to do what is right according to the Scriptures.

See Appendix III for: *The Westminster Confession of Faith* Chapter VI Of the Fall of Man, of Sin, and of the Punishment Thereof

ELECTION:
THE MORMON VIEW

In the Reformed understanding, foreordination or predestination is the doctrine that because God is all-powerful, all-knowing, and completely sovereign, he "from all eternity did by the most wise and holy counsel of His own will, freely and unchangeably ordain whatsoever comes to pass," (from the Westminster Confession). "In him we have obtained an inheritance, having been predestined according to the purpose of him who works all things according to the counsel of his will." (Ephesians 1:11)

The Mormon view is an outright rejection of this biblical truth. Man in the Mormon system is ultimately responsible for his salvation. Man must do something, then God will act. Election in Mormonism is the result of the Mormon god looking forward in time and seeing man's efforts, then accordingly electing him. The cause is man's work or contribution. Man's self-effort is the cause of God's foreordination or election. Yet this is not foreordination or election at all in the biblical sense of the terms. As a result, there is no true grace in the Mormon system, since it is earned or given in response to man's actions or withheld as a result of inaction.

Let us survey some Mormon writers to examine their concept of election or foreordination. The first person we will consider is James E. Talmage.

Talmage has the following to say concerning this subject:

> Foreordination takes into consideration repen-
> tance, faith, and obedience on the part of man...
>
> Talmage, *Articles of Faith* p. 441.

Talmage is more careful than most Mormon writers in trying to do justice to certain biblical doctrines. Nevertheless, he clearly connects "repentance, faith, and obedience" on man's part with foreordination. It should be noted that Talmage later tries to have it both ways by teaching God's independence. Yet Talmage's semi-pelagianism (a system where man contributes his own faith or works to obtain salvation) destroys God's independence. In addition, semi-pelagianism teaches that humanity is tainted by sin, but not to the extent that man cannot cooperate with God's grace on his own.

A concept of foreordination that operates only after taking into account man's actions is not foreordination at all. It is rather something granted to man as a result of his works.

Brigham Young, in one of his sermons, states his belief that God responds to man's efforts:

> My faith is, when we have done all we can, then the
> Lord is under obligation...
>
> Brigham Young, *Journal of Discourses* Vol. 4, p. 91.

Young is quite clear that God has to work after man first works. Yet grace defined biblically cannot exist in this type of theology.

We will now consider three quotations from Bruce. R. McConkie:

> As with every basic doctrine of the gospel, the
> Lord's system of election [is] sic. based on pre-exis-
> tent faithfulness has been changed and perverted
> by an apostated Christendom.
>
> McConkie, *Mormon Doctrine* p. 216.

> By their foreordination the Lord merely gives them
> the opportunity to serve him and his purposes if
> they will choose to measure up to the standard he
> knows they are capable of attaining.
>
> McConkie, *Mormon Doctrine* p. 588.

> Predestination is the false doctrine that from all
> eternity God has ordered whatever comes to pass,
> having especial and particular reference to the sal-
> vation or damnation of souls. Some souls, accord-

ing to this false concept, are irrevocably chosen for salvation, others for damnation; and there is said to be nothing any individual can do to escape his predestined inheritance in heaven or in hell as the case may be.

McConkie, *Mormon Doctrine* p. 290.

It is quite clear that McConkie does not accept predestination or foreordination unless it is based upon man's works. Since McConkie rejects the biblical teaching concerning man's fall and sin, he can see no reason for the entire human race to be under the sentence of hell.

Predestination is God electing, out of the mass of fallen men, a great multitude of people to receive salvation based entirely upon God's free choice. Those who go to hell get what they deserve. The gospel is offered to them sincerely. They are free to choose the gospel or reject it. They reject it of their own choice because their natures are fallen or corrupt.

McConkie is a Pelagian (where man is unhindered by Adam's sin and can obtain salvation by following the necessary steps) as seen from his belief that foreordination is simply giving man the opportunity to save himself. God, according to McConkie, knows that man is capable of attaining salvation. All man has to do in McConkie's system is measure up to the standard that man is capable of attaining. It is interesting that McConkie and Talmage seem to disagree on this subject. Talmage appears to teach something closer to semi-pelagianism while McConkie is clearly a Pelagian. Both positions can be labeled as heretical or non-biblical.

Let us consider McConkie's father-in-law, Joseph Fielding Smith, to see another view on this subject:

No person is ever predestined to salvation or damnation. Every person has free agency.

Joseph F. Smith, *Doctrines of Salvation* Vol.1, p. 61.

The gospel of Christ is the gospel of mercy. It is also, the gospel of justice. It must be so, for it comes from a God of mercy, not from a cruel monster, who as some

religionists still believe and declare: By the decree of
God, for the manifestation of his glory some men
and angels are predestined unto everlasting life, and
others fore-ordained to everlasting death.

Joseph F. Smith, *Doctrines of Salvation* Vol. 3, p.
286, 287.

It seems that Smith is setting up a false dichotomy rather than dealing with the totality of scriptural teaching on this subject. The Scriptures set forth God's predestination and man's depravity
and at the same time man's responsibility. Because Smith does not have a biblical view of man's
depravity, he cannot accurately judge the doctrine he is rejecting. It is entirely likely that Smith
himself does not fully understand the belief that he is rejecting.

In addition, it is clear that Joseph Fielding Smith and his son-in-law, Bruce R. McConkie, believe
that man possesses the ability to effect his own salvation. It is important that words such as predestination should be interpreted in light of biblical teaching. Instead, Mormonism, which is
governed by subjective rationalism, rejects God's Word. But what does the Bible say about this
subject?

It will be easy to see a vast difference between Scripture and Mormonism. The reader should keep
this issue before him concerning the cause of election. Is election caused by an act of man or the
free act of God? Does God elect after seeing man's faith, repentance, or willingness? If God elects
after man contributes something, is this a works form of salvation? In light of the above teaching
from Scripture concerning man's depravity, what good thing could man contribute? Are even
man's seemingly good works motivated from false motives? There are many passages of Scripture
that teach man's responsibility for his actions. Do these Scriptures conflict with passages that
teach God's unconditional election? How? If someone holds Scripture to the standard of human
reason what doctrines will be rejected?

Should men hold to man as the ultimate standard of human reason? Hasn't human reason been
affected by sin? If so, can human reason ever be an infallible guide? Can human responsibility and
unconditional election both be true? If not, why not?

Does man contribute something meritorious in his election? Does God act freely, or does he
respond after man makes his contribution? If man causes God to elect, how many works are need-

ed to obtain election? Are faith and repentance gifts from God? If they are gifts from God, how can they be the human cause of election? For the most part, Mormons just rely on the "gospel-like" words of their leaders, rather than doing exegetical Scriptural or theological work in the area of understanding predestination and the fall of man.

Why do men want to contribute their own works toward salvation? Is it sinful to do this? We will now consider some of the Biblical passages concerning election. Try to keep in mind some of the questions that have been raised about the relationship of man's works and election. Do Mormons agree with the following Scriptures?

ELECTION:
THE CHRISTIAN VIEW

UNCONDITIONAL ELECTION

Is election to salvation caused by an act of man or the free act of God? Does God elect after seeing man's faith, repentance, or willingness? If God elects only after man contributes something, is this a 'works' form of salvation?

In the eternal counsel of God, with man's fall into sin in view, God appointed certain people to be saved. In this act or decree, God was totally free in deciding to show grace and mercy to some sinners, while passing other sinners by. Human works were not in view, nor were they the cause of God's election. Because of man's proclivity to sin resulting from the fall, God is under no obligation to save anyone. Thus, God has determined those who will be saved based on nothing foreseen in their works, including foreseen faith. Scripture clearly puts the basis of God's election entirely outside of man's attempts to be worthy.

Let's be clear, unconditional election means that man does not meet conditions in order to be elected to salvation. God does not look forward in time, and on the basis of some foreseen work on the part of man, elect him to salvation. If this were so, it could be said that God elects men after seeing them do something. God then would be responding to man's action. Salvation or election would be a debt that God owed to man, and in order to obtain salvation, man would have to do his part by first earning it himself.

The following Scriptural passages provide the rationale for affirming God's unconditional election:

And he spake unto Korah and unto all his company, saying, Even tomorrow the LORD will show who are his, and who is holy; and will cause him to come near unto him: even him <u>whom he hath chosen</u> will he cause to come near unto him. (Numbers 16:5)

For thou art an holy people unto the LORD thy God: the LORD <u>thy God hath chosen thee</u> to be a special people unto himself, above all people that are upon the face of the earth. The LORD did not set his love upon you, <u>nor choose</u> you, because ye were more in number than any people; for ye were the fewest of all people. (Deuteronomy 7:6-7)

Yet <u>I have left me seven thousand</u> in Israel, all the knees which have not bowed unto Baal, and every mouth which hath not kissed him. (I Kings 19:18)

Blessed is the man whom <u>thou choosest, and causest</u> to approach unto thee, that he may dwell in thy courts: we shall be satisfied with the goodness of thy house, even of thy holy temple. (Psalms 65:4)

O ye seed of Abraham his servant, ye children of Jacob <u>his chosen</u>. (Psalms 105:6)

Thy people <u>shall be willing in the day of thy power</u>, in the beauties of holiness from the womb of the morning: thou hast the dew of thy youth. (Psalms 110:3)

The <u>Preparations of the heart in man, and</u>

the answer of the tongue, is from the LORD. (Proverbs 16:1)

LORD, thou wilt ordain peace for us: for thou also hast wrought all our works in us. (Isaiah 26:12)

I, even I, am he that blotteth out thy transgressions for mine own sake, and will not remember thy sins. (Isaiah 43:25)

For Jacob my servant's sake, and Israel mine elect, I have even called thee by thy name: I have surnamed thee, though thou hast not known me. (Isaiah 45:4)

O LORD, I know that the way of man is not in himself: it is not in man that walketh to direct his steps. (Jeremiah 10:23)

I have surely heard Ephraim bemoaning himself thus; Thou hast chastised me, and I was chastised, as a bullock unaccustomed to the yoke: turn thou me, and I shall be turned; for thou art the LORD my God. Surely after that I was turned, I repented; and after that I was instructed, I smote upon my thigh: I was ashamed, yea, even confounded, because I did bear the reproach of my youth. (Jeremiah 31:18-19)

In those days, and in that time, saith the LORD, the iniquity of Israel shall be sought for, and there shall be none; and the sins of Judah, and they shall not be found: for I will pardon them whom I reserve. (Jeremiah 50:20)

Turn thou us unto thee, O LORD, and we shall be

turned: renew our days as of old. (Lamentation 5:21)

A new heart also will I give you, and a new spirit will I put within you: and I will take away the stony heart out of your flesh, and I will give you an heart of flesh. And I will put my spirit within you, and cause you to walk in my statutes, and ye shall keep my judgments, and do them. (Ezekiel 36:26-27)

For there shall arise false Christs, and false prophets, and shall show great signs and wonders; insomuch that, if it were possible, they deceive the very elect....And he shall send his angels with a great sound of a trumpet, and they shall gather together his elect from the four winds, from one end of heaven to the other. (Matthew 24:24, 31)

And except that the Lord had shortened those days, no flesh should be saved: but for the elect's sake, whom he hath chosen, he hath shortened the days. (Mark 13:20)

And shall not God avenge his own elect, which cry day and night unto him, though he bear long with them? (Luke 18:7)

Which were born, not of blood, nor of the will of the flesh, nor of the will of man, but of God. (John 1:13)

All that the Father giveth me shall come to me; and him that cometh to me I will no wise cast out.... And this is the Father's will which hath sent me, that of all which he hath given me I should lose nothing, but should raise it up again at the last day. And this is the will of him that sent me, that every one which seeth the Son, and believeth on him, may have everlasting life: and I will raise him up at the last day....<u>No man can come to me, except the Father which hath sent me draw him</u>; and I will raise him up at the last day....And he said, Therefore said I unto you, <u>that no man can come unto me, except it were given unto him of my Father</u>. (John 6:37, 39, 40, 44, 65)

I speak not of you all: <u>I know whom I have chosen</u>: but that the scriptures may be fulfilled, He that eateth bread with me hath lifted up his heel against me. (John 13:18)

Ye have not chosen me, but <u>I have chosen you</u>, and ordained you, that ye should go and bring forth fruit, and that your fruit should remain: that whatsoever ye shall ask of the Father in my name, he may give it you. (John 15:16)

As thou hast given him power over all flesh, that <u>he should give eternal life to as many as thou hast given him</u>. (John 17:2)

I pray for them: I pray not for the world, but for them <u>which thou hast given me</u>; for they are thine. (John 17:9)

For the promise is unto you, and to your children, and to all that are afar off, <u>even as many as the LORD our God shall call</u>. (Acts 2:39)

Forasmuch then <u>as God gave them the like gift</u> as he did unto us, who believed on the Lord Jesus Christ; what was I, that I could withstand God? (Acts 11:17)

And when the Gentiles heard this, they were glad, and glorified the word of the Lord: and <u>as many as were ordained to eternal life believed</u>. (Acts 13:48)

And a certain woman named Lydia, a seller of purple, of the city of Thyatira, which worshipped God, heard us: <u>whose heart the Lord opened</u>, that she attended unto the things which were spoken of Paul. (Acts 16:14)

And when he was disposed to pass into Achaia, the brethren wrote, exhorting the disciples to receive him: who, when he was come, helped them much <u>which had believed through grace.</u> (Acts 18:27)

For whom he did foreknow, he also <u>did predestinate</u> to be conformed to the image of his Son, that he might be the firstborn among many brethren.... Who shall lay anything to the charge of God's elect? It is God that justifieth. (Romans 8:29, 33)

For the children being not yet born, neither having done any good or evil, that the <u>purpose of God according to election might stand, not of works, but of him that calleth</u>; It was said unto her, The elder shall serve the younger. (Romans 9:11-12)

And that he might make known the riches of his glory on the vessels of mercy, <u>which he had afore prepared unto glory</u>. (Romans 9:23)

But Esaias is very bold, and saith, <u>I was found of them that sought me not</u>; I was made manifest unto them that asked not after me. (Romans 10:20)

Even so then at this present time also there is <u>a remnant according to the election of grace</u>. (Romans 11:5)

What then? Israel hath not obtained that which he seeketh for; but the election hath obtained it, and the rest were blinded. (Romans 11:7)

According as he hath chosen us in him before the foundation of the world, that we should be holy and without blame before him in love. Having predestinated us unto the adoption of children by Jesus Christ to himself, according to the good pleasure of his will....In whom also have obtained an inheritance, being predestinated according to the purpose of him who worketh all things after the counsel of his own will. (Ephesians 1:4-5, 11)

But God hath chosen the foolish things of the world to confound the wise; and God hath chosen the weak things of the world to confound the things which are mighty; And base things of the world, and things which are despised, hath God chosen, yea, and things which are not, to bring to nought things that are: That no flesh should glory in his presence. (1 Corinthians 1:27-29)

For God, who commanded the light to shine out of darkness, hath shined in our hearts, to give the light of the knowledge of the glory of God in the face of Jesus Christ. (2 Corinthians 4:6)

For unto you it is given in the behalf of Christ, not only to believe on him, but also to suffer for his sake. (Philippians 1:29)

Knowing, brethren beloved, your election of God. (1 Thessalonians 1:4)

For God hath not appointed us to wrath, but

to obtain salvation by our Lord Jesus Christ. (1 Thessalonians 5:9)

But we are bound to give thanks always to God for you, brethren beloved of the Lord, because God hath <u>from the beginning chosen you to salvation</u> through sanctification of the Spirit and belief of the truth. (2 Thessalonians 2:13)

I charge thee before God, and the Lord Jesus Christ, and <u>the elect angels</u>, that thou observe these things without preferring one before another, doing nothing by partiality. (1 Timothy 5:21)

<u>Who hath saved us, and called us</u> with an holy calling, not according to our works, but according to his own purpose and grace, which was given us in Christ Jesus before the world began. (2 Timothy 1:9)

Therefore I endure all things <u>for the elect's sakes,</u> that they may also obtain the salvation which is in Christ Jesus with eternal glory. (2 Timothy 2:10)

Paul, A servant of God, and an apostle of Jesus Christ, according to the faith <u>of God's elect</u>, and the acknowledging of the truth which is after godliness. (Titus 1:1)

Of <u>his own will begat he us</u> with the word of truth, that we should be a kind of first fruits of his creatures. (James 1:18)

<u>Elect according to the foreknowledge of God</u> the Father, through sanctification of the Spirit, unto obedience and sprinkling of the blood of Jesus Christ: Grace unto you, and peace, be multiplied. (1 Peter 1:2)

> But ye are a chosen generation, a royal priesthood, an holy nation, a peculiar people; that ye should show forth the praises of him who hath called you out of darkness into his marvellous light. (1 Peter 2:9)

> The church that is at Babylon, elected together with you, saluteth you; and so doth Marcus my son. (1 Peter 5:13)

> The beast that thou sawest was, and is not; and shall ascend out of the bottomless pit, and go into perdition: and they that dwell on the earth shall wonder, whose names were not written in the book of life from the foundations of the world, when they behold the beast that was, and in not and yet is. (Revelation 17:8)

Therefore, salvation by grace is the unmerited favor of God. The underlined portions of the above Scriptures highlight the emphasis on God's electing action. The doctrine of unconditional election makes the point that God's favor is unearned by man. It is solely God's free choice to elect or not elect, not ours. The cause of election is God's good pleasure. Salvation is determined by God's will, not man's will. This excludes all human works and prevents boasting. God's electing grace demonstrates the fact that salvation is not the result of human action of any kind; it is all of grace.

In closing, consider the great Baptist preacher Charles Haddon Spurgeon's thoughts:

> Join with me in prayer at this moment, I entreat you. Join with me while I put words into your mouths, and speak them on your behalf: "Lord, I am guilty, I deserve thy wrath. Lord, I cannot save myself. Lord, I would have a new heart and a right spirit, but what can I do? Lord, I can do nothing, come and work in me to will and to do thy good pleasure.

> Thou alone hast power, I know, To save a wretch like me; To whom, or whither should I go If I should run from thee?

But I now do from my very soul call upon thy name. Trembling, yet believing, I cast myself wholly upon thee, O Lord. I trust the blood and righteousness of thy dear Son...Lord, save me tonight, for Jesus' sake.

Iain Murray, *The Forgotten Spurgeon* (Edinburgh: Banner of Truth Trust, 1973), pp. 101f.

But, say others, "God elected them on the foresight of their faith." Now, God gives faith, therefore he could not have elected them on account of faith, which he foresaw. There shall be twenty beggars in the street, and I determine to give one of them a shilling; but will any one say that I determined to give that one a shilling, that I elected him to have the shilling, because I foresaw that he would have it? That would be talking nonsense. In like manner to say that God elected men because he foresaw they would have faith, which is salvation in the germ, would be too absurd for us to listen to for a moment.

Spurgeon, *On Doctrines of Grace* 41.42.317

Some, who know no better, harp upon the fore-knowledge of our repentance and faith, and say that, Election is according to the foreknowledge of God;" a very scriptural statement, but they make a very unscriptural interpretation of it. Advancing by slow degrees, they next assert that God fore-knew the faith and the good works of his people. Undoubtedly true, since he foreknew everything; but then comes their groundless inference, namely, that therefore the Lord chose his people because he foreknew them to be believers. It is undoubt-edly true that foreknown excellencies are not the causes of election, since I have shown you that the Lord foreknew all our sin: and surely if there were enough virtue in our faith and goodness to constrain him to choose us, there would have been enough demerit in our bad works to have constrained him to reject us; so that if you make foreknowledge to operate in one way, you must also take it in the other, and you will soon perceive that it could not have been from anything good or bad in us that we were chosen, but according to the purpose of his own will, as it is written, I will have mercy upon whom I will have mercy, and I will have compassion on whom I will have compassion.

Spurgeon, *Doctrines of Grace* 779.621

The above two quotes are from:
http://www.reformationtheology.com/2006/02/c_h_spurgeon_quotes_on_the_doc.php

THE ATONEMENT:
THE MORMON VIEW

In the Scriptures, Christ's atonement is a doctrine that describes how human beings can be reconciled to God. Specifically, atonement refers to the forgiving or pardoning of sin through the death of Jesus on the cross and His subsequent resurrection. Man's sins were paid for by Christ, and His righteousness was imputed or transferred to man, accomplishing the reconciliation between God and man.

How do Mormons view the atonement? We will consider a couple of Mormon quotations that are representative of Mormonism in general. As will be seen, these two Mormon quotes clearly place Mormonism into the stream of Universalism. It should be noted that Mormonism teaches universal salvation for virtually all people, except for a very small number who will end up with the Devil.

Even people who reject Christ by embracing false religions will be saved, according to Mormonism's view of the atonement. All people, they say, are saved by Christ's atonement irrespective of personal beliefs. The 'human works' aspect of Mormonism is seen in their belief of works earning eternal life, which, according to them, means attaining godhood. Everyone gets some measure of salvation because of Christ's universal atonement. Eternal exaltation for the Mormon is determined solely on the basis of man's own efforts.

Let us consider what Mormon leader Joseph F. Smith had to say about the extent of the atonement:

> Also, through the atonement, not only Adam, but all his posterity were redeemed from the temporal effects of the fall, and shall come forth in the resurrection to receive immortality.

> Joseph F. Smith, *Doctrines of Salvation* Vol. 1, p. 112.

Immortality is the opposite of eternal death. In historic Christianity, eternal life is the same as immortality.

The apostle Paul proves this clearly in the following passage:

> For this corruptible must put on incorruption, and this mortal must put on immortality. So when this corruptible shall have put on immortality, then shall be brought to pass the saying that is written, Death is swallowed in victory. (1 Corinthians 15:53-54)

This blessing comes only to those who believe. It is not indiscriminate or ubiquitous in its extent. Paul is speaking specifically to believers in these passages. This is proved from verse fifty in which Paul is addressing "brethren."

Let us consider what James E. Talmage said on this topic.

Talmage has this to say:

> The extent of the atonement is universal, applying alike to all descendants of Adam. Even the unbeliever, the heathen, and the child who dies before reaching the years of discretion, all are redeemed

by the Savior's self-sacrifice from the individual
consequences of the fall.

Talmage, *Articles of Faith* p. 77.

It is clear that Talmage believes in the universal extent of the atonement. He says that unbelievers
and the heathen are redeemed by Christ's sacrifice. Talmage says everyone is redeemed by Christ's
sacrifice. Is this biblical?

It should be noted that Mormon universalism is similar to the version promoted by modern day
semi-pelagians. Semi-pelagians believe in a universal atonement, and as a result cannot effectively
challenge the Mormon view. In both views, man cannot receive the benefits of the atonement
unless he first does something, namely, believe.

The apostle Paul declares in Romans 2:6-7 that God "will render to every man according to his
deeds: To them who by patient continuance in well doing seek for glory and honor and immortality, eternal life."

Christians believe that after the Last Judgment, those who have been spiritually regenerated will
live forever in the presence of God, and those who were never regenerated will be lost to a never-ending consciousness of guilt, separation from God, and punishment for sin. Eternal death is
depicted in the Bible as a realm of constant physical and spiritual anguish in a lake of fire, and a
realm of darkness, away from God.

To summarize the Mormon view of the atonement it can be said: in order for Christ's atonement
to be effective, the Mormon must have faith in Christ, repent of his sins, and be baptized. Christ's
atonement for the Mormon is not effective unless he adds his works to it.

THE ATONEMENT:
THE CHRISTIAN VIEW

The Scriptures cited in this section will clearly refute the Mormon view along with the semi-pelagian view, i.e., the more modern position also known as Arminianism. If one accepts the idea
that the atonement is universal, it is impossible to escape the conclusion that everyone will ultimately be saved. It is fair to say that Mormons are more consistent than are present-day adherents

of Arminian theology. Mormon universalism makes for an attractive man-pleasing theology. The question is asked again: Is this position biblical?

In the Scriptures that follow, it will be seen clearly that the atonement is limited, or particular. It is limited to those for whom it was designed. God certainly has a design or plan. It should be remembered that no one is able to lay any rightful claim upon God for salvation. All men are "by nature children of wrath" (Ephesians 2:3) and are therefore unworthy of anything except eternal judgment. If it were God's design to save all men, there is no doubt that all men would be saved. But the Scriptures teach that not all men will be saved. Some ask, "why are not all saved?" This is the wrong question. The question that should be asked is "why are any saved?" No one deserves salvation. All deserve death. We have all earned it. Death is the wages of sin. When one keeps asking, "why are not all saved?" One must conclude this question arises as a result of a deficient view of sin and the fall. We prefer to leave this question to the secret counsel of God (see Deuteronomy 29:29).

It would be helpful at this point to touch briefly on the traditional Christian conception of immortality, or eternal life, since Christ's atonement secures this for the believer.

Immortality in Scripture involves the complete man who consists of both body and soul. The Christian view of immortality involves salvation from the sentence of death which came upon all mankind because of the fall. Immortality is a state of eternal blessedness, the result of Christ's atonement, which secures eternal life for the believer. Immortality or eternal life involves the believer's restoration to God's image and deliverance from sorrow, pain, and death in the eternal state.

A THOUGHT PROVOKING INTRODUCTION
TO THE EXTENT OF THE ATONEMENT

The doctrine of limited atonement or particular redemption will be the focus of this brief introductory and hopefully thought-provoking look at the extent of Christ's atonement. The doctrine of limited atonement may be an emotional shock to some. Unfortunately, it is usually the case, that those who disagree with the biblical doctrine of limited atonement assume their position to be true and then fall back on emotionalism when challenged. What must be determined, however, is if this teaching is Scriptural? This section will provide an objective look at the Scripture without resorting to emotional reasoning or arguments that can't be proven from the Bible. At the end of this study, I will provide links to classic Reformed studies on this topic that will provide meat for the serious student of God's Word.

The word "atonement" covers words that we find in Scripture such as redemption, redeem, purchase, satisfy, propitiation, and ransom. In addition, theologians use the word "substitutionary" or "vicarious" to describe Christ's atonement. Atonement in essence means acting on behalf of or representing another. At the most fundamental level, God has acted to bring reconciliation and salvation to lost sinners. Was this atonement universal in scope or limited? Does Christ's atoning death save everyone? Or, is the atonement limited in scope only to those who believe? If you believe that Christ's death was universal in scope, you are forced to limit its effectiveness to actually save anyone.

Did Christ die for everyone's sins on the cross? Many modern day evangelicals would say yes to this. When asked, does this mean that everyone will go to heaven, they say emphatically no, because not everyone has faith. Is this lack of faith or unbelief a sin? If so, is it a sin that Christ died for on the cross? If this sin of unbelief is a sin along with all other sins that were atoned for by Christ's death, surely this means that everyone is going to heaven. If you would say no, not everyone is going to heaven, then you must answer, what sins are still unaccounted for that would prevent someone from going to heaven?

Again, is unbelief a sin Christ died for or not? A person who believes in a universal, unlimited atonement is trapped in an inescapable circle of un-biblical thought that robs the Biblical words that cover the concept of the atonement of all meaning. In essence, the system of universal atonement, however emotionally pleasing it may sound, saves no one. The atonement is a historic fact. It is something that is objectively real. It is a completed and accomplished fact. The atonement has a specific design to it. It is limited to whom it is designed for. The atonement is effective to save those for whom it was intended. Limited atonement or particular redemption expresses the biblical concept that Christ's redeeming work was intended to save God's elect and actually secures salvation for them, not just hypothetically.

The famous Baptist preacher, Charles Haddon Spurgeon, makes a strong case for limited atonement by exposing the affront to divine justice universal atonement implies:

> Some persons love the doctrine of universal atonement because they say, "It is so beautiful. It is a lovely idea that Christ should have died for

all men; it commends itself," they say, "to the instincts of humanity; there is something in it full of joy and beauty." I admit there is, but beauty may be often associated with falsehood. There is much which I might admire in the theory of universal redemption, but I will just show what the supposition necessarily involves. If Christ on His cross intended to save every man, then He intended to save those who were lost before he died. If the doctrine be true, that He died for all men, then He died for some who were in hell before He came into this world, for doubtless there were even then myriads there who had been cast away because of their sins. Once again, if it was Christ's intention to save all men, how deplorably has He been disappointed, for we have His own testimony that there is a lake which burneth with fire and brimstone, and into that pit of woe have been cast some of the very person who, according to the theory of universal redemption, were bought with His blood. That seems to me a conception a thousand times more repulsive than any of those consequences which are said to be associated with the Calvinistic and Christian doctrine of special and particular redemption. To think that my Saviour died for men who were or are in hell, seems a supposition too horrible for me to entertain. To imagine for a moment that He was the substitute for all the sons of men, and that God, having first punished the Substitute, afterwards punished the sinners themselves, seems to conflict with all my ideas of Divine justice. That Christ should offer an atonement and satisfaction for the sins of all men, and that afterwards some of those very men should be punished for the sins for which Christ had already atoned, appears to me to be the most monstrous iniquity that could ever be imputed to Saturn, to Janus, to the goddess of the Thugs, or to the most diabolical heathen deities. God forbid that we should ever think thus of Jehovah, the just and wise and good!

Charles Haddon Spurgeon, *Autobiography* 2 Vol., (Edinburgh: Banner of Truth Trust, 1962) 1:172.

The following Scriptures establish what is known as particular or definite redemption:

Surely he hath borne our griefs, and carried our sorrows: yet we did esteem him stricken, smitten of God, and afflicted. But he was wounded <u>for our transgressions</u>; he was bruised <u>for our iniquities</u>: the chastisement of our peace was upon him; and with his stripes <u>we are healed</u>. (Isaiah 53:4-5)

He shall see of the travail of his soul, and shall be satisfied: by his knowledge shall my righteous servant <u>justify many</u>; for he shall <u>bear their iniquities</u>. Therefore will I divide him a portion with the great, and he shall divide the spoil with the strong; because he hath poured out his soul unto death: and he was numbered with the transgressors; and <u>he bare the sin of many</u>, and made intercession for the transgressors. (Isaiah 53:11-12)

We see clear qualifiers in these two passages that restrict Christ's death, using words like <u>many</u> (not all) <u>bare their</u> sin (again, not all). Also, Christ was wounded <u>for our</u> transgressions, not everyone's. And she shall bring forth a son, and thou shalt call his name JESUS: for he shall <u>save his people</u> from their sins. (Matthew 1:21)

Matthew could not be clearer; Jesus "<u>shall save his people</u>." Jesus effectively paid for the sins of His people. Even as the Son of man came not to be ministered unto, but to minister, and to give his life a <u>ransom</u> <u>for many</u>. (Matthew 20:28)

> The Son of man came to be "<u>a ransom for many</u>"
> (not all). For this is my blood of the new testament,
> which is <u>shed for many</u> for the remission of sins.
> (Matthew 26:28)

> And he said unto them, This is my blood of the new
> testament, which is "<u>shed for many</u>." (Mark 14:24)

In these two passages, Christ says His blood is "<u>shed for many</u>" (not everyone). If Christ's atonement was universal this type of restrictive language makes no sense.

> I am the good shepherd, and <u>know my sheep</u>, and
> am known of mine. As the Father knoweth me,
> even so know I the Father: and I lay down my life
> <u>for the sheep</u>. (John 10:14-15)

Christ lays down His life <u>for the sheep</u>, not the goats.

> I have manifested thy name unto the men which
> thou gavest me out of the world: thine they were,
> and thou gavest them me; and they have kept thy
> word....I pray for them: <u>I pray not for the world,</u>
> <u>but for them which thou hast given me</u>; for they
> are thine....And all mine are thine, and thine are
> mine; and I am glorified in them....And for their
> sakes I sanctify myself, <u>that they</u> also might be sanc-
> tified through the truth....Neither pray I for these
> alone, but for them also which shall believe on me
> through their word....Father, I will <u>that they</u> also,
> whom thou hast given me, be with me where I am;
> that they may behold my glory, which thou hast
> given me: for thou lovedst me before the founda-
> tion of the world. (John 17:6, 9-10, 19-20, 24)

Christ's high priestly intercessory prayer is only for those (they) whom the Father had given Him. Not every person who has ever lived or will live.

> And when the Gentiles heard this, they were glad, and glorified the word of the Lord: and <u>as many as were ordained to eternal life believed</u>. (Acts 13:48)

Only those who <u>were ordained to eternal life believed</u>. Christ's atoning sacrifice was intended for and effective for those who were ordained to eternal life.

> Take heed therefore unto yourselves, and to all the flock, over which The Holy Ghost hath made you overseers, to feed <u>the church of God, which he hath purchased with his own blood</u>. (Acts 20:28)

The Church, not the world was purchased <u>with his own blood</u>.

> He that spared not his own Son, <u>but delivered him up for us all</u>, how shall he not with him also freely give us all things? (Romans 8:32)

God delivered up his Son for <u>us all</u>, the elect.

> But we speak the wisdom of God in a mystery, even the hidden wisdom, which God ordained before the world <u>unto our glory</u>. (1 Corinthians 2:7)

> For He hath made him <u>to be sin for us</u>, who knew no sin, that we might be made the righteousness of God in him. (2 Corinthians 5:21)

> Christ bears the sins of His people by actually paying for our sins to the satisfaction of the Father. In whom <u>we have redemption through his blood</u>, the forgiveness of sins, according to the riches of his grace. (Ephesians 1:7)

Our redemption involves the delivering us from our sins. Christ's blood was the redemption price that paid for our salvation according to the riches of his grace. This redemption is real and effective for those for whom it was intended.

> Husbands love your wives, even as Christ, also <u>loved the church</u>, and <u>gave himself for it</u>. (Ephesians 5:25)

Christ gave himself for the His Church, not everyone indiscriminately.

As noted in the underlining from the above scriptural passages, it is quite clear that the design of the atonement was limited. Christ is said to have died for His people, i.e. the church. In John chapter seventeen, the intercessory prayer of the Lord Jesus Christ was restricted to His people. It was not a universal prayer for every person on earth.

AN OBJECTION TO THIS TEACHING:

The most common argument against the doctrine of limited atonement are passages that speak of Christ's atoning death in a universal sense. Some passages of this nature are where the apostle says; "And he is the propitiation for our sins: and not for ours only, but also for the sins of the <u>whole world</u>" in 1 John 2:2. The apostle also tells us that Jesus is called the <u>Saviour of the world</u> in John 4:42, and in another passage; The next day John seeth Jesus coming unto him and saith, Behold the Lamb of God, <u>which taketh away the sin of the world</u> (John 1:29). The apostle Paul also appears to suggest a universal view of the atonement when he says: <u>Who gave himself a ransom for all</u> (1 Timothy 2:6).

It should be noted, that these verses are easily found to be in harmony with other passages that support the doctrine of limited atonement by understanding that the Scriptures use the words; "world," or "all" in a restricted or qualified sense. There is nothing in the larger context of Scripture that demands these passages have to mean every person in the whole world. This is unmistakable, especially when other scriptural passages are taken into account that act as qualifiers. For example, we see that; And it came to pass in those days, that there went out a decree from Caesar Augustus that <u>all the world</u> should be taxed (Luke 2:1), And <u>all went to be taxed</u>, every one into his own city (Luke 2:3). Obviously, these passages could not be talking about every individual in the whole world. This decree of Caesar did not pertain to the indigenous Indians in the Americas and to those in Africa.

Moreover, when the Pharisees said, Do you see how you can do nothing? "behold, the world is gone after him." (John 12:19), can anyone maintain that every person in the world went after or followed Christ? Clearly, there is a restriction or limit here to use of the word "world." The word "world" by the context has to be limited to what happening in the nation of Israel during the first century. It should be abundantly clear that the word or phrases "all" or "all the world" do not mean every person on the planet. These types of objections fail to mitigate against the doctrine of limited atonement because they take certain words out of context by forcing an absolute universal meaning onto the words.

In the beginning, I raised the question, Did Jesus die for everyone's sins? Everyone who affirms this is trapped into a circle of contradictory thought by saying that non-belief keeps men from going to heaven, even though Christ died for the sin of non-belief. The Puritan, John Owen, raised these questions with far greater precision which prove the atonement, properly understood, could not be universal in scope, and if it were so, it would not be efficient to save anyone. I would encourage those who doubt this teaching on the extent of the atonement to read John Owen's *The Death of Death in the Death of Christ*. This work has never been biblically refuted by any type of Universalist, Arminian, or Semi-Pelagian.

Consider just one of John Owen's arguments:

"The Father imposed His wrath due unto, and the Son underwent punishment for, either:

1. All the sins of all men.

2. All the sins of some men, or

3. Some of the sins of all men.

In which case it may be said:

That if the last be true, all men have some sins to answer for, and so, none are saved.
That if the second be true, then Christ, in their stead suffered for all the sins of all the elect in the whole world, and this is the truth.
But if the first be the case, why are not all men free from the punishment due unto their sins?

You answer, "Because of unbelief."

I ask, is this unbelief a sin, or is it not? If it be, then Christ suffered the punishment due unto it, or He did not. If He did, why must that hinder them more than their other sins for which He

died? If He did not, He did not die for all their sins!"
John Owen, *The Death of Christ* (The Banner of Truth Trust, Carlisle, Penn. 1978), p. 173-174.

Owen's work is the most thorough biblical examination on the subject of the extent of the atonement ever printed. The claims of ignorance by Arminian and Semi-Pelagians concerning the existence of this work and this particular argument are not a substitute for refuting it.

In conclusion, it can be said that the atonement is limited by God who determines that certain ones will be saved as a result of His election. God determined that Christ should die for the elect alone. All whom God has elected and Christ has died for will absolutely be saved, or as stated: "Neither are any other redeemed by Christ, effectually called, justified, adopted, sanctified, and saved, but the elect only." (Chapter 3, paragraph 6 of the *Westminster Confession of Faith*)

The serious reader should take advantage of the material that can be accessed with the following links:

The classic and important Introductory Essay to John Owen's The Death of Death in the Death of Christ by theologian J. I. Packer. http://www.undergroundnotes.com/Packer.htm

Download a copy of John Owen's The Death of Death in the Death of Christ in PDF file format. http://undergroundnotes.com/graphics2/JohnOwen.pdf

PROPITIATION IN I JOHN 2:2 (A Doctrinal Study on the Extent of the Atonement) by Dr. Gary D. Long.
http://www.undergroundnotes.com/Long.htm

Particular Redemption audio lecture by Dr. Cornelis Venema.
http://undergroundnotes.com/mp3/ParticularRedemptionDr.CornelisVenema3.mp3

IRRESISTIBLE GRACE:
THE MORMON VIEW

How is grace defined in Mormonism? Is it defined as unmerited favor? Is it humanly resistible? Is it something that man works for? If man works to obtain it, can it be called grace?

We will consider three quotations from Bruce R. McConkie:

> Grace is granted to men proportionately as they conform to the standards of personal righteousness that are part of the gospel plan.
>
> McConkie, *Mormon Doctrine* p. 339.
>
> Conditional or individual salvation, that which comes by grace coupled with gospel obedience, consists in receiving an inheritance in the celestial kingdom of God.
>
> McConkie, *Mormon Doctrine* p. 669.
>
> However, one of the untrue doctrines found in modern Christendom is the concept that man can gain salvation (meaning in the kingdom of God) by grace alone...Salvation in the celestial kingdom of God, however, is not salvation by grace alone.
>
> McConkie, *Mormon Doctrine* p. 671.

In these quotations one can see clearly Mormonism's two tier, or first class and second class, salvation schemes. God's grace is insufficient to bring men into the kingdom of God. Man according to McConkie must do something. Man must add his works.

What does the *Book Of Mormon* say concerning this matter?

In 2 Nephi we find the following:

> For we labor diligently to write, to persuade our children, and also our brethren, to believe in Christ, and to be reconciled to God, for we know that it is by grace that we are saved, after all we can do.
>
> Joseph Smith, *Book Of Mormon* 2 Nephi 25:23, p. 92.

This is a rather incredible statement. It would be impossible to know if you could be saved. How can a man know that if he had done all that he could do? When would grace kick in?

Let us look at another Mormon book to see if this concept appears elsewhere:

> For I the Lord cannot look upon sin with the least
> degree of allowance; Nevertheless, he that repents
> and does the commandments of the Lord shall
> be forgiven.
>
> Joseph Smith, *Doctrine And Covenants* (Salt Lake
> City, The Church of Jesus Christ of Latter-Day
> Saints, 1977), 1:31, 32, p. 3.

We see this same idea again, namely, man must work to receive forgiveness.

Let us look at another passage from the *Doctrine And Covenants*:

> For if you keep my commandments you shall
> receive of his fullness, and be glorified in me as
> I am in the Father, therefore, I say unto you, you
> shall receive grace for grace.
>
> Joseph Smith, *Doctrine And Covenants* 93:20 p. 159.

This continues the Mormon concept of meeting conditions in order to obtain grace. Grace is not grace within this system. Grace is merited in Mormonism. If meeting conditions attains grace, then it follows that man can choose not to respond to it. Grace in this system is not irresistible. Grace does not transform or change the sinner. It is not effective. Even if God wants to save the sinner, He cannot, unless the sinner does something. When considering Mormonism's universal scheme, we find that grace is further distorted into a heretical doctrine. Within Mormonism's conditional exaltation scheme the definition of grace is radically redefined into something inherently self-contradicting.

IRRESISTIBLE GRACE:
THE CHRISTIAN VIEW

Irresistible Grace is defined as; the Holy Spirit effectively bringing salvation to every sinner that God calls to salvation in Christ, through the preaching of the gospel. 1. The Holy Spirit inescapably applies salvation to every sinner that God has elected to save. 2. It is the Holy Spirit who effectively brings those whom God has chosen to believe in Christ. 3. This teaching of "irresistible grace" is also described as "effectual calling" or as "efficacious grace" by theologians. In short, the doctrine says that God's will is in the end, irresistible. This is because God is the sovereign ruler over all creation, including man. The Scriptures declare God's sovereignty emphatically.

The doctrine of irresistible grace <u>does not mean</u> that everything the Holy Spirit does cannot be opposed or resisted. Men do fight against and resist God. However, even this resistance falls within God's secret or hidden will. "The secret things belong unto the LORD our God: but those things which are revealed belong unto us and to our children forever, that we may do all the words of this law" (Deuteronomy 29:29). The doctrine <u>does mean</u> that the Holy Spirit can overcome all unwillingness and opposition, thus making His grace irresistible.

The doctrine of irresistible grace means that God is Sovereign and can overcome all resistance to His will as the Scriptures declare: "And all the inhabitants of the earth are reputed as nothing: and he doeth according to his will in the army of heaven, and among the inhabitants of the earth: and none can stay his hand, or say unto him, What doest thou?" (Daniel 4:35) "But our God is in the heavens: he hath done whatsoever he hath pleased." (Psalms 115:3)

To further clarify, in Reformed theology there is a general or outward call to salvation. This call is made indiscriminately to everyone who hears the gospel. The Holy Spirit provides to God's elect a special inward or irresistible call that inescapably brings them to salvation. The external or outward call of the gospel is made to everyone, and can be, and is oftentimes rejected. The internal call is made only to the elect, and cannot be rejected because it is efficacious and in accordance with the sovereign will of God.

The Westminster Confession of Faith, in a similar fashion, makes the distinction of the "visible" and "invisible" church. The visible church is made up of the truly elect, along with others who unite with the church for reasons other than true conversion. Reasons for non-believers doing this may be things such as respect in the community, social standing, human works for salvation and a host of other humanistic motivations. In contrast, the invisible church is made up only of the elect, who responded to the inward call of gospel made efficacious by the Holy Spirit.

Consider the following scriptural passages in which we see God's irresistible will:

> And God said unto him in a dream, Yea, I know
> that thou didst this in the integrity of thy heart; <u>for</u>

I also withheld thee from sinning against me: therefore suffered I thee not to touch her. (Genesis 20:6)

And they journeyed: and the terror of God was upon the cities that were round about them, and they did not pursue after the sons of Jacob. (Genesis 35:5)

This day will I begin to put the dread of thee and the fear of thee upon the nations that are under the whole heaven, who shall hear report of thee, and shall tremble, and be in anguish because of thee. (Deuteronomy 2:25)

And the LORD thy God will circumcise thine heart, and the heart of thy seed, to love the LORD thy God with all thine heart, and with thy soul, that thou mayest live. (Deuteronomy 30:6)

And Samson went down to Timnath, and saw a woman in Timnath of the daughters of the Philistines. And he came up, and told his father and his mother, and said, I have seen a woman in Timnath of the daughters of the Philistines: now therefore get her for me to wife. Then his father and his mother said unto him, Is there never a woman among the daughters of thy brethren, or among all my people, that thou goest to take a wife of the uncircumcised Philistines? And Samson said unto his father, Get her for me; for she pleaseth me well. But his father and his mother knew not that it was of the LORD, that he sought an occasion against the Philistines: for at that time the Philistines had dominion over Israel. (Judges 14:1-4)

Now in the first year of Cyrus king of Persia, that

the word of the LORD by the mouth of Jeremiah might be fulfilled, <u>the LORD stirred up the spirit of Cyrus king of Persia</u>, that he made a proclamation throughout all his kingdom, and put it also in writing, saying,..Then rose up the chief of the fathers of Judah and Benjamin, and the priests, and the Levites, with <u>all them whose spirit God had raised, to go up to build the house of the LORD</u> which is in Jerusalem. (Ezra 1:1, 5)

<u>The LORD bringeth the counsel of the heathen to nought</u>: he maketh the devices of the people of none effect. (Psalms 33:10)

<u>Blessed is the man whom thou choosest, and causest to approach unto thee</u>, that he may dwell in thy courts: we shall be satisfied with the goodness of thy house, even of thy holy temple. (Psalms 65:4)

That saith <u>of Cyrus, He is my shepherd, and shall perform all my pleasure</u>: even saying to Jerusalem, Thou shalt be built; and to the temple, Thy foundation shall be laid. (Isaiah 44:28)

<u>A new heart also will I give you, and a new spirit will I put within you: and I will take away the stony heart out of your flesh, and I will give you an heart of flesh. And I will put my spirit within you, and cause you to walk in my statutes, and ye shall keep my judgements</u>, and do them. (Ezekiel 36:26-27)

<u>And the LORD stirred up the spirit of Zerubbabel</u> the son of Shealtiel, governor of Judah, and the spirit of Joshua the son of Josedech, the high priest, and the spirit of all the remnant of the peo-

ple; and they came and did work in the house of the LORD of hosts, their God, (Haggai 1:14)

For as the <u>Father raiseth up the dead, and quickeneth them</u>; even so <u>the Son quickeneth whom he will</u>. (John 5:21)

As thou hast <u>given him power over all flesh, that he should give eternal life to as many as thou hast given him</u>. (John 17:2)

And when the Gentiles heard this, they were glad, and glorified the word of the Lord: <u>and as many as were ordained to eternal life believed</u>. (Acts 13:48)

And a certain woman named Lydia, a seller of purple, of the city of Thyatira, which worshipped God, heard us: <u>whose heart the Lord opened</u>, that she attended unto the things which were spoken of Paul. (Acts 16:14)

But <u>by the grace of God I am what I am</u>: and his grace which was bestowed upon me was not in vain; but I laboured more abundantly than they all: yet not I, but the grace of God which was with me. (1 Corinthians 15:10)

Therefore <u>if any man be in Christ, he is a new creature</u>: old things are passed away; behold, all things are become new. And all things are of God, who hath reconciled us to himself by Jesus Christ, and hath given to us the ministry of reconciliation. (2 Corinthians 5:17-18)

<u>For he that wrought effectually in Peter</u> to the apostleship of the circumcision, the same was mighty in me toward the Gentiles. (Galatians 2:8)

> And You hath he quickened, who were dead in
> trespasses and sins.... Even when we were dead in
> sins, hath quickened us together in heavenly with
> Christ, (by grace ye are saved; (Ephesians 2:1, 5)

> For it is God which worketh in you both to will
> and to do of his good pleasure. (Philippians 2:13)

> For that ye ought to say, If the Lord will, we shall
> live, and do this, or that. (James 4:15)

After reading these Scriptures, you will have noticed by the underlined emphasis the words and phrases such as "circumcise," "give," "put," "opened her heart," "gives life," "ordained," "believed," "he made alive," "all this is from God," and "you hath He quickened." These verses clearly teach that God's action or his grace is the responsible agent for our conversion and that God's will is always accomplished; thus, His grace is irresistible.

As we saw from the passage from Ezekiel, how Ezekiel taught that we had hearts of stone before our conversion. In addition, the apostle Paul teaches that we were slaves in bondage to sin. Dead people are incapable of responding to anyone. Because of sinner's conversions, we must conclude that God's actions for us are irresistible and effective. Because God's grace is effective, people are saved. God works irresistibly and sinners are converted to the inward call by the outward preaching of the gospel. This is the plain teaching of the above Scriptures.

In contrast, Mormonism holds the concept of performing works to obtain grace. Grace is not "grace" within a system such as this. This is not unmerited favor; it is works. Because fallen man thinks he is doing something meritorious (or not doing anything at all) by his choice, grace in this system is mistakenly thought to be resistible. If man has to add something, then it follows that man can also add nothing, leading to the erroneous idea that he can resist the sovereign will of God. Grace, in the Mormon teaching, does not transform or change the sinner. It is not effective grace, nor is it biblical grace.

To repeat two passages again in closing, the doctrine of irresistible grace means that God is sovereign and can overcome all resistance to His will as the Scriptures declare:

> And all the inhabitants of the earth are reputed as
> nothing: and he doeth according to his will in the

army of heaven, and among the inhabitants of the
earth: and none can stay his hand, or say unto him,
What doest thou? (Daniel 4:35)

But our God is in the heavens: he hath done whatsoever he hath pleased. (Psalms 115:3)

God is not limited by man's will in His work of applying salvation, nor is He dependent upon
man's cooperation for success. The Spirit graciously enables and causes the elect sinner to cooperate, to believe, to repent, to come freely and willingly to Christ. God's grace, therefore, is invinci-
ble; it never fails to result in the salvation of those to whom it is intended. This is the essence of
the doctrine of irresistible grace, or the efficacious call of the gospel. Amen!

If man has to add something, then it follows that man can resist and he can withhold his works.
Grace is not grace is the Mormon system, since it can be resisted. Biblically speaking, it is a spiritual impossibility for a person to come to Christ aside from the Father's calling. (John 6:44) Stated
another way, it is a spiritual impossibility for the person given by the Father, to His Son, not to come.

Perseverance:
The Mormon View

Perseverance, or preservation of the saints, is a teaching that asserts that once a person is truly
"born of God," or "regenerated," nothing can separate him or her from the love of God. As Paul
says "For I am persuaded, that neither death, nor life, nor angels, nor principalities, nor powers,
nor things present, nor things to come, nor height, nor depth, nor any other creature, shall be
able to separate us from the love of God, which is in Christ Jesus our Lord" (Romans 8:38-39).
Perseverance is the continuance, in grace, of people elected to eternal salvation that is completely
dependent upon God's work for its outworking.

We will now survey several quotations that are relevant to this discussion. We will see that perseverance in Mormonism is completely dependent upon man's effort. It should be remembered
that as far as Mormon universalism is concerned, nearly everyone would attain some measure of
salvation. Mormon exaltation is contingent completely upon man's works. Mormon exaltation
means attaining a position in the Kingdom of God. In historic Christianity, being in God's eternal Kingdom is the same thing as being saved.

Let us now look at two passages from Mormon Scriptures.

The first passage glories in man's free will and the important role it plays in attaining eternal life or choosing death:

> ...free forever, knowing good from evil; to act for themselves and not to be acted upon...And they are free to choose liberty and eternal life, through the great mediation of all men, or to choose captivity and death...

> Joseph Smith, *Book Of Mormon* 2 Nephi 2:26, 27, p. 55.

> But there is a possibility that man may fall from grace and depart from the living God.

> Joseph Smith, *Doctrine and Covenants* 20:32.

The two above quotations clearly leave open the possibility that men may fall from grace. This possibility is contingent upon man's alleged free will. Mormons never prove this free will from Scripture, let alone define the term. Mormons just repeat this idea in various ways with no Scriptural or historical basis.

Bruce R. McConkie has more to say on this subject:

> Even sanctified persons, however, have no absolute guarantee that they will be saved.

> McConkie, *Mormon Doctrine* p. 676.

This says much about McConkie's god. The Mormon god cannot guarantee salvation to anyone. In Mormonism, even a sanctified person can be lost. Sanctification in Mormonism does not equate to a person having salvation.

Brigham Young continues this idea:

> ...for if you are the elect, it would be a great pity to have you led astray to destruction.

Brigham Young, *Journal of Discourses* Vol. 6, p. 45.

If all people are given some measure of salvation, destruction in Mormonism just means that they cannot progress to greater degrees of glory. Also, in my opinion, "a great pity" is pretty weak language on Young's part to describe the end result for an unsaved person.

These brief quotations should make it clear that in the Mormon system there is no guarantee that anyone who is elect can stay in grace and be eternally saved. What does the Bible say about this topic?

Perseverance: The Christian View

The tenacity of God for his people

The following scriptural study is intended to help believers have confidence in our great God's protection and care that He has for His people. He is tenacious on our behalf. There are responsibilities and duties that God requires of His people because of His covenantal relationship with man. This section will focus on the Sovereign God who opens and softens hearts, who brings men to conversion and who is more than capable of holding on to His people and protecting them by His grace through the omnipotent power of the Holy Spirit. We should never forget that grace is a gift and not something earned. The Scriptures declare that faith is a gift of God's grace "For by grace are ye saved through faith; and that not of yourselves: it is the gift of God: Not of works, lest any man should boast" (Ephesians 2:8-9). Grace is God's unmerited favor. We exercise faith but it is one of God's gracious gifts that cannot be claimed by man as a work or contribution on his part.

Doctrinal considerations: justification and covenant:

Of utmost importance is the question of how man is made righteous or justified before the Holy God of Scripture. Most misunderstandings in this area happen because of a confusion between justification and sanctification. Sanctification is a process that starts once a person becomes regenerate and lasts through the entirety of the Christian life. Justification, in contrast, is a judicial or forensic one-time act of God that involves the pardoning and forgiving of our sins, and accepting us as righteous in His sight because of what Christ accomplished for us. Moreover, justification is unequivocal or absolute for eternity. Our sins (the breaking of God's law) were imputed to Christ in that he experienced God's judgment on our behalf, and because of this, Christ's righteousness (keeping the law perfectly) is imputed to us. We are therefore pardoned and counted as righteous for His sake. It is not a legal fiction as some may say; it is a fact in the courts of heaven based upon Christ's perfect propitiatory sacrifice and accomplishment at Golgotha.

In further consideration, biblical justification involves the Hebrew verb *tsayke*, to which both the Greek word *dikaioun* and the Latin *justificare* refer, and is used in Scripture when dealing with passages on forensic or declared judicial righteousness. As noted, the Hebrew verb is forensic, and means to absolve someone in a trial, or to hold or to declare just, as opposed to the verb to condemn and to incriminate. See Exodus 23:7; Deuteronomy 25:1; Job 9:3; Psalms 143:2; Proverbs 17:15; Luke 18:14, Romans 4:3-5; and Acts 13:39. The Scriptures are unequivocal in establishing our justification because of how Christ bore the wrath of God for us (see Romans 4:1-7). Justification does not happen over and over again. Christ's died once for all of our sins (not just some) and His death was accepted by the Father on our behalf. It is a finished fact!

In addition, and of particular importance for this study, is the doctrine of God's covenantal dealings with man in Scripture and how this explains God's transactions with man. What is a covenant? In short, a covenant is an agreement or contract between two parties. The word "covenant" is translated from the Hebrew word *berith*. It literally means "to cut." In the Scripture there are covenants made between men, and there are covenants made between God and man, such as the covenant God made with Abraham in Genesis 15:9-18, 17:2.

It should be noted that there are two types of covenants: unconditional and conditional. A conditional covenant obligates both God and specifically man to certain responsibilities. In the case of a conditional covenant, God's promises are contingent upon man meeting his part of the agreement such as the land promises made with Israel. Historically, Israel was removed from the Promised Land by Nebuchadnezzar, king of Babylon, for her unfaithfulness to God's covenant. By way of contrast, in an unconditional covenant, God obliges Himself to certain expressed responsibilities for the fulfilling of the contract regardless of how man responds. An unconditional covenant is a promise made by God to man that is not contingent upon man fulfilling any obligation or conditions. Genesis 15:9-18 is a perfect example of this, where we see the cutting of the animals into pieces and God alone walking between the pieces of animals in the form of a smoking furnace and a burning lamp in verse 17, thus guaranteeing the eternal covenant would be fulfilled because of His action. If God did not keep the covenant made with Abraham and ultimately his spiritual descendants in Christ, God is saying that He Himself would be cut in pieces, or bear the judgment for violation of the covenant, which is an impossibility.

God is our strong tower. He has hedged us about with protection from outside forces. He has graciously placed his Holy Spirit within us to protect us from inward uncertainties. He is even there to protect us from our own failings. God has purchased our salvation by the death of His Son on the cross and He gives us assurance of our salvation by the fact that we are indwelt by the Holy Spirit which is said in Scripture to be "the earnest of our inheritance until the redemption of the purchased possession." We are God's purchased possession which is written in the past tense, thus solidifying the reality of our salvation. We have God's earnest money, or God's down payment, which is the Holy Spirit. Jesus said that He would never leave us or forsake us. He really meant this! Some may raise a question at this point about us forsaking Him. Is this possible in light of the indwelling Holy Spirit and the strong promises of God in Christ? For those that raise this question, consider the testimony of God's promises.

Consider the overwhelming evidence from Scripture of God's tenacious care for us:

> And he [a believer] shall be like a tree planted by
> the rivers of water, that bringeth forth his fruit in
> his season; his leaf also shall not wither; and what-
> soever he doeth shall prosper. (Psalms 1:3)

This passage teaches that the believer will bring forth fruit in his season and his leaf shall not wither and in fact shall prosper. Why? This is because the increase is God's doing and not ours. He is our strength and He is responsible for our fruitfulness. The next verse in the Psalm says that: "The ungodly are not so." What a contrast between the godly and ungodly. There are certainties for both the believer and non-believer.

> The angel of the LORD encampeth round
> about them that fear him, and delievereth them.
> (Psalms 34:7)

Many believe from what we learn in Genesis 16:7 that the angel of the LORD is none other than the Lord Jesus Christ. Consider Joshua's encounter with the Commander of the Lord's army as this will show us how God encamps about his people:

> He said, 'No, but as Commander of the army of the Lord I have now come.' And Joshua fell on his face to the earth and worshiped, and said to Him, 'What does my Lord say to His servant?' Then the Commander of the Lord's army said to Joshua, 'Take your sandal off your foot, for the place where you stand is holy.' And Joshua did so. (Joshua 5:14-15)

It is interesting that Joshua worshiped the Commander of the Lord's army. If he been simply a created angel he would not have done this, neither would this Commander have received worship if he had been a created angelic being. This makes many believe that this is none other than Christ himself. This passage in Psalm 34 is telling us that Christ himself and His heavenly hosts encamp around us to protect us and deliver us. What a blessed defense! We truly do not need to fear!

> For this God is our God for ever and ever: he will be our guide even unto death. (Psalms 48:14)

The passage says that God will be our God, who is a loving Savior forever and ever. Because of God's covenant this loving relationship is permanent. He will lead us across the river of death and onto the resurrection and the heavenly city. We will see death swallowed up in victory!

> They that trust in the LORD shall be as mount Zion, which cannot be removed, but abideth for ever. As the mountains are round Jerusalem, so the LORD is round about his people from henceforth even for ever. (Psalms 125:1-2)

We see permanency here as the Scriptures comfort us with the assurance that LORD is round about us "even forever."

> The LORD will perfect that which concerneth me: thy mercy, O LORD, endureth for ever: forsake

not the works of thine own hands. (Psalms 138:8)

The LORD will complete His work in us. We are the work of His hands. We can be sure that He will not forsake us, i.e. the work of His own hands!

> For the mountains shall depart, and the hills be
> removed; but my kindness shall not depart from
> thee, neither shall the covenant of my peace be
> removed, saith the LORD that hath mercy on thee.
> (Isaiah 54:10)

God's UN-changeability or immutability is seen in this verse by the contrast between the LORD and His creation. Again, as in Psalm 125 we see permanency, and as Isaiah says, "the mountains may depart and the hill may be moved," but God's mercy would never cease for His covenant people. If mountains departing are seemingly next to impossible, it should magnify in our minds the strength of this unbreakable promise. God Himself makes this contrast with the seemingly impossible and the absolute impossibility of His kindness and the peace of His covenant departing from His people.

> And I will make an everlasting covenant with them,
> that I will not turn away from them, to do them
> good; but I will put my fear in their hearts, that
> they shall not depart from me. (Jeremiah 32:40)

In this passage there is clearly an unconditional aspect of God's covenant made with His people, which is one reason it is said to be everlasting! God guarantees this by saying that He will not turn away from us and He will ensure this by putting His fear in our hearts so as to keep us from departing from Him. The New Covenant in Christ is built upon the fulfillment of the Older Testament Covenants. It is also seen to be an everlasting covenant because it is said that God's law is written on the heart, where God's spirit dwells in the hearts of redeemed men (See Joel 2:28). And I will betroth thee unto me forever, yea I will betroth thee unto me in righteousness, and in judgment, and in lovingkindness, and in mercies. I will even betroth thee unto me in faithfulness: and thou shalt know the LORD. (Hosea 2:19-20)

Betrothal historically was a contract or a ceremonial state of engagement considered to be just as binding as marriage. Using covenantal language in this passage, the LORD binds Himself to His people forever.

> How think ye? if a man have an hundred sheep,
> and one of them be gone astray, doth he not leave
> the ninety and nine, and goeth into the mountains,
> and seeketh that which is gone astray? And if so be
> that he find it, verily I say unto you, he rejoiceth
> more of that sheep, than of the ninety and nine
> which went not away. Even so it is not the will of
> your Father which is in heaven, that one of these
> little ones should perish. (Matthew 18:12-14)

We learn of the Father's revealed will in this passage, namely, that not one of these little ones should perish. What a comfort this revelation is to the sheep, His people.

> For there shall arise false Christs, and false proph-
> ets, and shall show great signs and wonders; inso-
> much that, if it were possible, they shall deceive
> the very elect. (Matthew 24:24)

The implication in this passage is that the elect cannot be lost since Christ says this could happen only if impossible things could happen. In establishing this, we must consider the promises of God for His elect: one, his grace for them; two, their safety in Christ; and finally, third, their protection by God's power. We can rightly agree that in light of the promises of Christ, the elect's deception is impossible.

> For God so loved the world, that he gave his
> only begotten Son, that whosoever believeth in
> him should not perish, but have everlasting life.
> (John 3:16)

For the one who truly believes it is said, "should not perish, but have everlasting life." In the second phrase "but have" is in the present tense meaning that this everlasting life is now a reality. In addition, the verb, "should not perish" means will not ever perish; and following directly the text says, "but have everlasting life." This strengthens and proves that "everlasting life" is to be savored as a reality by the believer right here and now.

> He that believeth on the Son hath everlasting life...
> (John 3:36)

This everlasting life the apostle speaks of is something that the believer possesses now as a real present possession! There is a future aspect to this obviously, yet awaiting the future final fulfillment does not diminish the present pleasure of this gift and all the enjoyment it brings in the here and now.

> But whosoever drinketh of the water that I shall
> give him shall never thirst... (John 4:14)

This phrase "shall never thirst" helps us understand that the water Christ is giving is eternal life. We have a strong symbol of God's security for his people in this passage.

> Verily, verily, I say unto you, He that heareth my
> word, and believeth on him that sent, hath ever-
> lasting life, and shall not come into condemnation;
> but is passed from death unto life. (John 5:24)

Again in this passage, we have the comfort of knowing that eternal life is a present possession that the believer enjoys now. And to add to the blessings of knowing this, the part of the passage that says "shall not come into condemnation" guarantees the future. We are secure in Christ. We have everlasting life now!

> And this is the Father's will which hath sent me,
> that of all which he hath given me I should lose
> nothing, but should raise it up again at the last day.
> And this is the will of him that sent me, that every
> one which seeth the Son, and believeth on him,
> may have everlasting life: and I will raise him up at
> the last day. (John 6:39-40)

We see in this verse God's choice or the election of His people, which is the strong guarantee of our preservation. The promise of Christ is sure, He will raise us up on the last day!

> And I give unto them eternal life; and they shall
> never perish, neither shall any man pluck them out

> of my hand. My Father, which gave them me, is
> greater than all; and no man is able to pluck them
> out of my Father's hand. (John 10:28-29)

Christ gives us eternal life now as a present possession along with the unmovable promise that the believer shall never perish. Christ not only protects His people, He adds the guarantee of the Father who is greater than all.

> That he should depart out of this world unto the
> Father, having loved his own which were in the
> world, he loved them unto the end. (John 13:1)

We see the heart of Christ towards His people in His unceasing care for His sheep.

> And I will pray the Father, and he shall give you
> another Comforter, that he may abide with you for
> ever. (John 14:16)

Our Mediator, Christ, prays for His people giving us great assurance. The Holy Spirit the third person of the triune Godhead has promised to stay with us forever. Some translations call the Comforter (the Holy Spirit) our Helper.

> While I was with them in the world, I kept them
> in thy name: those that thou gavest me I have kept,
> and none of them is lost, but the son of perdition;
> that the scripture might be fulfilled. (John 17:12)

We see in this passage our Lord's perfect protection of His people. Of those the Father gave to the Son, Christ says "none of them is lost." We can be assured that not any of Christ's sheep given Him by the Father can or will be lost!

> But God commendeth his love toward us, in that,
> while we were yet sinners, Christ died for us. Much
> more then, being now justified by his blood, we
> shall be saved from wrath through him. For if,
> when we enemies, we were reconciled to God by

the death of his Son, much more, being reconciled,

we shall be saved by his life. (Romans 5:8-10)

Christ died for us while we were in a spiritual state of unbelief characterized by a heart of stone that hated and rejected God's testimony. Not only this, Christ has surrounded us at every moment, in our innermost being and consciousness, as well as in all of creation. In light of this, how can anyone doubt that we will be given the grace to persevere, and be saved eternally, and be glorified, after being justified by His blood?

There is therefore now no condemnation to them

which are in Christ Jesus, who walk not after the

flesh, but after the Spirit. (Romans 8:1)

If you are truly justified, you will walk after the Spirit. It is part of our new nature to do so. We are indwelt by the Holy Spirit, who leads us in the ways of life, and calls us to repentance, and gives us His strength each day. The apostle makes it clear, "There is therefore now no condemnation."

For I am persuaded, that neither death, nor life,

nor angels, nor principalities, nor powers, nor

things present, nor things to come. Nor height,

nor depth, nor any other creature, shall be able

to separate us from the love of God, which is in

Christ Jesus our Lord. (Romans 8:38-39)

The apostle is persuaded that nothing will be able to "separate us from the love of God." We should agree and be thankful.

For the gifts and calling of God are without repen-

tance. (Romans 11:29)

Salvation is a gift of God that He gives without repentance. Due to His ongoing protection guaranteed by the indwelling Holy Spirit, it is a gift that cannot be lost.

Who shall also confirm you unto the end, that

ye may be blameless in the day of our Lord Jesus

Christ. God is faithful, by whom ye were called

unto the fellowship of his Son Jesus Christ our
Lord. (1 Corinthians 1:8-9)

Christ Himself shall "confirm us unto the end." And furthermore, the passage says that God is
faithful to keep us blameless to the end at the coming of the Lord Jesus Christ.

There hath no temptation taken you but such as
is common to man: but God is faithful, who will
not suffer you to be tempted above that ye are able;
but will with the temptation also make a way to
escape, that ye may be able to bear it. (1 Corinthians 10:13)

In this passage we see God's guarantee to give us grace to escape fatal temptations.

Knowing that he which raised up the Lord Jesus
shall raise up us also by Jesus, and shall present us
with you. (2 Corinthians 4:14)

The passage encourages the believer by the fact that it is God who will raise us up. In addition,
we are further encouraged of the certainty of our resurrection to life because of the fact that God
raised up the Lord Jesus.

Having predestinated us unto the adoption of children by Jesus Christ to himself, according to the
good pleasure of his will....ye were sealed with that
Holy Spirit of promise, which is the earnest of our
inheritance until the redemption of the purchased
possession, unto the praise of his glory. (Ephesians
1:5, 13-14)

The apostle says that we have been sealed with the Holy Spirit and this act on God's part is the
"earnest" or certainty of our redemption.

Being confident of this very thing, that he which
hath begun a good work in you will perform it

until the day of Jesus Christ. (Philippians 1:6)

Paul tells us that God will perform or accomplish this work which He began in us until Christ comes. Our confidence is in God's work, not our own.

> For ye are dead, and your life is hid with Christ in
> God. When Christ, who is our life, shall appear,
> then shall ye also appear with him in glory.
> (Colossians 3:3-4)

When Christ appears or comes in His glory, we are told that "ye shall appear" with Him in glory!

> And the very God of peace sanctify you wholly; and
> I pray God your whole spirit and soul and body be
> preserved blameless unto the coming of our Lord
> Jesus Christ. Faithful is he that calleth you, who
> also will do it. (1 Thessalonians 5:23-24)

We are assured that God is faithful who calls us and He will also preserve us until the coming of our Lord Jesus Christ. Our salvation rests upon God's faithfulness, not ours!

> But the Lord is faithful, who shall stablish you,
> and keep you from evil. (2 Thessalonians 3:3)

Again we learn that the Lord is faithful, by the fact that He shall establish us and keep us from evil.

> Having obtained eternal redemption for us....And
> for this cause he is the mediator of the new tes-
> tament, that by means of death, for the redemp-
> tion of the transgressions that were under the first
> testament, they which are called might receive the
> promise of eternal inheritance. (Hebrews 9:12, 15)

It is a fact: Christ has "obtained eternal redemption for us!" Again, we see our salvation is a present reality.

> For by one offering he hath perfected for ever them

that are sanctified. (Hebrews 10:14)

Our perfection in Christ is complete and forever!

> Who [believers] are kept by the power of God
> through faith unto salvation ready to be revealed
> in the last time. (1 Peter 1:5)

Since we are kept by the power of God through faith which is a gift of grace and not our own work we do have to fear. Our salvation is grounded in the power of God!

> These things have I written unto you that believe
> on the name of the Son of God; that ye may know
> that ye have eternal life, and that ye may believe on
> the of the Son of God. (1 John 5:13)

John tells us that we "can know" and that "ye have eternal life." Eternal life is therefore a present possession of believers in Christ. If it can be lost, it would not be eternal.

> To them that are sanctified by God the Father, and
> preserved in Jesus Christ, and called.... All believ-
> ers are sanctified by God the Father. And we are
> preserved in Jesus Christ! Now unto him that is
> able to keep you from falling, and to present you
> faultless before the presence of his glory with
> exceeding joy. (Jude 1:1, 24)

God Himself is able to keep us from falling and more than able to present us before the presence of His glory. Our eternal salvation rests upon God's power, not ours! If anyone still maintains that God will respect our so-called free will and allow us to depart from Christ, hopefully the following thoughts in the next paragraph will be of value.

In summary:

When a person chooses Christ, one must ask, why did the person do this? Was it his decision on his own apart from God's action? Or, does man act or choose for Christ as a result of God changing his heart by the power of the Holy Spirit? The Scripture declares that unbelievers are dead (not just sick) and have hearts of stone. Christ, through the work of the Holy Spirit, changes our heart of stone into a heart of flesh. As has been said, unbelievers are dead spiritually, and Christ quickens us or makes us alive. We are raised from the dead when Christ regenerates us. Regeneration happens before we can exercise faith.

Therefore, Christ gets the credit for our decision to believe in Him. Unbelievers do not choose Christ, because they in their fallen state hate him and are spiritually dead. And furthermore, it should be noted that fallen man's nature is corrupt, and fallen man freely chooses in harmony with his fallen nature to reject Christ.

Remember, we were the servants or slaves of sin. We yielded ourselves to sin because this was the inclination of our fallen nature. We are now the servants of righteousness and no longer the slaves of sin. Our innate, sinful natures have been supernaturally changed. The apostle Peter confirms this when he says: "ye might be partakers of the divine nature..." (2 Peter 1:4) The believer now has a new nature. We still make choices or decisions. Since we have a new nature, our desires have been changed. We are now slaves of righteousness.

Both the non-believer and the believer make choices, but they are determined by either a corrupt nature or a changed, divinely regenerated nature. Man's will can only be said to be free if it is understood that this freedom is always in accord with the desires of man's nature.

It can be said that the will is bound, yet free. The believer is now a new creation in Christ. We follow Christ because we love Him and want to please Him. The Holy Spirit lives in the believer and guides us and convicts us to do what is right according to the Scriptures.

WHAT ABOUT THOSE
WHO SEEM TO HAVE FAITH
AND FALL AWAY?

One of the characteristics of fallen man is to hide his sin like Adam did in the garden in Genesis 3:7. The Pharisees were prime examples of outwardly religious men. What did Christ say about them? "But when he saw many of the Pharisees and Sadducees come to his baptism, he said unto them, 'O generation of vipers, who hath warned you to flee from the wrath to come?'" (Matthew 3:7) It is clearly possible for people to act religiously with secretly selfish motives and still be dead in their sins. For example: Not everyone that saith unto me, Lord, Lord, shall enter into the kingdom of heaven; but he that doeth the will of my Father which is in heaven. Many will say to me in that day, Lord, Lord, have we not prophesied in thy name? And in thy name have cast out devils? And in thy name done many wonderful works? And then will I profess unto them, I never knew you: depart from me, ye that work iniquity. (Matthew 7:21, 22-23)

Here we have individuals mentioned who did things in Christ's name and yet Jesus says, "I never knew you." Outwardly religious works may be done in order to hide one's rebellion against God and remain respectable in the community.

It is my prayer that these Scriptures, and reasoning based upon Scripture, will convince the reader that God is truly sovereign in our salvation. If He were not sovereign in our salvation, no one would be saved. What has been covered in the above section are known historically in Reformed Churches as the "Doctrines of Grace."

CHAPTER 5

CHRIST'S KINGDOM AND ESCHATOLOGY

THE APOSTASY OF CHRIST'S CHURCH: THE MORMON VIEW

he Christian understanding of apostasy is the falling away from the Christian faith, or is the rejection of Christ by one who formerly professed Christianity. It can even describe a whole religious body that repudiates the corpus of biblical teaching.

Bruce R. McConkie explains the Mormon concept of apostasy:

> This universal apostasy began in the days of the ancient apostles themselves...With the loss of the gospel, the nations of the earth went into a moral eclipse called the Dark Ages. Apostasy was universal. "Darkness covereth the earth, and gross darkness the minds of the people, and all flesh has become corrupt before my face."

> And this darkness still prevails except among those who have come to a knowledge of the restored gospel.

> McConkie, *Mormon Doctrine* p. 43-44.

McConkie continues to set forward this idea that Christianity in its true form vanished from the earth:

> That portion of the world in which so-called Christianity prevails – as distinguished from heathen or Mohammedan lands – is called Christendom. The term also applies to the whole body of supposed

Christian believers; as now constituted this body is properly termed apostate Christendom.

McConkie, *Mormon Doctrine* p. 131.

McConkie, speaking of the creeds and the confessions of what he has called apostate Christendom, says:

> The most charitable thing that can be said of them is that they are man made.... When the Father and the Son appeared to Joseph Smith to usher in the dispensation of the fullness of times, the young Prophet asked which of all the sects was right and which he should join. In answer he was told to "join none of them, for they were all wrong; and the Personage who addressed me," he explained," said that all their creeds were an abomination in his sight.

McConkie, *Mormon Doctrine* p. 171.

Do McConkie's assertions have any basis in reality?

CHRIST'S KINGDOM
AND ESCHATOLOGY

The God of Holy Scripture is sovereign. Right now, He is governing this world by the word of His power. He is presently giving covenantal blessings and cursing according to his good pleasure. None can stay his hand. He controls all things including history. Men should fear and tremble before him.

The Scriptures set forth a much different view of history than many would like to believe. God not only controls history but has planned it as well. (See Daniel 4:34-35 and Ephesians 2:11.) There is a continual advancement of redemptive history in the Bible. God's purposes are not thwarted.

Satan will not be a winner in human history. Christ Jesus has gained the victory. Satan's power has been broken. He is presently chained. He has always been restricted to doing only what God Almighty has permitted. Will Jesus be the winner in history or Satan? What sayeth the Scriptures?

We will survey Old and New Testament passages to see the continual advancement of redemptive history. The Kingdom of Christ in history will subdue all others. Then and only then the end will come. At that point, death itself will be forever defeated and the kingdom turned over to God the Father. Let us start in the book of Genesis. The first passage we will consider is Genesis 3:15. This verse is significant because it sets forth God's promise of redemption and the defeat of Satan:

> And I will put enmity between thee and the woman, and between thy seed and her seed; it shall bruise thy head, and thou shalt bruise his heel.
> (Genesis 3:15)

This verse is recognized as the first messianic prophecy. The verse speaks of the war between the followers of righteousness and Satan. From the seed of the woman, Christ would come and defeat Satan. Satan appears to gain the victory when Christ is crucified. Christ then rises victoriously from the grave and crushes Satan's head. Eve says that she had gotten a man from the Lord. It is significant that Adam and Eve named their first son Cain (to possess, or to bring forth). (See Genesis 4:1). The meaning of Cain's name evidences the fact that Adam and Eve understood God's promise of a redeemer who would come forth from Eve and would defeat Satan. They thought that this promise would be fulfilled immediately as evidenced by their first born son's name. They thought God would, through Cain, bring forth deliverance from the curse.

It is important to see the promises of growth of the godly seed in human history. The verses that follow will continue to set forth the theme begun in Genesis 3:15 of the Messianic victory in history:

> And I will bless them that bless thee, and curse him that curseth thee: and in thee shall all families of the earth be blessed. (Genesis 12:3)

> And I will make thy seed as the dust of the earth: so that if a man can number the dust of

the earth, then shall thy seed also be numbered. (Genesis 13:16)

And he brought him forth abroad, and said, Look now toward heaven, and tell the stars, if thou be able to number them: and he said unto him, So shall thy seed be. And he believed in the LORD; and he counted it to him for righteousness. (Genesis 15:5-6)

And I will make thee exceedingly fruitful, and I will make nations of thee, and kings shall come out of thee. (Genesis 17:6)

That in blessing I will bless, and in multiplying I will multiply thy seed as the stars of heaven, and as the sand which is upon the sea shore; and thy seed shall possess the gate of his enemies; And in thy seed shall all the nations of the earth be blessed; because thou hast obeyed my voice. (Genesis 22:17-18)

And, behold the LORD stood above it, and said, I am the LORD God of Abraham thy father, and the God of Isaac: the land whereon thou liest, to thee will I give it, and to thy seed; And thy seed shall be as the dust of the earth, and thou shalt spread abroad to the west, and to the east, and to the north, and to the south: and in thee and in thy seed shall all the families of the earth be blessed. (Genesis 28:13-14)

The above verses set forth the clear promises of victory for the godly seed. Consider the following points that we see from the above passages: 1. All families would be blessed 2. All nations would be blessed 3. It would be impossible to number the Godly seed 4. Nations and kings (plural) would come forth 5. The godly will possess the gates of their enemies.

The following New Testament passages prove that the Abrahamic promises are fulfilled in Christ:

> That the blessing of Abraham might come on the Gentiles through Jesus Christ; that we might receive the promise of the Spirit through faith....And if ye be Christ's, then are ye Abraham's seed, and heirs according to the promise. (Galatians 3:14, 29)

> Ye are the children of the prophets, and of the covenant which God made without fathers, saying unto Abraham, And in thy seed shall all the kindreds of the earth be blessed. Unto you first God, having raised up his Son Jesus, sent him to bless you, in turning away every one of you from his iniquities. (Acts 3:25-26)

The universal Abrahamic promises of victory flow right into the New Covenant of Christ. These promises are fulfilled through the preaching and teaching of the gospel.

There are other important messianic promises to consider:

> Why do the heathen rage and the people imagine a vain thing? The kings of the earth set themselves, and the rulers take counsel together, against the LORD, and against his annointed saying, Let us break their bands asunder, and cast away their cords from us. He that sitteth in the heavens shall laugh; the Lord shall have them in derision. Then shall he speak unto them in his wrath, and vex them in his sore displeasure. Yet have I set my king upon my holy hill of Zion. I will declare the decree: the LORD hath said unto me, Thou art my Son,

this day have I begotten thee. Ask of me, and I shall give thee the heathen for thine inheritance, and the uttermost parts of the earth for thy possession. Thou shalt break them with a rod of iron; thou shalt dash them in pieces like a potter's vessel. Be wise now therefore, O ye kings: be instructed, ye judges of the earth. Serve the LORD with fear, and rejoice with trembling. Kiss the Son, lest he be angry, and ye perish from the way, when his wrath is kindled but a little. Blessed are all they that put their trust in him. (Psalms 2:1-12)

All the ends of the world shall remember and turn unto the LORD: and all the kindreds of the nations shall worship before thee. For the kingdom is the LORD's: and he is governor among the nations. (Psalms 22:27-28)

He shall have dominion also from sea to sea, and from the river unto the ends of the earth. They that dwell in the wilderness shall bow before him, and his enemies shall lick the dust. The kings of Tarshish and of the isles shall bring presents: the kings of Sheba and Seba shall offer gifts. Yea, all kings shall fall down before him: all nations shall serve him. (Psalms 72:8-11)

The LORD said unto my Lord, Sit thou at my right hand, until I make thine enemies thy footstool. The LORD shall send the rod of thy strength out of Zion: rule thou in the midst of thine enemies. (Psalms 110:1-2)

These Messianic Psalms clearly show Christ's dominion over all of the earth.

In 2 Samuel we see the promise of the Davidic covenant:

> He shall build an house for my name, and I will
> stablish the throne of his kingdom for ever...And
> thine house and thy kingdom shall be established
> for ever before thee: thy throne shall be established
> for ever. (2 Samuel 7:13, 16)

The Davidic promise shows there will be a kingdom and One who sits upon a throne forever. This is fulfilled in the New Covenant of Christ. The earthly throne of David was a type, foreshadowing and depicting the heavenly throne.

Christ now sits upon this throne and rules:

> This Jesus hath God raised up, whereof we all
> are witnesses. Therefore being by the right hand
> of God exalted, and having received of the Father
> the promise of the Holy Ghost, he hath shed forth
> this, which ye now see and hear. For David is not
> ascended into the heavens: but he saith himself,
> The LORD said unto my Lord, Sit thou on my
> right hand, Until I make thy foes thy footstool.
> (Acts 2:32-35)

It is significant that Peter quotes Psalm 110:1 as proof that this is now happening. Christ is now ruling and exercising dominion. Christ does this through the preaching of the gospel. Men and women are converted, and begin doing what he has commanded. Those converted are part of Christ's inheritance. (See Matthew 28:20 and Psalm 2.)

There are more passages that show Christ's dominion:

> And it shall come to pass in the last days, that the
> mountain of the LORD's house shall be estab-
> lished in the top of the mountains, and shall flow
> unto it. And many people shall go and say, Come
> ye, and let us go up to the mountain of the LORD,

> to the house of the God of Jacob, and he will teach
> us of his ways, and we will walk in his paths: for
> out of Zion shall go forth the law and the word
> of the LORD from Jerusalem. And he shall judge
> among the nations, and shall rebuke many people:
> and they shall beat their swords into plowshares,
> and their spears into pruning hooks: nation shall
> not lift up sword against nation; neither shall they
> learn war any more. (Isaiah 2:2-4)

The above verse shows Christ's victory and rule in history. The phrase "last days" has specific reference to the end of the old Jewish world order. (See 1 Corinthians 10:11 and Hebrews 9:26.) These verses speak of the end of the world, as it relates to the end of Old Testament Covenant order. 1 Peter 4:7 speaks of the Old Covenant as ready to pass away. Hebrews 1:2 says specifically that the Christians in the first century were living in the "last days." We see the destruction of the Jewish temple in 70 A.D., and the end of the Old Testament sacrificial system. We are now living in the New Covenant world order, which is characterized by the rule of Christ in history through the preaching of the gospel and its effects in history.

Isaiah has more to say concerning Christ's dominion:

> For unto us a child is born, unto us a son is given:
> and the government shall be upon his shoulder:
> and his name shall be called Wonderful, Counsel-
> lor, The mighty God, The everlasting Father, The
> Prince of Peace. Of the increase of his government
> and peace there shall be no end, upon the throne
> of David, and upon his kingdom, to order it, and
> to establish it with judgment and with justice from
> henceforth even for ever. The zeal of the LORD of
> hosts will perform this. (Isaiah 9:6-7)

The phrase "no end to his government" presents a powerful argument against the concept of the defeat of Christ's kingdom before the second coming. Mormons, like all premillennialists, say, "yes there will be an end to Christ's government."

Consider the next verse:

> They shall not hurt nor destroy in all my moun-
> tain: for the earth shall be full of the knowledge of
> the LORD, as the waters cover the sea. And in that
> day there shall be a root of Jesse, which shall stand
> for an ensign of the people, to it shall the Gentiles
> seek: and his rest shall be glorious. (Isaiah 11:9-10)

This passage speaks of the gospel age. The phrase "...to it shall the Gentiles seek" clearly finds fulfillment during the gospel age. The phrase "...the earth shall be full of the knowledge of the LORD" speaks of the extent of the influence of the gospel. There is no hint of the defeat of Christ's kingdom.

> For, behold, I create new heavens and a new earth:
> and the former shall not be remembered, nor come
> into mind. But be ye glad and rejoice for ever in
> that which I create: for, behold, I create Jerusalem
> a rejoicing, and her people a joy. And I will rejoice
> in Jerusalem, and joy in my people: and the voice
> of weeping shall be no more heard in her, nor the
> voice of crying. There shall be no more thence an
> infant of days, nor an old man that hath not filled
> his days, for the child shall die an hundred years old,
> but the sinner being an hundred years old shall be
> accursed. And they shall build houses, and inhabit
> them, and they shall plant vineyards, and eat the
> fruit of them. They shall not build, and another
> inhabit, they shall not plant, and another eat: for
> as the days of a tree are the days of my people, and
> mine elect shall long enjoy the work of their hands.
> They shall not labour in vain, nor bring forth for
> trouble, for they are the seed of the blessed of the
> LORD, and their offspring with them. And it shall
> come to pass, that before they call, I will answer,

and while they are yet speaking, I will hear. The
wolf and the lamb shall feed together, and the lion
shall eat straw like the bullock: and dust shall be
the serpent's meat. They shall not hurt nor destroy
in all my holy mountain, saith the LORD. (Isaiah
65:17-25)

This passage in Isaiah 65 is not talking about heaven because it is said there are still sinners and
death. It is also interesting to note that Jesus is not said to be physically present upon earth, which
constitutes a powerful argument against a premillennial interpretation of these passages. These verses should be understood in a figurative sense. Some premillennialists believe these verses are talking
about the millennium, but it should be noted that the word millennium is not even mentioned.

Revelation 20 contains the only passages in the Bible that use the word millennium. Sound
hermeneutical principles demand that we do not use obscure passages, which utilize apocalyptic
writing, to interpret clearer portions of Scripture. This is exactly what the proponents of premi-
llenialism do.

Isaiah, in Old Testament figurative language, sets forth the blessings of Christ's gospel upon the
earth during the New Covenant Church age.

**In the book of Ezekiel we can see the growth of the church and the spread of the gospel
utilizing Old Testament forms:**

Afterward He brought me again unto the door of
the house, and, behold, waters issued out from
under the threshold of the house eastward: for the
forefront of the house stood toward the east, and
the waters came down from under from the right
side of the house, at the south side of the altar...
Afterward he measured a thousand, and it was a
river that I could not pass over: for the waters were
risen, waters to swim in, a river that could not be
passed over... Then said he unto me, These waters
issue out toward the east country, and go down

into the desert, and go into the sea: which being brought forth into the sea, the waters shall be healed. And it shall come to pass, that every thing that liveth, which moveth, whithersoever the rivers shall come, shall live: and there shall be a very great multitude of fish, because these waters shall come thither: for they shall be healed, and every thing shall live whither the river cometh. (Ezekiel 47:1, 3, 5, 8-9)

The passages in both Isaiah and Ezekiel show an advancement of God's redemptive purposes in history. We do not see defeat for God's Kingdom in history.

In the book of Daniel we see that Christ's Kingdom will defeat all human kingdoms:

Thou, O king, sawest, and behold a great image. This great image, whose brightness was excellent, stood before thee, and the form thereof was terrible. This image's head was of fine gold, his breast and his arms of silver, his belly and his thighs of brass, His legs of iron, his feet part of iron and part of clay. Thou sawest till that a stone was cut out without hands, which smote the image upon his feet that were of iron and clay, and brake them to pieces. Then was the iron, the clay the brass, the silver, and the gold, broken to pieces together, and became like the chaff of the summer threshing floors, and the wind carried them away, that no place was found for them: and the stone that smote the image became a great mountain, and filled the whole earth. (Daniel 2:31-35)

I saw in the night visions, and, behold, one like the Son of man came with the clouds of heaven, and came to the Ancient of days, and they brought

> him near before him. And there was given him
> dominion, and glory, and a kingdom that all peo-
> ple, nations and languages, should serve him: his
> dominion is an everlasting dominion, which shall
> not pass away, and his kingdom that which shall
> not be destroyed. (Daniel 7:13-14)

Jesus identified himself as the very person of Daniel 7. Matthew 26:64 provides biblical proof of this. The Jews knew the significance of this claim as evidenced by their reaction in verse 65. The Jews delivered Christ to the Romans to be crucified, seemingly giving Satan the victory. Remember Genesis 3:15. Christ rose from the dead victorious and is now seated on the heavenly throne (Acts 7:55). Satan's power has been broken:

> And he said unto them, I beheld Satan as lightning
> fall from heaven. (Luke 10:18)

> Or else how can one enter into a strong man's
> house, and spoil his goods, except he first bind
> the strong man? And then he will spoil his house.
> (Matthew 12:29)

> And having spoiled principalities and powers, he
> made a show of them openly, triumphing over
> them in it. (Colossians 2:15)

> And I saw an angel come down from heaven, hav-
> ing the key of the bottomless pit and a great chain
> in his hand. And he laid hold on the dragon, that
> old serpent, which is the Devil, and Satan, and
> bound him a thousand years. (Revelation 20:1-2)

The above four selections are a reality now. The passage in Revelation is not something that will happen in the future; it is a present reality. Some comments concerning the time frame when this book was written will be necessary. This is because futuristic interpreters inadvertently undermine the clear teaching of Scripture that Satan is bound or restricted. The texts that reveal when the prophecy of this book will take place are called time indicator texts. They show that the book of

Revelation is historical, not eschatological. (See Revelation 1:1, 3 and Revelation 22:6, 10.) In John 22:10 is told "...seal not the sayings of the prophecy of this book: for the time is at hand." The reader should compare Revelation 22:10 with Daniel 12:4. Daniel is told to "shut up the words, and seal the book."

The burden of Daniel's prophecy deals with the coming of the Messiah. See Daniel 9:24-27. This would happen in approximately 500 years after the prophecy was given. Daniel is told to "seal the book" and John is told "seal not...the prophecy of this book. These two commands are exact opposites, proving that John's Revelation was fulfilled in the first century. The Biblical conclusion is that as the time indicator texts of Revelation show "The time is at hand" 1:1, 3, and "...which must shortly be done," and "Behold, I come quickly," in 22:6-7. Many Old Testament prophecies have already been fulfilled and bring glory to God and build the faith of God's people. The prophecy of Revelation is fulfilled like the prophecy of the virgin birth.

It will be important to consider the extent of Christ's power. Does He only have partial control of the universe or sovereign control?

Consider the two following verses:

> And Jesus came and spake unto them, saying, All power is given unto me in heaven and earth. (Matthew 28:18)

> And what is the exceeding greatness of his power to us-ward who believe, according to the working of his mighty power. Which he wrought in Christ, when he raised him from the dead, and set him at his own right hand in the heavenly places. Far above all principality, and power, and might, and dominion, and every name that is named, not only in this world, but also in that which is to come: And hath put all things under his feet, and gave him to be head over all things to the church, Which is his body, the fulness of him that filleth all in all. (Ephesians 1:19-23)

What did Jesus teach concerning the growth of his Kingdom? Consider two parables:

> Another parable put he forth unto them, saying,
> The kingdom of heaven is like to a grain of mus-
> tard seed, which a man took, and sowed in his
> field: Which indeed is the least of all seeds: but
> when it is grown, it is the greatest among herbs,
> and becometh a tree, so that the birds of the air
> come and lodge in the branches thereof. Another
> parable spake he unto them, The kingdom of heav-
> en is like unto leaven, which a woman took, and
> hid in three measures of meal, till the whole was
> leavened. (Matthew 13:31-33)

These parables set forth an identical teaching as Daniel 2:31-35 showing how Christ's Kingdom
will subdue all other kingdoms.

**Now let us turn to an important passage that ends the debate concerning the alleged earthly
defeat of Christ's Kingdom in history:**

> For he must reign, till he hath put all enemies under
> his feet. The last enemy that shall be destroyed is
> death. For he hath put all things under his feet.
> But when he saith all things are put under him,
> it is manifest that he is excepted, which did put
> all things under him. And when all things shall be
> subdued unto him then shall the Son also himself
> be subject unto him that put all things under him,
> that God may be all in all. (1 Corinthians 15:25-28)

The Scripture is clear: right now Christ is reigning.
His Kingdom is moving forward in history. He will
continue reigning until all things are put under him.
Not until then, and only then, will this present age
of the gospel close. It is time for Christians to renew

their efforts of preaching the gospel and discipling
the nations. We have good reasons to believe that
our efforts will be successful. Our reasons are found
in the promises of God who cannot lie.

We also have seen repeatedly in Scripture the fulfillment of prophecy, which provides encouragement for our efforts:

> Go ye therefore, and teach all nations, baptizing
> them in the name of the Father, and of the Son, and
> of the Holy Ghost: Teaching them [the nations] to
> observe all things whatsoever I have commanded
> you: and, lo I am with you always, even unto the
> end of the world. Amen. (Matthew 28:19-20)

Will our efforts to fulfill the great commission and the discipling of the nations be successful? It should be noted that this commission comes with a promise. The stone of Daniel 2:35 will never be destroyed. The stone becomes a mountain and fills the whole earth. This is the Kingdom that can never be destroyed. (Daniel 2:44) This is Christ's Church. The mustard seed (the Church) will become a great tree.

Let us close with the two following Scriptures:

> And I say also unto thee, That thou art Peter, and
> upon this rock I will build my Church, and the gates
> of hell shall not prevail against it. (Matthew 16:18)

> Unto him be glory in the church by Christ Jesus
> throughout all ages, world without end. Amen.
> (Ephesians 3:21)

I will close with the words of one of the great Christian hymns. It is again time in our churches to sing and take seriously the words of this great hymn that so clearly sets forth the teaching of the Bible concerning Christ's victory over the nations. This hymn was composed during a time when believers took seriously Christ's command to disciple the nations.

The following hymn is an inspirational Church of England processional hymn, which is similar to a marching song in civilian life. It beautifully encapsulates the advancement of Christ's Kingdom:

Onward, Christian soldiers,

Marching as to war,

With the cross of Jesus Going on before.

Christ the royal Master leads against the foe

Forward into battle, See, his banners go.

At the sign of triumph Satan's host doth flee. On then,

Christian soldiers On to victory.

Hell's foundations quiver At the shout of praise.

Brothers, lift your voices, Loud your anthems raise

Like a mighty army Moves the church of God,

Brothers, we are treading Where the saints have trod,

We are not divided, All one body we, One in hope and

doctrine, One in charity.

Crowns and thrones may perish, Kingdoms rise and

wane, But the church of Jesus Constant will remain,

Gates of hell can never Gainst that church prevail

We have Christ's own promise, And that cannot fail.

On ward, then, ye people, Join our happy throng,

Blend with ours your voices In the triumph song Glory,

laud and honor Unto Christ the King

This through countless ages Men and angels sing.

Onward

Christian soldiers Marching as to war, with the cross of

Jesus going on before.

Sabine Baring-Gould, 1865.

Amen!

THE TRINITY

THE TRIUNE NATURE OF GOD AND THE DEITY OF CHRIST STATED

n my dealings with various individuals over the years it is has been rare to find someone who could accurately state the Christian doctrine of the triune nature of God and at the same time reject it. It speaks volumes when someone rejects a position without understanding the position being rejected. If someone cannot state an opposing position, he or she does not understand it. The common reason for many in rejecting the triune nature of God is that they claim to not understand or comprehend that kind of being. If God is God and we are men it should not surprise us that we cannot completely comprehend God. If we could do this, then God would be nothing more than a finite entity.

The standard for rejecting a belief should not necessarily be an inability to comprehend it entirely. Why? For example, most people cannot understand or comprehend how their own brains function. Why not reject our brains? In this respect, many individuals are operational rationalists. Rationalism is a philosophy where human reason becomes the standard of truth. For the Christian, the Bible is our standard of truth. This does not mean that Christians are irrational for believing in the triune nature of God. Nothing could be further from the truth.

The next paragraph appears in Chapter Twelve, *Witnessing to Mormons using a Reformed Presuppositional Apologetic*. It is repeated here for the convenience of the reader.

It should be noted that epistemology is the study of how we know things. There are generally understood to be three types or theories of gaining knowledge: 1. empiricism (a view that experience, especially the senses, is the only source of knowledge) 2. rationalism (a view that appeals to man's independent reason as the source of knowledge) and 3. dogmatism, or scripturalism (all knowledge must be contained within a system and deduced from its starting principles, in the Christian case, the Bible). The Bible contains the Christian's starting principles or presuppositions.

To begin, the triune nature of God can be simply stated as:

1. There is only one God.

2. There are three equally divine, distinct and eternal Persons called God.

3. Therefore, these three equally divine and eternal Persons are the one God.

Louis Berkhof's *Systematic Theology* correctly defines the doctrine of God's triune nature.

The doctrine is stated in a series of propositions:

1. There is in the Divine Being but one indivisible essence

2. In this one Divine Being there are three Persons or individual subsistences, Father, Son, and Holy Spirit

3. The whole undivided essence of God belongs equally to each of the three persons

4. The subsistence and operation of the three persons in the Divine Being is marked by a certain definite order

5. There are certain personal attributes by which the three persons are distinguished.

Louis Berkhof, *Systematic Theology* (Grand Rapids: Eerdmans Publishing Company, 1979), pp. 87-89.

A definition that is more suited to the lay person would be:

Within the nature of the one true God, there are three eternal Persons, the Father, the Son, and the Holy Spirit. Or, it could be said that God is one with respect to His nature or substance and three in respect to Persons.

The Father is not the Son, the Son is not the Father; the Son is not the Spirit; and the Father is not the Spirit. God **is not** one person who manifests or reveals himself in three different modes, or three gods who are one in purpose. There is only one God in essence, who truly exists as three divine persons. The Christian is honestly handling the Word of God by saying there is only one God. The Christian is indeed correct in saying that there are three persons who are God, the Father, Son, and Holy Spirit.

The Magisterial *Westminster Confession of Faith* states:

> In the unity of the Godhead there are three persons, of one substance, power and eterni-

ty: God the Father, God the Son, and God the Holy Ghost. The Father is of none, neither begotten nor proceeding; the Son is eternally begotten of the Father; the Holy Ghost eternally proceeding from the Father and the Son. *The Westminster Confession Of Faith* Chap. II, 3.

The following Scriptures demonstrate that there is a plurality of persons in the Godhead, in other words, you see more than one divine person in each passage listed:

Genesis 1:26; 3:22; 11:7; Isaiah 6:8; 48:16; 61:1-2; Jeremiah 23:5-6; Zechariah 10:12; Matthew 28:19; Luke 4:18-19; John 1:1-3; John 14:23; 2 Corinthians 13:14; Colossians 2:2; Hebrews 1:8-10; Hebrews 3:7-11; 1 Peter 1:2; and 1 John 2:24.

Yet, the Bible makes it indisputable that there is only one God:

Hear, O Israel: The LORD our God is one LORD. (Deuteronomy 6:4)

I am he: before me there was no God formed. Neither shall there be after me, I, even I, am LORD, And beside me there is no saviour. (Isaiah 43:10)

I am the first, and I am the last; and beside me there is no God. (Isaiah 44:6)

Is there a God beside me? Yea, there is no God; I know not any? (Isaiah 44:8)

The Bible teaches the Father is God in the following verses:

To all that be in Rome, beloved of God, called to be saints: Grace to you and peace from God our Father, and the Lord Jesus Christ. (Romans 1:7)

Grace be unto you, and peace, from God our Father, and from the Lord Jesus Christ. (1 Corinthians 1:3)

Grace be to you and peace from God our Father, and from the Lord Jesus Christ. (2 Corinthians 1:2)

The Father is *Jehovah*:

In Exodus 3:13-14 God (*Elohim*) reveals Himself as the "I Am" or *Jehovah* the Lord.

The Father is both *Jehovah* and *Elohim*:

the earth when they were created, in the day that the LORD [*Jehovah*] God [*Elohim*] made the earth and the heavens. (Genesis 2:4)

And the LORD [*Jehovah*] God [*Elohim*] planted a garden Eastward in Eden; and there he put the man whom he had formed. (Genesis 2:8)

And Moses said unto God, Behold, when I come unto the children of Israel, and shall say unto them, The God (*Elohim*) of your fathers hath sent me unto you; and they shall say to me, What is his name? What shall I say unto them? And God said unto Moses, I AM THAT I AM: and he Said, Thus shalt thou say unto the children of Israel, I AM [*Jehovah*] hath sent me unto you. (Exodus 3:13-14)

The Son is proved to be God by the following verses:

But unto the Son he saith, Thy throne, O God, is for ever and ever: a scepter of righteousness is the sceptre of thy kingdom. (Hebrews 1:8)

For in him dwelleth all the fulness of the Godhead bodily. (Colossians 2:9)

And we know that the Son of God is come, and

hath given us an understanding, that we may know him that is true, and we are in him that is true, even in his Son Jesus Christ. This is the true God, and eternal life. (1 John 5:20)

Looking for that blessed hope, and the glorious appearing of the great God and our Saviour Jesus Christ; (Titus 2:13)

Jesus is *Jehovah*:

Jesus said unto them, Verily, verily, I say you, before Abraham was, I am. [*Jehovah*] (John 8:58)

Jesus is using the divine name from Exodus 3:14. The Septuagint (Greek translation of the Old Testament) uses *Ego eimi* for *Jehovah* (I AM) in this verse. John 8:58 in the Greek uses the same formulation, *Ego eimi*. It is inescapable that Jesus is *Jehovah*.

Isaiah 45:23 says "That unto <u>me</u> [*Jehovah*] every knee shall bow..." The New Testament in Philippians 2:10 tells us that this verse speaks of Jesus. Jesus is *Jehovah*.

The following passage speaks of *Jehovah*:

Thou hast ascended on high, thou hast led captivity captive: thou hast received gifts for men; yea, for the rebellious also, that the LORD God might dwell among them. (Psalms 68:18)

The next verse from Ephesians speaks of Jesus with the wording from Psalms 68:18. This makes Jesus *Jehovah*.

Wherefore he saith, when he ascended up on high, he led captivity captive, and gave gifts unto men. (Ephesians 4:8)

Jeremiah the prophet records:

I the LORD search the heart, I try the reins, even to

give every man according to his ways, and according to the fruit of his doings. (Jeremiah 17:10)

What does the New Testament teach about Jesus that identifies him with *Jehovah* of whom Jeremiah spoke?

Consider what John says in Revelation 2:23:

I am he which searcheth the reins and hearts: and
I will give unto every one of you according to your
works. (Revelation 2:23)

More passages could be cited from the Old Testament which the New Testament writers apply to
Christ. The above two examples should be sufficient.

In addition, consider Christ's following claim:

I and my Father are one. (John 10:30)

"Then the Jews took up stones again to stone him." (John 10:31) Why? Jesus was clearly claiming
to be *Jehovah* God in this verse. Is this true?

The Jews said:

The Jews answered him; saying, for a good work we
stone thee not; but for blasphemy: and because that
thou, being a man, <u>makest thyself God</u>. (John 10:33)

The Holy Spirit is called God in the following verses:

But Peter said, Ananias, why hath Satan filled
thine heart to lie to the Holy Ghost, and to keep
back part of the price of the land? ...thou hast not
lied unto men, but unto God. (Acts 5:3-4)

Know ye not that ye are the temple of God, and that
the Spirit of God dwelleth in you? (1 Corinthians 3:16)

> Wherefore (as the Holy Ghost saith, Today if ye
> will hear his voice, Harden not your hearts, as in
> the provocation, in the day of temptation in the
> wilderness. (Hebrews 3:7-8) (See Psalm 95:7-8).

As seen clearly from Acts 5:3-4, the Holy Spirit is a person who can be lied to. In John 14:26, the Holy Spirit is sent to teach the apostles and bring things to their remembrance. This is proof that the Holy Spirit is an intelligent member of the Godhead, hence a person.

The Holy Spirit is *Jehovah*:

> Now the Lord [*Kyrios*] is that Spirit: and where the
> Spirit of the Lord [*Kyrios*] is, there is liberty. (2 Cor-
> inthians 3:17)

The Greek word *Kyrios* is used in the Septuagint (Greek translation of the Old Testament) to translate *Jehovah*. *Kyrios* is translated in English with the word "Lord."

God is the creator. All three persons are involved in creation:

> But to us there is but one God, the Father, of
> whom are all things, and we in him, and one Lord
> Jesus Christ, by whom are all things, and we by
> him. (1 Corinthians 8:6) (Father)

> All things were made by him; and without him was
> not any thing made that was made. (John 1:3) (Son)

> The spirit of God hath made me, and the breath of
> the Almighty hath given me life. (Job 33:4) (Spirit)

All three persons share the attributes of deity.

For example, all three persons are omniscient:

> Known unto God are all his works from the begin-
> ning of the world. (Acts 15:18) (Father)

And he said unto him, Lord thou knowest all things; thou knowest that I love thee. (John 21:17b) (Son)

But God hath revealed them unto us by his Spirit: for the Spirit searcheth all things, yea, the deep things of God. (1 Corinthians 2:10) (Spirit)

All three persons are omnipotent:

And I heard as it were the voice of a great multitude, and as the voice of many waters, and as the voice of mighty thunderings, saying, Alleluia: for the Lord God omnipotent reigneth. (Revelation 19:6) (Father)

And Jesus came and spake unto them, saying, All power is given unto me in heaven and in earth. (Matthew 28:18) (Son)

And the angel answered and said unto her, The Holy Ghost shall come upon thee, and the power of the Highest shall overshadow thee:...For with God nothing shall be impossible. (Luke 1:35-37) (Spirit)

All three persons are omnipresent:

Can any hide himself in secret places that I shall not see him? saith the LORD. Do not I fill heaven and earth? (Jeremiah 23:24) (Father)

...and, lo, I am with you always, even unto the end of the world, Amen. (Matthew 28:20) (Son)

Wither shall I go from thy spirit? Or whither shall I flee from thy presence? (Psalms 139:7) (Spirit)

The Father, Son, and the Holy Spirit are all eternal:

> But now is made manifest, and by the scriptures of the prophets, according to the commandment of the everlasting God, made known to all nations for the obedience of faith: (Romans 16:26) (Father)

> Jesus Christ the same yesterday, and today, and forever. (Hebrews 13:8) (Son)

> How much more shall the blood of Christ, who through the eternal Spirit... (Hebrews 9:14) (Spirit)

All three persons of the Trinity dwell in us. Only God can do this:

> Jesus answered and said unto him, if a man love me, he will keep my words: and my Father will love him, and we will come unto him, and make our abode with him. (John 14:23) (Father)

> That Christ may dwell in your hearts by faith; that ye being rooted and grounded in love. (Ephesians 3:17) (Son)

> Even the Spirit of truth; whom the world cannot receive, because it seeth him not, neither knoweth him: but ye know him, for he dwelleth with you, and shall be in you. (John 14:17) (Spirit)

All three persons of the Trinity were involved in the resurrection of Christ from the dead. Only God can raise the dead:

> Paul, An apostle, not of men, neither by man, but by Jesus Christ, and God the Father, who raised him from the dead: (Galatians 1:1) (Father)

> Jesus answered and said unto them, "Destroy this

temple, and in three days I will raise it up".... But he spake of the temple of his body. (John 2:18-20) (Son)

For Christ also hath once suffered for sin, the just for the unjust, that he might bring us to God, being put to death in the flesh, but quickened by the Spirit: (1 Peter 3:18) (Spirit)

We see all three persons at the baptism of Christ. These are persons, not modes of existence:

And Jesus, when he was baptized, went up straightway out of the water: and, lo, the heavens were opened unto him, and he saw the Spirit of God descending like a dove, and lighting upon him: And lo a voice from heaven, saying, This is my beloved Son, in whom I am well pleased. (Matthew 3:16-17)

We see all three persons at the Great Commission:

Go ye therefore, and teach all nations, baptizing them in the name of the Father, and of the Son, and of the Holy Ghost. (Matthew 28:19)

We see all three persons in Paul's letter:

The grace of the Lord Jesus Christ, and the love of God, and the communion of the Holy Ghost, be with you all. Amen. (2 Corinthians 13:14)

How many gods are there in the Bible? The Bible is abundantly clear on this.

Two verses are sufficient to put an end to polytheism:

...Is there a God beside me? Yea, there is no God; I know not any. (Isaiah. 44:8)

And the scribe said unto him, Well, Master, thou

> hast said the truth: for there is one God; and there
> is none other but he. (Mark 12:32)

The Bible teaches that there are three persons who are called God, and yet the Bible is emphatic that there is only one God.

In conclusion, theologian Norman Geisler summarizes:

- All three Persons possess the attribute of omnipresence (that is, all three are every-where-present): the Father (Matthew 19:26), the Son (Matthew 28:18), and the Holy Spirit (Psalm 139:7).

- All three have the attribute of omniscience: the Father (Romans 11:33), the Son (Matthew 9:4), and the Holy Spirit (1 Corinthians 2:10).

- All three have the attribute of omnipotence (that is, all three are all powerful): the Father (Jeremiah 32:27), the Son (Matthew 28:18), and the Holy Spirit (Romans 15:19).

- Holiness is ascribed to each of the three Persons: the Father (Revelation 15:4), the Son (Acts 3:14), and the Holy Spirit (John 16:7-14).

- Eternity is ascribed to all three Persons: the Father (Psalm 90:2), the Son (Micah 5:2; John 1:2; Revelation 1:8, 17), and the Holy Spirit (Hebrews 9:14).

- Each of the three Persons is individually described as the truth: the Father (John 7:28), the Son (Revelation 3:7), and the Holy Spirit (1 John 5:6).

- As well, each of the three is called Lord (Romans 10:12; Luke 2:11; 2 Corinthians 3:17), everlasting (Romans 16:26; Revelation 22:13; Hebrews 9:14), almighty (Genesis 17:1; Revelation 1:8; Romans 15:19), and powerful (Jeremiah 32:17; Hebrews 1:3; Luke 1:35).

Indeed, the Holy Spirit was present at the same time, revealing that they coexist. Further, the fact that they have separate titles (Father, Son, and Spirit) indicate that they are not one person. Also, each member of the Trinity has special functions that help us to identify them. For example, the Father planned salvation (John 3:16; Ephesians 1:4); the Son accomplished it on the cross (John 17:4; 19:30; Heb. 1:1-2) and at the resurrection (Rom. 4:25; 1 Cor. 15:1-6), and the Holy Spirit applies it to the lives of the believers (John 3:5; Ephesians 4:30; Titus 3:5-7). The Son submits to the Father (1 Cor. 11:3; 15:28), and the Holy Spirit glorifies the Son (John 16:14).

Norman L. Geisler, *Baker Encyclopedia of Christian Apologetics* pp. 731-732.

In a further response to rationalist critics of God's triune nature, Geisler says:

Critics make a point of computing the mathematical impossibility of believing there is a Father, Son and Holy Spirit in the Godhead, without holding that there are three gods. Does not 1+1+1=3? It certainly does if you add them, but Christians insist that the triunity of God is more like 1x1x1=1. God is triune, not triplex. His one essence has multiple centers of personhood. Thus, there is no more mathematical problem in conceiving the Trinity that there is in understanding 1 cubed (13). Norman L. Geisler, p. 732.

There is one God Deuteronomy 6:4 and Jesus is *YAHWEH*

Job 33:4		John 1:3
Isaiah 40:28	**Creator**	Colossians 1:16-17
Genesis 1:1		Hebrews 1:10-12
Psalms 106:21		John 4:42
Isaiah 45:21-23	**Savior**	1 John 4:14
Isaiah 43:3, 11		Acts 4:12
Jeremiah 10:10		Matthew 2:1-6
Isaiah 44:6	**King**	Luke 23:3
Psalms 47:8		John 19:21
Joel 3:12		2 Timothy 4:1
Genesis 18:25	**Judge**	2 Corinthians 5:10
Hebrews 12:23		Romans 14:10

Exodus 3:14	**I Am**	John 8:24
Isaiah 43:10		John 8:58
Deuteronomy 32:39		John 13:19
		John 18:5
Isaiah 17:10	**Rock**	1 Corinthians 10:4
2 Samuel 22:32		1 Peter 2:6-8
Deuteronomy 32:4		Numbers 20:10-11
Isaiah 17:10	**Shepherd**	John 10:11
Psalms 100		Hebrews 13:20
Psalms 23		1 Peter 5:4
Isaiah 60:20	**Light**	John 8:12
Psalms 27:1		Luke 2:23
		John 1:9
Isaiah 48:12	**First and Last**	Revelation 1:17
Isaiah 44:6		Revelation 2:8
Isaiah 41:4		Revelation 22:13

This chart shows that there is only one God. Jesus in Revelation 1:17 is said to be the first and last. *YAHWEH* in Isaiah 41:4 is the first and last. Therefore, there is only one God.

A Comparison of the Mormon and Christian View of God

he Mormon view of God the Father, Jesus and the Holy Spirit is compared with Scripture and found wanting. If you have the wrong view of God, if you don't believe in the one <u>true</u> God, you have no hope for eternal salvation!

Joseph Smith, in *The History of the Church*, tells us what is still today the view of God within Mormonism:

> Many men say there is one God; the Father, the Son, and the Holy Ghost are only one God! I say that is a strange God anyhow~three in one, and one in three! It is a curious organization.... He would be a wonderfully big God~ he would be a giant or a monster.
>
> Joseph Smith, *History of the Church* Vol. 6, p. 476.

Mormon founder Joseph Smith in the above quotation evidences that his knowledge of Christianity's doctrine of God is inaccurate.

In the Provo, Utah, paper *The Herald* we find Mormon apostle Bruce McConkie's ideas concerning biblical teaching. In this devotional speech given at Brigham Young University McConkie is discussing the major heresies of Christianity.

The quotation is the words of the paper, and McConkie himself as quoted by the paper:

> The first great heresy, he said, pertains to the nature of God, the doctrine of the trinity. McConkie said the doctrine of a "three-in-one" God filled the uni-

194

verse after Christ died, and the adoption of the false image destroyed the true worship of God.

Bruce R. McConkie, *The Herald* (Provo: The Herald, January 12, 1984), p. 21.

McConkie is a fairly recent Mormon apostle. He makes it clear that he is no friend of Christian Trinitarian theology.

In the book *The Teachings of the Prophet Joseph Smith,* we have Mormon founder Joseph Smith's view concerning God:

> God himself was once as we are now, and is an exalted man, and sits enthroned in yonder heavens! . . . for I am going to tell you how God came to be God. We have imagined and supposed that God was God from all eternity. I will refute that idea, and take away the veil, so that you may see.... It is the first principle of the Gospel to know for a certainty the Character of God, and to know that we may converse with him as one man converses with another, and that he was once a man like us; yea that God himself, the Father of us all dwelt on an earth, the same as Jesus Christ himself did; and I will show it from the Bible.
>
> Joseph Smith, *The Teachings of the Prophet Joseph Smith* p. 345-346.

In this quotation of Joseph Smith, it is abundantly clear that the god of Mormonism cannot by any stretch of the imagination be the God of Scripture.

Mormon apostle James E. Talmage in his work *Articles Of Faith* tells us about the Father-god of Mormonism:

> His person cannot be in more than one place at

any time. Admitting the personality of God, we are compelled to accept the fact of His materiality.

Talmage, *Articles Of Faith* p. 39.

Talmage also makes it abundantly clear that the god of Mormonism is corporeal and finite.

In the *Doctrine and Covenants* we learn this about the Mormon god:

The Father has a body of flesh and bones as tangible as man's; the Son also; but the Holy Ghost has not a body of flesh and bones, but is a personage of Spirit.

Joseph Smith, *Doctrine And Covenants* p. 238.

The Mormon scriptures concur with this unbiblical notion of an embodied deity.

In the *Journal of Discourses* Mormon leader Wilford Woodruff tells us this about God:

God himself is increasing and progressing in knowledge, power, and dominion, and will do so worlds without end.

Wilford Woodruff, *Journal of Discourses* Vol. 6, p. 120.

This is blatant heresy. In this quotation Woodruff attacks God's attributes of omniscience and omnipotence.

In the Mormon work *History of the Church* we learn more about Smith's views concerning God. Not only does Smith's god change, polytheism is a position that is also promoted.

Smith tells us here about his polytheistic beliefs:

I will preach on the plurality of Gods. [sic] I have selected this text for that express purpose. I wish to declare I have always and in all congregations when I have preached on the subject of Deity, it has been

the plurality of Gods. It has been preached by the
Elders for fifteen years.

Joseph Smith, *History of the Church* Vol. 6, p. 474.

Not only are there many gods in the universe, there are apparently just as many redeemers, tempt-
ers, and planets.

In the *Journal of Discourses* Brigham Young, second prophet of the Mormon religion, tells us this:

> He was the Lamb slain from the foundation of
> the world. Is it so on any other earth? On every
> earth. How many earths are there? I observed this
> morning that you may take the particles of matter
> composing this earth, and if they could be enumer-
> ated they would only be a beginning to the number
> of the creations of God; and they are continually
> coming into existence, and undergoing changes
> and passing through the same experience that we
> are passing through....Consequently every earth
> has its redeemer, and every earth has its tempter.
> Brigham Young, *Journal of Discourses* Vol. 14, p. 71.

**Early Mormon leader Orson Pratt, faithfully following Joseph Smith in his book titled *The Seer*,
tells about the Mormon scheme of reality:**

> We were begotten by our Father in Heaven; the
> person of our Father in Heaven was begotten on a
> previous heavenly world by His Father; and again,
> He was begotten by a still more ancient Father;
> and so on, from generation to generation, from
> one heavenly world to another still more ancient,
> until our minds are wearied and lost in the mul-
> tiplicity of generations and successive worlds,
> and as a last resort, we wonder in our minds,
> how far back the genealogy extends, and how

the first world was formed and the first father was begotten.

Orson Pratt, *The Seer* p. 132.

Contemporary Mormon writer W. Cleon Skousen in his book *The First 2000 Years* has drawn together some of these teachings and brought out the implications that this view of reality holds:

From the scriptures it is obvious that the Father was somehow subject to an impelling circumstance which made it impossible for Him to bring us back into His presence by acting directly or through His own initiative.... God is omnipotent, but only within the circumscribed boundaries of law, truth and justice. He cannot violate these or He would cease to be God....In other words, if eternal principles were violated, God could cease to be God... Through modern revelation we learn that the universe is filled with vast numbers of intelligences, and we further learn the Elohim is God simply because all of these intelligences honor and sustain Him as such. In other words, as God extended His power and influence throughout His great kingdom, He did so by obtaining the voluntary cooperation and support of vast concourses of intelligences.... Therefore, the Father is actually dependent upon their sustaining influence or honor to accomplish His purposes....His glory and power is something which He slowly acquired until today "all things bow in humble reverence." But since God "acquired" the honor and sustaining influence of "all things" it follows as a corollary [sic] that if He should ever do anything to violate the confidence or "sense of justice" of these intel-

ligences, they would promptly withdraw their support, and the "power" of God would disintegrate....
Our Heavenly Father can do only those things
which the intelligences under Him are voluntarily
willing to support Him in accomplishing.

W. Cleon Skousen, *The First 2000 Years* p. 354-356.

In summary, it could be said that the Mormon god was once a man. He somehow became a god.
There are other gods in the universe. These gods have physical bodies. These physical gods are
limited to being in only one place at a time. They progress or change and become more powerful
in their knowledge and their dominion.

Let us now conduct a brief survey of Scripture. Does the testimony of Scripture support these Mormon ideas? Or, does Scripture contradict these Mormon notions? Keep in mind that the Mormon
position involves three major concepts:

1. Polytheism; 2. A finite god with a body; 3. Eternal progression. The Mormon concept makes
God into someone who is not unique. He is simply one god among many, and dependent upon
forces outside himself for his status as God.

THE CHRISTIAN
VIEW OF GOD

Hear, O Israel the LORD our God is one LORD.
(Deuteronomy 6:4)

This is called the *Shema*, the central confession of faith of the Old Testament covenant people. This
was a distinctive belief of the people of Israel, setting them apart from all pagan concepts of god.

All of the following verses will clearly demonstrate that the God of the Bible is completely different from the Mormon god, who changes and is essentially nothing more than a big man. The
following verses prove God's spiritual nature and his attributes that set Him apart from finite or
limited men. Numerous passages prove that God is not a man because of the fact that God is the

creator. God sets himself apart from sinful men by clear declarations. How many verses does it take to prove that God is not a man who changes? Consider carefully the passages in this section to see if the quotations by various Mormons are in harmony with the Bible.

> God is not a man, that he should lie; neither the son of man, that he should repent. (Numbers 23:19)

> Who hath wrought and done it, calling the generations from the beginning? I the LORD, the first, and with the last; I am he. (Isaiah 41:4)

> Ye are my witnesses, saith the LORD, and my servant whom I have chosen: that ye may know and believe me, and understand that I am he: before me there was no God formed, neither shall there be after me. (Isaiah 43:10)

> I am the first, and I am the last; and beside me there is no God. (Isaiah 44:6)

> I am the LORD, and there is none else, there is no God beside me: I girded thee, though thou hast not known me: That they may know from the rising of the sun, and from the west, that there is none beside me, I am the LORD, and there is none else. (Isaiah 45:5-6)

> Remember the former things of old: for I am God, and there is none else; I am God, and there is none like me. (Isaiah 46:9)

God's omniscience is proved by the following verses:

> Great is our Lord, and of great power: his understanding is infinite. (Psalms 147:5)

> The eyes of the LORD are in every place, beholding the evil and the good. (Proverbs 15:3)

Produce your cause, saith the LORD; bring forth your strong reasons, saith the King of Jacob. Let them bring them forth, and show us what shall happen: let them show the former things, what they be, that we may consider them, and know the latter end of them; or declare us things to come. Show the things that are to come hereafter, that we may know that ye are gods: yea, do good, or do evil, that we may be dismayed, and behold it together. Behold, ye are of nothing, and your work of nought: an abomination is he that chooseth you. (Isaiah 41:21-24)

In the above verse God compares His knowledge with that of all false gods.

Known unto God are all his works from the beginning of the world. (Acts 15:18)

... And he said unto him, Lord, thou knowest all things; thou knowest that I love thee. Jesus saith unto him, Feed my sheep. (John 21:17)

Neither is there any creature that is not manifest in his sight: but all things are naked and opened unto the eyes of him with whom we have to do. (Hebrews 4:13)

For if our heart condemn us, God is greater than our heart, and knowest all things. (1 John 3:20)

God's omnipresence is seen in the following verses:

But will God in very deed dwell with men on the earth? Behold heaven and the heaven of heavens cannot contain thee: how much less this house which I have built! (2 Chronicles 6:18)

Wither shall I go from thy spirit? Or whither shall I flee from thy presence? (Psalms 139:7)

Thus Saith the LORD, The heaven is my throne, and the earth is my footstool: where is the house that ye build unto me? And where is the place of my rest? (Isaiah 66:1)

Can any hide himself in secret places that I shall not see him? saith the LORD. Do not I fill heaven and earth? (Jeremiah 23:24)

Though they dig into hell, thence shall mine hand take them; though they climb up to heaven, thence will I bring them down. (Amos 9:2)

God that made the world and all things therein, seeing that he is Lord of heaven and earth, dwelleth not in temples made with hands; Neither is worshipped with men's hands, as though he needed any thing, seeing he giveth to all life, and breath, and all things; And hath made of one blood all nations of men for to dwell on all the face of the earth, and hath determined the times before appointed, and the bounds of their habitation; That they should seek the Lord, if haply they might feel after him, and find him, though he be not far from every one of us: For in him we live, and move, and have our being; as certain as certain also of your own poets have said, For we are also his offspring. (Acts 17:24-28)

God's omnipotence is seen in the following verses:

All things were made by him; and without him was not anything made that was made. (John 1:3)

I am Alpha and Omega, the beginning and the ending, saith the Lord, which is, and which was, and which is to come, the Almighty. (Revelation 1:8)

Before the mountains were brought forth, or ever thou hadst formed the earth and the world, even from everlasting to everlasting thou art God. (Psalms 90:2)

These things hast thou done, and I kept silence; thou thoughtest that I was altogether such an one as thyself: but I will reprove thee, and set them in order before thine eyes. (Psalms 50:21)

I know that thou canst do everything, and that no thought can be withholden from thee. (Job 42:2)

Ah Lord God! behold, thou hast made the heaven and the earth by thy great power and stretched out arm, and there is nothing too hard for thee. (Jeremiah 32:17)

I will not execute the fierceness of mine anger, I will not return to destroy Ephraim: for I am God, and not man; the Holy One in the midst of thee: and I will not enter the city. (Hosea 11:9)

For all the gods of the nations are idols: but the Lord made the heavens. (Psalms 96:5)

For I am the LORD, I change not; therefore ye sons of Jacob are not consumed. (Malachi 3:6)

They shall perish, but thou shalt endure: yea all of them shall wax old like a garment; as a vesture shalt thou change them, and they shall be changed:

But thou art the same, and thy years shall have no end. (Psalms 102:26-27)

But Jesus beheld them, and said unto them, with men this is impossible; but with God all things are possible. (Matthew 19:26)

God's spiritual nature is proved by the following two verses:

God is a Spirit: and they that worship him must worship him in spirit and in truth. (John 4:24)

Behold my hands and my feet, that it is I myself: handle me, and see, for a spirit hath not flesh and bones, as ye see me have. (Luke 24:39)

It should be abundantly clear that the God of Holy Scripture is not the finite changeable god of Mormonism. One final Scripture reference will be given before going on to the next section.

Professing themselves to be wise, they became fools, And changed the glory of the uncorruptible God into an image made like to corruptible man, and to birds, and fourfooted beasts, and creeping things. (Romans 1:22-23)

Passages in the *Book Of Mormon* that teach one eternal God:

And now Abinadi said unto them: I would that ye should understand that God himself shall become down among the children of men, and shall redeem his people.

And because he dwelleth in flesh he shall be called the Son of God, and having subjected the flesh to the will of the Father, being the Father and the Son

The Father, because he was conceived by the power

of God; and the Son, because of the flesh; thus becoming the Father and Son

And they are one God, yea, the very Eternal Father of heaven and of earth. (Mosiah 15:1-4)

And Zeezrom said unto him: Thou sayest there is a true and living God?
And Amulek said: Yea, there is a true and living God.
Now Zeezrom said: Is there more than one God?
And he answered, No.
Now Zeezrom said unto him again: How knowest thou these things?
And he said: An angel hath made them known unto me.

Now, this restoration shall come to all, both old and young, both bond and free, both male and female, both the wicked and the righteous; and even there shall not so much as a hair of their heads be lost; but everything shall be restored to its perfect frame, as it is now, or in the body, and shall be brought and be arraigned before the bar of Christ the Son, and God the Father, and the Holy Spirit, which is one Eternal God, to be judged according to their works, whether they be good or whether they be evil. (Alma 11:26-31, 44)

The point of showing these passages from the *Book of Mormon* is that when considering the Mormon Standard Works (the *Book of Mormon*, *Doctrine and Covenants*, and *The Pearl of Great Price*) you see many contradictions between these Mormon-authoritative writings. *The Book of Mormon* sets forth a crude monotheism, whereas *the Pearl of Great Price* blatantly teaches polytheism.

For example, *The Pearl of Great Price* states in the *Book of Abraham*, "And they [the gods] said: let there be light and there was light. And they [the gods] comprehended the light . . . and the gods called the light Day and the darkness they called Night. . . ." In these chapters from the *Book of Abraham*, the word "gods" is used repeatedly. If language has any meaning, we must reject the polytheism of Mormonism.

THE NATURE OF CHRIST JESUS

In this section we will look at various things that different Mormons have taught about Jesus and then compare their concepts with Scripture.

THE MORMON JESUS

In his book *Gospel Through the Ages* Mormon authority Milton R. Hunter tells us about Jesus prior to coming to this earth:

> The appointment of Jesus to be the Savior of the world was contested by one of the other sons of God. He was called Lucifer, son of the morning. Haughty, ambitious, and covetous of power and glory, this spirit-brother of Jesus desperately tried to become the Savior of Mankind.
>
> Milton R. Hunter, *The Gospel Thru The Ages* (Salt Lake City: Deseret Book Company, 1957), p. 15.

Brigham Young, second prophet of the Mormon religion, gives us his views concerning Christ's birth:

> When the Virgin Mary conceived the child Jesus, the Father had begotten him in his own likeness. He was not begotten by the Holy Ghost.... Now remember from this time forth, and for ever, that Jesus Christ was not begotten by the Holy Ghost.
>
> Brigham Young, *Journal of Discourses* Vol. 1, p.50-51.

Mormon apostle Joseph Fielding Smith concurs with this un-biblical teaching:

> They tell us the *Book of Mormon* states that Jesus was begotten of the Holy Ghost. I challenge that statement. The *Book of Mormon* teaches no such thing! Neither does the Bible.
>
> Joseph F. Smith, *Doctrines Of Salvation* Vol. 1, p. 19.

It is quite clear that Mormonism rejects the biblical teaching concerning Christ's virgin birth.

Mormon apostle Bruce R. McConkie gives us this information on Christ's birth:

> Christ was begotten by an immortal Father in the same way that mortal men are begotten by mortal fathers.
>
> McConkie, *Mormon Doctrine* p. 547.

Early Mormon apostle Orson Hyde made the following startling statements:

> It will be borne in mind that once on a time, there was a marriage in Cana of Galilee, and on a careful reading of that transaction, it will be discovered that no less a person than Jesus Christ was married on that occasion. If he was never married, his intimacy with Mary, Martha, and the other Mary also whom Jesus loved, must have been highly unbecoming and improper to say the best of it.
>
> Orson Hyde, *Journal of Discourses* Vol. 4, p. 259.

This was not an isolated teaching of Hyde's. He taught on another occasion exactly who Christ supposedly married:

> Jesus Christ was married at Cana, that Mary, Martha and others were his wives, and that he begat children.
>
> Orson Hyde, *Journal of Discourses* Vol. 2, p. 210.

In present day Mormonism, marriage is seen as an essential requirement for exaltation, i.e., god-hood. The fact that Mormons believe that Jesus was married reveals much about their view of Christ. He was fulfilling the requirements of the Mormon program. In order for Christ to meet all the requirements to become a god, he had to be married. The Mormons do say that he was already a god when he was on earth. This is a contradiction in their system. Christ was supposedly born as a spirit child in Mormonism's "preexistent world." He, according to Mormon theology, was our elder brother. He was not always a god. He needed to meet the requirements that the following two quotations outline.

Consider the following statement of Joseph F. Smith:

> No exaltation without marriage.
>
> Joseph F. Smith, *Doctrines Of Salvation* Vol. 2, 1989, p. 65.

Bruce McConkie says basically the same thing:

> celestial marriage is the gate to exaltation.
>
> McConkie, *Mormon Doctrine* p. 118.

Jedediah M. Grant, another early Mormon leader, gives us more information of this Mormon teaching concerning plural marriage:

> The grand reason of the burst of public senti-ment in anathemas upon Christ and his disciples, causing his crucifixion, was evidently based upon polygamy, according to the testimony of the philos-ophers who rose in that age. A belief in the doc-trine of plurality of wives caused the persecution of Jesus and his followers. We might think they were Mormons. Jedediah M. Grant, *Journal of Discourses* Vol. 1, p. 346.

According to Mormonism, Jesus is really not all that different from us. He is just further along the path of eternal progression.

Brigham Young explains how Christ is not all that different from other men:

> When the time came that His first-born, the Saviour, should come into the world and take a tabernacle, the Father came Himself and favoured that spirit with a tabernacle instead of letting any other man do it. The Saviour was begotten by the Father of His spirit, by the same being who is the Father of our spirits, and that is all the organic differences between Jesus Christ and you and me.

> Brigham Young, *Journal of Discourses* Vol. 4, p. 218.

Since, according to Brigham Young, there is no real organic difference between Christ and us, it is not surprising to find out that Mormonism denies that Christ's blood is sufficient to save us from certain sins. Confessing Christ with our lips and believing in our hearts that the Father raised Jesus from the dead apart from works will be soul damning, according to Mormonism.

In the Mormon pamphlet *What the Mormons Think Of Christ,* we read:

> Christians speak often of the blood of Christ and its cleansing power. Much that is believed and taught on this subject, however, is such utter nonsense and so palpably false that to believe it is to lose one's salvation. For instance, many believe or pretend to believe that if we confess Christ with our lips and avow that we accept him as our personal Savior, we are thereby saved. They say that his blood, without any other act than mere belief, makes us clean.

> Tract, *What The Mormons Think Of Christ* (Salt Lake City: The Church of Jesus Christ of Latter-Day Saints, 1982), p. 19, 20.

Mormon leader Joseph F. Smith sets forth this idea:

> Joseph Smith taught that there were certain sins so grievous that man may commit, that they place the transgressors beyond the power of the atonement of Christ. If these offenses are committed, then the blood of Christ will not cleanse them from their sins even though they repent. Therefore, their only hope is to have their own blood shed to atone, as far is possible in their behalf.

Joseph F. Smith, *Doctrines Of Salvation* Vol. 1, p. 49-50.

The two above quotations tell us by implication much about the Mormon view of Christ. The Jesus of Mormonism is unable to save certain people by his sacrifice. Since according to Mormonism Jesus is basically the same as us, this would explain why his death is insufficient to save sinners. The sinner's own death and shed blood can do what Christ's cannot.

According to Mormonism, the Father and Son are two completely separate gods. The Father is *Elohim* and Jesus is *Jehovah*.

James E. Talmage sets forth the following:

> The purport of these scriptures is to the effect that God the Eternal Father, whom we designate by the exalted name-title "Elohim" is the literal Parent of our Lord Jesus Christ, and of the spirits of the human race.... With this meaning, as the context shows in every case, Jehovah who is Jesus Christ the Son of Elohim, is called "the Father," and even "the very eternal Father of heaven and of earth".... That Jesus Christ, whom we also know as Jehovah, was the executive of the Father, Elohim, in the work of creation is set forth in the book Jesus the Christ, chapter 4....

Talmage, *Articles Of Faith* p. 421.

In summary, it can be said that the Mormon Jesus is the spirit brother of the devil; the Holy Ghost did not beget him. He was married, had children, practiced polygamy, was crucified because of polygamy, he is organically the same as mortal men, his sacrifice is insufficient for certain sins, and he is *Jehovah* whereas the Father is *Elohim*.

THE CHRISTIAN
VIEW OF JESUS

The following Scriptures will make clear that Jesus could not have been the devil's brother. The first passage deals with Lucifer and his fall.

In the next passage from Ezekiel, we learn about Lucifer. Then we see the biblical teaching concerning Christ's divinity and creation activity. The biblical data makes it impossible for the Mormon theory of Christ and the devil to be brothers to be possible:

> Thou hast been in Eden the garden of God... Thou art the annointed cherub that covereth; and I have set thee so: thou wast upon the holy mountain of God; thou hast walked up and down in the midst of the stones of fire. Thou wast perfect in thy ways from the day that thou wast created, till iniquity was found in thee. (Ezekiel 28:13-15)

> For by him were all things created, that are in heaven, and that are in earth, visible and invisible, whether they be thrones, or dominions, or principalities, or powers: all things were created by him and for him. (Colossians 1:16)

> But to us there is but one God, the Father, of whom are all things, and we in him; and one Lord Jesus Christ, by whom are all things, and we by him. (1 Corinthians 8:6)

> All things were made by him; and without him was not any made that was made. (John 1:3)

Lucifer is a created being, according to the passage in Ezekiel. It is impossible to be the spirit brother of your own creation. The following two passages refute the Mormon denial of the virgin birth of Christ.

Please recall Joseph F. Smith's assertion that the Bible teaches "no such thing":

> Therefore the Lord himself shall give you a sign;
> Behold, a virgin shall conceive, and bear a son, and
> shall call his name Immanuel. (Isaiah 7:14)

> Then said Mary unto the angel, How shall this be,
> seeing I know not a man? And the angel answered
> and said unto her, The Holy Ghost shall come
> upon thee, and the power of the Highest shall over-
> shadow thee: therefore also that holy thing which
> shall be born of thee shall be called the Son of
> God. (Luke 1:34-35)

One text of Scripture will refute this story about Jesus getting married. It is the same one that Mormon apostle Hyde appeals to, when claiming "a careful reading of that transaction" will reveal that Jesus is getting married:

> And The third day there was a marriage in Cana
> of Galilee; and the mother of Jesus was there: And
> both Jesus was called, and his disciples, to the mar-
> riage. (John 2:1-2)

The NIV reads "invited" instead of "called." How can you be invited or called to your own wed-ding? Hyde talks about Christ's intimacy with Mary and Martha. Of course Christ loved them. The Scripture says as much. To say that when Christ loved Mary and Martha, it means Jesus had intimate sexual relations with them is to force ideas into the text that are simply unwarranted.

Other passages of Scripture refute polygamous and adulterous unions. There were cases in the Old Testament of marriages of this type but it was not God's intended order. The following pas-sages make it absolutely clear.

> And the LORD God said, It is not good that the

> man should be alone; I will make him an help
> meet for him.... Therefore shall a man leave his
> father and his mother, and shall cleave unto his
> wife: and they shall be one flesh. (Genesis 2:18, 24)

> Neither shalt thou take a wife to her sister, to vex
> her, to uncover her nakedness, beside the other in
> her life time. (Leviticus 18:18)

Consider the restrictions placed upon the high priest:

> And he shall take a wife in her virginity. A wid-
> ow, or a divorced woman, or profane, or an harlot,
> these shall he not take: but he shall take a virgin of
> his own people to wife. (Leviticus 21:13-14)

Consider also the restrictions placed upon the King:

> Neither shall he multiply wives to himself. (Deuter-
> onomy 17:17)

Jesus Christ was and is the true Prophet, Priest, and King so it is impossible for Jesus to have been a polygamist.

> And he answered and said unto them, Have ye not
> read, that he which made them at the beginning
> made them male and female, And said, For this
> cause shall a man leave father and mother, and
> shall cleave to his wife: and they twain shall be one
> flesh? Wherefore they are no more twain, but one
> flesh. What therefore God hath joined together,
> let not man put asunder. (Matthew 19:4-6)

Polygamy is forbidden to Church officers:

> A bishop then must be blameless, the husband of
> one wife. (1 Timothy 3:2)

The following passages bear much light about the effects of polygamous marriages: Genesis 35:22; Genesis 37:18-28; 1 Kings 11:1-12; 2 Samuel 13:1-29. Consider also Genesis 16:4-16 and Galatians 4:21-31. Paul refers to the Galatians passage in which he condemns works-righteousness. As you consult some of the above passages notice the evil results that happen to the people who practice these types of marriages. One thinks particularly of David and Solomon.

In response to Brigham Young's un-biblical ideas about the organic similarity that we have to Jesus, the following passages demonstrate that Jesus is the absolutely unique Son of God.

> In the beginning was the Word, and the Word was with God, and the Word was God.... And the Word was made flesh and dwelt among us, (and we beheld his glory, the glory as of the only begotten of the Father,) full of grace and truth. (John 1:1, 14)

> By the word of the LORD were the heavens made; and all the host of them by the breath of his mouth. (Psalms 33:6)

> Through faith we understand that the worlds were framed by the word of God, so that things which are seen were not made of things which do appear. (Hebrews 11:3)

The Mormon concept that Jesus is _Jehovah_ and the Father is _Elohim_ and thus, two completely separate Gods can be refuted by the following verses:

> Here, O Israel: The LORD [_Jehovah_] our God [_Elohim_] is one LORD:" [_Jehovah_] (Deuteronomy 6:4)

> "O LORD, [Jehovah] there is none like thee, neither is there any God [Elohim] beside thee, according to all that we have heard with our ears. (1 Chronicles 17:20)

But the LORD [Jehovah] is the true God, [*Elohim*]
he is the living God. (Jeremiah 10:10)

THE HOLY GHOST

THE MORMON VIEW

In this section we will briefly consider the Mormon view of the Holy Ghost. The <u>Mormons differ-entiate between the Holy Ghost and the Spirit of God.</u>

Bruce McConkie gives us the Mormon understanding of the Holy Ghost. Notice the limitation of this third member of the Mormon godhead:

> He is a Personage of Spirit, a Spirit Person, a Spirit
> Man, a Spirit entity. He can be in only one place at
> one time, and he does not and cannot transform
> himself into any other form or image that than of
> the Man whom he is.
>
> McConkie, *Mormon Doctrine* p. 359.

Joseph F. Smith concurs with McConkie's view:

> The Holy Ghost should not be confused with the
> Spirit which fills the immensity of space and which
> is everywhere present. This other Spirit is imper-
> sonal and has no size, nor dimension; it proceeds
> forth from the presence of the Father and the Son
> and is in all things. We should speak of the Holy
> Ghost as a personage as "he" and this other Spirit
> as "it," although when we speak of the power or
> gift of the Holy Ghost we may properly say 'it'.
>
> Joseph F. Smith, *Doctrines Of Salvation* Vol. 1, p. 49, 50.

In distinction from the Holy Ghost, under the heading Holy Spirit in McConkie's *Mormon Doctrine* the reader is referred to the Spirit of God.

McConkie, *Mormon Doctrine* p. 361.

Those unfamiliar with Mormonism may be somewhat startled to find out that Mormonism makes two separate entities out of the Holy Spirit and Holy Ghost. It is also a bit unusual to hear someone referring the Holy Spirit as an "it."

THE CHRISTIAN VIEW

In *Vine's Expository Dictionary Of New Testament Words* we read the following:

The Holy Spirit is spoken of under various titles in the N.T. (Spirit" and "Ghost" are renderings of the same word *pneuma*; the advantage of the rendering "Spirit" is that it can always be used, whereas "Ghost" always requires the "Holy" prefixed.)

W. E. Vine, *Vine's Expository Dictionary Of New Testament Words* (Iowa Falls: Riverside, 1952), p.1076.

On the same page, Vine goes on to say concerning the use or absence of the article:

The use or absence of the article in the original where the Holy Spirit is spoken of cannot always be decided by grammatical rules, nor can the presence or absence of the article alone determine whether the reference is to the Holy Spirit. Examples where the Person is meant when the article is absent are Matt. 22:43 (the article is used in Mark 12:36); Acts 4:25; R.V. (absent in some texts); 19:2, 6; Rom. 14:17; 1 Cor. 2:4; Gal. 5:25 (twice); 1 Pet. 1:2. Sometimes the absence is to be accounted for

by the fact the *Pneuma* (like *Theos*) is substantially a
proper name e.g., John 7:39.

Vine, p. 1076.

The Spirit is not an "it", but is the same person as the Holy Ghost. And furthermore, if *Pneuma* is substantially a proper name, the labeling of *Pneuma* as an "it" is a direct attack on the personality and deity of the third member of the Godhead.

Note how uses in the Pauline Epistles are translated "Spirit" and "Ghost" interchangeably:

Know ye not that ye are the temple of God, and the
Spirit [*Pneuma*] of God dwelleth in you? (1 Corinthians 3:16)

What? know ye not that your body is the temple of
the Holy Ghost [*Pneuma*] which is in you, which ye
have of God, and ye are not your own? (1 Corinthians 6:19)

Two more verses will be listed to demonstrate that the Holy Spirit and Holy Ghost are not two separate entities:

...for that which is conceived in her is of the Holy
Ghost [*Pneuma*]. (Matthew 1:20)

For as many as are led by the Spirit [*Pneuma*] of
God, they are the sons of God. (Romans 8:14)

PART II

PRIESTS, PROPHETS AND APOSTLES: A COMPARISON OF THEIR QUALIFICATIONS, ROLES AND RESPONSIBILITIES

CHAPTER 8
APOSTLES AND APOSTASY

CHAPTER 9
BEWARE OF FALSE PROPHETS

CHAPTER 10
MORMON PRIESTHOOD: ROBBING CHRIST
OF HIS ROYAL HIGH PRIESTLY POSITION

Food for Thought:

"The moral absolutes rest upon God's character. The moral commands He has given to men are an expression of His character. Men as created in His image are to live by choice on the basis of what God is. The standards of morality are determined by what conforms to His character, while those things which do not conform are immoral."
- Francis A. Schaeffer

"...to engage in philosophical discussion does not mean that we begin without Scripture. We do not first defend theism philosophically by an appeal to reason and experience in order, after that, to turn to Scripture for our knowledge and defense of Christianity. We get our theism as well as our Christianity from the Bible. The Bible is thought of as authoritative on everything of which it speaks. And it speaks of everything..."
*- Cornelius Van Til from **The Defense Of The Faith***

CHAPTER 8

APOSTLES
AND APOSTASY

nlike the teaching of the Bible concerning the choosing of apostles, in Mormonism one finds Joseph Smith, Oliver Cowdery, and David Whitmer choosing and ordaining those who are purported to be modern day apostles in Smith's writings.*

*Joseph Smith, *The Teachings Of The Prophet Joseph Smith* p. 307.

Were these men qualified to choose and ordain apostles?

Consider the following assessment of these two men who are listed inside the *Book of Mormon* as witnesses to its origin and truthfulness by Mormon founder, Joseph Smith:

> Such characters as ...David Whitmer, Oliver Cowdery...are too mean to mention; and we had liked to have forgotten them.

> Joseph Smith, *History of the Church* Vol. 3, (Salt Lake City: Deseret Book Company 1978), p. 232.

This sounds like very good advice. Unfortunately for Mormonism, Joseph Smith gives us good reason not to believe their testimony inside the *Book of Mormon*. Was Joseph Smith qualified to choose and ordain apostles? Did Joseph Smith have the biblical quality of humility?

Consider the following:

> The whole earth shall bear me witness that I, like the towering rock in the midst of the ocean, which has withstood the mighty surges of the warring waves for centuries, and am impregnable...I combat the errors of ages; I meet the violence of mobs; I cope with ille-

gal proceedings from executive authority; I cut the
gordian knot of powers, and I solve mathematical
problems of universities, with truth-diamond truth;
and God is my right hand man.

Joseph Smith, *History of the Church* Vol. 6, p. 78.

Smith's "superhuman powers" failed him miserably in the real world and should make it clear that
he had no authority to pick apostles for Christ's Church.

Do the Mormon apostles meet the biblical requirements for the office of apostle? What are the
biblical criteria for apostleship? Do the claims that someone is an apostle settle the question?
Many alleged apostles have followers with dogmatic testimonies. Is this sufficient in and of itself
to determine if the claims to apostleship are reliable? Should every claim to apostleship be unques-
tioningly accepted?

Consider the following warning from Scripture:

> For such are false apostles, deceitful workers, trans-
> forming themselves into apostles of Christ. And
> no marvel; for Satan himself is transformed into
> an angel of light. Therefore it is no great thing if
> his ministers also be transformed as the ministers
> of righteousness; whose end shall be according to
> their works. (2 Corinthians 11:13-15)

The Mormon apostles may appear to be ministers of righteousness. But are they? If they do not
meet the biblical requirements for apostleship, then they, in spite of appearances, are impostors.

Is there an apostolic office still in existence today? Were the original twelve Apostles supposed to
be replaced by twelve more and then more down through history? Consider the importance of the
following passage:

> And are built upon the foundation of the apostles
> and prophets, Jesus Christ himself being the chief
> cornerstone. (Ephesians 2:20)

Verse nineteen of this chapter says "ye." This is significant because it tells us who are built upon this foundation. We are built upon this foundation. Christ himself is the cornerstone of this holy building, called the Church. Christ himself is the true foundation and the apostles are part of that foundation. The Church has but one foundation. This fact puts to rest forever the notion that there is a continuous line of apostles. There is not a new foundation laid for every generation of believers in the history of the Church.

The Mormon Church makes much of their apostles. But do they meet the requirements of biblical apostleship? Again, what are the biblical criteria for apostleship?

1. A true apostle had to be a personal witness to the work of Christ and had to be chosen of God.

The twelve had to personally eat a meal with Christ, and they were commanded to perform specific tasks assigned by him:

> And we are witnesses of all things which he did both in the land of the Jews, and in Jerusalem... (Acts 10:39)

> But unto witnesses chosen before God, even us, who did eat and drink with him after he rose from the dead. (Acts 10:41)

> And he commanded us to preach... (Acts 10:42)

2. The apostles had to be personally called by Christ:

> And when it was day, he called unto him his disciples: and of them he chose twelve, whom also he named apostles. (Luke 6:13)

3. The apostles had to be personally instructed by Christ himself:

> He shall teach you all things, and bring all things to your remembrance, whatsoever I have said unto you. (John 14:26)

4. True apostles of Christ had to work miracles:

> And fear came upon every soul: and many wonders
> and signs were done by the apostles. (Acts 2:43)

It is hard to imagine how Mormons can believe that their leaders can meet these requirements. Not only do Mormon apostles fail these tests; they also fail to meet the level of training that has been historically required of ministers. One example is that none of the present Mormon apostles have ever demonstrated an ability to understand Biblical Greek or Hebrew. A Mormon leader's inability to understand biblical Greek and Hebrew is similar to Roman Catholic priests in the Middle Ages who read from Latin Bibles but didn't understand the language. Teachers who can't understand the primary source material are a huge danger to souls.

What about Mormon claims of apostolic succession?

> Now therefore ye are no more strangers and for-
> eigners, but fellow citizens with the saints, and of
> the household of God; And are built upon the
> foundation of the apostles and prophets, Jesus
> Christ himself being the chief corner stone. (Ephe-
> sians 2:19-20)

Systematic theologian Charles Hodge's comments on Ephesians 2:20 are instructive:

> There is a true and obvious sense in which the
> apostles are the foundation of the church; secondly
> they are expressly so called in Scripture — as in Rev.
> 21:14, besides the disputed passage, Matt. 16:18;
> and thirdly, the figure here demands this interpre-
> tation. In this particular passage Christ is the cor-
> ner stone, the apostles the foundation, believers
> the edifice.
>
> Charles Hodge, *Commentary on the Epistle to the
> Ephesians* (Eerdmans: Grand Rapids Michigan,
> reprinted 1994), p. 150.

Therefore, there are no apostles after the death of the biblical apostles in the First Century. The biblical ones continue to serve as the foundation of the Christ's Church through their inspired scriptural writings recorded in the Bible.

What about Ephesians 4:11?

> And he gave some, apostles; and some, prophets; and some, evangelists; and some, pastors and teachers. (Ephesians 4:11)

Does the passage from Ephesians 4:11 contradict Ephesians 2:20?

Charles Hodge's comments on Ephesians 4:11 are important:

> First, the apostles, the immediate messengers of Christ, the witnesses for him, of his doctrines, his miracles, and of his resurrection; infallible as teachers and absolute as rulers in virtue of the gift of inspiration and of their commission. No man, therefore, could be an apostle unless — 1. He was immediately appointed by Christ. 2. Unless he had seen him after his resurrection and had received the knowledge of the Gospel by immediate revelation. 3. Unless he was rendered infallible by the gift of inspiration. These things constituted the office and were essential to its authority. Those who without these gifts and qualifications claimed the office, are called "false apostles."
>
> Charles Hodge, *Commentary on the Epistle to the Ephesians* (Eerdmans: Grand Rapids Michigan, reprinted 1994), pp. 222-223.

In conclusion, Ephesians 2:19 says "ye." This is significant because it tells us who are built upon the apostolic foundation. We, those who believe in Christ, are built upon this foundation. Christ himself is the cornerstone of this holy building, called the Church. Christ himself is the chief cornerstone and the apostles are the foundation. The Church has one foundation. This fact puts to rest forever the notion that there is a continuous line of apostles. There is not a new foundation laid for every generation of believers in the history of the Church.

For a response to Roman Catholic claims to apostolic succession, see: http://turretinfan.blogspot.com/2011/02/solo-scriptura-sola-scriptura-and.html

Is the doctrine of apostolic succession true? How is apostolic authority claimed, considering that there are no present day apostles in Christ's Church? In 2 Timothy 2:2 Paul instructs Timothy to commit what he had learned to faithful men. In short, apostolic authority or apostolic succession is continued in the True Church when local churches continue in the doctrine taught by the apostles.

BEWARE
OF FALSE PROPHETS

e need to be clear, that once the canon of Scripture is closed, additional books cannot be added or existing books removed. This represents historic Protestant belief that revelation has ended and the text of Scripture is complete. Because of the implications for any person or religion claiming continued revelation, the issue of a completed canon was settled at the outset of this study. Joseph Smith lived well after the canon of Scripture was closed. This is reason enough to reject him as a prophet.

1. Considering the biblical tests to determine if someone is a prophet.

God has given His covenant people some very clear guidelines on how to evaluate or test an individual who claims to be a prophet. We will look at the Scriptural teachings relevant to these tests under several different headings and examine Joseph Smith's teachings, character and prophecies in light of the Scriptures.

2. Agreement with the testimony of Scripture.

> To the law and to the testimony: if they speak not
> according to this word, it is because there is no
> light in them. (Isaiah 8:20)

If Joseph Smith is a prophet, his teachings should be in harmony with the testimony of Scripture.

In the book *The Teachings of the Prophet Joseph Smith,* we have Mormon founder Joseph Smith's view concerning God.

For example, we have Smith teaching the following:

> God himself was once as we are now, and is an

exalted man, and sits enthroned in yonder heavens! . . . for I am going to tell you how God came to be God. We have imagined and supposed that God was God from all eternity. I will refute that idea, and take away the veil, so that you may see.... It is the first principle of the Gospel to know for a certainty the Character of God, and to know that we may converse with him as one man converses with another, and that he was once a man like us; yea that God himself, the Father of us all dwelt on an earth, the same as Jesus Christ himself did; and I will show it from the Bible.

Joseph Smith, *Teachings of the Prophet Joseph Smith*, pp. 345-346.

Mormon leader Wilford Woodruff agrees and says:

God himself is increasing and progressing in knowledge, power and dominion and will do so, worlds without end.

Wilford Woodruff, *Journal of Discourses* Vol. 6, p. 120.

According to Smith, God is a limited or finite corporeal being (with a body) who progressed to godhood and will ever be learning and increasing in knowledge. Men today are fundamentally no different than Smith's god, just not as far up the scale of being as the Mormon deity.

In contrast, the doctrine of God as set forth in Scripture:

Hear, O Israel the LORD our God is one LORD.
(Deuteronomy 6:4)

This is called the Shema, the central confession of faith of the Old Testament covenant people. This was a distinctive belief of the people of Israel, setting them apart from all pagan concepts of god.

In addition, the following verses will clearly demonstrate that the God of the Bible is completely different from the Mormon god, who changes and is essentially nothing more than a big man. The following verses prove God's eternal existence which set him apart from finite or limited men. I will cite a few of the many passages in Scripture that prove God is not a man. God sets himself apart from sinful men by clear declarations. Consider carefully the passages in this section to see if the quotations by Joseph Smith are in harmony with the Bible.

> God is not a man, that he should lie; neither the son of man, that he should repent... (Numbers 23:19)

> Who hath wrought and done it, calling the generations from the beginning? I the LORD, the first, and with the last; I am he. (Isaiah 41:4)

> Ye are my witnesses, saith the LORD, and my servant whom I have chosen: that ye may know and believe me, and understand that I am he: before me there was no God formed, neither shall there be after me. (Isaiah 43:10)

> I am the first, and I am the last; and beside me there is no God. (Isaiah 44:6)

> I am the LORD , and there is none else, there is no God beside me: I girded thee, though thou hast not known me: That they may know from the rising of the sun, and from the west, that there is none beside me, I am the LORD, and there is none else. (Isaiah 45:5-6)

Do Mormon teachings speak "according to this word?" The above citations from Joseph Smith make it clear that Smith did not believe in the God of the Bible.

JOSEPH SMITH
AND HUMILITY

Jesus tells us:

> For whosoever exalteth himself shall be abased and
> he that humbleth himself shall be exalted. (Luke
> 14:11)

True godly humility is a trait that all legitimate church leaders should have. Does Joseph Smith meet this requirement? Consider Smith's own view of himself:

> I am learned, and know more than all the world
> put together.
>
> Joseph Smith, *Documentary History of the Church*
> pp. 307, 308.
>
> I have more to boast of than ever any man had. I
> am the only man that has ever been able to keep a
> whole church together since the days of Adam. A
> large majority of the whole have stood by me. Nei-
> ther Paul, John, Peter, nor Jesus ever did. I boast
> that No Man ever did such a work as I. The follow-
> ers of Jesus ran away from Him, but the latter-day
> Saints never ran away from me yet.
>
> Joseph Smith, *History of the Church*, Vol. 6, pp. 408, 409.

These assertions on Smith's part seem more like the ravings of a megalomaniac rather than a prophet of God. There is certainly no humility in these assertions. Again, remember the words of Christ, "For whosoever exalteth himself shall be abased and he that humbleth himself shall be exalted." (Luke 14:11) It is interesting to note that less than of year from some of these ravings, Smith was killed in a gun battle when angry citizens stormed the jail where Smith was being held for destroying a newspaper printing press that was critical of him.

WHAT IS JOSEPH SMITH'S
PLACE IN MORMONISM?

In the Christian faith, Christ Jesus is preeminent in man's salvation. Faith in Christ is indispensable for salvation.

In contrast, look at the preeminence Joseph Smith holds in Mormonism:

> No man or woman in this dispensation will ever enter into the celestial kingdom of God without the consent of Joseph Smith. From the day that the Priesthood was taken from the earth to the winding up scene of all things, every man and woman must have the certificate of Joseph Smith junior, as a passport to their entrance into the mansion where God and Christ are.
>
> Brigham Young, *Journal of Discourses* Vol. 7, p. 289.

> Well now, examine the character of the Savior, and examine the characters of those who have written the Old and New Testaments; and then compare them with the character of Joseph Smith, the founder of this work...and you will find that his character stands as fair as that of any man's mentioned in the Bible. We can find no person who presents a better character to the world when the facts are known than Joseph Smith, jun., the prophet...
>
> Brigham Young, *Journal of Discourses* Vol. 14, p. 203.

> There is no salvation without accepting Joseph Smith.
>
> Joseph Fielding Smith, *Doctrines of Salvation* Vol. 1, pp. 189-190.

These teachings about Joseph Smith show the shockingly unbiblical nature of the Mormon religion. Rather than Christ being exalted, Smith is set forth as indispensable for salvation.

The heart of the Gospel is that Jesus died for our sins, was buried, and rose again the third day according to the Scriptures (1 Corinthians 15:1-4). For by grace are ye saved through faith; and that not of yourselves: it is the gift of God: Not of works, lest any man should boast (Ephesians 2:8, 9). And, "For God so loved the world, that he gave his only begotten Son, that whosoever believeth in him should not perish, but have eternal life." (John 3:16)

A BIBLICAL EXAMINATION OF JOSEPH SMITH, POLYGAMY AND SPEAKING THE TRUTH

First, the Scriptures say:

> Thou shalt not bear false witness... (Exodus 20:16)

> Lie not one to another, seeing you have put off the old man with his deeds. (Colossians 3:9)

Was Joseph Smith a liar? Using the Mormon doctrine of polygamy as an example, let's consider what Smith said in public about this practice:

> In as much as this church of Christ has been reproached with the crime of fornication and polygamy; we believe one man should have one wife; and one woman but one husband, except in case of death; when either is at liberty to marry again.

> Joseph Smith, *Doctrine and Covenants* Section C1, p. 251.

> But, for the information of those who may be assailed by those foolish tales about two wives, we would say that no such principle ever existed among the Latter-day Saints, and never will; this

is well known to all who are acquainted with our books and actions, the Book of Mormon, Doctrine and Covenants; and also our periodicals are very strict and explicit on that subject, indeed far more so than the Bible.

Joseph Smith, *Millennial Star* Vol. 3, (Liverpool, England: Ward, Thomas, 1842), p. 74.

As we have lately been credibly informed, that an Elder of the Church of Jesus Christ, of Latter-day Saints by the name of Hiram Brown, has been preaching Polygamy, and other false doctrines, in the county of Lapeer, state of Michigan. This is to notify him and the Church in general, that he has been cut off from the church for his iniquity; and his further notified to appear at the Special Conference, on the 6th of April next, to make answer to these charges.

Joseph Smith, *Times & Seasons* Vol. 5, (Nauvoo, Illinois: John Taylor, 1844), p. 423.

In 1887, Mormon historian Andrew Jensen recorded in the publication the Historical Record Volume 6 on page 233 the marriages of Joseph Smith to: Louisa Beman, Zina D. Huntington, Prescinda L. Huntington, Eliza Roxey Snow, Sarah Ann Witney, Desdemona W. Fuller, Eliza M. Partridge, Emily D. Partridge, Lucy Walker, and Almera W. Johnson during the years of 1841 thru 1843.

Joseph Smith and the early Mormons were denying the practice of polygamy publicly and even went so far as to excommunicate one of their elders for this practice; all the while Joseph Smith was secretly practicing polygamy himself. This is what the Scripture call bearing a false witness, a violation of the 9th Commandment (Exodus 20:16). "Ye shall know them by their fruits..." (Matthew 7:16) Lying is bad fruit!

It should be noted that because of Mormonism's commitment to on-going new revelations, they have been forced to downplay previous revelations condemning polygamy.

PROPHECY

> Beware of false prophets, which come to you in
> sheep's clothing, but inwardly they are ravening
> wolves. Ye shall know them by their fruits.
> (Matthew 7:15-16)

It is important that we understand the role we play as fruit inspectors. Christians are called to discern between truth and error.

> If there arise among you a prophet, or a dream-
> er of dreams, and giveth thee a sign or a wonder,
> And the sign or the wonder come to pass, whereof
> he spake unto thee, saying, Let us go after other
> gods, which thou hast not known, and let us serve
> them; Thou shalt not hearken unto the words of
> that prophet, or that dreamer of dreams: for the
> LORD your God proveth you, to know whether ye
> love the LORD your God with all your heart and
> with all your soul. Ye shall walk after the LORD
> your God, and fear him, and keep his command-
> ments, and obey his voice, and ye shall serve him,
> and cleave unto him. And that prophet, or that
> dreamer of dreams, shall be put to death; because
> he hath spoken to turn you away from the LORD
> your God, which brought you out of the land
> of Egypt, and redeemed you out of the house of
> bondage, to thrust thee out of the way which the
> LORD thy God commanded thee to walk in. So
> shalt thou put the evil away from the midst of thee.
> (Deuteronomy 13:1-5)

We must ask, did any of the prophecies of Joseph Smith come to pass?

> But the prophet, which shall presume to speak a

word in my name, which I have not commanded
him to speak, or that shall speak in the name of
other gods, even that prophet shall die. And if
thou say in thine heart, How shall we know the
word which the LORD hath not spoken? When
a prophet speaketh in the name of the LORD, if
the thing follow not, nor come to pass, that is the
thing which the LORD hath not spoken, but the
prophet hath spoken it presumptuously: thou shalt
not be afraid of him. (Deuteronomy 18:20-22)

Did the prophecies of Joseph Smith come to pass? The next passages from Deuteronomy are
straight-forward and clear. The prophecies must come to pass or said another way, be fulfilled. A
biblical prophet is 100 percent accurate. This is the standard of Scripture.

Prophecies
of Joseph Smith:

Mormon founder Joseph Smith certainly tried to prophesy. Let's consider his track record.

Smith prophesied on February 14, 1835, that Jesus would return within 56 years:

President Smith then stated that the meeting had
been called, because God had commanded it; and
it was made known to him by vision and by the
Holy Spirit. He then gave a relation of some of
the circumstances attending us while journeying
to Zion - our trials, sufferings; and said God had
not designed all this for nothing, but He had it
in remembrance yet; and it was the will of God
that those who went to Zion, with a determination to lay down their lives, if necessary, should
be ordained to the ministry, and go forth to prune
the vineyard for the last time, for the coming of the

Lord, which was nigh - even fifty-six years should wind up the scene.

Joseph Smith, *History of the Church* Vol. 2, p. 189.

This prophecy is false because Jesus did not return within fifty-six years or by 1891. The outside time frame for this prophecy to be fulfilled was in 1891, which arrived without Christ's return.

Smith prophesied on September 14, 1835, that the temple would be built in Jackson County, Missouri within his generation:

> Yea, the word of the Lord concerning his church, established in the last days for the restoration of his people, as he has spoken by the mouth of his prophets, and for the gathering of his saints to stand upon Mount Zion, which shall be the city of New Jerusalem. Which city shall be built, beginning at the temple lot, which is appointed by the finger of the Lord, in the western boundaries of the State of Missouri, and dedicated by the hand of Joseph Smith, Jun., and others with whom the Lord was well pleased. Verily this is the word of the Lord, that the city New Jerusalem shall be built by the gathering of the saints, beginning at this place, even the place of the temple, which temple shall be reared in this generation. For verily this generation shall not all pass away until an house shall be built unto the Lord, and a cloud shall rest upon it, which cloud shall be even the glory of the Lord, which shall fill the house... Therefore, as I said concerning the sons of Moses for the sons of Moses and also the sons of Aaron shall offer an acceptable offering and sacrifice in the house of the Lord, which house shall be built unto the Lord in this generation, upon the consecrated spot as I have appointed.

Joseph Smith, *Doctrine and Covenants* Section
84:2-5, 31.

The Mormons were driven out of Jackson County in 1833. They were not gathered there in
accordance to this prophecy dealing with building the temple. The prophecy clearly states that
the generation present when the prophecy was given would not pass away until the temple was
built at the western boundaries of the state of Missouri which is in Independence. Therefore, this
prophecy is false!

**Smith prophesied on December 25, 1832 that All Nations would be involved in the War
Between the States:**

> Verily, thus saith the Lord concerning the wars that
> will shortly come to pass, beginning at the rebellion
> of South Carolina, which will eventually terminate
> in the death and misery of many souls; And the
> time will come that war will be poured out upon
> all nations, beginning at this place. For behold,
> the Southern States shall be divided against the
> Northern States, and the Southern States will call
> on other nations, even the nation of Great Britain,
> as it is called, and they shall also call upon other
> nations, in order to defend themselves against oth-
> er nations; and then war shall be poured out upon
> all nations.

Joseph Smith, *Doctrine and Covenants* Section 87:1-3.

Consider some historical details: Is this really a prophecy or just common knowledge that was in
the newspapers of the day? Smith gave this prophecy on December, 25, 1832. Yet he was simply
exaggerating news that had happened months earlier, in July.

On July 14, 1832 Congress passed a tariff act that South Carolina thought was so bad it declared
it null and void. Andrew Jackson alerted the U.S. Troops and the nation expected war. And, on
December 10, 1832 The Boston Daily Advertiser and Patriot printed extracts from the message
of the Governor of South Carolina at the opening of the Legislature in Boston on November 27,

1832 and "His message warned that South Carolina was prepared to resist the U.S. Government by force, if necessary."

The same day, December 10, 1832, Orson Hyde (the Mormon apostle) left Boston. On December 22, 1832, he arrived in Kirkland, Ohio where Smith was. Three days later Smith gave his civil war "prophecy" on the rebellion of South Carolina. This in reality was no big deal, because they had already rebelled on July 14. The fact that Smith predicted the Civil War is not incredible or an indicator that he had special revelatory knowledge. This was a common belief among many people who read the newspapers of the day. It is clearly another false prophecy, since all nations did not get involved in the American Civil War.

Smith prophesied on December 27, 1832:

> For not many days hence and the earth shall trem-
> ble and reel to and fro as a drunken man; and the
> sun shall hide his face, and shall refuse to give
> light; and the moon shall be bathed in blood; and
> the stars shall become exceedingly angry, and shall
> cast themselves down as a fig that falleth from off
> a fig-tree.
>
> Joseph Smith, *Doctrine and Covenants* Section 88:87.

The sun has not yet been hidden nor has the moon hidden its face. And it should be noted that this prophecy was given on December 27, 1832. Smith's prophecy failed because the time frame of prophecy when he said "Not many days hence."

Smith prophesied On September 1, 1842:

> ...for to this day has the God of my fathers delivered
> me out of them all, and will deliver me from hence-
> forth; for behold, and lo, I shall triumph over all
> my enemies, for the Lord God hath spoken it.
>
> Joseph Smith, *Doctrine and Covenants* Section 127:2.

In this case, Smith had prophesied that God would allow him to "triumph" over "all" his enemies.

However, less than two years later, his enemies attacked the Carthage, Illinois jail where Smith was being held prisoner for inciting his fellow Mormons to destroy the printing press of a newspaper that was critical of him. A group of angry citizens attacked the jail and Smith was killed. Smith fought back with a gun that had been smuggled into him and it should be noted that because of this (fighting back) he did not die as the martyr which Mormons claim he was. Martyrs do not die in blazing gun battles. Moreover, it is clear that Smith's "enemies" did "triumph" over him. Therefore, this is another false prophecy.

Smith prophesied about David W. Patten on April 17, 1838:

This revelation was concerning early Mormon leader David W. Patten, telling him to settle his business up so that he could go on a mission:

> Next spring...to testify of my name and bear glad
> tidings unto all the world.
>
> Joseph Smith, *Doctrine and Covenants* Section 114:1.

However, before Patten could settle his business, eight months after receiving this prophecy, Patten was killed leading Mormons in the Battle of Crooked River on October 25, 1838. He never went on the mission as prophesied. (See History of the Church Volume 3, page 171). Therefore, this is also a false prophecy.

Smith prophesied about early Mormon Oliver Granger on July 8th, 1838:

> His name shall be had in sacred remembrance
> from generation to generation, forever and ever,
> saith the Lord... let the blessings of my people be
> on him forever and ever.
>
> Joseph Smith, *Doctrine and Covenants* Section
> 117:12-15.

The problem is that Mormons today do not know anything about Oliver Granger, let alone keep his name in sacred remembrance, as the prophecy in the Doctrine and Covenants asserts. As far as the Mormon people are concerned, Oliver Granger has been forgotten rather than keeping his name in "sacred remembrance." This is clearly a failed prophecy!

Smith prophesied that the U.S. government would be destroyed on May 18, 1843:

> By virtue of the holy priesthood... and in the name
> of the Lord that if Congress or the United States
> will not redress the wrongs which the Mormons
> suffered in Missouri, and grant them protection,
> "the government will be utterly overthrown and
> wasted," they shall be "broken up as a government"
> and there will be nothing left of them.

> Joseph Smith, *History of the Church* Vol. 5, p. 394.

The United States rejected the Mormon petitions. Nor were their wrongs redressed and they were not protected from their enemies. The United States government was not overthrown as Smith predicted. This is another example of a false prophecy!

Smith prophesied on Apr 23, 1834 that the united order would be everlasting:

This is another revelation to establish a separate United Order in Missouri, which was to be:

> Everlasting," "immutable and unchangeable, and
> to benefit the church "until I come," "This is the
> way that I, the Lord, have decreed to provide for
> my saints...

> Joseph Smith, *Doctrine and Covenants* Section 104:1.

The United Order (a form of theocratic communism) failed, even though the Latter-day Saints tried to make it work. It was clearly not everlasting, nor was it immutable or unchangeable and it did not provide for the Latter-day Saints. Therefore, this is yet another false prophecy!

In closing, I would challenge any Mormon to supply me with one example of a prophecy of Joseph Smith that was fulfilled. I've made this challenge repeatedly over the years and have never received even one example. Remember, the Scriptures require prophetic accuracy.

> When a prophet speaketh in the name of the LORD,
> if the thing follow not, nor come to pass, that is the

thing which the LORD hath not spoken, but the
prophet hath spoken it presumptuously: thou shalt
not be afraid of him. (Deuteronomy 18:22)

Other Mormons leaders tried their hand at prophecy with about as much success.

For example, Mormon apostle Heber C. Kimball is recorded as saying:

> The Church and kingdom to which we belong will
> become the kingdom of our God and his Christ,
> and brother Brigham Young (second prophet of
> the Utah Mormon Church) will become President
> of the United States.
>
> Heber C. Kimball, *Journal of Discourses* Vol. 5, p. 219.

CHAPTER 10

MORMON PRIESTHOOD: ROBBING CHRIST OF HIS ROYAL HIGH PRIESTLY POSITION

his study will examine the Mormon claims to have restored the Aaronic and Melchizedek priesthoods to the New Covenant Church. The Mormon priesthood's authority claim is an example of trying to establish uniqueness to legitimize their church. Additionally, as the next two quotes demonstrate, Mormons do not believe orthodox Christians have the authority to act in the name of God or have spiritual authority to administer the sacraments or even to preach the gospel.

> The priesthood is the power and authority of God delegated to man on earth to act in all things pertaining to the salvation of men. It is the means whereby the Lord acts through men to save souls. Without this priesthood power, men are lost.
>
> Spencer W. Kimball, *The Teachings of Spencer W. Kimball* (Salt Lake City: Bookcraft, 1995), p. 494.

According to LDS doctrine:

> We must have priesthood authority to act in the name of God when performing the sacred ordinances of the gospel, such as baptism, confirmation, administration of the sacrament, and temple marriage.
>
> *Gospel Principles* (Salt Lake City: Church Of Jesus Christ of Latter-Day Saints, 2009), p. 67.

This analysis of the Mormon view of priestly authority requires a couple of initial observations. First, Mormonism has distorted the Older Covenant's Aaronic and Melchizedek priesthoods into offices to be held by self-appointed men. And second, today in the New Covenant church age, we are in the wrong time period to even have these offices in the church. In these two regards, Mormonism completely misunderstands the discontinuities between the Covenants.

We would be wise to consult the Scriptures to learn about the purpose of the priesthood's duties in the Older Covenant and take note of the changes that have taken place as the result of the inauguration of the New Covenant. This will be a relatively brief survey of biblical material regarding the duties and obligations of the Aaronic priesthood. Then in the following comparative sections I will emphasize important teachings of Scripture showing the New Covenant fulfillment by our Lord Jesus Christ that are relevant in demonstrating the untruthfulness of Mormon claims between them.

The purpose of my repeated emphasis is to drive home the fact that significant changes have been made in redemptive history when moving from the Older Covenant into the New Covenant Age. Of special note, I use the phrase Older Covenant frequently, which may seem unusual to those outside of Reformed Protestant tradition. This utilization is intended to stress the essential unity of the Covenants along with a proper understanding of legitimate continuities and discontinuities.

THE REQUIREMENTS OF LEVITICAL OR AARONIC PRIESTS

All Aaronic priests had to be from the tribe of Levi and the High Priests were required to be of the physical lineage of Aaron, the brother of Moses. This should make it clear that not just anyone could be a priest or perform the duties of a priest. It should be remembered that God rebuked Saul because he made a sacrificial offering, something only a priest from the tribe of Levi could do. (1 Samuel 13:1-15)

Note the specifics and details in the following passages:

> And take thou unto thee Aaron thy brother, and
> his sons with him, from among the children of
> Israel, that he may minister to me in the priest's
> office even Aaron Nadab and Abihu, Eleazar and
> Ithamar, Aaron's sons. (Exodus 28:1)

And the cloths of service, and the holy garments for Aaron the priest and the garments of his sons, to minister in the priest's office. (Exodus 31:10)

Bring the tribe of Levi near, and present them before Aaron the priest, that they may minister him. (Numbers 3:6)

The priests, the Levites, and all the tribe of Levi, shall have no part nor inheritance with Israel; they shall eat the offerings of the LORD made by fire, and his inheritance. (Deuteronomy 18:1)

Consider the detailed ordinances to be performed by the Levites, the sons of Aaron, from the *Pulpit Commentary* summary of Exodus 29:1-37:

> Verses 1-37. - THE CONSECRATION OF THE PRIESTS. From the description of the priestly attire, the Divine Law-giver passed to the form of priestly consecration, whereof investiture in the "holy garments" was a part. The ceremony of consecration was to consist of four things:
>
> 1. Ablution;
> 2. Investiture;
> 3. Chrism or Anointing with oil; and
> 4. Sacrifice.
>
> In the directions given, we have, first, the preparation of the offerings (vers. 1-3); secondly, directions for the ablutions (ver. 4); thirdly, directions for the investiture of Aaron (vers. 5, 6), of his sons (vers. 8, 9); fourthly, directions for the anointing (ver. 7); and fifthly, directions as to the mode in which the sacrifices should be offered and disposed of (vers. 10-34). A command is then given that the ceremonies

should be repeated every day for a week (ver. 35); and another, that the altar should receive consecration at the same time as the priests (vers. 36, 37). Additional light is thrown on most of these matters by the account contained in Leviticus (ch. 8.), of the manner in which Moses carried out the directions here given to him. Verse 1. - This is the thing that thou shalt do to them - i.e., "This is the ceremonial that thou shalt use on the occasion." There is a tacit reference to verse 41 of ch. 28, which had announced that the priests were to be consecrated. Take one young bullock. The offerings were to be provided beforehand, so as to be in readiness when the investiture and anointing were over. Hence they are mentioned first; rams without blemish, literally "perfect." On the offense to God of offering him blemished offerings, see Malachi 1:6-14.

H. D. M. Spence, Joseph S. Exell (Editors), *The Pulpit Commentary*, Exodus 29:1-37, EBook PDF Format (Grace Works, Multi-Media Labs), 2010.

More instructions on sacrifices, offerings and other detailed rites of cleanliness and purification that were required of the Aaronic priests, found in the book of Leviticus:

The Burnt Offering: Leviticus 1:3-17; 6:8-13

The Grain Offering: Leviticus 2:1-6; 6:14-18; 7:12, 13.

The Fellowship Offering: Leviticus 3:1-17; 7:11-21, 28-34.

The Day of Atonement offerings: Leviticus 16:8-34; 23:27-32.

Clean and Unclean Food: Leviticus 11:1-46. Purification after Childbirth: Leviticus 12:1-8.

What has been surveyed so far is a small fraction of the elaborate regulations and rites for the Older Covenant priesthood. Of special note is the fact that the Older Covenant people of God received detailed specific principles and instructions governing their approach to a holy God.

THE REGULATIVE
PRINCIPLE OF WORSHIP

The Regulative Principle States this: True worship is only that which is commanded by God; false worship is anything not commanded.

Consider Chapter 21, paragraph 1, in the *Westminster Confession*:

> The light of nature showeth that there is a God, who hath lordship and sovereignty over all, is good, and doth good unto all, and is therefore to be feared, loved, praised, called upon, trusted in, and served, with all the heart, and with all the soul, and with all the might.[1] But the acceptable way of worshiping the true God is instituted by himself, and so limited by his own revealed will, that he may not be worshiped according to the imaginations and devices of men, or the suggestions of Satan, under any visible representation, or any other way not prescribed in the Holy Scripture.
>
> 1. Romans 1:20; Psalms 19:1-4a; 50:6; 86:8-10; 89:5-7; 95:1-6; 97:6; 104:1-35; 145:9-12; Acts 14:17; Deuteronomy 6:4-5
>
> 2. Deuteronomy 4:15-20; 12:32; Matthew 4:9-10; 15:9; Acts 17:23-25; Exodus 20:4-6, John 4:23-24; Colossians 2:18-23

The regulative principle is closely tied to the example of the Levitical priesthood as is primarily seen in the book of Leviticus and other portions of Scripture, along with God's punishment for its violation. Consider the following examples:

Strange fire or worship condemned:

> And Nadab and Abihu, the sons of Aaron, took either of them his censer, and put fire therein, and put incense thereon, and offered strange fire before the LORD, which he commanded them not. And there went out fire from the LORD, and devoured them, and they died before the Lord. (Leviticus 10:1-2)

Uzzah's error punished:

> And they set the ark of God upon a new cart, and brought it out of the house of Abinadab that was in Gibeah: and Uzzah and Ahio, the sons of Abinadab, drave the new cart. And they brought it out of the house of Abinadab which was at Gibeah, accompanying the ark of God: and Ahio went before the ark. . . . And when they came to Nachon's threshing floor, Uzzah put forth his hand to the ark of God, and took hold of it; for the oxen shook it. And the anger of the LORD was kindled against Uzzah; and God smote him there for his error; and there he died by the ark of God. (2 Samuel 6:3-7)

Man-made worship condemned:

> And they have built the high places of Tophet, which is in the valley of the son of Hinnom, to burn their sons and their daughters in the fire; which I commanded them not, neither came it into my heart. (Jeremiah 7:31) See also, Jeremiah 19:5.

> And it shall be unto you for a fringe, that ye may
> look upon it, and remember all the command-
> ments of the LORD, and do them; and that ye seek
> not after your own heart and your own eyes, after
> which ye use to go a whoring: that ye may remem-
> ber, and do all my commandments, and be holy
> unto your God. (Numbers 15:39-40)

God is very specific: unauthorized or man-made worship is condemned and even punishable by death. When the Mormons distort the office of the Aaronic priesthood into an office to be con-tinued in the New Covenant Church, being held by young boys not from the tribe of Levi they are in clear violation of the Regulative Principle of worship. This is dangerous territory to be in. While it is admitted that it is out of the norm for God to execute sinners today like the examples above, nevertheless God still brings about spiritual judgments for violation of the Regulative Prin-ciple. See Paul's warning to the Corinthian Church in 1 Corinthians 11:17-32.

THE OLDER COVENANT
AARONIC PRIESTHOOD COMPARED:

In Mormonism's version of the Aaronic priesthood, young boys at the age of 12 are ordained. In Mormonism, these young boys collect fast-offerings on the first Sunday of each month, pre-pare the sacramental elements (white bread and water), and pass the microphone around at testimony meetings.

In contrast to the Mormon Church's teachings, the Scriptures surveyed thus far quite clearly put forth a different system of rules concerning the Aaronic priesthood. It will now be helpful to look at some additional details of the Older Aaronic priesthood and its fulfillment in Christ. To start, as was previously noted, the Aaronic or Levitical priesthood was limited to male members of Israel from the tribe of Levi, and who were also descendants of Aaron's lineage (Exodus 28:1; Numbers 3:5-13; Hebrews 7:4-7). Said another way, the priesthood was conveyed by descent through the genealogy of Aaron.

Furthermore, Aaron's priesthood could never be received or passed on by ordination through the laying on of Mormon hands. This is because the *goyim* or gentiles by their very nature were prohibited from holding the priesthood. It should also be noted that there is not one example of the Aaronic priesthood being practiced in the New Covenant. Mormons are gentiles, despite the claims in their patriarchal blessings to be descendants of Ephraim or Manasseh. Mormons have to resort to their extra-biblical "revelation" in an attempt to substantiate such a practice. Even if Mormons could substantiate that they somehow were descendants of Joseph's sons, Ephraim or Manasseh, they would still not be qualified since they are not of Aaron's lineage.

Getting at the central issue involving redemption, the Aaronic priests had to offer sacrifices for themselves and then for the people. Mormon boys who hold this priesthood have nothing to offer similar to the Aaronic priests of the Older Covenant. It should be emphasized that these sacrifices covered their sins only temporarily until the individual sinned again. Then another sacrifice would have to be made.

The Bible tells us:

> For it is not possible that the blood of bulls and goats could take away sins. (Hebrews 10:4)

> The blood of Jesus Christ His Son cleanses us from all sin. (1 John 1:7)

> But this man [Jesus], after he had offered one sacrifice for sins forever, sat down on the right hand of God. (Hebrews 10:12)

What is more, the Aaronic priesthood was done away in Christ. Jesus or *Yeshua* is the final High Priest (Hebrews 7:11, 12). *Yeshua* is his Hebrew name, and the English spelling is "Joshua." *Iesous* is the Greek transliteration of his Hebrew name, and the English spelling is "Jesus."

He fulfilled the Law as our Eternal High Priest (Hebrews 7:11-28; 8:6, 7). The Old Testament priests were human intermediaries, but now in the New Covenant administration, Jesus is the only mediator between men and God.

This is clearly seen in the following passages:

> For there is one God, and one mediator between God and men, the man Christ Jesus." (1 Timothy 2:5)

For there is one God, and one mediator between
God and men, the man Christ Jesus. (1 Timothy
2:5) But this man, because he continueth ever, hath
an unchangeable priesthood. Wherefore he is able
also to save them to the uttermost that come unto
God by him, seeing he ever liveth to make intercession for them, (Hebrews 7:24, 25) and Jesus saith
unto him, I am the way, the truth, and the life: no
man cometh unto the Father, but by me. (John 14:6)

Therefore, there is no need for the Older Covenant Aaronic priesthood today, because Jesus'
Priesthood has fulfilled and superseded it. Also note, The High Priest's work had special signif-
icance. A specific example being when the Chief Priest in the Older Covenant would enter the
Kodesh Hakodashim, the "Holy of Holies," which was the most revered site in the Older Covenant.
This was the inner sanctuary within the Tabernacle. Later on in Israel's history, the High Priest
would go into the "Holy of Holies" every year which was located in Solomon's temple. The High
Priest, once each year, would make a sacrifice for his own sins and then for the rest of the nation.

And Aaron shall make an atonement upon the
horns of it once in a year with the blood of the
sin offering of atonements: once in the year shall
he make atonement upon it throughout your generations: it is most holy unto the LORD. (Exodus
30:10; see also Hebrews 9:7, 19-22).

Jesus put an end to the representation of the work of salvation by the High Priestly atonement
in the "Holy of Holies," along with the on-going sacrifices which merely foreshadowed His truly
effectual redemptive work. (Hebrews 3:1; 9:11-12, 25-26) It is clear that God accepted the sacrificial redemptive work of His Son when we read, "And the veil of the temple was rent in twain from
the top to the bottom." (Mark 15:38)

Furthermore, one of the most significant historical acts that took place is the judgment that came
upon Jerusalem which culminated in the destruction of the temple in 70 AD.

And Jesus went out, and departed from the temple:

and his disciples came to him for to shew him the buildings of the temple. And Jesus said unto them, See ye not all these things? verily I say unto you, There shall not be left here one stone upon another, that shall not be thrown down. And as he sat upon the Mount of Olives, the disciples came unto him privately, saying, Tell us, when shall these things be? And what shall be the sign of thy coming, and of the end of the world? Verily I say unto you, this generation shall not pass, till all these things be fulfilled. (Matthew 24:1-2, 34)

God himself, after tearing the veil, providentially brought about the destruction of the Temple along with the Aaronic priesthood sacrificial system. Nothing could be clearer; the Older Covenant age had ended. With the temple gone, the Levitical priesthood could no longer function. The everlasting priesthood of Christ was vindicated and established.

In closing this section of our study we should note that since Christ's work is finished, there is now no need for a High Priest on earth after the Older Covenant order. Christ is the only mediator and High Priest who now resides in heaven and is spoken of this way by the writer of Hebrews:

Now of the things which we have spoken this is the sum: We have such a high priest, who is set on the right hand of the throne of the Majesty in the heavens; A minister of the sanctuary, and of the true tabernacle, which the Lord pitched, and not man. For every high priest is ordained to offer gifts and sacrifices: wherefore it is of necessity that this man have somewhat also to offer. For if he were on earth, he should not be a priest, seeing that there are priests that offer gifts according to the law: Who serve unto the example and shadow of heavenly things, as Moses was admonished of God when he was about to make the tabernacle: for, See, saith he, that thou make all things according to the pattern shewed

to thee in the mount. But now hath he obtained
a more excellent ministry, by how much also he is
the mediator of a better covenant, which was established upon better promises. (Hebrews 8:1-6)

Is the Melchizedek priesthood still an office for today?

The Mormon's second, or higher, priesthood is called the Melchizedek priesthood. Does the biblical record indicate that this is a New Covenant office or order to be held by men? Thankfully, the biblical record is rich in detail about the Melchizedek priesthood, which is now held exclusively by our Lord Jesus Christ.

What about the Melchizedek Priesthood in light of the Scriptures?

First, there is no mention in the Bible about an ongoing order of Melchizedek priests in the New Covenant, as the Mormons claim. Melchizedek is mentioned briefly in the Older Covenant in two places, namely Genesis 14:18-20 and Psalms 110:4. In Genesis 14, Melchizedek is revealed as a king and priest who blesses Abraham and to whom Abraham pays tithes. Psalm 110, composed by David, is known as a Messianic Psalm, and David in this Psalm applies this priesthood of Melchizedek to Jesus! Psalm 110:1 is speaking prophetically about Jesus. It is indisputable that this prophecy is about Christ. Nowhere in the Older or New Covenants do we see the practice of ordaining men to the office of the Melchizedek priesthood. Jesus alone is mentioned in the New Covenant as a priest after the order of Melchizedek. (Hebrews 6:20)

It is edifying to read Simon J. Kistemaker's comments on Hebrews 6:20:

> Where Jesus, who went before us, has entered on
> our behalf. He has become a high priest forever, in
> the order of Melchizedek.
>
> Our hope is pinned on Jesus, who has entered
> the heavenly sanctuary. An anchor lies unseen at
> the bottom of the sea; our hope lies unseen in the
> highest heaven. "For in this hope we were saved,"
> writes Paul. "But hope that is seen is no hope at
> all" (Rom. 8:24). Our anchor of hope has absolute
> security in that Jesus in human form, now glorified,

has entered heaven. And he has entered heaven in his humanity as a guarantee that we, too, shall be with him. This guarantee is indicated by the phrase who went before us. (In the Greek the equivalent expression is the word prodromos, which means "forerunner.") He goes ahead and we follow. Also note that the name Jesus and not Christ (5:5) occurs—a distinct reminder of the earthly life of the Lord. Jesus ascended in his glorified human body to heaven and entered the presence of God. As Jesus' human body has come into God's presence, so our bodies will enter heaven. That is our hope. Jesus "has become a high priest forever." This rather short sentence is filled with meaning.

a. Jesus has become a high priest. He did not become high priest when he ascended into heaven. Rather, he took his place at the right hand of God the Father because he accomplished his atoning work on the cross. He indeed was the sacrificial Lamb of God offered for the sin of the world; as the writer of Hebrews puts it, "Christ was sacrificed once to take away the sins of many people" (9:28).

b. Jesus has become a high priest. The writer has called Jesus high priest in Hebrews 2:17; 3:1; 4:14-15; and 5:5, 10. He will explain the concept high priest in succeeding chapters, but in 6:20 the author stresses that Jesus entered heaven as high priest, as the one who atoned for the sins of God's people. He opened the door to heaven because of his high- priestly work.

c. Jesus has become a high priest forever. An Aaronic high priest served in the capacity of high priest for a limited duration. Jesus serves forever. The high priest entered the Most Holy Place once a year. Jesus is in heaven forever. "Because Jesus lives forever, he has a permanent priesthood" (7:24). Constantly he intercedes for us (Rom. 8:34; Heb. 7:25; 9:24).

By his death on the cross, Jesus fulfilled the responsibilities of the Aaronic priesthood. But as a high priest he had to belong to a different order. The writer of Hebrews showed that according to Psalm 110:4 God designated Jesus as high priest forever in the order of Melchizedek (5:6, 10).

Simon J. Kistemaker, *New Testament Commentary, Hebrews* (Baker Book House, Grand Rapids, Michigan, 1984), pp. 176-177.

Kistemaker's comments are very concise and a powerful summary of Christ's work and eternal mediatorial office. We should further ask, why is only Jesus qualified for this order? Jesus, because he "continueth [for] ever," hath an unchangeable priesthood. "This man" refers to none other than Christ, and His priesthood is "unchangeable," which also means perpetual (Hebrews 7:24). In fact, Hebrews 7 gives us an important comparison of the priesthoods of Aaron and Melchizedek. The whole chapter shows the reader that the Levitical priesthood has ceased to exist and has been replaced by the superior Melchizedek priesthood held by one, namely, Jesus Christ. Mormon men do not live forever, so it is impossible for them to hold the Melchizedek priesthood.

WHY ONLY CHRIST CAN NOW HOLD THE MELCHIZEDEK PRIESTHOOD

Abraham is known to believers as "the father of faith" and is blessed by Melchizedek who is the greater. (Hebrews 7:7) Hebrews also tells us unmistakably that "The lesser [Abraham] is blessed by the better" [Melchizedek]. Melchizedek even received tithes from Abraham, proving that he [Melchizedek] is the greater. Not only did Abraham pay tithes to Melchizedek (which is an act of worship), he then received a blessing from Melchizedek in Hebrews 7:4-5, 8-9. Since the tribe of Levi would come through Abraham's linage, they also paid tithes to Melchizedek, even though they were not yet born. These descendants were as the Scriptures said: "For [Levi] was yet in the loins of his father." (Hebrews 7:10) Our unparalleled, unique High Priest is none other than Christ Jesus, who would afterward appear, and of whom Melchizedek was a type. Jesus is superior to Melchizedek and also to all of the Aaronic priests.

The Puritan scholar John Gill's comments are *apropos*:

> And without all contradiction the less is blessed of the greater. This is a self-evident truth, and is undeniable; it admits of no controversy, and cannot be gainsaid, that he that blesseth is greater in that respect than he that is blessed by him; as the priests were greater in their office than the people who were blessed by them; and so Melchizedek, as a priest of the most high God, and as blessing Abraham, was greater than he; and so must be greater than the Levites, who sprung from him; and his priesthood be more excellent than theirs; and consequently Christ, his antitype, and who was of his order, must be greater too; which is the design of the apostle throughout the whole of his reasoning.
>
> John Gill, *Exposition of the Old and New Testaments* Hebrews (Grace Works, Multi-Media Labs), 2011, p. 113.

In light of Dr. Gill's comments, it can be said with certainty that the writer of Hebrews in his epistle has explained in great detail what it meant to be a priest "in the order of Melchizedek." The Aaronic or Levitical Priesthood, which was necessary under the law as a foreshadowing of Christ, has been set aside under the New Covenant. In the New Covenant, we do not have a priesthood designed after the Older Covenant, which in reality served only as a type. The Melchizedek priesthood in the New Covenant is held by one person, namely, Jesus Christ. It is Jesus who is the only priest of the order of Melchizedek because He, being God, lives forever. This is something that the priests of the Older Covenant could not do, since they were mere men.

Moreover, since Christ never dies, there is no need to transfer His priesthood on to someone else as a replacement. In the Older Covenant a priest was a mediator who presented sacrifices to God on behalf of sinful men. Under the Older Covenant, this function was specifically fulfilled by members of the Aaronic priesthood. Under the administration of the New Covenant, Jesus became the only high priest. Jesus accomplished this by sacrificing Himself "once for all" for the forgiveness of sin on the behalf of His people, the church. Consequently, there is no need for any other mediators. The Older Covenant saints had to look in faith beyond the temporal sacrifices, to the true sacrificial Lamb (Jesus), to the True Mediator of the Covenant to be saved.

THE PRIESTHOOD
OF ALL BELIEVERS

There are many solid scriptural reasons that the Church has believed in the priesthood of all believers. Most noticeably, the Bible teaches that all believers have a priestly role. (1 Peter 2:5, 9; Revelation 1:6; 5:10; 20:6) As seen from these texts, we can assert that the New Covenant revelation definitely speaks of the priesthood of all believers. This is problematic for the Mormon concept of priesthood, since all of the Saints in Christ make up this priesthood.

To specify, this believers priesthood is clearly seen in Peter's first epistle where Peter, speaking to believers in Christ, calls all believers, both men and women, "a holy priesthood." In 1 Peter 2:5, we read, "you are a chosen generation, a royal priesthood, an holy nation, a peculiar people: that ye should show forth the praises of him how hath called you out of darkness into his marvelous light" in 1 Peter 2:9. Also, John tells us that "Unto him that loved us, and washed us from our sins in his own blood," and He "has made us kings and priests to His God and Father, to Him be glory and dominion forever and ever. Amen." (Revelation 1:5, 6) This priesthood of all believers overthrows the unbiblical Mormon concept of an Older Covenant priesthood order in the New Covenant era.

MORMONS AND TEMPLES

The Mormon temple is another aberration and confused discontinuity in the history of redemption and theology, primarily because the temple had a specific purpose and function in the older covenant; it is out of place in the New Covenant.

Alfred Edersheim was a scholar of Jewish lineage who lived in the 1800. He converted to Christianity and used his substantial theological knowledge to build up Christ's Church. *The Temple - Its Ministry and Services* (as they were at the time of Christ) by Alfred Edersheim will put to rest the idea that there are any similarities between Jewish Temples and Mormon temples. By even glancing at the chapter outline of Edersheim's book on the Temple, the reader can see this with clarity:

Chapter 1 — A First View of Jerusalem, and of the Temple.

Chapter 2 — Within the Holy Place.

Chapter 3 — Temple Order, Revenues, and Music.

Chapter 4 — The Officiating Priesthood.

Chapter 5 — Sacrifices: Their Order and their Meaning.

Chapter 6 — The Burnt-Offering, the Sin-and Trespass-Offering, and the Peace-Offering.

Chapter 7 — At Night in the Temple.

Chapter 8 — The Morning and the Evening Sacrifice.

Chapter 9 — Sabbath in the Temple.

Chapter 10 — Festive Cycles and Arrangement of the Calendar.

Chapter 11 — The Passover.

Chapter 12 — The Paschal Feast and the Lord's Supper.

Chapter 13 — The Feast of Unleavened Bread and the Day of Pentecost.

Chapter 14 — The Feast of Tabernacles.

Chapter 15 — The New Moons: The Feast of the Seventh New Moon, or of Trumpets, or New Year's Day.

Chapter 16 — The Day of Atonement.

Chapter 17 — Post-Mosaic Festivals.

Chapter 18 — On Purification.

Chapter 19 — On Vows— Nazarite's Vow. The Offering of the First-Fruits in the Temple.

The Temple of the Older Covenant, with its sacrificial system, was a shadow of heavenly realities and is brought to reality through the once-for-all sacrifice of Christ that redeems us from our transgressions.

> Know ye not that ye are the temple of God, and
> that the Spirit of God dwelleth in you? If any man

defile the temple of God, him shall God destroy;
for the temple of God is holy, which temple ye are.
(1 Corinthians 3:16)

The Church is "built upon the foundation of the apostles and prophets, Jesus Christ himself being the chief corner stone; In whom all the building fitly framed together groweth unto an holy temple in the Lord: In whom ye also are builded together for an habitation of God through the Spirit." (Ephesians 2:20-22) The Church of Christ is God's temple, not a house made with hands.

In Conclusion

It is clear that the priesthood has been changed (Hebrews 7:12) and it is Christ who now holds an eternal priesthood after the order of Melchizedek. The Scriptures are emphatic that only Jesus can hold this priesthood (Hebrews 7:24). Additionally, Christ's eternal priesthood is far superior to the priesthood in the Older Covenant. Why? The Older Covenant's sacrifices were deficient in that as Hebrews says:

> For it is not possible that the blood of bulls and
> goats should take away sins. (Hebrews 10:4)

Consider our better position in Christ:

> How much more shall the blood of Christ, who
> through the eternal Spirit offered Himself with-
> out spot to God, purge your conscience from dead
> works to serve the living God. (Hebrews 9:14)

The Levitical rituals of the Older Covenant revealed to Moses by God were reflective of the New Covenant realities. In and of themselves, the priestly rituals of the Older Covenant could not perfect the Older Covenant saints as Christ has now done. The Levitical rituals were nothing more than a shadow of the good things to come in Christ (See Hebrews 10:1).

The completed work of Christ Jesus is now established, so we no longer apply the Older Covenant's laws regulating the various ceremonies and sacrifices performed by the Aaronic priesthood in the same way. There is an unmistakable discontinuity between the covenants. Moreover, we are warned against returning to the imperfection of the Older administration's application of the Mosaic law, which was meticulously required in the Older Levitical system. With the coming of Christ and His perfect High-priestly work, the Levitical priesthood was, by necessity changed. (Hebrews 7:12) Thus, the sacrifices and feasts of the Older Covenant are not binding upon the New Covenant believer/priests of today as in their older or former shadow forms. (Colossians 2:13-17) There is however, an unmistakable continuity of fulfillment of these sacrifices and priestly duties today by faith in Christ, our Eternal High Priest.

Finally, the New Covenant saints have this special assurance: "...if we walk in the light, as he is in the light, we have fellowship one with another and the blood of Jesus Christ his son cleanses us from all sin" (1 John 1:7). It is unmistakable that the Mormons have distorted the priesthood of Melchizedek that Christ alone holds, by having made this an on-going office held by Mormon men. Furthermore, when Mormons attempt to lay claim to this priesthood, they are fighting against Christ, the sole possessor of the New Covenant Melchizedek priesthood. The Mormon priesthoods are nothing more than a fantasy that attempts to rob Christ of his Royal High Priestly position.

MORMON ATTEMPTS TO DEFEND THEIR SYSTEM OF PRIESTHOODS IN THE NEW COVENANT TIME PERIOD

The Mormon claim to have restored two priesthoods, the Aaronic and the other after the order of Melchizedek, is preposterous in light of what we have seen in the Scriptures and commentary above. The Scriptures are silent with regard to this supposed restoration of the priesthoods of Aaron and Melchizedek. This is believed by Mormons to have come as a result of Joseph Smith, Mormon founder, and Oliver Cowdrey, one of the three witnesses to the *Book of Mormon* receiving special visitations from Peter, James and John in upstate New York in 1829. Since the canon of Scripture is closed, Scripture does not allow for such an event.

Mormons have said that the Aaronic priesthood is an "everlasting" order, when attempting to convince prospects that the Aaronic priesthood is a continuing office in the New Covenant church. The Mormon correctly points out that the priesthood is said to be "everlasting" in Numbers 25:10-13, and yet Hebrews 7:12 makes it clear that the priesthood was changed. Is this a contradiction in the biblical record or is there an adequate explanation?

What about the Hebrew word *olam* which can be translated "everlasting"? Does this support the Mormon idea of an ongoing two-tier priesthood structure in the New Testament?

We should note that the Hebrew word *olam* can be translated in different ways. Some examples are forever, perpetual, everlasting, eternal, or permanent. The word "forever" does not necessarily mean never ending in Scripture, but can also be understood to mean as lasting only as long as a time period or age. Since the Mormons are appealing to Scripture in the defense of one of their peculiar doctrines, we should briefly respond to this argument about the "everlasting" nature of the Aaronic priesthood.

Does this mean that a practice commanded in Scripture will last forever? First, we can admit that it's possible when dealing with the usage of *olam* that a practice mentioned may last forever. However, the context of a passage is important when making this determination. Admitting that 'olam may literally mean forever does not invalidate the fact the there are numerous indicators that 'olam can also be used to describe a practice that will end or change forms going from the Older Covenant into the New. In particular, *olam* is used regarding ordinances in the Older Covenant which were to be kept by the people of Israel and not carried over into the New Covenant church practice in their Older Covenant forms. It should be noted that there are significant discontinuities and continuities in redemptive history when moving from the Older Covenant into the New Covenant era.

Examples of the time limitations of *olam*:

For example:

> Then his master shall bring him unto the judges; he
> shall also bring him to the door, or unto the door
> post; and his master shall bore his ear through with
> an awl; and he shall serve him forever. (Exodus 21:6)

In this passage 'olam stresses permanence and that the man would be a servant forever. This verse is explicit in conveying the idea of a limitation of time. The *prima facie* limitation in this verse is the life-span of the servant.

Another example is the Feast of Unleavened Bread:

> So you shall observe the Feast of Unleavened

> Bread, for on this same day I will have brought
> your armies out of the land of Egypt. Therefore
> you shall observe this day throughout your gener-
> ations as an everlasting ordinance. (Exodus 12:17)

The discontinuity is that the New Covenant church no longer celebrates the Feast of Unleavened Bread. The continuity is that this Feast is fulfilled in Christ.

Consider the Passover:

> Now this day will be a memorial to you, and you
> shall celebrate it as a feast to the Lord; throughout
> your generations you are to celebrate it as a perma-
> nent ordinance. (Exodus 12:14)

The discontinuity is that the New Covenant church no longer celebrates the Passover feast. The continuity is that all of the Older Covenant feasts including the Passover find fulfillment in the Lord's Supper.

Then there is the example of circumcision:

> And I will establish my covenant between me and
> thee and thy seed after thee in their generations for
> an everlasting covenant, to be a God unto thee, and
> to thy seed after thee. And I will give unto thee, and
> to thy seed after thee, the land wherein thou art a
> stranger, all the land of Canaan, for an everlasting
> possession; and I will be their God. And God said
> unto Abraham, Thou shalt keep my covenant there-
> fore, thou, and thy seed after thee in their generations.
> This is my covenant, which ye shall keep, between me
> and you and thy seed after thee; Every man child
> among you shall be circumcised. (Genesis 17:7-10)

The discontinuity is that circumcision is no longer required in the New Covenant. The continuity is that circumcision is replaced by baptism in the New Covenant era as the mark of the covenant.

The Sabbath Day to be kept on the seventh day:

> Therefore the children of Israel shall keep the
> Sabbath, to observe the Sabbath throughout their
> generations as a perpetual covenant. It is a sign
> between Me and the children of Israel forever; for
> in six days the Lord made the heavens and the
> earth, and on the seventh day He rested and was
> refreshed. (Exodus 31:16-17)

The discontinuity is that the day has been changed to the first day of the week in celebration of the resurrection of Christ. The continuity is that God's people are to still honor Him by resting for our labors after six days of work. (Hebrews 4:9) In the Greek text, the word for "rest" in Hebrews 4:9 is *sabbatismos*. It means "a Sabbath rest." *Young's Literal Translation* captures this well: "There doth remain, then, a sabbatic rest to the people of God" (Hebrews 4:9).

Nothing could be clearer than the New Covenant's emphasis that the Aaronic priesthood has been set aside, or more properly, it has been completed, since it was part of the types and shadows that prefigured Christ's work. Attempting to return to the observances and rites of the Older Covenant which have been completed in Christ can be described as, "But now, after that ye have known God, or rather are known of God, how turn ye again to the weak and beggarly elements, whereunto ye desire again to be in bondage?" (Galatians 4:9) It is clear from the above survey of the scriptural use of the Hebrew word *olam*, it is readily seen that appealing to one possible understanding of the word is of no use to Mormonism in defending their view of the on-going nature of the Aaronic priesthood in the New Covenant Church.

ADDITIONAL PROBLEMS
FOR MORMON PRIESTHOOD AUTHORITY

The Mormons claim that in 1829, Joseph Smith and Oliver Cowdery were ordained to these priesthoods by John the Baptist and the apostles Peter, James, and John, resulting in a restoration of the Priesthood authority that was allegedly lost from the earth at the time of the death of the First-Century apostles.

According to the Mormon Church: "In restoring the gospel, God again gave the Priesthood to men. John the Baptist came in 1829 to ordain Joseph Smith and Oliver Cowdery to the Aaronic Priesthood. (*Doctrine and Covenants* 13; 27:8) Then the First-Century apostles Peter, James, and John came and gave Joseph Smith and Oliver Cowdery the Melchizedek Priesthood; (*Doctrine and Covenants* 27:12, 13)

This is problematic because the *Doctrine and Covenants* says that a man must have the priesthood before he can see God:

> And without the ordinances thereof, and the authority of the Priesthood, the power of godliness is not manifest unto men in the flesh; For without this no man can see the face of God, even the Father, and live.
>
> Joseph Smith, *Doctrine and Covenants*, Section 84:21-22.

Since Joseph Smith didn't possess priesthood authority when he claimed to see God in 1820 in the first vision story, why did he not die? Which is true, the *Doctrine and Covenants* 84:21-22 or Joseph Smith's first vision story?

Another significant problem is

Section 7 of the *Doctrine and Covenants* and 3rd Nephi 28:7-8 say that the apostle John and three Nephite disciples would remain on the earth alive until Jesus returns to set up his kingdom. If this is true, how could there be a total apostasy as the Mormons say? In the *Journal of Discourses* Volume 9 on page 88 we find that if one elder remains alive he has power to reorganize the church. If this is true, why did not God ask the apostle John and the Nephite disciples to reorganize the church? According to Mormonism's own teaching, John and the Nephite disciples already had priesthood authority.

Many additional questions can be raised about inconsistencies and contradictions in Mormon priesthood theology. However, these two problems are insurmountable for Mormonism and will suffice to conclude this point of the study.

This scriptural evaluation of the Mormon priesthood claims we will close with a good summary from Simon J. Kistemaker from Hebrews chapter 10:

Doctrinal Considerations in 10:1–10

For readers of Jewish origin who considered the law of God their most precious possession, the author's assertion—"the law is only a shadow of the good things that are coming"—must have been astounding. If the law was their treasured possession, it would be difficult to imagine that far more desirable things were in store for them. The writer of Hebrews calls these things "the realities themselves," and he explains that they consist of Christ and his redemptive work. Writing to Jewish readers in Colosse about religious observances, Paul says almost the same thing. He writes, "These [regulations] are a shadow of the things that were to come; the reality, however, is found in Christ" (Col. 2:17).

By quoting and applying the verses from Psalm 40, the author of Hebrews shows that Christ has come to do God's will. In doing that will, Christ offered his body as a sacrifice, fulfilled the requirements of the Aaronic priesthood, and terminated the Levitical sacrifices. If Christ had fulfilled only the demands of the Aaronic priesthood, however, there would not have been a new covenant. The writer of Hebrews teaches that after Christ had offered himself without blemish to God, he became the mediator of a new covenant. He cleansed the consciences of the members of this covenant, "so that we may serve the living God!" (9:14). This refers to a higher priesthood that is eternal; it is called the priesthood in the order of Melchizedek. Christ fulfilled the requirements of this priesthood in his dedication to do God's will.

When Christ came into the world, "he [set] aside the first to establish the second" (Heb. 10:9). The author of Hebrews uses the terms first and another, new, or second when he discusses the covenant (8:7, 13; 9:1, 15, 18). Explaining the psalm quotation in 10:8-9, the writer first quotes the words about the sacrificial system of the Aaronic priesthood and then cites the words pertaining to Christ's perfect obedience to God's will. These two verses, in effect, describe the two covenants and the two phases of Christ's priesthood. To atone for the sins of his people (2:17), Christ had to sacrifice his body once for all (10:10). He fulfilled the demands of the first covenant and terminated the first phase of his priesthood; that is, the Aaronic priesthood. Christ established the second covenant when he came to do God's will. Then he also established the second phase of his priesthood, the one of Melchizedek. The Aaronic priesthood typifies Christ's passive obedience; the priesthood of Melchizedek, Christ's active obedience.

Simon J. Kistemaker, *New Testament Commentary, Hebrews* (Baker Book House, Grand Rapids, Michigan, 1984), p. 278.

PART III

WITNESSING TO MORMONS

CHAPTER 11
K.I.S.S. – KEEP IT SIMPLE SAINTS

CHAPTER 12
WITNESSING TO MORMONS
USING PRESUPPOSITIONAL APOLOGETICS

Food for Thought:

It is of critical importance in the current scene that a consistently Reformed apologetic be set forth. The non-Christian point of view is much more self-consciously hostile to Christianity than it has ever been. The fact that the assumption of human autonomy is the root and fountain of all forms of non-Christian thought is more apparent than it has ever been in the past. Any argument for the truth of Christianity that is inconsistent with itself should not expect to have a hearing. Only a position which boldly and humbly challenges the wisdom of the world and, with the Apostle Paul, brings out that it has been made foolishness with God will serve the purpose. Only such a method which asks man to serve and worship the Creator rather than the creature honors God and assigns to him the place that he truly occupies. Only such a method is consistent with the idea that the Holy Spirit must convict and convince the sinner. The Holy Spirit cannot be asked to honor a method that does not honor God as God. - Cornelius Van Til in A Christian Theory of Knowledge

If we first allow the legitimacy of the natural man's assumption of himself as the ultimate reference point in interpretation in any dimension we cannot deny his right to interpret Christianity itself in naturalistic terms. - Cornelius Van Til from The Defense Of The Faith

CHAPTER 11

K.I.S.S. -
KEEP IT SIMPLE SAINTS

KEEP IT SIMPLE SAINTS

STAY FOCUSED ON WHAT'S IMPORTANT! DO NOT DEVIATE FROM THE FOLLOWING FOUR POINTS.
1. THE AUTHORITY OF SCRIPTURE AS OPPOSED TO EXPERIENCES AND FALSE REVELATION.
2. THE NATURE OF GOD AND CHRIST.
3. MAN THE CREATURE AND HIS FALLEN CONDITION.
4. THE GOOD NEWS.

BASIC POINTERS

tart your witnessing opportunities by stating that the Word of God in the Old and New Testaments is the authority for all of your life and beliefs. Make it clear that you do not accept any other revelations. Let Mormons know that you would love to talk with them and hear what they have to say. Also acknowledge that you know that they would like to see you give up your beliefs and adopt theirs. Take control of the situation by saying, "If you want me to give up my beliefs and adopt yours you will have to convince me from the Bible." Make it clear that the Bible is the only authority that you accept. Restrict your discussions to the Bible. If the Mormons attacks the reliability of the Bible, ask them, "Can you tell me what the ordinary standards are for evaluating ancient historical documents?" If they do not answer, then raise the question, "Why do you feel qualified to make statements attacking the historicity and reliability of the Bible?"

For the most part, Mormons use the same theological terms that Christians use. You must get beyond these surface similarities. Ask questions such as, "What do you mean?" Or, "How do you know that?" The question "What do you mean?" forces the individual to define their terms. This gets beyond the surface similarities or the "language barrier." The question "How do you know that?" forces the Mormon to give a basis for their beliefs. It will show that their beliefs are based upon sources outside of the Bible. These questions are extremely important when dealing with the nature of God.

THE RELIGION THAT STARTED IN A HAT

Make sure that Mormons understand where you are coming from. Have them restate your position so that you know that they understand you.

1. THE QUESTION OF AUTHORITY

The Christian must be committed to the sufficiency and absolute authority of Scripture. The Mormon is committed to Joseph Smith. The Mormon religion stands or falls with Joseph Smith. It is necessary to apply the biblical test of a prophet to Joseph Smith. (Deuteronomy 13:1-5; 18:20-22)

How do we know truth? Should we let feelings or experiences guide us?

The Bible gives us clear answers to the above two questions. "Whoso despiseth the word shall be destroyed; but he that feareth the commandment shall be rewarded." (Proverbs 13:13) "The grass withereth, the flower fadeth; but the word of our God shall stand forever." (Isaiah 40:8) "Heaven and earth shall pass away, but my words shall never pass away." (Matthew 24:35) "The Scriptures cannot be broken..." (John 10:35) "These were more noble minded than those in Thessalonica, in that they received the word with all readiness of mind, and searched the Scriptures daily, whether those things were so." Acts 17:11 and Hebrews 1:1-2 are important verses on the cessation of prophecies.

1 Corinthians 4:6 warns us not to go beyond what is written (NIV).

The Mormon testimony is nothing more than a strong feeling that what they believe is right. "There is a way which seemeth right unto a man, but the end thereof are the ways of death" (Proverbs 14:12). "He that trusteth in his own heart is a fool" (Proverbs 28:26). "The heart is deceitful above all things, and desperately wicked; who can know it." (Jeremiah 17:9)

2. THE DOCTRINE OF GOD

Discussion of the doctrine of God is of the utmost importance. Remember the above two questions that force the Mormon to define and defend their beliefs. As you proceed to probe the Mormon's doctrine, it will be clearly seen that the Mormon deity is one finite god among many gods and is definitely not the God of the Bible. Be prepared with biblical passages such as Isaiah 43:10; 44:5, 8; and 46:9 to refute the Mormon doctrine of the plurality of gods. In addition, Mormons believe that God and man are of the same family. Use passages of Scripture that make it clear that God is not a man and never has been. "God is not a man..." (Numbers 23:19)

Call the Mormon to repentance for the idolatry of believing in a false god. Romans 1:22-23 are important verses for this.

3. Man's condition

Mormons reject the doctrine of original sin (Romans 5:12-19) and man's depravity (Romans 3:9-19). There are many passages in Scripture, such as Psalm 51:5 and Jeremiah 17:9 that establish the fact of man's fallen condition and guilt before a Holy God. Use these and other passages frequently in your witnessing to Mormons.

4. The Good News

Mormons have a warped and degenerate view of grace. In 2 Nephi 25:23 on page 92 in the *Book of Mormon,* in we find this incredible doctrine set forth:

> For we labor diligently to write, to persuade our children, and also our brethren, to believe in Christ, and to be reconciled to God, <u>for we know it is by grace that we are saved, after all that we can do</u>. (Emphasis mine)

Mormons can never know if they will be saved. How could anyone be sure that they had done enough? Grace does not take over in their system until you have done "all that we can do." This is not grace, but a system of works. The Mormon is working to obtain grace. This is the sin of Cain (Genesis 4:3).

Give a biblical definition of grace that shows that grace is unmerited favor. Use passages such as Ephesians 2:8-9 to show that salvation is a gift from God.

Ask the Mormon, "do you know if you have eternal life?" 1 John 5:13 reads: "These things have

I written unto you that believe on the name of the Son of God; <u>that ye may know that ye have eternal life</u>, and that ye may believe on the name of the Son of God." Tell the Mormon that God will reject his doctrine of works just like Cain's. God has provided redemption for sinners in Jesus Christ. It is not some kind of general salvation that gets man out of the grave. It is a real redemption set forth in Romans 5:8-10.

Consider the following possible dialogue with a Mormon to illustrate a point:

You tell the Mormon that you are a Mormon but you don't believe that Joseph Smith was a prophet, nor do you believe that the *Book of Mormon* is Scripture. You tell the Mormon that you do not believe God has a body. And you do not believe the Mormon Church is a true church and yet you say, "I am a Mormon." The Mormon will be completely taken back and at some point will express doubt that you could possibly be a Mormon.

You then say that you agree; that you could not be a Mormon if you don't believe Mormon beliefs. You then politely say to the Mormon that you don't accept them as a Christian because they don't believe Christian beliefs such as the Triune nature of God, that there is only one God, that the Bible is complete and trustworthy, and that any additional so-called revelations are not only unnecessary, but are indeed contrary to Scripture.

Concluding observation

Over the years I have challenged a number of Mormons, including university professors to forsake their false faith. At times when interacting with BYU professors the debate has become somewhat technical. These encounters are out of the norm for most people witnessing to Mormons. The K.I.S.S. method is the best approach for almost every witnessing encounter with an average Mormon.

CHAPTER 12

WITNESSING TO MORMONS
USING A REFORMED
PRESUPPOSITIONAL APOLOGETIC

o we witness to Mormons and other non-believers by appealing to a body of supposed neutral facts and then ask them to objectively consider the evidence and
then expect them to embrace the Christian faith? This may sound reasonable, but
it does not take into account the nature of fallen man. Will someone with a fallen
nature be able to objectively look at the claims and demands set forth in the Word of God? If not,
how do we get beyond this seemingly insurmountable problem? I will attempt to deal with these
questions as we move through the material. To start, let's consider the dynamics of what happens
in a typical encounter between a Mormon and Christian.

Many times both the Mormon and the Christian appeal to evidence, or a supposed common body
of neutral knowledge or facts that exist. Let me say at the outset that facts are not neutral. There
are no such things as brute or neutral facts. There are God-interpreted facts! We must seek to
understand God's interpretation of facts. A fact can only be properly apprehended to the degree
that it is viewed through the lens of God's sovereignty and aligns with all of His other attributes.
It is only within the realm of the nature of God that we can define a fact as true and applicable
to our worldview. When we consider God's version or interpretation of facts, we are dealing with
truth, since God cannot lie. (Hebrews 6:18)

As Christians, we need to be aware of our worldview. We need to understand and hold to a dis-
tinctively Christian theory of knowledge. We also need to understand that fallen man has a fundamentally different worldview than redeemed man. Or it could be said that we as Christians need
to be epistemologically self-conscious. Epistemology is the study of how we know things. There are
generally understood to be three primary types or theories of gaining knowledge: 1. Empiricism;
a view that experience, especially the senses, is the only source of knowledge. 2. Rationalism; a
view that appeals to man's independent reason as a source of knowledge. And 3. Dogmatism, or
Scripturalism; all knowledge must be contained within a system and deduced from its starting
principles, in the Christian case, the Bible.

To be clear, we are talking about presuppositions as they relate to epistemology, and we are talking about faulty epistemology. The point of the matter is that the epistemological paradigm of the Mormon is not the same as the Christian. (* See below: What is Presuppositionalism?)

What usually happens in witnessing encounters is that Mormons will appeal to his or her testimony; he or she knows the Mormon Church is true and Joseph Smith is a prophet from their subjective "burning in the bosom" sensation. They also appeal to the authority of the Mormon priesthood and to alleged archaeological discoveries in support of Mormonism. Many times, the Christian likewise appeals to evidence. Does this approach get anywhere?

It seems to me that what is taking place many times between Christians and Mormons is that both sides end up batting evidence back and forth without either side seeing the real fundamental differences involved. To understand this we must first understand that the real issue between Mormons and Christians is one that involves a fundamental difference in presuppositions or a difference in worldviews. Evidence must be interpreted within the framework of a worldview or by presuppositions in order to have any meaning.

Why is this? Two people looking at the same evidence from different presuppositions or worldviews can and do get very different interpretations to the same evidence. For example, Psalm 19:1 says: "The heavens declare the glory of God; and the firmament sheweth his handywork." We as Christians see evidence for God's existence everywhere in God's creation. Non-believers, however, when looking at the same evidence, would reject the testimony of Psalm 19 and claim to see nothing in support of God's existence.

When two opposing sides seem to agree on a particular interpretation it may be only a superficial agreement. When you get below the surface by defining terms, the agreement often disappears. At many times you have the non-Christian becoming inconsistent, borrowing from the Christian worldview in order to function. Non-believers find it difficult to consistently live out the implications of their belief system, given ultimate materialistic assumptions. Non-believers are challenged to show how their presuppositions or materialistic world-view can account for the laws of logic, ethics and science. (See Appendix 1, *The Importance and Necessity of Special Revelation* for a pressupositional defense of Scripture).

I want to emphasize the point: we are talking about the fundamental commitments and how those commitments inform the worldviews of Mormons and Christians.

It cannot be stated strongly enough that the Mormon and the Christian have rather obvious differences in their worldviews. To say this another way, the Christian and Mormon have different fundamental commitments. The Christian is committed to dependence upon God's complete revelation revealed in the Old and New Testaments of the Bible. The Mormon, on the other hand, is committed ultimately to independence from and rejection of God's revealed Word found in the Bible. I say this in spite of Mormon protests that they do believe in the Bible. I reply to this protest by pointing out that Mormons always qualify their belief in the Bible by saying "as far as it is translated correctly." This qualification reveals Mormonism's rejection of the absolute authority of Scripture.

The Mormon or the non-Christian commitment is a commitment of independence from God and His Word. You can call this commitment to independence "sinful human autonomy." Human autonomy is the starting principle of how sinful or fallen man operates. He has set himself in the place of God. He tries to be the measure of all things. This is also the essence of humanism. In contrast, the Christian person acknowledges that God and His Word are the measure and standard of all things.

If we are going to be biblical and consistent in our approach to Mormons we must challenge their false commitment, which is ultimately a rejection of God and His Word. The only way to have true knowledge and certainty is to be dependent upon God and His Word. I say this since God is the creator of all things, including all facts in the universe. For us to have true knowledge, we must have the interpretation of facts that God gives to them. Any interpretation of facts that refuses God's interpretation will be false.

Where do we find God's interpretation of the world? In the Bible which is God's revelation to man. It comes down to either the Bible, or our thoughts and feelings in disregard for God's revelation. We are either dependent upon God or we are committed to sinful human autonomy. The only thing that can cause the Mormon to forsake his sinful human autonomy is the Holy Spirit working through the preaching of the Gospel. If we are batting evidence back and forth without ever preaching the Gospel to them, our efforts are in vain. The very least we can do is give them a gospel tract.

THE IMPORTANCE AND ISSUE AT STAKE

As Paul tells us, the heart of the Gospel is that "Jesus died for our sins, was buried, and rose again the third day according to the Scriptures." (1 Corinthians 15:1-4) "For by grace are ye saved through faith; and that not of yourselves: it is the gift of God: Not of works, lest any man should boast." (Ephesians 2:8-9) This is truly good news! Mormonism is a complex system involving a works-for-salvation scheme, and because of this, they have no certainty of salvation or good news.

If you've studied Mormonism at all you have seen some of the many changes, contradictions and outright rejection of biblical truth within its structure. These contradictions are the result of their rejection of God and His Word. Man-made religious systems will always be full of contradictions, errors, inconsistencies and absurdities. This will always be so in light of the fact that they are mis-interpreting the world that God has ordained and made.

Let me summarize what has been said so far: I believe many times Christians and Mormons end up batting evidence around that is interpreted differently because of our different worldviews or presuppositions. There are no neutral facts because God is the creator of all things. The Christian's commitment is to God and His Word and because of this we must stress that there are no neutral facts; there are only God interpreted facts. The Christian worldview and how we interpret evidence is controlled by our presupposition of the absolute authority of Scripture. The Bible is our starting point. We argue from Scripture.

In contrast, the Mormon worldview and how evidence is interpreted is controlled by a presupposition that rejects the absolute authority of Scripture. They have set themselves up as the authority to determine truth. Romans 8:7 tells us "The mind is set on the flesh is hostile toward God; for it does not subject itself to the law of God, for it is not even able to do so."

We can expose and disprove Mormonism by using a series of questions that function as a *reductio ad absurdum* argument because it reduces and shows Mormonism to be holding absurd and contradictory positions in its commitment to ultimate truth. These questions can be used against any system that rejects the absolute authority of God's Word.

Most importantly, our goal is to challenge the Mormon through gospel preaching to forsake his false independence from God and His Word - an independence that keeps him in darkness and confusion. We should then challenge the Mormon to believe the Gospel and become dependent upon God and His Word.

THE LANGUAGE BARRIER

As an example of the language barrier, a Mormon will say, "I believe in God the eternal Father and in His Son Jesus Christ and in the Holy Ghost." What is wrong with this statement? It sounds good on the surface. But we need to cut through the language barrier that is there. How can we do this?

There are three questions that I like to use when challenging Mormons beliefs. These questions are good for any debate or witnessing encounter, and help us: First, get past the language barrier or superficial meaning of words. Second, to show Mormons that their beliefs are not biblical and that they can have no assurance or confidence in the finite Mormon deity. Third, also show the Mormon that he can have no confidence in the area of knowledge or epistemology.

The Three Questions:

1. What do you mean?
   This question forces Mormons to define their terminology and gets beyond surface similarity.

2. How do you know that?
   This forces them to give reasons for their definitions. Are they parroting things that they heard? Are their definitions biblical?

3. What are the implications of this?
   This question forces them to look at the absurdities of their belief system and where it leads.

Areas to apply these questions and examples of questions:

Normally I like to start with epistemology since we need to know how we can know anything. In the case of Mormonism, I start with ontological questions since questions in this area quickly reveal the finite nature of the Mormon deity and then allow you to contrast this finite god with scriptural passages on God's nature and attributes.

Ontology or metaphysics, the ultimate nature of reality:

What do you mean by God? Has he always been God? Where did he come from? Are there other gods in the universe like your god? Does your god have a body? If he is a glorified man with a body, is he limited or finite? How does he travel? A space ship? How does he communicate with the other gods in the universe? Intergalactic phone service? Celestial conferences?

Keep contrasting the Mormon's answers with scriptural passages on God's attributes. Also remember that they want you to surrender your beliefs and adopt theirs. Keep asking the question, "How do you know that?" to expose their lack of biblical understanding. It is also helpful at different points in the discussion to say, "I'm not sure what you mean, go on."

The Mormon god is finite or limited because of his body. Some additional questions you could ask to expose the implications of this are: "Has your god with a body traveled everywhere in the universe? If so, when? How long would it take him to do this? Does your god know everything? If he has not been everywhere in the universe, how could he? Could your god ever be overthrown by other gods from a different part of the universe that have a different agenda than his? If not, how do you know that? Can you give me a guarantee of this? Based upon what? Is there a creator/creature distinction? Do men and the gods exist in a realm of being in general? Is God further up the scale of being than man? Are there two types of being: created/uncreated? Is reality ultimately one (a unity), or many (a diversity)? How do the universals relate to the particulars?"

The Christian God cannot be overthrown since there are no other gods! Our God is omnipotent (all powerful) and He is omnipresent (everywhere present) and He is omniscient (all knowing).

Keep pressing questions like: If there are more senior gods in the universe, why not put my faith in one of them? Why put my faith in a junior god? Could your god ever step down from being god? If he became a god, it is conceivable that he could quit someday.

After pressing them with questions for awhile you can summarize their position. You could say: "I think you are saying that your god was once a man and now is god. There are other gods in the universe like the god you worship and you may become a god yourself in the future." Contrast what they tell you with biblical verses on God and His attributes, and that God declares that there are no other gods.

EPISTEMOLOGY

Are Mormons and their gods empiricists, rationalists, or irrationalists, or do they hold to some other concept of gaining knowledge? Former Utah University professor, Sterling McMurrin, on page eleven of his book, *Theological Foundations of the Mormon Religion*, states that Mormons and their gods are basically empiricists [gaining knowledge through experience and sensations]. Is McMurrin correct in his perception of Mormon epistemology? Are the revelations of the Mormon god empirically-based revelations?

Aristotle, John Locke, David Hume, George Berkeley, and Bertrand Russell were all empirical thinkers. They would all agree that knowledge comes through the senses in the following order: (a) sensations (b) perceptions (c) memory images, (d) development of abstract ideas. Perceptions are inferences from sensations. How do you know valid from invalid inferences? About five percent of the population does not have any memory images at all. How can these people be empiricists? What about studies which deal in the areas of the threshold of sensations? These studies show how unreliable the senses can be, especially sight (colors), and hearing (sound). Also, can fatigue, drugs, or optical illusions deceive the senses? What about the deceitfulness of sin or demonic deception?

Empirical epistemology has its roots in the pagan philosopher Aristotle. Why do Mormons incorporate pagan thinking into their understanding Christianity?

ETHICS

Mormon ethics are derived from what they call the *Four Standard Works:* the *Bible*, the *Book of Mormon; Doctrine and Covenants; The Pearl of Great Price;* and most importantly, the pronouncements from their church leaders in the official church magazine, *Ensign*, and General Conference meetings. Because of their extra-biblical revelations, Mormonism has opened a can of worms, philosophically speaking, which can be seen in the questions below and also in sections dealing with epistemology, ontology and teleology.

Is there a law structure above your god that he is accountable to? If so, how do you know he's interpreting if correctly? Where did this law structure come from? If there are eternal laws in the universe above the Mormon god, wouldn't this law structure be God? Do all the gods interpret it the same? Are there evil gods in the universe? If not, how do you know? If so, could they destroy or defeat the good gods?

Do you believe that the free will argument is a solution to save your god from being weak, and responsible for evil and its results? How would you respond to Gordon Clark in his book, *Religion, Reason, and Revelation* that such a thing as free will cannot save your god from being responsible? See also Antony Flew's *God and Philosophy* for similar rejections of the "free will argument" to allegedly protect God from being responsible for evil. Antony Flew is a non-Christian philosopher.

TELEOLOGY

Mormonism teaches that history is endless, involving eternal progression of men to godhood and new worlds being formed by councils of the gods.

Is history linear or endless? Is eternal progression a concept of history that involves endlessness? Will the Mormon god ever defeat evil in the universe? Why haven't the more senior gods defeated it yet? Will time ever cease to exist in the part of the universe your god rules over? What about other parts of the universe? Is there any real difference between eternal progression and the Hindu teleological concept of history? What is the difference, if any? Does your god control history? In what way? Partially or completely? What is the ultimate purpose of creation? In what way does evolutionary theory differ from eternal progression? In what ways are they similar?

Be careful not to be sarcastic when asking questions like these. We don't want make fun of the Mormon. However, the Mormon is obligated to answer these questions. Remember you got them at the outset to agree that they wanted you to surrender your beliefs and adopt theirs.

I can assure you that you will never get answers to questions like these. These questions demonstrate the finite non-biblical nature of the Mormon god. The finite gods of Mormonism cannot save anyone. The Mormon god is really just a big man who is surrounded by ultimate mystery and contingency in the universe. Since the Mormon worldview incorporates contingency or chance, it is possible that the Mormon god could literally become lost in space.

The Mormon worldview is unable to provide a coherent account for anything, due to its lack of absolute truth, which only the Christian worldview provides. The reader is encouraged to read the following philosophical critique of Mormon worldview problems by Francis Beckwith:

Philosophical Problems with the Mormon Concept of God, by Francis Beckwith at Christian Research Institute, Article ID: DM410 http://www.equip.org/articles/philosophical-problems-with-the-mormon-concept-of-god/

Don't let the Mormon use words like sovereignty, omnipresence, omniscience, and omnipotence. These words cannot be accurately used to describe a finite god. Make them define their use of words biblically. The Mormon will have to explain how a finite god with a body can have biblically defined attributes of deity applied to him. You can cite numerous Mormon leaders and scholars who have admitted that the Mormon deity has limitations in every one of the aforementioned divine attributes.

The Mormon's use and appeal to God's divine attributes is an emotional appeal or a smoke screen to throw you off track. We are trying to get Mormons to face the implications of their belief in a finite deity. We do this by pressing the antithesis or huge chasm between the Mormon and Christian world-views. As you talk with Mormons you will quickly experience numerous examples of Mormons asserting absolutes and omniscient statements within the framework of a system that does not allow absolutes. When Mormons, without biblical authority, asserts absolute or omniscient statements, they are indefensible.

In contrast, the Christian God is transcendent above and beyond creation and the creator of all things. The Christian God is not surrounded by mystery since He is the author, creator and controller of history and the space/time universe. The transcendence of God should be understood as being connected to His divine sovereignty. The transcendence of God means that He is above, different than, and separate from His creation.

The Christian God is also immanent. This means that God is within or near His creation. Immanence is intimately related to God's omnipresence, in that God is always present within the universe, though separate from it. God is within the universe and is its sustaining cause.

To argue for God's transcendence only and deny God's immanence leads to deism. On the other hand, to deny His transcendence and argue for His immanence leads to pantheism. Transcendence and immanence are terms that cannot in any way be applied to the Mormon finite deity.

In conclusion, are these questions just some kind of philosophical game? I would emphatically say, most certainly not. Elijah used questions like these to mock the false prophets of his day. Elijah said to the false prophets about their so-called god, "Is he asleep, or on a journey? Then wake him up."

Again, raising questions of this nature allows us to contrast the biblical doctrine of God with the Mormon finite deity. We are showing the antithesis between Mormonism and Christianity. By doing this we can more effectively challenge the Mormon to forsake his finite idols for the infinite God of Christianity who is holy and will judge all idolaters and has power to save those who put their faith in Him.

Again, I want to express my indebtedness to Alan Myatt, Ph.D., Adjunct Associate Professor of Theology and Missions at Gordon-Conwell Theological Seminary, for teaching me this method.

What is Presuppositionalism?

Worldview apologetics, or Presuppositionism, sets forth the biblical basis for Christianity by contrasting it with other worldviews and establishing its superiority. It points out and questions the inconsistencies and absurdities of alternative worldviews. It does this by using the *reductio ad absurdum* argument.

Let's consider Cornelius Van Til, one of the preeminent defenders of Presuppositionalism:

> The Reformed apologist throws down the gauntlet and challenges his opponent to a duel of life and death from the start. He does not first travel in the same direction and in the same automobile with the natural man for some distance in order then mildly to suggest to the driver that they ought perhaps to change their course somewhat and follow a road that goes at a different slant from the one they are on. The Reformed apologist knows that there is but one way to the truth and that the natural man is traveling it, but in the wrong direction.
>
> Cornelius Van Til, *The Defense of the Faith*, (Phillipsburg, New Jersey: Presbyterian & Reformed, 1955), p. 113.
>
> To engage in philosophical discussion does not mean that we begin without Scripture. We do not first defend theism philosophically by an appeal to reason and experience in order, after that, to turn to Scripture for our knowledge and defense of Christianity. We get our theism as well as our Christianity from the Bible. The Bible is thought of as authoritative on everything of which it speaks. And it speaks of everything.
>
> Cornelius Van Til, *The Defense of the Faith*, (Phillipsburg, New Jersey: Presbyterian & Reformed, 1955), p.

8.

If he (the unbeliever) is asked to use his reason as the judge of the credibility of the Christian revelation without at the same time being asked to renounce his view of himself as ultimate, then he is virtually asked to believe and to disbelieve in his own ultimacy at the same time and in the same sense.

Cornelius Van Til, *The Defense of the Faith*, ed. Scott Oliphint (Phillipsburg, New Jersey: Presbyterian & Reformed, 1955), p. 107.

Richard Pratt's explanation of a worldview apologetic will conclude the definition of Presuppositionalism:

Once the biblical defense has been given it is necessary to expose the fact that the non-Christian rejects the Christian evidence because of his commitment to independence. Every thought contrary to Christianity which the unbeliever has results from his desire to set himself up as the independent judge of truth. We live in a day when many non-Christians think they are neutral and objective. So, their basic commitment must be exposed. This can be done by a series of questions. If the Christian wishes to show the non-Christian that he has committed himself to independence he may simply assert that it is the case and then ask, "Why do you believe that?" or "How do you know that?" again and again until the point becomes obvious. The unbeliever thinks and believes as he does because he has determined it to be correct independently. For instance, the unbeliever may argue that the Christian God does not exist. When asked "Why?" he may say, "You have shown me no convincing evidence." When asked why he thinks the evidence is unconvincing, he will have to admit that the evidence does not meet with his independent criterion of truth. When asked why he accepts his criterion of truth he can be shown that it is the result of his own independent decision to look at things without submission to the Bible and to God.

By exposing the commitment of the unbeliever, the Christian reveals the truth that all men have either chosen for Christ or against Him. The line of division is clearly drawn and the door is opened for demonstrating the hopelessness of the non-Christian way of thinking.

Richard L. Pratt Jr., *Every Thought Captive*, (Phillipsburg, New Jersey: Presbyterian & Reformed, 1979), p. 91.

A theologian's epistemology controls his interpretation of the Bible. If his epistemology is not Christian, his exegesis will be systematically distorted. If he has no epistemology at all, his exegesis will be unsystematically distorted.

Gordon H. Clark, *The Incarnation*, (Jefferson, Maryland: The Trinity Foundation, 1988), pp. 46-47.

The Christian can say, if you start with a non-Christian syllogism or presupposition, you will never arrive at a Christian conclusion. All non-believing assumptions ultimately lead to skepticism. Fallen man cannot live consistently with the end result of where his worldview takes him. This is why a presuppositional apologetic argues that the beliefs of non-Christians force them to borrow from and believe certain things about the world, which in reality they have stolen from the Christian worldview.

Biblically speaking, holding philosophical beliefs that contain internally self-refuting contradictions is an expression of irrationalism. It can also be a case of inexcusable ignorance. Ultimately, all non-Christian philosophy starts with bold rationalistic assertions about reality and ends up in irrationalism.

As Christians we have a coherent theory of knowledge. God has spoken. This is certain: God speaks to us in the Scriptures with human language utilizing logically structured sentences in which He tells us the difference between right and wrong. In fact, and because of this, presuppositionalists argue that Christianity is true because of the impossibility of the contrary.

SCRIPTURE PASSAGES TO USE
IN WITNESSING ENCOUNTERS WITH MORMONS

God is omnipotent (all powerful):

> In the beginning God created the heaven and the earth. (Genesis 1:1)

> I know that thou canst do every thing, and that no thought can be withholden from thee. (Job 42:2)

> The heavens declare the glory of God; and the firmament sheweth his handiwork. (Psalms 19:1)

> These things hast thou done, and I kept silence; thou thoughtest that I was altogether such an one as thyself: but I will reprove thee, and set them in order before thine eyes. (Psalms 50:21)

> Before the mountains were brought forth, or ever thou hadst formed the earth and the world, even from everlasting to everlasting thou art God. (Psalms 90:2)

For all the gods of the nations are idols: but the Lord made the heavens. (Psalms 96:5)

They shall perish, but thou shalt endure: yea all of them shall wax old like a garment; as a vesture shalt thou change them, and they shall be changed: But thou art the same, and thy years shall have no end. (Psalms 102:26-27)

Ah Lord God! behold, thou hast made the heaven and the earth by thy great power and stretched out arm, and there is nothing too hard for thee. (Jeremiah 32:17)

I will not execute the fierceness of mine anger, I will not return to destroy Ephraim: for I am God, and not man; the Holy One in the midst of thee: and I will not enter the city. (Hosea 11:9)

For I am the LORD, I change not; therefore ye sons of Jacob are not consumed. (Malachi 3:6)

But Jesus beheld them, and said unto them, With men this is impossible; but with God all things are possible. (Matthew 19:26)

And Jesus looking upon them saith, With men it is impossible, but not with God: for with God all things are possible. (Mark 10:27)

All things were made by him; and without him was not any thing made that was made. (John 1:3)

I am Alpha and Omega, the beginning and the ending, saith the Lord, which is, and which was, and which is to come, the Almighty. (Revelation 1:8)

And I heard as it were the voice of a great multitude, and as the voice of many waters, and as the voice of mighty thunderings, saying, Alleluia: for the Lord God omnipotent reigneth. (Revelation 19:6)

God is omnipresent (everywhere present):

But will God in very deed dwell with men on the earth? Behold, heaven and the heaven of heavens cannot contain thee: how much less this house which I have built! (2 Chronicles 6:18)

Where can I go from Your Spirit? Or where can I flee from Your presence? If I ascend into heaven, You are there; if I make my bed in hell, behold, You are there. If I take the wings of the morning, and dwell in the uttermost parts of the sea, even there Your hand shall lead me, and Your right hand shall hold me. (Psalm 139:7–10)

Thus saith the LORD, The heaven is my throne, and the earth is my footstool: where is the house that ye build unto me? And where is the place of my rest? (Isaiah 66:1)

Can any hide himself in secret places that I shall not see him? saith the LORD. Do not I fill heaven and earth? (Jeremiah 23:24)

Though they dig into hell, thence shall mine hand take them; though they climb up to heaven, thence will I bring them down. (Amos 9:2)

God is omniscient (all knowing):

Great is our Lord, and of great power: his understanding is infinite. (Psalms 147:5)

The eyes of the LORD are in every place, behold-ing the evil and the good. (Proverbs 15:3)

Are not two sparrows sold for a farthing? And one of them shall not fall on the ground without your Father. But the very hairs of your head are all num-bered. (Matthew 10:29, 30)

Neither is there any creature that is not manifest in his sight: but all things are naked and opened unto the eyes of him with whom we have to do. (Hebrews 4:13)

God is transcendent:

For my thoughts are not your thoughts, neither are your ways my ways, declares the LORD. As the heavens are higher than the earth, so are my ways higher than your ways and my thoughts than your thoughts. (Isaiah 55:8-9)

God is immanent:

God that made the world and all things therein, seeing that he is Lord of heaven and earth, dwel-leth not in temples made with hands; Neither is worshipped with men's hands, as though he need-ed any thing, seeing he giveth to all life, and breath, and all things; And hath made of one blood all nations of men for to dwell on all the face of the earth, and hath determined the times before appointed, and the bounds of their habitation; That they should seek the Lord, if haply they might feel after him, and find him, though he be not far from every one of us: For in him we live, and move, and have our being; as certain also of your own poets have said, For we are also his offspring. (Acts 17:24-28)

There is only one God:

Who hath wrought and done it, calling the generations from the beginning? I the LORD, the first, and with the last; I am he. (Isaiah 41:4)

Ye are my witnesses, saith the LORD, and my servant whom I have chosen: that ye may know and believe me, and understand that I am he: before me there was no God formed, neither shall there be after me. (Isaiah 43:10)

I am the first, and I am the last; and beside me there is no God. (Isaiah 44:6)

I am the LORD , and there is none else, there is no God beside me: I girded thee, though thou hast not known me: That they may know from the rising of the sun, and from the west, that there is none beside me, I am the LORD, and there is none else. (Isaiah 45:5-6)

FOOD FOR THOUGHT

Paul infallibly declares in Colossians 2:3-8 that "all the treasures of wisdom and knowledge are hid in Christ." Note that he says all wisdom and knowledge is deposited in the person of Christ - whether it be about the war of 1812, water's chemical composition, the literature of Shakespeare, or the laws of logic! Every academic pursuit and every thought must be related to Jesus Christ, for Jesus is the way, the truth, and the life. (John 14:6) To avoid Christ in your thought at any point, then, is to be misled, untruthful, and spiritually dead. To put aside your Christian commitments when it comes to defending the faith or sending your children to school is willfully to steer away from the only path to wisdom and truth found in Christ. It is not the end or outcome of knowledge to fear the Lord; it is the beginning of knowledge reverence Him (Proverbs 1:7-9). - Greg L. Bahnsen in *Always Ready.*

PART IV

A HOUSE DIVIDED

Food for Thought:

God is thus the principle of definition, of law, and of all things. He is the premise of all thinking, and the necessary presupposition for every sphere of thought. It is blasphemy therefore to attempt to "prove" God; God is the necessary presupposition of all proof. To ground any sphere of thought, life, or action, or any sphere of being, on anything other than the triune God is thus blasphemy. Education without God as its premise, law which does not presuppose God and rest on His law, a civil order which does not derive all authority from God, or a family whose foundation is not God's word, is blasphemous. - R.J. Rushdoony, The Institutes of Biblical Law

CHAPTER 13

INSURMOUNTABLE PROBLEMS WITH THE MORMON RELIGION: AN OVERVIEW

or the purpose of this overview, the term Mormonism should be understood as the umbrella under which all the followers of Joseph Smith and the *Book of Mormon* can be grouped or classified. Joseph Smith was the founder of the Mormon religion. However, there are many competing factions within the Mormon religion. The term Mormonism encompasses the Utah Mormon Church as well as the Reorganized Church of Jesus Christ of Latter Day Saints, now called The Community of Christ, the Church of Christ Temple Lot, the polygamous Kingston, and Mexican *Bautista* groups, to name a few. Mormonism is a biblical imitation religion. It claims that God gave revelation along with prophecies and miraculous events to authenticate this new revelation.

THE FIRST VISION

The Mormon religion stands or falls with Joseph Smith. If Smith was a charlatan, then the Mormon religion is fraudulent and nothing more than an elaborate fabrication. The foundation event for Mormonism is its "first vision" story. This is where Smith claimed he encountered a heavenly visitation that would alter his life. First of all, did this happen? What was the message Smith supposedly received during this vision? Smith claimed that God the Father and Jesus Christ both in bodily form appeared to him in bodily form.

This was what the heavenly beings reportedly told him:

> I was born in the year of our Lord one thousand
> eight hundred and five...[Smith was fourteen] ...I
> saw <u>two personages</u>, whose brightness and glory
> defy all description, standing above me in the air.
> One of them spake unto me by name and said,

pointing to the other-This is My Beloved Son. Hear Him! My object in going to inquire of the Lord was to know which of all the sects was right, that I might know which to join. No sooner, therefore, did I get possession of myself, so as to be able to speak, than I asked the Personages who stood above me in the light, which of all the sects was right-and which I should join. I was answered that I must join none of them, [all existing churches] for they were all wrong; and the Personage who addressed me said that all their creeds were an abomination in his sight; that those professors were all corrupt; that: they draw near to me with their lips, but their hearts are far from me, they teach for doctrine the commandments of men, having a form of godliness, but they deny the power thereof.

Joseph Smith, *Pearl Of Great Price* pp. 46, 48.

With one swipe Smith's two deities labeled all of Christianity apostate. There are numerous problems with this story. To begin with, it contradicts Scripture. The gospel in John 1:18 and 1st Timothy 6:16 makes it clear that men do not see God the Father, only the Son does. (John 1:18, "No man hath seen God at any time; the only begotten Son, which is in the bosom of the Father, he hath declared him." 1st Timothy 6:15b-16 "...the blessed and only Potentate, the King of kings, and Lord of lords; Who only hath immortality, dwelling in the light which no man can approach unto; whom no man hath seen, nor can see: to whom be honour and power everlasting. Amen.)

The setting of this "first vision" story was in Palmyra, New York in 1820. According to Smith, in 1820 there was a great religious revival in the Palmyra area. The events surrounding this revival caused the young fourteen-year old Smith to go into the woods and ask God in prayer, which of the churches he should join. He then encountered a heavenly visitation in answer to his prayer. Smith's 1820 revival started through the work of Rev. Lane, a Methodist, and Rev. Stockton, a Presbyterian. Is this accurate? The records from both denominations make it clear that neither Rev. Lane nor Rev. Stockton were assigned to the Palmyra area until 1824. Denominational church records actually show membership losses in 1820. For an excellent in-depth study of this first vision story, see the book: *Inventing Mormonism Tradition And The Historical Record.* *

*H. Michael Marquardt & Wesley P. Walters, *Inventing Mormonism Tradition And The Historical Record* (Salt Lake City: Smith Research Associates, 1994), pp. 15-41.

On September 21, 1823, Smith was supposedly having another heavenly visit from the angel Nephi. This second vision was to inform Joseph Smith about the existence of golden plates, which contained the record of people who once lived on this continent. Smith was to eventually gain temporary custody of these plates in order to make a translation of the record contained on them. Regarding the name of the angel a Mormon would say, "The name of the angel is not Nephi, its Moroni."

According to the original 1851 edition of the *Pearl of Great Price* * (one of the four standard works of the Mormon Church) Nephi was the name of this angel who appeared to Smith at this time. *Joseph Smith, *Pearl Of Great Price* (Salt Lake City: Modern Microfilm Company, A photo reprint of the Original 1851 edition), p. 41.

In the biography by Joseph Smith's mother titled *Biographical sketches of Joseph Smith The Prophet and His Progenitors for many Generations* * we find another source that identifies this angel as Nephi. *Jerald & Sandra Tanner, *Joseph Smith's History By His Mother* (Salt Lake City: Modern Microfilm Company, A photo-mechanical Reprint of the Original 1853 edition), p. 79.

This belief that Nephi was the angel is recorded in Smith's mother's book. Now Moroni is the angel with officially approved status as of 1889. Moroni will probably never be debunked, in light of the fact that there are too many golden replicas of the angel Moroni on Mormon temples around the world. In light of this contradiction of which angel appeared, the whole first vision story is called into question.

Back to the "first vision story;" another insurmountable problem with this story is getting it straight.

One account, told by Brigham Young was as follows:

> The Lord did not come... But He did send His angel to this same obscure person, Joseph Smith jun., who afterwards became a Prophet, Seer, and Revelator, and informed him that he should not join any of the religious sects of the day, for they

were all wrong.

Joseph Smith, *Journal of Discourses* Vol. 2, p. 171.

In Young's version only one personage appeared. The message given makes it clear that the "first vision" account is being spoken of. Another version of this account goes like this:

> The Lord heard my cry in the wilderness and while
> in the attitude of calling upon the Lord in the 16th
> year of my age a piller of light above the brightness
> of the sun at noon day comes down from above
> and rested upon me and I was filled with the spirit
> of god and the Lord opened the heavens upon me
> and I saw the Lord and he spake unto me saying
> Joseph my son thy sins are forgiven thee...
>
> Cited in *The Changing World Of Mormonism* pp.
> 152, 153, Joseph Smith, *Brigham Young University
> Studie*, (Provo: Spring 1969), p. 281.

According to this version, Smith was sixteen instead of fourteen, and only one person appeared instead of the two in today's official version. Also, nothing is said about not joining the ostensibly apostate churches. What is significant is that this account is the earliest known version of the "first vision" and it is written in Smith's own handwriting. There are numerous accounts of this story that are radically different from one another. The accounts vary in regard to who appeared, what the message was, how old Smith was, and the historical setting. Because of these different contradictory accounts it is an inescapable conclusion that this whole story was made up by Smith and evolved into the present official version which has no basis in reality. Biblically speaking, this first vision account is a violation of the ninth commandment, (Exodus 20:16) because it is a case where an organization is speaking official lies or the bearing of a false witness. The Scriptures clearly say, "You shall not circulate a false report." (Exodus 23:1)

Besides these contradictory versions, a more fundamental problem exists for this story. What was Smith doing after having received these earth-shattering visions? Was he preparing himself by becoming a godly individual to receive the golden plates? You would think that this was what Smith would have or should have been doing. What was he really doing?

SMITH AND DIVINE GIFTS

On March 20, 1826, just three years after his alleged second heavenly visitation, Smith was convicted in court in the state of New York for tricking people into giving him money in exchange for his services to locate golden treasures that were supposedly buried in the earth. Smith was convicted as a "glass-looker" in the town of South Bainbridge, NY.* Judge Albert Neely presided over this trial. Smith was convicted and fined, and asked to leave the county. It was revealed in the trial that Smith would use a magic peep-stone as a device to locate buried treasure. *H. Michael Marquardt & Wesley P. Walters, *Inventing Mormonism Tradition And The Historical Record* (Salt Lake City: Smith Research Associates, 1994), pp. 63-87.

How was this done? Smith would place his peep-stone in his hat and then place his face into the hat blocking out all light. The peep-stone would then show where the buried treasure was located. Unfortunately for those who paid, when Smith's peep-stone identified the location where the treasure was buried, the diggers could never reach it. Smith would claim that a special magical enchantment would cause the treasure to sink deeper into the earth. Smith's gold treasures-hunting never produced anything of lasting interest except a criminal record.

It is interesting to note that Smith also used a peep-stone in his hat when translating the *Book of Mormon* from the mysterious gold plates. Smith claimed that as a prophet he had the power of revelator and translator.

David Whitmer, one of the three witnesses listed inside the cover to the *Book of Mormon*, explains the translation method of the *Book of Mormon* like this:

> I will now give you a description of the manner in which the Book of Mormon was translated. Joseph would put the seer stone into a hat, and put his face in the hat, drawing it closely around his face to exclude light; and in the darkness the spiritual light would shine. A piece of something resembling parchment would appear, and on that appeared the writing.
>
> David Whitmer, *An Address To All Believers In Christ* (Richmond, Missouri: 1887, reprinted by Pacific Publishing Company, 1959), p. 12.

This is not a translation; it is an example of a spiritualist medium, or someone who has a familiar spirit. This activity is expressly forbidden in Leviticus 20:27. Along this same line, consider some additional incriminating evidence about Smith.

According to the *Book of Commandments,* now called the *Doctrine And Covenants,* we learn of another gift that Smith allegedly possessed:

> Now this is not all, for you have another gift, which is the gift of working with the rod: behold it has told you things: behold there is no other power save God, that can cause this rod of nature, to work in your hands.
>
> Joseph Smith, *Book of Commandments* Chapter 7:3 (Zion, Missouri: W.W. Phelps & Co. reprinted by Wilford C. Wood, Publisher 1962), p. 19.

This embarrassment of working with a spiritualist divining rod has been deleted from the modern *Doctrine and Covenants*. If these examples of superstitious magic were not enough, consider Smith's magic Jupiter's talisman. Dr. Reed Durham, director of the LDS Institute of Religion at the University of Utah, explains Smith's use of his talisman in a lecture given to the Mormon History Association on April 20, 1974. The information given in this lecture is devastating to the adherents of Mormonism. It proves that Smith was an occult practitioner.

This is a portion of the lecture given by Dr. Reed:

> ...I should like to initiate all of you into what is perhaps the strangest, the most mysterious, occult-like esoteric, and yet Masonically oriented practice ever adopted by Joseph Smith.... All available evidence suggests that Joseph Smith the Prophet possessed a magical Masonic medallion, or talisman, which he worked during his lifetime and which was evidently on his person when he was martyred....His talisman is in the shape of a silver dollar and is probably made of silver or tin....[this talisman] can now be identified as a Jupiter talisman....

> When properly invoked, with Jupiter being very powerful and ruling in the heavens, these intelligences by <u>the power of ancient magic</u> guaranteed to the possessor of this talisman the gain or riches, and favor, and power, and love and peace; and to confirm honors, and dignities, and councils. Talismatic magic further declared that anyone who worked skillfully with this Jupiter Table would obtain the power of stimulating anyone to offer his love to the possessor of the talisman whether from a friend, brother, relative, or <u>even any female</u>.
>
> Cited in *The Changing World Of Mormonism* pp. 89, 90, *Mormon Miscellaneous* published by David C. Martin, Vol. 1, Number 1, October 1975, pp. 14-15.

This talisman supposedly gave Smith tremendous influence over people. See pictures of Smith's court record and his talisman inside the back cover.

The book *Early Mormonism and the Magic World View* by former Brigham Young University (BYU) professor Dr. D. Michael Quinn provides evidence that some of Smith's key distinctive doctrinal concepts were plagiarized from the Jewish Cabala. The Jewish Cabala is an occultist system of magic. Smith's King Follett funeral sermon in particular is an example where ideas were borrowed that have become distinctive or defining concepts of Utah Mormonism.

Some peculiar concepts that were plagiarized by Smith are:

1. A head God calling a council of the other gods for the purpose of creating the world

2. Smith's belief in the plurality of gods

3. That God is corporeal or has a human form

4. Smith's rejection of the Hebrew Christian belief in the creation of the world by God *ex nihilo*.

These and other ideas are seemingly taken from Eisenmenger's *Traditions of the Jews* 1748, and John Allen's 1816 *Modern Judaism*.* The book by Eisenmenger is an example of Jewish cabalistic occultism.

*D. Michael Quinn, *Early Mormonism and the Magic World View*, (Salt Lake City: Signature Books, 1998), pp. 296-306.

Dr. Quinn provides pictures of some of the Smith family's collection of magic and occultic parchments and artifacts.* For example, Smith's dagger was inscribed on the blade towards the hilt with Scorpio's astrological symbol along with the magic symbol for the "Intelligence of Mars." Astrologically, Mars was the ruling planet of Joseph Smith's father.

*D. Michael Quinn, *Early Mormonism and the Magic World View* (Salt Lake City: Signature Books, 1998), figures 43, 50, 51, 52, 53, 55-59.

SMITH AND MASONRY

We must make a necessary digression to set the stage for the further evaluation of Smith and his work. First of all, we should know that the Scriptures forbid us to join secret religious societies where allegiance is pledged to a source other than the God of Holy Scripture. Is it acceptable for Christians to join Freemasonry?

Dr. Albert G. Mackey the author of the *Encyclopedia of Freemasonry* declares on pages 618 and 619 of this work:

> I contend, without any sort of hesitation, that Masonry is, in every sense of the word... an eminently religious institution....The religion of Masonry is not sectarian. It admits men of every creed within its hospitable bosom, rejecting none and approving none for his peculiar faith. It is not Judaism...it is not Christianity.
>
> Cited in Alva J. McClain, *Freemasonry and Christianity* (Winona Lake, Indiana: BMH Books, 1983), p. 9.

Dr. Mackey accuses Christianity of being sectarian in the above quote. It should be noted that Dr. Mackey says that Masonry is a religion and that "it is not Christianity."

In addition, Dr. Mackey says on page 439 of his encyclopedia that:

> If Masonry were simply a Christian institution, the Jew and the Moslem, the Brahman and the Buddhist could not conscientiously partake of its illumination, but its universality is its boast. In its language, citizens of every nation may converse; at its altar men of all religions may kneel; to its creed, disciples of every faith may subscribe.
>
> McClain, *Freemasonry and Christianity* p. 439.

We should especially notice that members of Masonry "partake of its illumination," "converse at its altar," and "kneel to its creed." This is clearly religious terminology. It is also noteworthy that this religion boasts of its universality. These ideals of Freemasonry are foreign and completely antithetical to Christianity. The Christian can kneel at no foreign altar and remain faithful to Christ.

Paul in 2 Corinthians 6:14-15 warns the believer "Do not be unequally yoked together with unbelievers. For what fellowship has righteousness with lawlessness? And what communion has light with darkness? And what accord has Christ with Belial? Or what part has a believer with an unbeliever?" Should Christians be involved in a religion other than Christianity? Of course not! In Galatians 1:8-9 Paul tells us that the curse of God is upon false religions that promote false gospels.

Did Smith regard these teachings of Scripture? No! Smith joined the Masonic Lodge in 1842. Masonic rituals were a major source of influence in the development of Mormon temple ceremony. Mormonism shows the unmistakable influence of Masonry in its temple architecture. Some similarities are the sun, moon and stars, the two right hands clasped in fellowship, the All-seeing eye, and the beehive. Mormons use secret handshakes like the Masons. Mormon temple rituals parallel Masonic rites in a number of areas.*

*Jerald & Sandra Tanner, *The Changing World Of Mormonism* (Chicago: Moody Press, 1981), pp. 536-547.

> The capstone for the temple that the Mormons were going to build in Nauvoo, Illinois was a picture of Baal as the Sun face with its extending rays.

> When Smith was killed in Illinois, he gave the
> Masonic signal of distress. Smith raised his hands
> and arms to the elbows, perpendicularly, one on
> each side of the head, the elbows, forming a square.
> The words accompanying this sign, in case of dis-
> tress, are, "O Lord my God! Is there no help for the
> widow's son?*

> *Jerald & Sandra Tanner, *Mormonism, Magic and
> Masonry* (Salt Lake City: Utah Lighthouse Ministry,
> 1983), p. 52.

This is clear evidence that Smith did not trust in God, but rather the flesh. Considering Smith's heavy involvement with magic, this may have been essentially a magic incantation on his part for deliverance. If so, then this is another example of occultism. Occultism is clearly condemned in Deuteronomy 18:9-14, and Galatians 5:19-21.

Amazingly, the *Book of Mormon* claims to have a familiar spirit:

> For those who shall be destroyed shall speak unto
> them out of the ground, and their speech shall be
> low out of the dust, and their voice shall be as one
> that hath a familiar spirit....For thus saith the Lord
> God: They shall write the things which shall be
> done among them, and they shall be written and
> sealed up in a book,...

> Joseph Smith, *Book of Mormon* pp. 93-94.

This speech from the dust will be written in a book, which will be the *Book of Mormon*. A familiar spirit is a demonic spirit. The Scriptures warn us against familiar spirits in Leviticus 19:31; 20:6; 2 Kings 21:6; 1 Chronicles 10:13-14; 2 Chronicles 33:6; and Isaiah 19:3.

SMITH THE TRANSLATOR

In 1835, Joseph Smith acquired some Egyptian papyrus writing from a man named Michael Chandler in Kirtland, Ohio. To the excitement of the Mormons, Smith announced that this Egyptian papyrus contained the writing of Abraham in Egypt. At this time, Egyptian as a language was little understood, so Smith was relatively safe in making his assertions. Who could double-check him? It is interesting to note that with the passage of time, men like Smith are exposed. Smith claimed to have translated this papyrus, which in reality was an Egyptian funeral document for a man named Hor. In addition to this translation, Smith produced his own Egyptian alphabet and grammar. His alphabet and grammar have no relationship to any accepted or known meaning of Egyptian hieroglyphics. This spurious alphabet and grammar are an on-going source of embarrassment for members of the various Mormon religious groups. The Mormons lost the original Egyptian papyrus, which Smith claimed to have translated. As a result, Mormons would not accept criticism of Smith's translation, which was published in their *Pearl of Great Price.*

Incredibly, this papyrus turned up in the Metropolitan Museum of Art in New York City in 1967. A number of prominent Egyptologists have looked at this document and stated conclusively that it has nothing to do with Abraham in Egypt. The correct English translation of this funeral document yields ninety words. Smith's translation yielded over 2,000 English words about Abraham in Egypt. Smith did not even get one word right in his whole preposterous translation. Charles Larson's book *…by his own hand upon papyrus,* is a serious scholarly work in which Smith's fraudulent claim to be a translator of Egyptian hieroglyphics is debunked.

*Charles M. Larson, *…by his own hand upon papyrus*, (Grand Rapids, Michigan: Institute for Religious Research, 1992).

After realizing a golden opportunity, nine citizens of Kinderhook, Illinois certified that a man named R. Wiley had unearthed some mysterious plates with what appeared to be ancient writing on them from a large mound. The plates were brought to Smith in 1843 who announced that he could read the writing on them. He was soon "busy in translating them." Unfortunately for Smith, these plates were a forgery intended to trap him. Smith actually began to translate these plates. This is how he described his work:

> I have translated a portion of them, and find they
> contain the history of the person with whom they

> were found. He was a descendant of Ham, through
> the loins of Pharaoh, king of Egypt.

Joseph Smith, *History of the Church* Vol. 5, p. 372.

Smith died in a blazing gun battle in June of 1844 so we never will see the completed translation. The plates had ancient looking forged characters but said nothing. Like other embarrassing endeavors of Smith, the Mormon Church has swept this episode under the rug. Commenting on Smith's work as a translator, a man named Charles A. Shook observed: "Only a bogus prophet translates bogus plates."*

*Jerald & Sandra Tanner, Archeology *and the Book of Mormon* (Salt Lake City: Modern Microfilm Company, 1969), p. 31.

In the *Book of Mormon*, Smith said the following:

> I told the brethren that the Book of Mormon was
> the most correct of any book on earth, and the key-
> stone of our religion, and a man would get nearer to
> God by abiding by its precepts, <u>than any other book.</u>

Joseph Smith, *History of the Church* Vol. 4, p. 461.

If this was true about the *Book of Mormon*, why have there been over four thousand changes and corrections made in it since its publication in 1830? Significantly, some of these changes involved doctrinal changes. As stated earlier the Mormon religion stands or falls with Joseph Smith. What can be said about the reliability and truthfulness of the *Book of Mormon*? Not anything in the opinion of this writer!

As was seen, Smith's abilities as a translator of ancient documents were duplicitous. If Smith was a fraud, certainly his book must be called into question. Does the *Book of Mormon* show evidence of divine or human authorship? These are some questions to keep in mind as we begin to evaluate Joseph Smith's book. Mormons reject the idea that Joseph Smith wrote the *Book of Mormon*. Yet, inside the original 1830 edition of the *Book of Mormon* Joseph Smith is listed as the author.

In 1831, Alexander Campbell, in a publication called the *Millennial Harbinger* on page 93, wrote an assessment of the *Book of Mormon* that is highly perceptive.

His assessment, while brief, is devastating:

> This prophet Smith through his stone spectacles
> wrote on the plates of Nephi, in his Book of Mor-
> mon every error, and almost every truth discussed
> in New York for the last ten years. He decides all
> the great controversies;-infant baptism, ordination,
> the Trinity, regeneration, repentance, justification,
> the fall of man, atonement, fasting, penance, and
> even the question of Freemasonry, republican gov-
> ernment, and the rights of man.
>
> Cited in Jerald & Sandra Tanner, *The Changing World
> of Mormonism* (Chicago: Moody Press, 1981), p. 111.

This makes the *Book of Mormon* highly suspect. To believe that an ancient document would examine and decide all the religious controversies in nineteenth century New York is not only laugh-
able it is ludicrous.

The three witnesses
to the *Book of Mormon's*
authenticity

After Smith translated the golden plates, the angel Moroni or Nephi took the plates back. So
there is really no way to verify if there were any golden plates. Inside the front cover of the *Book
of Mormon* there are three witnesses listed, Martin Harris, Oliver Cowdery, and David Whitmer.
Since there are no golden plates to examine we are left with the word of these three men. Is their
word reliable? What did Smith think?

All three of these witnesses fell into apostasy with regards to their membership in the Mormon
Church. Smith called David Whitmer "a dumb ass."*

*Joseph Smith, *History of the Church* Vol. 3, p. 228.

Smith claimed in a letter, which is recorded in his *History of the Church* that such characters as "...

David Whitmer, Oliver Cowdery, and Martin Harris are to mean to mention; and we had liked to have forgotten them."*

*Joseph Smith, *History of the Church* Vol. 3, p. 232.

That about sums it up for the credibility of the three witnesses.

Why did the angel take the golden plates back to heaven? Smith did not say. If the Mormon Church had the plates today, it would be a powerful piece of evidence for the truthfulness of their religion. Since the plates are gone, exegetical work is absolutely impossible.

THE BIBLE AND
THE *BOOK OF MORMON*

The *Book of Mormon* was published in 1830. This book was supposedly translated from gold plates containing writings in Reformed Egyptian hieroglyphics of the Jewish people in the Old World. The *Book of Mormon* record was engraved on golden plates, relating events that were supposed to have happened between 600 BC and 33 AD. It is important to note that the King James Version was published in 1611. There are over four hundred parallels in the *Book of Mormon*'s Old Testament section where verses from the 1611 New Testament King James Version are copied or plagiarized.*

*Jerald & Sandra Tanner, *The Changing World of Mormonism* (Chicago: Moody Press, 1981), pp. 116-124.

Mark Twain even commented on the *Book of Mormon*'s plagiarism of biblical material on page 110 of his book *Roughing It*.

Mark Twain said that the *Book Of Mormon*:

> Seems to be merely a prosy detail of imaginary history, with the Old Testament for a model; followed by a tedious plagiarism of the New Testament.
>
> Cited in Jerald & Sandra Tanner, *The Changing World of Mormonism* (Chicago: Moody Press, 1981), p. 116.

A translation of ancient Egyptian or Semitic writing made during the 1800's would not translate into and read like seventeenth century Elizabethan English.

In "Mosiah" chapter fourteen in the *Book of Mormon*, Isaiah chapter fifty-three is copied word for word, including the italicized words that the King James translators added for clarity! There are sixteen italicized words from the King James Bible in "Mosiah" fourteen.*

*See Joseph Smith's plagiarism from Isaiah in, *Book Of Mormon* pp. 162, 163.

The list of italicized words are <u>and</u> (three times), <u>there is</u>, <u>our</u>, <u>was</u> (twice), <u>he was</u>, <u>was any</u>, <u>his</u> (twice), <u>a portion (once)</u>. How did these italicized words from a 1611 translation get into a document that was supposedly written before the time of Christ? The answer is obvious: Smith copied them when plagiarizing the King James translation of the prophet Isaiah.

Linguistic
AND HISTORICAL PROBLEMS

Listed below is a brief summary of some significant problems contained in the *Book of Mormon*. Utah Mormon Apostle B. H. Roberts discovered a number of serious linguistic, anthropological, cultural, and historical problems in the *Book of Mormon* during the earlier part of this century. A manuscript by Roberts outlining these problems was published by the Tanners.*

*Jerald & Sandra Tanner, *Roberts Manuscript Revealed: A photographic reproduction of Mormon Historian B.H. Roberts,* Secret *Studies on the Book of Mormon* (Salt Lake City: Modern Microfilm Company, 1980).

Since Roberts, a Mormon, first identified them, these problems all the more significant. After considering these problems and many others not dealt with below, he concluded that the *Book of Mormon* showed evidence in numerous places that it was the product of an underdeveloped mind. I have tried to summarize just a few of the multitudinous problems that Roberts noticed, pertinent to the credibility of the *Book Of Mormon,* from the manuscript published by the Tanners.

In 600 B.C. a small group of Nephites from Jerusalem come to the New World to establish a colony. Centuries earlier, the Jaredites had come from the Old World. This Jaredite civilization left no evidence of their existence aside from twenty-four plates that contained their history.

The time frame of *Book of Mormon* peoples in the New World is from 600 B.C. to 420 A.D.

The *Book of Mormon* represents the Nephites and the Lamanites (peoples who broke away from the Nephites and became sinful and subsequently were punished with dark skin) as having written correspondence in the Hebrew language until the time of the Nephite destruction in 420 A.D. by the Lamanites. The Lamanites were the ancestors of the American Indians.

The *Book of Mormon* represents these peoples as inhabiting all of North, Central, and South America. These inhabitants all spoke and wrote in the Hebrew language, except for the Nephite's religious history. This was written in Reformed Egyptian Hieroglyphics.

The Europeans came to the New World beginning in 1492.

This means that all linguistic development, including the primitive forms of language found in the Americas, must be accounted for between 420 A.D. and the arrival of the Europeans 1000 years later or by assuming some sort of massive migrations to the New World during this same time period. There is no evidence of extensive migrations of this nature.

In North, Central, and South America by the early 19th century linguists had identified over 169 different language stocks that show very little common relationship to each other, no more than between English and German.

The New World languages show no relationship to the Old World languages.

The development of the different language stocks and their accompanying dialects could not possibly have arisen during this 1000-year period from a single form of Hebrew.

How does one derive these 169 language stocks from a single form of Hebrew that existed as late as 420 A.D.? The Mormon has no answers for these questions.

ANTHROPOLOGICAL
AND CULTURAL PROBLEMS:

Anthropologists have shown evidence that demands a great antiquity or length of time for man in America. The *Book of Mormon* has the Nephites coming fairly recently to the Americas that had never been inhabited except for the previous Jaredites.

The Nephites had an iron and steel age culture.

When the Europeans came to the Americas, the Indians were no further developed than the polished Stone Age.

The *Book of Mormon* has a culture of peoples who had wheels, glass windows with glazing, steel for swords, and oars for sea going vessels.

The *Book of Mormon* has animal husbandry that included elephants, horses, cows, oxen, asses, and sheep. Agriculturally among the *Book of Mormon* peoples, there was ostensibly silk, wheat, barley, corn, and grapes. However, the Europeans introduced the agriculture and animal husbandry that the *Book of Mormon* assumes to have existed prior to 1420.

Therefore, the cultural picture given in the *Book of Mormon* is invalidated when compared to known archaeological and historical research. In addition, amateur Mormon archaeologists have attempted to mislead the public concerning the ruins of the Aztec and Inca civilizations. *Book of Mormon* archaeological tours routinely take trips to the Aztec ruins in Mexico and Central America, leaving the impression that these were in reality Mormon civilizations. By contrast, non-religious and scientific groups have sought to distance themselves from any association with the religion. Consider this official statement from the Smithsonian. "The Smithsonian Institution has never used the *Book of Mormon* in any way as a scientific guide. Smithsonian archaeologists see no direct connection between the archeology of the New World and the subject matter of the book."*

*National Museum of Natural History Smithsonian Institution, (Washington, D.C. "Press Statement", 1982), p. 1.

THE *BOOK OF MORMON*:
EVIDENCE OF A HUMAN AUTHOR –
REPETITION, CONTRADICTIONS AND ABSURDITIES

There is a lack of coherent perspective regarding the information that the *Book of Mormon* represents as history. This points quite clearly to an uneducated mind as its origin.

The book proceeds in characteristic disregard of conditions necessary to its reasonableness. Numerous parallels and repetitions evidence this. The same stories are told over and over again, the only difference being the characters.

Both the Nephites and earlier Jaradites colonies had identical stories. Both colonies came to an uninhabited continent and then populated all of the Americas numbering in the millions. Both colonies ultimately had wars of annihilation at the hill Cummorah (upstate New York).

Both colonies came to the New World on the same types of submerged barges. Could these barges have carried elephants and horses? Both stories stress the smallness and lightness of the barges.

There is an utter disregard for consistency in the story of the Nephites building a temple like Solomon's temple (2 Nephi 5:15-16). Verse fifteen says the temple was built with precious metals because there was much to be found in the land. Verse sixteen says the temple did not have all the precious metals because there was none to be found upon the land. The Nephite colony only had one hundred people. How could they build a temple like Solomon's?

There are super miraculous events in battles that strain the credibility of the story.

Absurdities of expression, lapses of mind, speech lapses, and serious grammatical problems are common. Here are just a few examples:

Nephi, a Jew living all his life in Jerusalem, keeps a sacred religious record in the Egyptian language (1 Nephi 1:2). Nephi's father, Lehi, was a devout Jew who lived in Jerusalem and his spoken language was Egyptian (1 Nephi 1:2). This is historically and linguistically unlikely. In 1 Nephi 7:6 there is an individual named Sam, not Samuel. Is this a Hebrew or Yankee name? Jacob 7:27 ends with the French word *adieu*. In 3 Nephi 9:18 supposedly written in Reformed Egyptian you find the Greek words *Alpha* and *Omega*. Alma 7:10 has Jesus being born in Jerusalem. Ether 7:9 says, "He did molten out of the hill and made swords out of steel." The steel industry would like to find a hill like this. Alma 30:2 says: "...it was in the sixteenth year of the reign of the judges...there began a continual peace throughout all the land." But in the eighteenth year "...thus commenced a war..." Alma 35:13. So much for the continual peace.

As stated, Brigham H. Roberts, editor of *History of the Church* and author of *A Comprehensive History of The Church of Jesus Christ of Latter-day Saints,* discovered many of the above problems.

In light of these and other serious problems he studied, Roberts raised the following question concerning the *Book of Mormon*:

> Is all this sober history inspired, written and true, representing things that actually happened? Or is it a wonder-tale of an immature mind, unconscious of what a test he is laying on human credulity when asking men to accept his narrative as solemn history?
>
> B.H. Roberts, *Studies Of The Book Of Mormon* Edited by Brigham D. Madsen, (Urbana and Chicago: University of Illinois Press, 1985), p. 283.

Roberts also studied the relationship between the nineteenth-century book *View of the Hebrews* written by Ethan Smith in 1825 just a few miles from Smith's home. The *View of the Hebrews* was published five years before the *Book of Mormon* and purported to be historical research. This work by Ethan Smith attempts to show how the American Indians, allegedly Israelites, migrated to the New World. The parallels between the *Book of Mormon* and the *View of the Hebrews* are astonishing. Did the book *View of the Hebrews* provide the framework and source material for the *Book of Mormon*? Mormon apostle Roberts catalogs numerous significant parallels in a manuscript that he secretly worked on. The following is a brief summary of the parallels in the *Book of Mormon*, which can only be explained by postulating the thesis that Smith used the book the *View of the Hebrews* to provide the framework and source material for his own book.

Some of the parallels:

Both books contain the idea that the American Indians are really Israelites.

Both works put forth the notion that the Indians were once knowledgeable in writing, culture, and religion.

There is a similar emphasis on the prophet Isaiah and the restoration of Israel.

Both books believe that the European Christians who settled America were called to evangelize the Indians.

Both books have the Israelites coming to America and subsequently degenerating into the American Indians. Both books have the Israelites coming to America from the Old World by following long migration routes.

Both books teach that after the Israelites come to the New World they eventually separate into two separate peoples.

Both books teach that the American Indians once had an Iron Age culture.

Both works assert that all the languages in the New World were corrupted from an original Hebrew.

Both books talk about a lost Indian book buried in a hill.

Both books set forth the idea that the original inhabitants started off with a Monarchy, which eventually became a Republican form of government.

The religious conversions in both books are reminiscent of conversion scenes in nineteenth century New England.

Roberts concludes his shocking and consequential study of the parallels between Ethan Smith's book and the *Book of Mormon* with this question:

> Can such numerous and startling points of resemblance and suggestive contact be merely coincidence?
>
> B.H. Roberts, *Studies Of The Book Of Mormon* edited by Brigham D. Madsen, (Urbana and Chicago: University of Illinois Press, 1985), p. 242.

Smith's Inspired Version of the Bible:

The Reorganized Mormon Church uses this version of the Bible. To call it a biblical translation would be worse than a misnomer. This "inspired version" of the Bible is essentially the King James Bible with the verses changed that were in conflict with Smith's new and constantly evolving theology.

For example, the inspired version in John 4:26 reads "For unto such hath God promised his Spirit"* instead of "God is a Spirit..." (John 4:24 KJV).

*Joseph Smith, *Inspired Version* (Independence, Missouri: Herald Publishing House, 1974), p.1025.

Smith's inspired version changes the wording and inserts into the text material that is not in the Greek manuscript. Smith believed God was an embodied being, which is why he felt compelled to change the text. Smith claimed to have the power of God as Seer and Revelator to interpret foreign languages. There is absolutely no support in the text for the interpretation "Hath God promised his Spirit." He had to make his own translation since there was no way he could twist the original Greek or the English translation into this particular wording. Most heretics will fallaciously appeal to the original language or make some kind of flawed grammatical argument. Not Smith, he was a bold heretic. His approach was, if it does not fit, just rewrite it with the help of his seer-stone.

To demonstrate how far Smith would go, consider what he did to the book of Genesis:

> A Seer shall the Lord my God raise up, who shall be a choice seer unto the fruit of my loins. Thus saith the Lord God of my fathers unto me, a choice seer will I raise up out of the fruit of thy loins, he shall be esteemed highly among the fruit of thy loins; and unto him will I give commandment that he shall do work for the fruit of thy loins, his brethren.... And that seer will I bless, and they that seek to destroy him shall be confounded; for this promise I give unto you, for I will remember you from generation to generation; and <u>His name shall be called Joseph, and it shall be the name of his father</u>.

> Joseph Smith, *Inspired Version* (Independence, Missouri: Herald Publishing House, 1974), p. 79.

This wording is not in the Hebrew text; Smith just adds numerous words and a prophecy of himself into Scripture. Mormons believe that this phrase "his name shall be called Joseph, and it shall be the name of his father" is a prophecy about Joseph Smith. Mormons do not distance themselves from this rewriting of the Bible. They actually believe this is a prophecy of Smith recorded in Scripture. The judgment of Revelation 22:18 with respect to adding to Scripture will fall on Smith!

A sampling of contradictory prophetic nonsense:

Is this quote correct? "For I know that God is not a partial God, neither a changeable being; but he is unchangeable from all eternity to all eternity"* (Moroni 8:18).

*Joseph Smith, *Book Of Mormon* p. 517.

Or is this quote correct? "We have imagined and supposed that God was God from all eternity. I will refute that idea, and take away the veil, so that you may see."*

*Joseph Smith, *Teachings of the Prophet Joseph Smith* p. 345

Is this quote correct? "Behold, David and Solomon truly had many wives and concubines, which thing was abominable before me, saith the Lord."* (Jacob 2:24).

*Joseph Smith, *Book Of Mormon* p. 111.

Or is this quote correct? "... I, the Lord, justified my servants Abraham, Isaac, and Jacob, as also Moses, David, and Solomon, my servants, as touching the principle and doctrine of their having many wives and concubines."* (*Doctrines and Covenants* 132:1).

*Joseph Smith, *Doctrine And Covenants* p. 239.

Members of the Reorganized Mormon Church are offended that Smith has been labeled as a polygamist. They are willing to accept the following statement from Smith as the truth. Was Smith lying when he said the following in 1844?

> What a thing it is for a man to be accused of committing adultery, and having seven wives, when I can only find one, I am the same man, and as innocent as I was fourteen years ago; and I can prove them all perjurers.
>
> Joseph Smith, *History of the Church* Vol. 6, p. 411.

It is a probable that Joseph Smith may have been secretly married to at least 48 different women when making these public statements.*

*Joseph Smith, *History of the Church* Vol. 6, p. 411.

Some of these women were: 1. Louisa Beman in 1841, 2. Fanny Alger, 3. Lucinda Harris, 4. Zina D. Huntington in 1841, 5. Prescindia L. Huntington in 1841, 6. Eliza Roxey Snow in 1842, 7. Sarah Ann Whitney, in 1842, 8. Desdemona W. Fullmer in 1842, 9. Helen Mar Kimball in 1843, 10. Eliza D. Partridge in 1843, 11. Emily D. Partridge in 1843, 12. Lucy Walker in 1843, and 13. Almera W. Johnson also in 1843, 14. Malissa Lott, in 1843, 15. Fanny Young, in 1843, 16. Maria Lawrence, in 1843, 17. Sarah Lawrence, in 1843, 18. Hannah Ells, in 1843, 19. Flora Ann Woodworth, 20. Ruth D. Vose, 21. Mary Elizabeth Rollins, 22. Olive Frost, 23. Rhoda Richards, 24. Sylvia Sessions, 25. Maria Winchester, 26. Elvira A. Cowles, and 27. Sarah M. Cleveland.*

*Jerald & Sandra Tanner, *Joseph Smith and Polygamy* (Salt Lake City: Modern Microfilm Company), pp. 233, 234. A photo-mechanical reprint of an article written by Andrew Jensen, Assistant L.D.S. Church Historian published in the Historical Record, Vol. 6, 1887.

These women all admitted being married to Smith. Many of these marriages were secret. To members of the Reorganized Mormon Church we must ask, were these women all lying? Smith's public denials, while secretly practicing the very thing he denied, are hypocritical. It is clear from Smith's actions that he had no regard for the truth or the people he lied to.

PROPHETIC DEBACLES

In Deuteronomy 18:21-22, we find the standard to judge prophets. One hundred percent accuracy is the standard set forth. Did Smith meet this standard?

In the *Doctrine And Covenants* 104:1 we read about a revelation that was allegedly given to Smith in April 23, 1834.

It reads as follows:

> Verily I say unto you, my friends, I give unto you counsel, and a commandment, concerning all the properties which belong to the order which I commanded to be organized and established, to be a united order, and an everlasting order for the benefit of my church, and for the salvation of men until I come.

Joseph Smith, *Doctrine And Covenants* pp. 182, 183.

This revelation was given to establish a Mormon socialist economy where the Church was owner of all properties. This order was to continue until Christ came. The everlasting united order did not last very long, thus showing it to be a false revelation.

In the *Doctrine And Covenants* 111:1-4, we read about Salem, Massachusetts. This alleged prophecy was given August 6, 1836.

It reads:

> I, the Lord your God, am not displeased with your coming this journey, notwithstanding your follies. I have much treasure in this city for you, for the benefit of Zion, and many people in this city, whom I will gather out in due time for the benefit of Zion through your instrumentality. Therefore, it is expedient that you should form acquaintance with men in this city, as you shall be led, and as it shall be given you. And it shall come to pass in due time that I will give this city into your hands, that you shall have power over, insomuch that they shall not discover your secret parts; and its wealth pertaining to gold and silver shall be yours.

Joseph Smith, *Doctrine And Covenants* p. 205.

This revelation says that Smith would obtain the gold and silver in Salem, Massachusetts. History shows that this never happened.

Doctrine And Covenants 114:1 is a purported revelation given on April 17, 1838. It reads:

> Verily thus saith the Lord: It is wisdom in my servant David W. Pattern, that he settle up all his business as soon as he possibly can, and make a disposition of his merchandise, that he may perform

a mission unto me next spring, in company with
others, even twelve including himself, to testify of
my name and bear glad tidings unto all the world.

Joseph Smith, *Doctrine And Covenants* p. 208.

According to the Mormon work *History of the Church* Vol. 3, page 171, we find that Patten died
in the fall of 1838. Therefore, this is a false revelation given by Smith. Smith, on a number of
occasions, had revelations concerning individuals and what they were to do. An individual who
was the subject of one of Smith's revelations would find it difficult to refuse to fulfill the direction
given for them and remain in the good graces of Smith. Receiving revelations regarding what individuals were to do gave Smith incredible control over his followers. If you were the subject of one
of Smith's revelations and refused, you were, in essence, in rebellion against the Lord.

Doctrine And Covenants 117:12 contains a revelation given on July 8, 1838, saying:

And again, I say unto you, I remember my servant
Oliver Granger; behold, verily I say unto him that
his name shall be had in sacred remembrance from
generation to generation, forever and ever, saith
the Lord.

Joseph Smith, *Doctrine And Covenants* p. 211.

The problem is that today Mormons do not remember who he is, let alone keep his name in
sacred remembrance.

An interesting prophecy of Smith is mentioned in the *History of the Church* Vol. 2. The date of
this is February of 1835.

In this work we read:

President Smith then stated it was the will of God
that those who went to Zion with a determination
to lay down their lives, if necessary, should be
ordained to the ministry, and go forth to prune
the vineyard for the last time, or the coming of the

> Lord, which was nigh even 56 years should wind
> up the scene.
>
> Joseph Smith, *History of the Church* Vol. 2, p. 182.

According to this prophecy, Christ should have come by 1891.

Evidently, Smith also believed and taught that the moon was inhabited. This was recorded in the "Young Women's Journal" by an Oliver B. Huntington.

Huntington stated it like this:

> As far back as 1837, I know that he [Joseph Smith] said the moon was inhabited by men and wom-en the same as this earth, and that they lived to a greater age than we do, that they live generally to near the age of a 1000 years.
>
> Cited in Jerald & Sandra Tanner, *The Changing World of Mormonism* (Chicago: Moody Press, 1981), p. 25.

Huntington went on in this article to talk about how the moon men dressed and that Smith told him in his patriarchal blessing that he himself would go to evangelize these moon men.

More prophecies of Smith could be looked at. These, however, should be sufficient to demonstrate that Smith had no prophetic abilities. Some of his followers such as Mr. Huntington were extremely gullible. The biblical standard of a prophet requires one hundred percent accuracy. This standard for prophetic accuracy is set forth in Deuteronomy 18:21-22. Therefore, it is clearly seen that Smith is a false prophet.

Now we will look at some of Smith's views on the Bible.

Smith, in the work *The Teachings Of The Prophet Joseph Smith*, relates his views concerning the Bible:

> From sundry revelations which had been received, it was apparent that many important points touch-

ing the salvation of men, had been taken from the
Bible, or lost before it was compiled.

Joseph Smith, *The Teachings of the Prophet Joseph
Smith* pp. 9-10.

**In this same work, in a small section titled "Errors in the Bible," we find more of Smith's views
about the reliability of the Bible:**

Ignorant translators, careless transcribers, or
designing and corrupt priests have committed
many errors.

Joseph Smith, *The Teachings of the Prophet Joseph
Smith* p. 327.

Smith never provides evidence of errors in the Bible. He just asserts it. In light of his own book's
numerous mistakes, errors, problems, and absurdities it is disingenuous for Smith to attack any
literature, especially the Bible.

Smith on salvation:

For we know that it is by grace that we are saved
after all we can do (2 Nephi 25:23)

Joseph Smith, *Book Of Mormon* p. 23.

Verily it is a day of sacrifice, and a day for the tith-
ing of my people; for he that is tithed shall be not
be burned at his coming. (Doctrine And Covenants 64:23)

Joseph Smith, *Doctrine And Covenants* p. 106.

It is clearly seen that Smith's system of salvation is one of works. In contrast, Ephesians 2:8, 9
reads, "For by grace are ye saved through faith; and that not of yourselves: it is the gift of God. Not
of works lest any man boast."

SMITH'S VIEWS ON GOD

In the *History of the Church* we learn of Smith's view regarding the Christian God:

> Many men say there is one God; the Father, the
> Son, and the Holy Ghost are only one God! I say
> that is a strange God anyhow - three in one, and
> one in three! It is a curious organization....He
> would be a wonderfully big God - he would be a
> giant or a monster.
>
> Joseph Smith, *History of the Church* Vol. 6, p. 476.

Smith's comments are offensive mocking statements against God. They have a light-hearted tone, making large assertions with no biblical or historical grounding. God is not mocked. Smith died the very same year he said these things.

Smith's *Book of Mormon* is best described as confused heretical anti-Trinitarian monotheism.

For example, we read:

> And he said unto me, Behold, the virgin which
> thou seest, is the mother of God, after the manner
> of flesh.... And the angel said unto me, behold the
> Lamb of God, yea, even the Eternal Father!
>
> Joseph Smith, *Book Of Mormon* (Palmyra, NY: E.B.
> Grandin, 1830), reprinted by Wilford C. Wood,
> Publisher 1958, p. 25.

> And now Abinadi saith unto them, I would that
> ye should understand that <u>God himself</u> shall
> come down among the children of men, and shall
> redeem his people; and because he <u>dwelleth in
> flesh, he shall be called the Son of God</u>: and hav-

ing subjected the flesh to the will of the Father, <u>being the Father and the Son; the Father, because he was conceived by the power of God; and the Son, because of the flesh; thus becoming the Father and the Son: and they are one God,</u> yea, the very Eternal Father of Heaven and of Earth...

Joseph Smith, *Book Of Mormon* (Palmyra, NY: E.B. Grandin, 1830), reprinted by Wilford C. Wood, Publisher 1958, p. 186.

In the above two quotations, it is clearly seen how Smith confuses the Father and Son. Modern editions of this "most correct book" read entirely different. The first citation now simply reads "yea, even the Son of the Eternal Father." This first citation from 1st Nephi is a significant example of the doctrinal changes made in the "most correct book on earth." It is interesting that modern editions of this "most correct book" do not inform the reader with a footnote of any kind that changes have been made. Yet there is an ethical necessity to inform readers when doctrinal changes of this magnitude are made.

Consider the following example of Smith's polytheistic beliefs:

I will preach on the plurality of Gods. I have selected this text for that express purpose. I wish to declare I have always and in all congregations when I have preached on the subject of Deity, it has been the plurality of Gods. It has been preached by the Elders for fifteen years.

Joseph Smith, *The Teachings of the Prophet Joseph Smith* p. 370.

It should be clear that Smith is promoting a non-biblical religion.

In the King Follett funeral sermon given in 1844, Smith sets forth a bizarre teaching concerning the origins of this world.

He states it like this:

> In the beginning, the head of the Gods, called a
> council of the Gods; and they came together and
> concocted a plan to create the world and people it.

> Joseph Smith, *The Teachings of the Prophet Joseph
> Smith* p. 349.

We should not forget *Early Mormonism and the Magic World View* mentioned earlier by Dr. Quinn, which provides evidence that portions of this sermon are plagiarized from the Cabala.

Did Smith's god possess omniscience (all-knowledge)? According to Mormon Apostle Wilford Woodruff:

> God himself is increasing and progressing in
> knowledge, power, and dominion, and will do so,
> worlds without end.

> Wilford Woodruff, *Journal of Discourses* Vol. 6, p. 120.

If this is true, will the Mormon god ever gain a complete knowledge of things? If so, when?

Is Smith's god the eternal God of Scripture? Consider these teachings by Smith:

> God himself was once as we are now, and is an
> exalted Man, and sits enthroned in yonder heav-
> ens. That is the great secret...it is necessary that
> we should understand the character and being of
> God, and how he came to be so; for I am going
> to tell you how God came to be God. We have
> imagined and supposed that God was God from
> all eternity. I will refute that idea...

> Joseph Smith, *The Teachings of the Prophet Joseph
> Smith* p. 345.

This is a continuation from the King Follett funeral sermon from which Smith stole concepts from the Cabala. Not only does the occultic Cabala teach that God is corporeal or embodied, so does Greek Stoic philosophy.

Smith on metaphysics:

Smith taught in his *Book of Mormon* an ethical dualism. This is how it is stated:

> For it must needs be, that there is an opposition in all things. If not so, my first-born in the wilderness, righteousness could not be brought to pass, neither wickedness, neither holiness nor misery, neither good nor bad. Wherefore, all things must needs be a compound in one; wherefore, if it should be one body it must needs remain as dead, having no life neither death, nor corruption nor incorruption, happiness nor misery, neither sense nor insensibility.

> Joseph Smith, *Book Of Mormon* p. 53.

This is not simply saying that there are such things as good and evil. Smith is teaching that there are eternal principles of good and evil, which govern the universe. Smith believes these principles are equally ultimate. These principles are supposedly independent of God and above Him. If these principles are independent and above God, would not they be the ultimate source of authority in the Universe? Where does this type of thinking lead? The same chapter in verse twenty-seven concludes with a declaration of man's autonomy or ability, which reads "free forever, knowing good from evil; to act for themselves and not to be acted upon...." Thus, Smith is teaching that man not only has the power within himself to determine right from wrong, but also to make choices and act upon them accordingly as his will pleases. This is nothing more than the ancient heresy of Pelagianism. This ancient heresy says in effect that man can save himself through his own strength.

Smith rejects God creating the world *ex nihilo*, out of nothing:

> You ask the learned doctors why they say the world
> was made out of nothing; and they will answer,

"Doesn't the Bible say He created the world?" And they infer, from the word create, that it must have been out of nothing. Now, the word create came from the word baurau which does not mean to create out of nothing; it means to organize; the same as a man would organize materials and build a ship. Hence, we infer that God had materials to organize the world out of chaos-chaotic matter, which is element, and in which dwells all the glory. Element had an existence from the time he had. The pure principles which can never be destroyed; they may be organized and re-organized, but not destroyed. They had no beginning, and can have no end.

Joseph Smith, *The Teachings of the Prophet Joseph Smith* p. 350-352.

The verb *bara* does not of itself and absolutely preclude the use of existing material; (cf. Isaiah 65:18) However, when no existing material is mentioned. . . no such material is implied. Consequently, this passage teaches creation *ex nihilo*, creation out of nothing, a doctrine otherwise also clearly taught by the Scriptures; Rom. 4:17; Heb. 11:3; cf. also Ps. 33:6,9; Amos 4:13. The verb is never used of other than divine activity.*

*Leupold, *Exposition of Genesis* (Columbus, Ohio: The Wartburg Press, 1942), pp. 40-41.

As stated previously, Dr. Quinn traces this rejection of creation *ex nihilo* to the influence of the occultic Cabala in Smith's thinking.

In the quotations that follow, does Smith sound like a prophet?

Jesus said in Matthew 7:20, "Wherefore by their fruits ye shall know them."

God made Aaron to be a mouth piece for the children of Israel, and He will make me be god to you in His stead, and the Elders to be mouth for me; if you don't like it, you must lump it.

Joseph Smith, *History of the Church* Vol. 6, pp. 319, 320.

I have more to boast of than ever any man had, I am the only man that has ever been able to keep a whole church together since the days of Adam. A large majority of the whole have stood by me. Neither Paul, John, Peter, nor Jesus ever did it. I boast, that no man ever did such a work as I.

Joseph Smith, *History of the Church* Vol. 6, pp. 408, 409.

The whole earth shall bear me witness that I, like the towering rock in the midst of the ocean, which has withstood the mighty surges of the warring waves for centuries, am impregnable...I combat the errors of ages; I meet the violence of mobs; I cope with illegal proceedings from executive authority; I cut the gordian knot of powers, and I solve mathematical problems of universities, with truth-diamond truth and God is my right hand man.

Joseph Smith, *History of the Church* Vol. 6, p. 78.

I am a lawyer; I am a big lawyer and comprehend heaven, earth and hell, to bring forth knowledge that shall cover up all lawyers, doctors and other big bodies.

Joseph Smith, *History of the Church* Vol. 5, p. 289.

Don't employ lawyers, or pay them money for their

knowledge, for I have learned that they don't know
anything. I know more than they all.

Joseph Smith, *History of the Church* Vol. 5, p. 467.

It is dismaying that anyone would ever try to justify and defend such statements. Yet, this is exactly what the followers of Smith do.

In conclusion, we should note some introductory comments from John L. Brooke, Associate Professor of History at Tufts University, in his book *The Refiner's Fire The Making of Mormon Cosmology, 1644-1844*. In his book, Professor Brooke makes some perceptive observations, where he thoroughly documents the beginnings of Mormon cosmology. This work by Professor Brooke is profound and significant.

Some of Professor Brooke's introductory comments to his important study are as follows:

> This book argues that Joseph Smith went through
> two critical transformations. He began his engage-
> ment with the supernatural as a village conjurer but
> transformed himself into a prophet of the "Word,"
> announcing the opening of a new dispensation.
> Then, moving beyond his role as prophet and reve-
> lator, Smith transformed himself and the Mormon
> priesthood into Christian-hermetic magi, a role pre-
> viously manifested in the medieval alchemist, the
> Renaissance hermetic philosopher, and the perfec-
> tionist sectarians of the Radical Reformation.
>
> John L. Brooke, *The Refiner's Fire The making of
> Mormon Cosmology 1644-1844*, (Cambridge: Cam-
> bridge University Press, 1996), p. 4.

Hermeticism, of which alchemy was involved, taught that man could regain or obtain the supposed divine powers that man lost in the fall of Adam. Magic, witchcraft, alchemy, and Freemasonry are manifestations of hermeticism. It is interesting that Smith was involved with elements of all of these. Smith did not really escape his role as village conjurer; he expanded it into a bogus nationwide seer.

Considering this brief look at Smith's character, distorted theology, plagiarized sources, false revelations, and his deluded self-image, those who still believe that this man is a prophet of God are clearly outside of the Christian faith. The testimony of Joseph Smith and his work must be repudiated. Any testimony that lifts up Joseph Smith is false.

CHAPTER 14

HOW DID JOSEPH SMITH TRANSLATE THE BOOK OF MORMON?

 number of Joseph Smith's contemporaries said that he put his face into a hat that contained a magic rock, or seer stone, as a means of translating the *Book of Mormon*. This sounds shocking, but readers will see from the testimony of men who are listed as witnesses to the authenticity inside its front cover that this is how it was supposedly accomplished.

In the *Comprehensive History of the Church*, Mormon Apostle, Brigham H. Robert's citation of Martin Harris, one of the three witnesses to the authenticity to the *Book of Mormon* is most revealing.

Martin Harris explains in his eye-witness account of how Smith performed this translation* process that:

The seer stone Smith possessed was a

> chocolate-colored, somewhat egg-shaped stone which the Prophet found while digging a well in company with his brother Hyrum.
>
> B.H. Roberts, *Comprehensive History of the Church* Vol. 1. (Brigham Young University Press, Provo, Utah, 1965), p. 1:129.

Harris continues:

> Joseph was able to translate the characters engraven on the plates.
>
> B.H. Roberts, *Comprehensive History of the Church* Vol. 1. p. 1:129.

In his book *An Address to All Believers in Christ,* David Whitmer, another witness to the authenticity of the *Book of Mormon* writes:

> I will now give you a description of the manner in which the Book of Mormon was translated. Joseph Smith would put the seer stone into a hat, and put his face in the hat, drawing it closely around his face to exclude the light; and in the darkness the spiritual light would shine. A piece of something resembling parchment would appear, and under it was the interpretation in English. Brother Joseph would read off the English to Oliver Cowdery, who was his principal scribe, and when it was written down and repeated to brother Joseph to see if it was correct, then it would disappear, and another character with the interpretation would appear.
>
> David Whitmer, *An Address to All Believers in Christ* (Richmond, Missouri: n.p., 1887), p. 12.

Emma Hale Smith, Joseph's wife, was the first person to serve as his scribe. In her testimony as told to her son Joseph Smith III, we read:

> In writing for your father I frequently wrote day after day, often sitting at the table close by him, he sitting with his face buried in his hat, with the stone in it, and dictating hour after hour with nothing between us.
>
> Joel Tiffany, *Interview with Martin Harris* May 1859 p. 163-170.

Was Joseph Smith into Occultism?

Consider Joseph Smith's history of using a magic rock when hunting for buried treasure:

Again we learn from Martin Harris, when he described Smith's involvement in this dishonorable occultic practice in an interview he gave to "Tiffany's Monthly."

Harris says:

> Joseph had had this stone for some time. There was a company there in that neighborhood, who were digging for money supposed to have been hidden by the ancients. Of this company were old Mr. Stowel~I think his name was Josiah~also old Mr. Beman, also Samuel Lawrence, George Prop~ er, Joseph Smith, jr., and his father, and his broth~ er Hiram Smith. They dug for money in Palmyra, Manchester, also in Pennsylvania, and other places.

> Joseph Smith, *Rough Stone Rolling* pp. 51-52.

Notes from the March, 1826 court appearance in South Bainbridge, New York shed light on the Smith family's attitude towards treasure seeking before receiving the golden plates:

> Peter Bridgeman, nephew of Josiah Stowell, entered a complaint against Joseph Smith Jr. as a disorder~ ly person in South Bainbridge, Chenango Coun~ ty, New York. New York law specified that anyone pretending to have skill in discovering lost goods should be judged a disorderly person. . . . Presum~ ably, Bridgeman believed that Joseph was trying to cheat the old man by claiming magical powers.

> Joseph Smith, *Rough Stone Rolling* p. 52.

In the court record, Stowell said that he

> had the most implicit faith in the Prisoners skill, implying that was the reason for hiring Joseph Smith.

> Excerpt from 1826 *Bill of Justice Albert Neely* (Cour~

tesy Clerk of the Board of Supervisors, Chenango
County Office Building, Norwich, New York.)

Joseph Smith's involvement in magic practices had always been denied by the LDS Church until 1971, when Presbyterian pastor, Wesley P. Walters, discovered two original documents which proved that Joseph Smith was a "glass looker" and was arrested and examined before a justice of the peace in Bainbridge, N.Y. in 1826. One of the documents is Justice Albert Neeley's bill to the county showing the costs involved in several hearings held in 1826. The fifth item from the top of Neeley's bill mentions the examination of "Joseph Smith The Glass Looker."

More on Joseph Smith being arrested as a glass-looker:

A thoroughgoing account of this evidence is given by former Brigham Young University history professor D. Michael Quinn in his book *Early Mormonism and the Magic World View.*

> Indeed, in 1826, four years before the publication of the Book of Mormon, Joseph was arrested, jailed, and examined in court in Bainbridge, New York on the charge of being "a disorderly person and an impostor" in connection with his use of a peep stone to search for buried treasure. While the evidence indicates he was found guilty of this charge, the young Joseph was apparently released on the condition that he leave the area.
>
> Quinn, pp. 44ff.; and H. Michael Marquardt and Wesley P. Walters, *Inventing Mormonism: Tradition and the Historical Record* (Salt Lake City: Smith Research Associates, 1994), pp. 70ff.

This court record discovered by pastor Walters is incredibly damaging to the truthfulness of Mormonism. This discovery means that Joseph Smith was engaged in a glass-looking or a money-digging operation with the same magic seer stone in 1826, at the very time in which according to Joseph's "First Vision story" he was being given the golden plates by the angel. The reason this magic seer stone story is suppressed in Mormonism today is that it would be a major hindrance for potential prospects in accepting the truthfulness of the *Book of Mormon* as Scripture if it was known to have been "translated" using a magic rock placed in a hat.

According to P. T. Barnum, "There's a sucker born every minute." Today, even most suckers or gullible people will find this "magic rock in a hat used to translate an historical book from golden plates" fiction a little hard to swallow.

Again, it should be noted that Joseph Smith also used a magic "seer stone" for some years prior to publication of the *Book of Mormon*:

It has been well documented by Mormon historians that for a number of years before he produced the *Book of Mormon*, Joseph Smith was heavily involved in various magic-occultic practices, including the use of a magic "seer stone" or "peep stone.*

*Michael Quinn, *Early Mormonism and the Magic World View* (Salt Lake City: Signature Books, 1987; revised, expanded 1998), pp. 41-ff.

Moreover, let it be widely proclaimed to the followers of Joseph Smith, in light of this brief study dealing with the occultic practices that resulted in the *Book of Mormon* being published:

> Regard not them that have familiar spirits, neither
> seek after wizards, to be defiled by them: I am the
> LORD your God. (Leviticus 19:31)

Professor D. Michael Quinn's book titled *Early Mormonism and the Magic World View* details the extensive occultic involvement that the Smith family was into. In addition it will be well worth your time to consult: *The Locations of Joseph Smith's Early Treasure Quests* by Dan Vogel. The reader should also consult *The Method of Translation of the Book of Mormon* by James E. Lancaster

In contrast, how Bible translation is done, from the Wycliffe Translators:

In the narrow sense, Bible translation is the actual process of drafting, checking, polishing and producing a final version of vernacular Scriptures for publication. It is a specialized, step-by-step effort with technical terminology.

First draft: A preliminary, tentative translation, for testing and improving. Several successive drafts are produced as improvements and revisions are made.

Reviewer Check: A read-through of the translation by other speakers of the indigenous language to get their corrections and suggested improvements.

Consultant Check: An advisor with special skills, such as expertise in the original Hebrew or Greek, and/or broader background and experience, reviews the draft. The consultant discusses the translation verse-by-verse with the translators, shares how problem passages have been handled by others, and advises on general aspects of the text.

Exegetical Check: Compares the indigenous language translation draft with the original Greek or Hebrew text. This ensures accuracy and faithfulness in the translation. NOTE: "Exegesis" is the explanation or critical interpretation of the text.

Consistency Check: Reviews the translation of key biblical terms, important theological concepts, Bible names, and parallel passages throughout the entire text and evaluates rationale for any variations.

Format and Style Check: Reviews the preface, introductions to the books, glossary and footnotes. Spelling, punctuation, verse and chapter numbers, paragraphing, maps, pictures and captions are also checked.

Proofreading: Checking of the entire manuscript, including all the details listed under format and style, above, is a long, intense and tedious job.

Oral read-through: Reading of the entire manuscript to determine whether anything sounds wrong or is missing. This is often done by a group of native speakers.

People Involved in the Process: Translators are those who participate in the work of Bible translation. This includes the following activities: preparing the first draft of the translation, reviewing the work of others on the team, testing the translation with other speakers of the language, receiving, studying and assessing their comments making a revised draft checking the final manuscript for publication

The review committee is a group of native speakers and other workers (expatriates and/or nationals) who do the revision steps referred to above.

Revisions: Are made in the translation to make it more faithful to the original meaning, more natural in expression, more accurate and readable. Every translation goes through many revisions.

Back-translation: Is translating a Scripture text back into a language of wider communication, from the indigenous language, word-by-word or phrase-by-phrase. It reflects as closely as possible the meaning and grammatical structure of the indigenous language text, so that consultants who do not know the indigenous language can evaluate how accurate and adequate the translation is.

Support Wycliffe at: https://www.wycliffe.org/

CHAPTER 15

MORMONISM AND LOGICAL CHOICES: A HOUSE DIVIDED

n logic, the law of non-contradiction is stated that "one cannot say of something that it is and that it is not in the same respect and at the same time."

The following is an exercise in elementary logic using the law of non-contradiction to analyze select teachings of Mormonism that appear to be in opposition. During this exercise in Section One, I'm not trying to get Mormons to answer what they think the official doctrine of their church is. It is admitted that a Mormon leader may engage in speculation and as such should be given liberty to have speculative statements accepted as such. But usually, when the Mormon brings up the issue of speculation, it is simply a cop-out for not wanting to deal with the challenge at hand.

However, the assertions that are contrasted, both of which claim to explain something about ultimate reality, cannot both be true if they are mutually contradictory. Truth may be in one or the other, or neither, but they cannot both be true if they contradict each other.

When considering the following citations from Section One, which person or source is correct? Is there a fundamental contradiction in the statements contrasted in each column? A Christian will obviously have a third choice, namely, that neither citation is correct. Only one choice can be correct in Section Two.

SECTION ONE:
MORMONISM AGAINST ITSELF

Adam was made from the dust of an earth, but <u>not from the dust of this earth</u>. Brigham Young, *Journal of Discourses*, Vol. 3, p. 319.

The *Book of Mormon*, the Bible, the *Doctrine and Covenants*, and the *Pearl of Great Price* all declare that Adam's body was created from the dust of this ground, that is, <u>from the dust of this ground, this earth</u>. Joseph Fielding Smith, *Doctrines of Salvation*, Vol. 1 p. 90.

For I know that God is not a partial God, neither a changeable being; but he is unchangeable from all eternity to eternity. (Moroni 8:18)

We have imagined and supposed that God was God from all eternity. I will refute that idea, and take away the veil, so that you may see.

Joseph Smith, *The Teachings of the Prophet Joseph Smith*, p. 345.

And Zeezrom said unto him: Thou sayest there is a true and living God? And Amulet said: Yea, there is a true and living God. Now Zeesrom said: Is there more than one God? And he answered, No. (Alama 11:26-29)

How many Gods there are, I do not know. But there was never was a time when there were no Gods. Brigham Young, *Journal of Discourses*, Vol. 7, p. 333.

Behold, David and Solomon truly had many wives and concubines, which thing was a abomination before me, saith the Lord. (Jacob 2:24)

I, the Lord, justified my servants Abraham, Issac, and Jacob, as also Moses, David and Solomon, my servants as touching the principle and doctrine of their having many wives and concubines.

Doctrine and Covenants, Section 132:1

God himself is increasing and progressing in knowledge, power and dominion, and will do so worlds without end.

Wilford Woodruff, *Journal of Discourses*, Vol. 6, p. 120

It seems very strange to me that members of the Church will hold to the doctrine, "God increases in knowledge as time goes on." "I think this kind of doctrine is very dangerous.

Joseph Fielding Smith, *Doctrines of Salvation*, Vol. 1 pp. 7, 8.

And I did teach my people to build buildings, and to work in all manner of wood, and of iron, and of copper, and of brass, and of steel, and of gold, and of silver, and of precious ores, which were in great abundance. (2 Nephi 5:15)

And I, Nephi, did build a temple; and I did construct it after the manner of the temple of Solomon save it were not built of so many precious things; for they were not to be found upon the land, wherefore, it could not be built like unto Solomon's temple. (2 Nephi 5:16, Ibid., p. 66)

"Christ Not Begotten of Holy Ghost."

Christ was born of God. He was not born without the aid of man and that man was God.

Joseph Fielding Smith, *Doctrines of Salvation*, Vol. 1 p. 18

They tell us the Book of Mormon states that Jesus was begotten of the Holy Ghost. I challenge that statement. The Book of Mormon teaches no such thing! Neither does the Bible.

Joseph Fielding Smith, *Doctrines of Salvation*, Vol. 1 p. 19.

God is a Spirit

And now when Aaron heard this, his heart began to rejoice, and he said: Behold, assuredly as thou livest, O king, there is a God.

And the king said: Is God that Great Spirit that brought our fathers out of the land of Jerusalem?

And Aaron said unto him: Yea, he is that Great Spirit, and he created all things both in heaven and in earth. Believest thou this?

And he said: Yea, I believe that the Great Spirit created all things, and I desire that ye should tell me concerning all these things, and I will believe thy words." (Alma 22:8-11)

God Has a Body

The Father has a body of flesh and bones as tangible as man's; the Son also; but the Holy Ghost has not a body of flesh and bones, but is a personage of Spirit. Were it not so, the Holy Ghost could not dwell in us.

Doctrine and Covenants, Section 130:22

God Dwells in man's Heart

And this I know, because the Lord hath said he dwelleth not in unholy temples, but in the hearts of the righteous doth he dwell; yea, and he has also said that the righteous shall sit down in his kingdom, to go no more out; but their garments should be made white through the blood of the Lamb. (Alma 34:36)

God Does Not Dwell in man's Heart

John 14:23—The appearing of the Father and the Son, in that verse, is a personal appearance; and the idea that the Father and the Son dwell in a man's heart is an old sectarian notion, and is false. Doctrine and Covenants Section 130:3

Creation of the World by One God

And now, my sons, I speak unto you these things for your profit and learning; for there is a God, and he hath created all things, both the heavens and the earth, and all things that in them are, both things to act and things to be acted upon. (2 Nephi 2:14)

For behold, by the power of his word man came upon the face of the earth, which earth was created by the power of his word. Wherefore, if God being able to speak and the world was, and to speak and man was created, O then, why not able to command the earth, or the workmanship of hishands upon the face of it, according to his will and pleasure? (Jacob 4:9)

Creation of the world by Many Gods

Pearl of Great Price

AND then the Lord said: Let us go down. And they went down at the beginning, and they, that is the Gods, organized and formed the heavens and the earth.

And the earth, after it was formed, was empty and desolate, because they had not formed anything but the earth; and darkness reigned upon the face of the deep, and the Spirit of the Gods was brooding upon the face of the waters.

And they (the Gods) said: Let there be light; and there was light.

Book of Abraham, Chapter 4:1-3

Murder Can Be Forgiven

"Turn, all ye Gentiles, from your wicked ways; and repent of your evil doings, of your lyings and deceivings, and of your whoredoms, and of your secret abominations, and your idolatries, and of your murders, and your priestcrafts, and your envyings, and your strifes, and from all your wickedness and abominations, and come unto me, and be baptized in my name, that ye may receive a remission of your sins, and be filled with the Holy Ghost, that ye may be numbered with my people who are of the house of Israel." (3 Nephi 30:2)

Murder Cannot be Forgiven

"And now, behold, I speak unto the church. Thou shalt not kill; and he that kills shall not have forgiveness in this world, nor in the world to come. *Doctrine and Covenants,* Section 42:18

God's Word Unchangeable	God's Word is Subject to Change
Now, <u>the decrees of God are unalterable</u>; therefore, the way is prepared that whosoever will may walk therein and be saved. (Alma 41:8)	Wherefore <u>I, the Lord, command and revoke, as it seemeth me good</u>; and all this to be answered upon the heads of the rebellious, saith the Lord. *Doctrine and Covenants*, Section 56:4

SECTION TWO:
MORMONISM AGAINST THE BIBLE

CHRISTIAN DOCTRINE	MORMON DOCTRINE
There is only one God: Ye are my witnesses, saith the LORD, and my servant whom I have chosen: that ye may know and believe me, and understand that I am he: before me there was no God formed, neither shall there be after me." (Isaiah 43:10). "...I am the first, and I am the last; and beside me there is no God." (Isaiah 44:6) "I am the LORD , and there is none else, there is no God beside me: I girded thee, though thou hast not known me: That they may know from the rising of the sun, and from the west, that there is none beside me, I am the LORD, and there is none else. (Isaiah 45:5-6)	And they (the Gods) said: Let there be light: and there was light. *Book of Abraham* 4:3 I will preach on the plurality of Gods. [sic] I have selected this text for that express purpose. I wish to declare I have always and in all congregations when I have preached on the subject of Deity, it has been the plurality of Gods. It has been preached by the Elders for fifteen years. Joseph Smith, *History of the Church*, Vol. 6, p. 474.

God has always been God:

Before the mountains were brought forth, or ever thou hadst formed the earth and the world, even from everlasting to everlasting, thou art God. (Psalms 90:2)

God himself was once as we are now, and is an exalted man, and sits enthroned in yonder heavens! . . . We have imagined that God was God from all eternity. I will refute that idea and take away the veil, so that you may see.

Joseph Smith, *The Teachings of the Prophet Joseph Smith,* p. 345.

God is a spirit without flesh and bones:

God is a Spirit: and they that worship him must worship him in spirit and in truth." John 4:24 "Behold my hands and my feet, that it is I myself: handle me, and see; for a spirit hath not flesh and bones, as ye see me have. (Luke 24:39)

The Father has a body of flesh and bones as tangible as man's," (Doctrine and Covenants 130:22; "Therefore we know that both the Father and the Son are in form and stature perfect men; each of them possesses a tangible body . . . of flesh and bones.

Talmage, *Articles of Faith,* p. 38.

The Trinity is the doctrine that there is only one God and that He exists eternally in three persons. The Father, the Son, and the Holy Spirit are the one and God and they share the same nature and essence. The triune nature of God can be simply stated as:

1. There is only one God

2. There are three equally divine, distinct and eternal Persons called God

3. Therefore, these three equally divine and eternal Persons are the one God

The trinity is three separate Gods: The Father, the Son, and the Holy Ghost. "That these three are separate individuals, physically distinct from each other, is demonstrated by the accepted records of divine dealings with man. Talmage, *Articles of Faith,* p. 35.

The following Scriptures, demonstrate that there is a plurality of persons in the God-head, in other words, you see more than one divine person in each passage listed: (Genesis 1:26, 3:22; 11:7; Isaiah 6:8; 48:16; 61:1-2; Jeremiah 23:5-6; Zechariah 10:12; Matthew 28:19; Luke 4:18-19; John 1:1-3; John 14:23; 2 Corinthians 13:14; Colossians 2:2; Hebrews 1:8-10; Hebrews 3:7-11; 1 Peter 1:2; and 1 John 2:24).

Jesus was born of the virgin Mary: "Therefore the Lord himself shall give you a sign; Behold, a virgin shall conceive, and bear a son, and shall call his name Immanuel." (Isaiah 7:14) "Behold, a virgin shall be with child, and shall bring forth a son, and they shall call his name Emmanuel, which being interpreted is, God with us." (Matthew 1:23)

The birth of the Saviour was as natural as are the births of our children; it was the result of natural action. He partook of flesh and blood - was begotten of his Father, as we were of our fathers. Brigham Young, *Journal of Discourses,* Vol. 8, p. 115 Christ was begotten by an Immortal Father in the same way that mortal men are begotten by mortal fathers. McConkie, *Mormon Doctrine,* p. 547.

Jesus is the eternal Son. He is second person of the Trinity. He has a human and divine nature. He is God in flesh and a true man "In the beginning was the Word, and the Word was with God, and the Word was God. And the Word was made flesh, and dwelt among us, (and we beheld his glory, the glory as of the only begotten of the Father,) full of grace and truth." (John 1:1;14)

Jesus is the literal spirit-brother of Lucifer, a creation.

Milton R. Hunter, *Gospel Through the Ages,* p. 15.

It will be seen that the great Messiah who was the founder of the Christian religion, was a polygamist.

Orson Pratt, *The Seer,* p. 172.

Who is the image of the invisible God, the firstborn of every creature: <u>For by him [Jesus] were all things created, that are in heaven, and that are in earth, visible and invisible, whether they be thrones, or dominions, or principalities, or powers: all things were created by him, and for him.</u>

And he is before all things, and by him all things consist." (Colossians 1:15-17) "For in him dwelleth all the fulness of the Godhead bodily (Colossians 2:9).

How can Jesus be the spirit-brother of His own creation as Hunter asserts? And furthermore, it is blasphemous to teach that Jesus was a polygamist!

Jesus Christ was married at Cana, that Mary, Martha and others were his wives, and that he begat children. Orson Hyde, *Journal of Discourses*, Vol. 2, p. 210.

The Holy Spirit is the third person of the Trinity.

He is not a force, He is a person:

"But Peter said, Ananias, why hath Satan filled thine heart to lie to the Holy Ghost, and to keep back part of the price of the land? Whiles it remained, was it not thine own? and after it was sold, was it not in thine own power? why hast thou conceived this thing in thine heart? thou hast not lied unto men, but unto God. (Acts 5:3-4) "As they ministered to the Lord, and fasted, the Holy Ghost said, Separate me Barnabas and Saul for the work whereunto I have called them. (Acts 13:2)

Mormonism distinguishes between the Holy Spirit (God's presence via an essence) and the Holy Ghost (the third god in the Mormon doctrine of the godhead). He [the Holy Ghost] is a being endowed with the attributes and powers of Deity, and not a mere force, or essence. Talmage, *Articles of Faith*, p. 144.

Biblical salvation involves the forgiveness of sin and deliverance from hell. It is a <u>free gift</u> received by God's grace:

For by grace are ye saved through faith; and that [faith] not of yourselves: it is the gift of God" (Ephesians 2:8). "For the wages of sin is death; but the gift of God is eternal life through Jesus Christ our Lord." (Romans 6:23) And it cannot be earned. "And if by grace, then is it no more of works: otherwise grace is no more grace. But if it be of works, then it is no more grace: otherwise work is no more work. (Romans 11:6)

Salvation has two meanings in Mormonism. There is a universal resurrection involving first a general salvation for everyone and then a individual salvation determined by works. The first effect [of the atonement] is to secure to all mankind alike, exemption from the penalty of the fall, thus providing a plan of *General Salvation*. The second effect is to open a way for *Individual Salvation* whereby mankind may secure remission of personal sins.

Talmage, *Articles of Faith,* p. 78-79.

Salvation is not by works:

For by grace are ye saved through faith; and that [faith] not of yourselves: it is the gift of God" (Ephesians 2:8). "But to him that <u>worketh not</u>, but believeth on him that justifieth the ungodly, <u>his faith is counted for righteousness.</u>" (Romans 4:5) "I do not frustrate the grace of God: for <u>if righteousness come by [keeping] the law</u>, then Christ is dead in vain. (Galatians 2:21)

As these sins are the result of individual acts it is just that forgiveness for them should be conditioned on individual compliance with prescribed requirements - obedience to the laws and ordinances of the Gospel.

Talmage, *Articles of Faith,* p. 79.

The Bible is the inspired inerrant word of God. All Scripture is given by inspiration of God, and is profitable for doctrine, for reproof, for correction, for instruction in righteousness. (2 Timothy 3:16)

We believe the Bible to be the word of God as far as it is translated correctly. . .

8th Article of Faith of the Mormon Church

In addition to the clear violation of the law of non-contradiction seen in the above comparative quotes in Section One Mormonism Against Itself, the astute reader will not be able to miss another fallacy that is very common within Mormon writings, namely, the fallacy of equivocation.

Stated simply, the fallacy of equivocation occurs when a word switches meaning in the middle of an argument or when it expresses one concept in one premise and another concept in another premise or in the conclusion.

Not only do Mormons equivocate by the usage of words, they will also lie when you talk to them about their controversial beliefs, which sets them far apart from historic Christianity.

See the YouTube video titled: <u>Mormon Missionaries Taught to Lie!</u>
<u>http://www.youtube.com/watch?v=uFqPVOkfmmI</u>

CUTTING THROUGH
THE FALLACIES

There are three questions that I like to use when challenging Mormons beliefs. These questions are good for any debate or witnessing encounter and help us to (1.) get past the language barrier or surface meaning of words, and (2.) show the Mormon that his beliefs are not biblical and that he can have no assurance or confidence in the finite Mormon deity and (3.) also show the Mormon that he can have no confidence in the area of knowledge.

Now for a refresher on the method for questioning Mormons:

1. **What do you mean?**
   This question forces the Mormon to define their terminology and gets beyond surface similarity.

2. **How do you know that?**
   This forces them to give reasons for their definitions. Are they parroting things that they heard? Are their definitions biblical?

3. **So what are the implications of this?**
   This question forces them to look at the absurdities of their belief system and where it leads.

CHAPTER 16

ADAM-GOD
AND BLOOD ATONEMENT

THE ADAM-GOD DOCTRINE

righam Young, the second prophet of the Mormon religion, taught that the first man, Adam was God and the biological father of the Lord Jesus in the flesh. It is well documented that Brigham Young taught this for many years, even with ongoing attempts by the Mormon hierarchy to hide this embarrassing reality. Why hide it if Brigham Young taught this? This suppression's Young's teaching is because Mormons including their leaders recognize such a teaching as blatant heresy with even a cursory reading of Scripture.

For example:

> We warn you against the dissemination of doc-
> trines which are not according to the scriptures
> and which are alleged to have been taught by some
> of the General Authorities of past generations.
> Such for instance is the Adam-god theory. We
> denounce that theory and hope that everyone will
> be cautioned against this and other kinds of false
> doctrine.
>
> Spencer W. Kimball, *Church News* October 9, 1976.

Spencer W. Kimball was the twelfth prophet of the Mormon religion.

We can certainly agree with Kimball that the Adam-god doctrine is false. We cannot agree with Kimball when he tries to hide the fact that this doctrine was taught authoritatively by early day Mormons, most notably by Brigham Young.

As a matter of fact, Mormon apostle Bruce R. McConkie admitted in a letter to Eugene England from Brigham Young University on February 19, 1981 that Brigham Young did teach the Adam-God doctrine.

See Utah LightHouse Ministry for more on this letter in their publication: "APOSTLE McCONKIE ADMITS BRIGHAM YOUNG TAUGHT ADAM-GOD DOCTRINE" Part One of their article and ordering information at Utah Light House Ministry: http://www. utlm.org/newsletters/no49.htm#McCONKIE

McConkie says:

> Yes, President Young did teach that Adam was the father of our spirits, and all the related things that the cultists ascribe to him. This, however, is not true. He expressed views that are out of harmony with the gospel. But, be it known, Brigham Young also taught accurately and correctly, the status and position of Adam in the eternal scheme of things. What I am saying is, that Brigham Young, contradicted Brigham Young, and the issue becomes one of which Brigham Young we will believe. The answer is we will believe the expressions that accord with the teachings in the Standard Works.
>
> **Part One of their article and ordering information at Utah Light House Ministry** http://www. utlm.org/newsletters/no49.htm#McCONKIE

Later in this same letter he says:

> I think you can give me credit for having a knowledge of the quotations from Brigham Young relative to Adam, and of knowing what he taught under the subject that has become known as the Adam God Theory.

This admission by McConkie that Brigham Young did in fact teach the Adam God doctrine should resolve the issue of whether this theory was taught or not.

The fact that Brigham Young taught this shocking heresy which is now denounced by Mormon leaders today raises an insurmountable problem for their religion. Namely, a major prophetic figure of their religion taught heresy on the doctrine of who God is. It does not get any more important than this. If Brigham Young taught false doctrine on the very nature of God, how can he still be considered a prophet? A true prophet does not teach people to believe in false gods.

Because of these differences in major doctrines, one can ask: is the whole body of Mormon writing a living document? That's how it seems, since they change or cancel or denounce various pieces at various times. How can this be reconciled with their belief that the church leaders speak with apostolic authority? How can they hope to keep believers from being blown back and forth by the winds of every new leader? After many years of researching Mormonism, I've never seen a satisfying response to questions of this nature.

Consider:

> If there arises among you a prophet or a dreamer of dreams, and he gives you a sign or a wonder, and the sign or the wonder comes to pass, of which he spoke to you, saying, 'Let us go after other gods'~ which you have not known~'and let us serve them,' you shall not listen to the words of that prophet or that dreamer of dreams, for the Lord your God is testing you to know whether you love the Lord your God with all your heart and with all your soul. You shall walk after the Lord your God and fear Him, and keep His commandments and obey His voice, and you shall serve Him and hold fast to Him. (Deuteronomy 13:1-4)

This heretical doctrine produces a dilemma for Mormonism. If a Mormon claims that Brigham Young is a true prophet, he must accept all of his authoritative teachings of which the Adam-god doctrine was an important one. According to Deuteronomy, a prophet must have true teaching regarding the nature of God. If the modern Mormon cannot accept Brigham Young's Adam-god doctrine, then the Mormon must conclude that Brigham Young was a false prophet.

If there is any doubt, consider the following references from his own writings where Young taught the Adam-god doctrine:

> Adam came into the garden of Eden with a celestial body and one of his many wives, he is our Father and God. The Father, not the Holy Spirit, conceived Jesus with the Virgin Mary.
>
> Brigham Young, *Journal of Discourses* Vol. 1, p. 50.

> Jesus, our elder brother, was begotten in the flesh by the same character that was in the garden of Eden, and who is our Father in Heaven.
>
> Brigham Young, *Journal of Discourses* Vol. 1, p. 51.

> God is so near to us as Father Adam.
>
> Brigham Young, *Journal of Discourses* Vol. 5, p. 331

> Mankind are here because they are the offspring of parents who were brought here from another planet. Brigham Young, *Journal of Discourses* Vol. 7, p. 285.

Scriptural refutation of Brigham Young's Adam-god doctrine:

> And the LORD God called unto Adam, and said unto him, Where art thou? (Genesis 3:9)

Who did God call? Adam. Who called Adam? God. In light of this passage, only a madman would claim that Adam is God.

There is no way out of this dilemma. In fact, if Brigham Young was a false prophet, all other subsequent prophets of the Mormon religion are false. All subsequent Mormon leaders claim Brigham Young was a true prophet, and claim their leadership is in a succession of prophets starting with Joseph Smith who has already been shown to be fraud. The Mormon leadership succession structure is like a house of cards. One breath of truth will cause this house of cards to fall.

BRIGHAM YOUNG'S DOCTRINE
OF BLOOD ATONEMENT

According to this doctrine there are certain sins which place the sinner beyond the forgiving power of the blood of Christ. The only way the sinner can have forgiveness is to have his or her own blood shed.

It is easy to demonstrate from Young's own writings that he taught this un-biblical theory of blood atonement made possible from the sinner's own impure shed blood:

According to Young, Mormon people are even called on to redeem other people by shedding their blood, as the fourth quote will demonstrate.

> There is not a man or woman, who violates the covenants made with their God, that will not be required to pay the debt. The blood of Christ will never wipe that out, your own blood must atone for it.
>
> Brigham Young, *Journal of Discourses* Vol. 3, p. 247.
>
> There are sins that men commit for which they cannot receive forgiveness in this world, or in that which is to come, and if they had their eyes open to see their true condition, they would be perfectly willing to have their blood spilt upon the ground.
>
> Brigham Young, *Journal of Discourses* Vol. 4, p. 3.
>
> It is true that the blood of the Son of God was

shed for sins through the fall and those committed by men, yet men can commit sins which it can never remit.

Brigham Young, *Journal of Discourses* Vol. 4, p. 54.

For some the only way to be saved and exalted with the Gods is to have their own blood shed. Will you love your brothers or sisters likewise, when they have committed a sin that cannot be atoned for without the shedding of blood? Will you love that man or woman well enough to shed their blood?

Brigham Young, *Journal of Discourses* Vol. 4, p. 219.

I could refer you to plenty of instances where men have been righteously slain, in order to atone for their sins. Brigham Young, *Journal of Discourses* Vol. 4, p. 220.

Scriptural refutation:

In whom we have redemption through his blood, the forgiveness of sins, according to the riches of his grace. (Ephesians 1:7)

In whom we have redemption through his blood, even the forgiveness of sins. (Colossians 1:14)

In conclusion, the shed blood of man, which is impure because of sin, cannot save. Only Christ's shed blood joined by faith in an elect sinner makes salvation possible. Said another way in Scripture, forgiveness is by grace through faith joined to the shed blood of Jesus Christ.

CHAPTER 17

DOES THE *BOOK OF MORMON*
HAVE A FAMILIAR SPIRIT?

WHAT IS
A FAMILIAR SPIRIT?

The following comes from the notes of the King James Bible on-line:

> Sorcerers or necormancers, who professed to call up the dead to" "answer questions, were said to have a "familiar spirit" (Deuteronomy 18:11; 2 Kings 21:6; 2 Chronicles 33:6; Leviticus 19:31; 20:6; Isaiah 8:19; 29:4). Such a person was called by the Hebrews an 'ob, which" properly means a leathern bottle; for sorcerers were regarded as vessels containing the inspiring demon. This Hebrew word was "equivalent to the pytho of the Greeks, and was used to denote" both the person and the spirit which possessed him (Leviticus 20:27; 1 Samuel 28:8; comp. Acts 16:16). The word "familiar" is from the Latin *familiaris*, meaning a "household servant," and was" intended to express the idea that sorcerers had spirits as their servants ready to obey their commands.

Mormon leader LeGrand Richards makes the remarkable claim:

> Truly it [*Book of Mormon*] has a familiar spirit...
>
> LeGrand Richards, *A Marvelous Work and a*

Wonder (Salt Lake City: Deseret Book Company, 1979), pp. 67-68.

As will be seen in this study, claiming the *Book Of Mormon* has a familiar spirit is truly bizarre, and yet I believe this claim is actually true.

Closely related to this claim about the *Book Of Mormon* having a familiar spirit, Mormons use Isaiah 29:4 as a proof text and argue that Isaiah prophesies the coming of the *Book Of Mormon* from the ground.

Mormon leader Joseph Fielding Smith has this to say:

> One of the most important predictions regarding the Book of Mormon is that found in the 29th chapter of Isaiah. The prophet here speaks of a people who should be like Ariel, the city where David dwelt. They should have heaviness and sorrow and should be brought down to speak out of the ground, and their speech was to be low out of the dust, and their voice was to be as of one that had a familiar spirit. Later in this same prophecy Isaiah refers to the words of "a book that is sealed, which men deliver to one that is learned, saying, Read this, I pray thee: and he saith, I cannot for it is sealed: And the book is delivered to him that is not learned, saying, Read this, I pray thee: and he saith, I am not learned." This prophecy was literally fulfilled when Martin Harris took copies of the engravings of the plates of the Book of Mormon to Professor Anthon in New York.
>
> Joseph Fielding Smith, *Doctrines of Salvation* Vol. 3, p. 213.

Is this understanding of the Mormons regarding Isaiah's prophecy true? To claim that a prophecy from Isaiah's time would be fulfilled in the 19th century, in upstate New York, is farcical.

Yes, God's Word absolutely has relevance to believers today. The difference is that Isaiah did not prophesy things that would come true in the 19th century. And furthermore, this type of interpretation reveals that Joseph Fielding Smith had no knowledge of the ordinary standards for evaluating historical documents. Moreover, the careful student of Scripture must use the grammatico-historical-hermeneutical method in determining its meaning.

This method of interpretation focuses attention not only on literary forms but upon grammatical constructions and historical contexts out of which the Scriptures were written. It is solidly in the 'literal schools' of interpretation, and is the hermeneutical methodology embraced by virtually all evangelical Protestant exegetes and scholars. The goal of biblical exegesis (to bring out) is to explore the meaning of the text which then leads to discovering its significance or relevance.

Edward J. Young was a Reformed theologian and an Old Testament scholar at Westminster Theological Seminary in Philadelphia, Pennsylvania from 1936 until his death. Professor Edward J. Young was a staunch defender of the grammatical-historical hermeneutical method. It will be interesting to see his comments on Isaiah.

Commenting on verse 4 in Isaiah chapter 29, Professor Young says:

> Continuing his address to the city, the Lord now declares that from her condition of defeat she will yet speak. The relationship of the first two verbs is interesting, and we may render, and thou shalt be brought low; from the earth thou shalt speak. These two verbs are coordinate, standing in an asyndetic relationship to one another. At the same time the first verb expresses the state or circumstances under which the action of the second takes place. Hence, we may render the first verb by an adverb. Low-thou shalt speak from the earth. When the city speaks, she has already been brought low, and her voice, which has been abased, comes from the dust. In this dust she is a mourner, perhaps also as one who is ready to plead that even now there may be a pardon and an averting of the

ultimate destruction. To emphasize how completely the people will fall the prophet states that when
the city speaks, its voice will be like that of a departed spirit and it words as mutterings that come
from the earth. The departed spirit is really one
that does not belong to this earth; for it does not
speak with a clear voice, but only with mutterings.
Such will be the voice of Judah. Once Judah was
filled with the voice of scorn and mocking; now its
voice will be like the whispering of shades (cf. 8:19).
A spirit without flesh or bones cannot speak with
a loud voice; nor will Judah when she is fallen.
Gone is the voice of arrogance; in its place, the
voice of one in humiliation.

Edward J. Young, *The Book of Isaiah* Vol. 2, (Grand
Rapids, Michigan, Eerdmans Publishing Company,
reprinted 1993), pp. 308, 309.

**Professor Young continues in his comments on verses 11 and 12 which are relevant to a proper
understanding of Isaiah's prophecy:**

11. "God has placed upon all the nation a deep
sleep with the result that the vision of all that I
have prophesied unto you has become like the
words of a sealed writing." The word all is not to be
restricted to what has just proceeded, but includes
the entire course of messages which have to do
with the fortunes of the nation. All God's purposes with His people are to thee people as a closed
book. The revelation was known to the nation,
but the nation had no understanding of and consequently no belief in the verity of that message.
From the time of his call Isaiah had carefully set
before the people both the nature of the danger

that threatened to destroy Judah and also the will of the Lord with respect to the deliverance which he purposed to accomplish. All of this, so earnestly and boldly proclaimed by the prophet, might as well have been a closed writing, inaccessible to anyone. The people walking about in darkness of a deep sleep, paid no attention to it.

The mention of a sealed writing goes back to 8:16, but from this language we are not necessarily to collude that the prophecy at this time was at hand in written form. The point is not that the prophecy was present in writing, but rather that the delivered revelations of the prophet are compared to a book that was sealed. In order to read it one would first have to break the seal and to unroll the writing. As long as the writing was sealed, there would be no possibility of reading it, and there would be no point in asking a learned person to read such a writing. Weber, however, takes the reference to sealing in a figurative sense. It is the writing itself, he thinks, that is mysterious. Even a learned person, who knows the art of reading and writing is unable to understand the writing; for although he may be able to to make out the letters and to pronounce the words, nevertheless, the meaning is sealed to him so that he does not understand what he is reading. The reply of the learned one, however, "I cannot (i.e. read it) for it is sealed," seems to imply not a lack of ability to read but simply that one cannot read for he does not know what to read. The thing to be read is sealed.

12. Not merely the learned ones cannot read, but also the ignorant. The writing is given over to one

who does not know writing, and a similar command is placed upon him. His reply is that he does not know writing. Whether he actually sees the words of the book or not he does not attempt to read for he is ignorant. The learned man could not read, for the book was sealed; the ignorant cannot read, for he does not know how to read. All among the people, therefore, are unable to read. Before them the revelation of God had been presented in clear words. To the learned and wise of this world it was meaningless, for it was to them as a sealed writing; to the ignorant it came as without meaning for they did not even have the ability to understand revelation. All, therefore, without exception, were spiritually obtuse. Before them all the Revelation of God, proclaimed through His faithful prophets, shone forth in the majesty and glory of the powerful Word; but over the entire people a deep sleep had fallen. It was a nation drunken and tottering about, groping, but never able to find the truth.

This is perhaps as sad a picture as is to be found anywhere in the Old Testament. When one considers all the manifold and rich gifts that the gracious God had given to this people, when one reflects that it was His design to make of this people a "kingdom of priests and a holy nation," and then reads of the rebellion and apostasy that characterized the nation, one can but wonder at the goodness and patience of God. Yet, God's purposes were not frustrated. Although in its entirety the nation turned its back upon Him, in His gracious wisdom God preserved alive in even the nation those that feared His Name, and in the fullness of

time sent forth His Son, about whom there would
be gathered those who loved His appearing and
who would be truly a "kingdom of priests and a
holy nation, a peculiar people; that ye should shew
forth the praises of him who hath called you out
of darkness into his marvelous light" (1 Peter 2:9).

Edward J. Young, *The Book of Isaiah* pp. 317-318.

After seeing what Professor Young has said about the prophecy of Isaiah, the Mormon understanding is nothing more than twisting the Scriptures to fit into a preconceived faulty explanation
of God's Word, in order to support the fanciful ideas about Joseph Smith and his Book of Mormon. The reason for the inhabitants of Jerusalem speaking "low out of the ground" has nothing to
do with the *Book of Mormon* being allegedly found by Joseph Smith in 19th Century upstate New
York; rather, Judah was being "brought down," because Jewish people were under God's judgment.

Concerning God judgment, Jesus gets right to heart of the matter when he quotes Isaiah:

"And in them is fulfilled the prophecy of *Esaias*," which said:

> By hearing you shall hear, and shall not understand;
> and seeing you shall see, and shall not perceive: For
> this people's heart is waxed gross, and their ears
> are dull of hearing, and their eyes they have closed;
> lest at any time they should see with their eyes and
> hear with their ears, and should understand with
> their heart, and should be converted, and I should
> heal them. (Matthew 13:14-15)

This is why the learned and unlearned could not read the sealed revelation. God had closed their
eyes and hearts.

Going on in this study, if the Mormons believe that the *Book Of Mormon* has a familiar spirit, then
they should be challenged to read what God has to say in Scripture about familiar spirits.

The teachings of Scripture are clear that a familiar spirit is something evil. We see that the

familiar spirit is condemned expressly in the following passages:

Regard not them that have familiar spirits, neither seek after wizards, to be defiled by them: I am the LORD your God. (Leviticus 19:31)

And the soul that turneth after such as have familiar spirits, and after wizards, to go a whoring after them, I will even set my face against that soul, and will cut him off from among his people. (Leviticus 20:6)

A man also or woman that hath a familiar spirit, or that is a wizard, shall surely be put to death: they shall stone them with stones: their blood shall be upon them. (Leviticus 20:27)

Or a charmer, or a consulter with familiar spirits, or a wizard, or a necromancer. (Deuteronomy 18:11)

Now Samuel was dead, and all Israel had lamented him, and buried him in Ramah, even in his own city. And Saul had put away those that had familiar spirits, and the wizards, out of the land. (1 Samuel 28:3)

Then said Saul unto his servants, Seek me a woman that hath a familiar spirit, that I may go to her, and enquire of her. And his servants said to him, Behold, there is a woman that hath a familiar spirit at Endor. And Saul disguised himself, and put on other raiment, and he went, and two men with him, and they came to the woman by night: and he said, I pray thee, divine unto me by the familiar spirit, and bring me him up, whom I shall name unto thee. And the woman said unto him, Behold, thou knowest what Saul hath done, how he hath cut off those that have familiar spirits, and the wizards, out of the land: wherefore then layest thou a snare for my life, to cause me to die? (1 Samuel 28:7-9)

And he made his son pass through the fire, and observed times, and used enchantments, and dealt with familiar spirits and wizards: he wrought much wickedness in the sight of the LORD, to provoke him to anger. (2 Kings 21:6)

Moreover the workers with familiar spirits, and the wizards, and the images, and the idols, and all the abominations that were spied in the land of Judah and in Jerusalem, did Josiah put away, that he might perform the words of the law which were written in the book that Hilkiah the priest found in the house of the LORD. (2 Kings 23:24)

So Saul died for his transgression which he committed against the LORD, even against the word of the LORD, which he kept not, and also for asking counsel of one that had a familiar spirit, to enquire of it; (1 Chronicles 10:13)

And he caused his children to pass through the fire in the valley of the son of Hinnom: also he observed times, and used enchantments, and used witchcraft, and dealt with a familiar spirit, and with wizards: he wrought much evil in the sight of the LORD, to provoke him to anger. (2 Chronicles 33:6)

And when they shall say unto you, Seek unto them that have familiar spirits, and unto wizards that peep, and that mutter: should not a people seek unto their God? for the living to the dead? (Isaiah 8:19)

And the spirit of Egypt shall fail in the midst there-

of; and I will destroy the counsel thereof: and they
shall seek to the idols, and to the charmers, and to
them that have familiar spirits, and to the wizards.
(Isaiah 19:3)

And thou shalt be brought down, and shalt speak
out of the ground, and thy speech shall be low out
of the dust, and thy voice shall be, as of one that
hath a familiar spirit, out of the ground, and thy
speech shall whisper out of the dust. (Isaiah 29:4)

After reading these scriptural passages, I cannot understand how anyone would want to promote
a book that has been said to have a familiar spirit. Every aspect of religion should be tied to other
aspects, having value and reasonableness. Choosing an aspect like the Mormons do without a reason is not only silly, it's intellectually lazy. In reality, the Mormons use the prophecy from Isaiah
as a proof text in an attempt to win converts.

What exactly does familiar spirit mean?

Familiar spirit is translated from the Hebrew word,
"*ob*", which means a necromancer.

Robert Young, *Analytical Concordance to the Holy
Bible* (London, Lutterworth Press, 1965), p. 327.

In the Jamieson-Fausset-Brown commentary on Leviticus 19:31, we learn:

Regard not them that have familiar spirits ~ The
Hebrew word, rendered "familiar spirit," signifies
the belly, and sometimes a leathern bottle, from its
similarity to the belly. It was applied in the sense
of this passage to ventriloquists, who pretended to
have communication with the invisible world. The
Hebrews were strictly forbidden to consult them as
the vain but high pretensions of those impostors
were derogatory to the honor of God and subversive

of their covenant relations with Him as His people.

neither seek after wizards ~ fortunetellers, who pretended, as the Hebrew word indicates, to prognosticate by palmistry (or an inspection of the lines of the hand) the future fate of those who applied to them.

Jamieson, Fausset and Brown, *Commentary on the Whole Bible* (Grand Rapids, Michigan, Zondervan, 1977), p. 101.

In addition we learn:

Familiar spirit, the spirit of a dead person, allegedly consulted by mediums who issued prophetic advice of a secular sort. Consultation of mediums was forbidden in the O.T. (Lev. 19:31, 20:6, 27; Deut. 18:11) as apostasy from Yahweh. Mediums were punishable by death. King Saul had put "those that had familiar spirits, and the wizards, out of the land" (1 Sam. 28:3)...Josiah put away familiar spirits, together with many other "abominations" (2 Kings 23:24). Isaiah (8:19, see also Isa. 19:3, 29:4) protested against consultation with those who had familiar spirits, and wizards that peep, and that mutter.

Madeleine S. and J. Lane Miller, *Harper's Bible Dictionary* (New York, Harper & Brothers, Publishers), 1988, pg. 185.

And finally, commenting on Leviticus 19:31, Keil-Delitzsh say:

True fear of God, however, awakens confidence in the Lord and His guidance, and excludes all superstitious and idolatrous ways and methods of discovering the future. This thought prepares the way for the warning against turning to familiar spirits, or seeking after wizards. בוא denotes a departed spirit, who was called up to make disclosures with regard to the future, hence a familiar spirit, spiritum malum qui certis artibus eliciebatur ut evocaret mortuorum manes, qui praedicarent quae ab eis petebantur (Cler.). This is the meaning in Isaiah 29:4, as well as here and in Leviticus 20:6, as is evident from Leviticus 20:27, "a man or woman in whom is an ob," and from 1 Samuel 28:7-8, baalath ob, "a woman with such a spirit." The name was then applied to the necromantist himself, by whom the departed were called up (1 Samuel 28:3; 2 Kings 23:24). The word is connected with ob, a skin. ידעני, the knowing, so to speak, "clever man" (Symm. γνώστης, Aq. γνωριστής), is only found in connection with ob, and denotes unquestionably a person acquainted with necromancy, or a conjurer who devoted himself to the invocation of spirits. (For further remarks, see as 1 Samuel 28:7.).

Keil-Delitzsch, *Commentary on the Old Testament, The Pentateuch* (Grand Rapids, Michigan, William B. Eerdmans Publishing Company, Reprinted 1985), p. 425.

If Mormons still want to claim the *Book of Mormon* has a "familiar spirit," then so be it. If so, we can actually agree with them on this. This becomes one of the many reasons to tell them to reject it.

Let it be widely proclaimed that the Bible itself should be the only infallible rule of faith and practice for the Christian.

CHAPTER 18

PAGAN INFLUENCE
UPON THE MORMON
WORLD VIEW

 n the pages that follow I will show areas of essential agreement between Mormonism and Greek philosophy. I am advancing this thesis primarily because any impartial research into this subject will confirm that there exists an essential agreement between Mormon theology and ancient pagan thought in a number of crucial areas. This will prove that the Mormon and Christian worldviews are incompatible. Secondarily, I have done this because of the astounding false accusations that have come out of Brigham Young University (B.Y.U.) in recent years about Neo-Platonism and its supposed influence upon Christianity.

One example of an attempt to connect Christianity with Neo-Platonic thought is an article titled "Early Christian Belief in a Corporeal Deity: Origen and Augustine as Reluctant Witnesses" by David L. Paulsen, Associate Professor of Philosophy at Brigham Young University. Mr. Paulsen sent me this article that he was preparing for publication. In the letter that accompanied this manuscript he solicited my "comments criticisms and especially suggestions for improvement."

In this article, prior to quoting Augustine, Mr. Paulsen prejudices the reader's mind by prefacing Augustine's remarks by saying:

> In his newly-found Neo-Platonic interpretation of
> Christian doctrine, He exults.[1]

In Paulsen's article, he did not admit that Augustine, as he matured in the faith, abandoned remnants of Greek philosophy from his own belief system. Therefore, I believe accusations of this nature by Paulsen reveal the shoddy research which B.Y.U. engages in, and also how far out of step the school is with the rest of the philosophical and theological academic world. The last serious attempts that tried to demonstrate the Gnostic and Neo-Platonic influence upon Christianity ended forty years ago. There is a whole body of literature that refutes any supposed relationship that liberal theologian, Rudolf Bultmann, and his like tried to conjure up. This "Johnny come lately" use of discredited arguments may impress the ignorant, but so far as adding anything of value to the scholarly debate, this thesis is very dubious. The books listed in the Bibliography of Section One represent only a small part of the body of literature that refutes the B.Y.U. revival of a discredited thesis.

Failure on the part of the B.Y.U. faculty to engage in serious interaction with the books listed in the Bibliography, as well as those in the appendix attached to my philosophical challenge, will reveal an apparent unwillingness or possibly an inability to interact with conservative scholarship. Can B.Y.U. be anything other than a sectarian indoctrination center if it fails to interact honestly with those who have refuted this discredited thesis? Serious scholarship has always interacted with differing points of view.

Please do not misunderstand me. I am not saying that Mormon theology is Greek philosophy, but that Mormonism appears much closer to ancient pagan thought than Christianity has been alleged to be. The following thirteen positions were clearly held by pagan philosophers. I maintain that Mormon leaders are teaching concepts that have their origin in ancient pagan thought. The apostle Paul warns us to:

> Beware lest any man spoil you through philosophy
> and vain deceit, after the tradition of men, after
> the rudiments of the world, and not after Christ.
> (Colossians 2:8)

It is my thesis that members of Mormonism have been spoiled through the vain philosophy of men. The following survey shows which philosophies have affected Mormonism.

1. Knowledge comes through sensations, i.e., experience. Empiricism is rooted in the pagan philosopher Aristotle. Particularly, this is seen in Aristotle's work *De Anima*.

In this work he deals with the types of senses. Aristotle starts this book by saying:

> That there is no sixth sense in addition to the five
> enumerated ~sight, hearing, smell, taste, touch ~
> may be established by the following considerations: [2]

He then goes on for several pages explaining the methods of receiving sensations and then reaches a conclusion that Mormon epistemology appears to have adopted. Aristotle concludes by saying that:

> Again, sensations are always true, imaginations are
> for the most part false.[3]

The philosopher Epicurus agrees with Aristotle. Epicurus explains it as follows:

> For the existence of bodies is everywhere attested
> by sense itself, and it is upon sensation that reason
> must rely when it attempts to infer the unknown
> from the known.[4]

In what ways has the Mormon religion bought into this empirical epistemology? Mormon revelation that was given by Joseph Smith simply assumes that sensations are reliable.

The *Book of Mormon* tells us how to find truth in the following way:

> And when ye shall receive these things, I would
> exhort you that ye would ask God, the Eternal
> Father, in the name of Christ, if these things are
> not true; and if ye shall ask with a sincere heart,
> with real intent, having faith in Christ, he will
> manifest the truth of it unto you, by the power of
> the Holy Ghost.[5]

Exactly how does the Mormon Holy Ghost reveal this truth to man?

Joseph Smith puts it this way in the *Doctrine And Covenants*:

> But, behold, I say unto you, that you must study it out
> in your mind; then you must ask me if it be right, and
> if it is right I will cause that your bosom shall burn
> within you; therefore, you shall feel that it is right.[6]

So truth for Mormonism is determined by a burning sensation. How a person can tell empirically the difference between valid and invalid inferences is unclear.

2. The finite (or limited) god concept. The idea of limited gods is seen throughout Greek philosophy.

For example, in Plato's *Parmenides,* we have this discussion:

> But will God, having absolute knowledge, have a knowledge of human things? Why not?.... And if God has this perfect authority and perfect knowledge, his authority cannot rule us, nor his knowledge know us, or any human thing; just as our authority does not extend to the gods, nor our knowledge know anything which is divine, so by parity of reason they, being gods, are not our masters, neither do they know the things of men.[7]

How is the Mormon deity finite, or limited?

Mormon leader Bruce R. McConkie tells us of the limits of one of the Mormon deities this way:

> The Holy Ghost is the third member of the Godhead. He is a Personage of Spirit, a Spirit Person, a Spirit Man, a Spirit Entity. He can be in only one place at one time, and he does not and cannot transform himself into any other form or image than that of the Man whom he is, though his power and influence can be manifest at one and the same time through all immensity.[8]

Mormon leader James E. Talmage places the same restrictions on the Father of the Mormon Godhead:

> His person cannot be in more than one place at anyone time.[9]

Both the Greek and Mormon deities are clearly finite in that their bodies limit them. Because of this, in my philosophical challenge to the leaders of Mormonism, I argue that their gods, just like the Greek gods, cannot know the future or have exhaustive knowledge of the universe.

3. The rejection of a sinful heart or nature.

In Aristotle's *Nicomachean Ethics* we learn about Socrates and his Pelagian like ideas concerning man's natural ability:

> For Socrates was entirely opposed to the view in question holding that there is no such thing as incontinence.[10]

Incontinent being defined as:

> Not continent; lacking in restraint, esp. over the sexual appetite.[11]

Christians have always believed that our sin has brought on dreadful consequences. We have lost our freedom to choose what is good. Our choices are in line with the desires of our nature. Our natures are sinful and as a result our choices always go toward the inclinations of our fallen natures. We choose, but these choices are always in harmony with our natural state.

Socrates believed in man's natural ability of restraint. In what ways have Mormon theologians argued for a position much closer to that of Socrates than that of Christianity?

Former Mormon Apostle LeGrand Richards explains his view of man's ability:

> Thus all nations and people have free agency and, according to their choice, the Lord will do unto them.... If all men are not saved, it will be because they, in the exercise of their free will, do not accept his gift of grace.[12]

Fallen man, according to Richards, is able to do many things. Through man's own choice he can be saved. If men are not saved it is because "they...do not accept his...grace." It is easy to detect Richard's emphasis upon man's ability. Socrates believed in the power of restraint, which would include man's ability to choose and evaluate the best choices.

4. Exceptional men becoming gods.

In Plato's *Gorgias* we have the story of mortals becoming judges, i.e., gods:

> I have made my sons judges: two from Asia, Minos
> and Rhadamanthus, and one from Europe, Aeacus.
> And these, when they are dead, shall give judgment
> in the meadow at the parting of the ways, whence
> the two roads lead, one to the Islands of the Bless-
> ed, and the other to Tartarus.... Rhadamanthus
> sends to the Islands of the Blessed. Aeacus does
> the same; and they both have sceptres, and judge;
> but Minos alone has a golden sceptre and is seated
> looking on, as Odysseus in Homer declares that he
> saw him...[13]

In Plato's *Apology* we learn more concerning this:

> He is delivered from the professors of justice in
> this world, and finds the true judges who are said
> to give judgement there, Minos and Rhadaman-
> thus and Aeacus and Triptolemus and other sons
> of God who were righteous in their own life. [14]

Mormon leaders have also taught that certain people in this world may become gods themselves.

Joseph Smith puts it this way:

> Here, then is eternal life to know the only wise and
> true God; and you have got to learn how to be
> Gods yourselves. [15]

Mormon authority Milton Hunter agrees with this, and tells about Joseph Smith's doctrine of men becoming gods in this way:

> No prophet of record gave more complete and
> forceful explanations of the doctrine that men may
> become Gods than did the American Prophet....[16]

Both the ancient Greek religion and Mormonism hold to the belief that certain men may be able to become gods.

5. The world or matter existing eternally and not created by God or the gods. Epicurus taught this idea.

Epicurus says:

> To begin with, nothing comes into being out of what is nonexistent. For in that case anything would have arisen out of anything, standing as it would in no need of its proper germs. And if that which disappears had been destroyed and become nonexistent, every thing would have perished, that into which the things were dissolved being non-existent. Moreover, the sum total of things was always such as it is now, and such it will ever remain. For there is nothing into which it can change.... Beyond bodies and space there is nothing which by mental apprehension or on its analogy can conceive to exist. When we speak of bodies and space, both are regarded as wholes or separate things, not as the properties or accidents of separate things. [he repeats this in the First Book and in Books fourteen and fifteen of the work "On Nature" and in the Large Epitome, of bodies some are composite, others the elements of which these composite bodies are made. These elements are indivisible and unchangeable, and necessarily so, if things are not all to be destroyed and pass into nonexistence, but are to be strong enough to endure when the composite bodies are broken up, because they possess a solid nature and are incapable of being anywhere or anyhow dissolved. It follows that the first beginnings must be indivisible, corporeal entities.... Of

all this there is no beginning, since both atoms and void exist from everlasting.[17]

Mormon founder Joseph Smith agrees completely with Epicurus:

> You ask the learned doctors why they say the world was made out of nothing; and they will answer, "Doesn't the Bible say He created the world?" And they infer, from the word create, that it must have been out of nothing. Now, the word create came from the word baurau which does not mean to create out of nothing; it means to organize; the same as a man would organize materials and build a ship. Hence, we infer that God had materials to organize the world out of chaos-chaotic matter, which is element, and in which dwells all the glory. Element had an existence from the time he had. The pure principles which can never be destroyed; they may be organized and re-organized, but not destroyed. They had no beginning, and can have no end.[18]

6. Pre-existence of souls and men.

Plato taught this belief. In the work called *Phaedrus* we read:

> This soul shall at her first birth pass, not into any other animal, but only into a man....[19]

The concept of pre-existence of the soul is a well known and undisputed teaching of Mormonism.

Mormon leader Bruce R. McConkie teaches the idea of pre-existence much like Plato. He has this to say:

> Pre-existence is the term commonly used to describe the premortal existence of the spirit children of God the Father.[20]

7. Polytheism or believing that more than one god exists.

In Plato's *Laws Book Ten* we read:

> If Cleinias and this our reverend company succeed
> in proving to you that you know not what you say
> of the Gods, then will God help you; but should
> you desire to hear more, listen to what we say to
> the third opponent, if you have any understanding
> whatsoever. For I think that we have sufficiently
> proved the existence of the Gods....[21]

This polytheism was part of the common philosophical belief of the Greeks. Mormonism shares this polytheistic outlook.

Joseph Smith agrees with Plato:

> In the beginning, the head of the Gods called a coun-
> cil of the Gods; and they came together and concoct-
> ed a plan to create the world and people it.[22]

Not only were there gods involved in the organization of this world, according to Mormonism, all faithful Mormon men are striving for god-hood or exaltation.

8. The corporeal or physical god concept is rooted in Stoicism.

Plotinus referring to the Stoic school says this about them:

> To a certain school, body-forms exclusively are the
> Real Beings, existence is limited to bodies; there is
> one only Matter, the stuff underlying the primal-
> constituents of the Universe: existence is nothing
> but this Matter: everything is some modification of
> this; the elements of the Universe are simply this
> Matter in a certain condition. The school has even
> the audacity to foist Matter upon the divine beings
> so that, finally, God himself becomes a mode of Mat-

ter - and this though they make it corporeal, describing it as a body, void of quality but a magnitude.[23]

The Mormon Scriptures called the *Doctrine And Covenants* agrees with and promotes this Stoic notion:

The Father has a body of flesh and bones as tangible as man's....[24]

Mormon leader James E. Talmage concurs with this teaching. He has this to say about it:

Admitting the personality of God; we are compelled to accept the fact of His materiality....[25]

In Mormon cosmology, matter is eternal. Along with eternal matter, Mormons believe that spirit intelligences have existed co-eternally with God. These intelligences have not fully progressed.

9. All men are children of God.

This notion comes from Stoicism. Epictetus tells us this about man's origin:

If the things are true which are said by the philosophers about the kinship between God and man, what else remains for men to do than what Socrates did? [26]

A little further into the chapter we learn this information:

The most comprehensive community is that which is composed of men and God, and that from God have descended the seeds not only to my father and grandfather, but to all beings which are generated on the earth and are produced, and particularly to rational beings for these only are by their nature formed to have communion with God, being by means of reason conjoined with Him - why should not such a man call himself a citizen of the world,

why not a son of God, and why should he be afraid
of anything which happens among men? Is kinship
with Caesar or with any other of the powerful in
Rome sufficient to enable us to live in safety, and
above contempt and without fear at all? and to
have God for your maker and father and guardian,
shall not this release us from sorrows and fears?....
And are we not in a manner kinsman of God, and
did we not come from Him? [27]

McConkie's position is identical with that of Epictetus:

All men are brothers in the sense of being the spirit
offspring of Deity.[28]

All people, according to Mormonism, were sexually procreated by the Mormon god and his wives
prior to coming to this earth.

10. The concept of free agency or free will.

The Epicureans promoted this pagan idea in particular.

**Lucretius informs us of the Epicurean thought. He does this by mocking the Stoics and their
doctrine of providence or God's control of the world:**

They would seek a refuge in handing over things to
the gods and supposing all things to be guided by
their nod.[29]

If the gods guide all things, what happens to free agency? Wouldn't man's choices also be guided?
For reasons like this, Mormons reject divine determination or God's providential control of all
things. In this sense, Mormons will join the Epicureans in mocking God's providential control
of the world.

Plotinus also tells us this about Epicureanism:

Epicurus denies a Providence....[30]

Why did he do this? Because according to Epicurus, providence and free will conflicted, or at least they appeared to.

McConkie explains man's free agency essentially the same as the Epicureans:

> Wherefore, men are free according to the flesh; and all things are given them which are expedient unto man. And they are free to choose liberty and eternal life, through the great mediation of all men, or to choose captivity and power of the devil; for he seeketh that all men might be miserable like unto himself. (2 Ne.2:26-30;10:23; Alma 13:3; Hela. 14:31.) [31]

11. A. The fall of man is necessary and B. souls come to this earth to learn good from evil, and C. then can return after meeting certain requirements, and D. attain salvation, i.e., becoming godlike.

Plotinus the third great master of Hellenistic thought taught this.

A. The fall of man is necessary

In the second *Ennead* Plotinus begins to explain man's fall this way:

> For our part, nature keeps us upon the work of the Soul as long as we are not wrecked in the multiplicity of the Universe: once thus sunk and held we pay the penalty, which consists both in the fall itself and in the lower rank thus entailed upon us: riches and poverty are caused by the combinations of external fact. [32]

In the fourth *Ennead* he gives us more information about this:

> With this comes what is known as the casting of the wings, the enchaining in body: the soul has lost that innocency of conducting the higher which it knew when it stood with the All-Soul, that earlier

state to which all its interest would bid it hasten
back. It has fallen.... Souls that take this way have
place in both spheres, living of necessity the life
there and the life here by turns . . . they must of
necessity experience birth.[33]

Mormon leader McConkie in essence agrees with this as stated:

In conformity with the will of the Lord, Adam fell
both spiritually and temporally . . . Temporal death
also entered the world, meaning that man and all
created things became mortal, and blood became
the life preserving element in the natural body....
Adam fell that men might be.[34]

B. souls come to this earth to learn good from evil

**Beginning in the fourth *Ennead*, Plotinus tells of man's task of learning good from evil, and
our benefit from it:**

If it [the soul] turns back quickly, all is well; it will
have taken no hurt by acquiring the knowledge
of evil and coming to understand what sin is....
Where the faculty is incapable of knowing without
contact, the experience of evil brings the clearer
perception of Good.[35]

James E. Talmage agrees and puts it this way:

Sin was introduced to the world by Satan; yet it
is by divine permission that mankind are brought
in contact with sin, the contrast between evil and
good thus being learned by experience.[36]

C. What type of requirements do we have to meet to advance from this life?

Plotinus in the first *Ennead* puts it this way. (Notice the emphasis on man's self effort of puri-

fication to meet the requirements in order to advance.)

> Since Evil is here, "haunting this world by necessary law," and it is the Soul's design to escape Evil, we must escape hence. But what is this escape? "In attaining Likeness to God," we read. And this is explained as becoming just and holy, living by wisdom, the entire nature grounded in Virtue.... And elsewhere he [Plato] declares all the virtues without exception to be purifications....The solution is in understanding the virtues and what each has to give: thus the man will learn to work with this or that as every several need demands. And as he reaches to loftier principles and other standards these in turn will define his conduct: for example, Restraint in its earlier form will no longer satisfy him, he will work for the final Disengagement; he will live no longer, the life of the good man such as Civic Virtue commends but, leaving this beneath him, will take up instead another life, that of the Gods....What art is there, what method, what discipline to bring us there where we must go? [37]

McConkie in essence agrees and explains it this way:

> Full salvation is attained by virtue of knowledge, truth, righteousness, and all true principles. Many conditions must exist in order to make such salvation available to men.... Salvation in the celestial kingdom of God, however is not salvation by grace alone. Rather, it is salvation by grace coupled with obedience to the laws and ordinances of the gospel.[38]

D. How do we achieve salvation and the status of god?

The final goal for Plotinus is as follows in the second *Ennead*:

> There is another life emancipated, whose quality is
> progression towards the higher realm, towards the
> good and divine, towards that Principle which no
> one possesses except by deliberate usage but so may
> appropriate, becoming each personally, the higher,
> the beautiful, the Godlike.[39]

Plotinus continues this idea in the sixth *Ennead*:

> For to be a god is to be integral with the Supreme....
> Thus we have all the vision that may be of Him and
> of ourselves; but is of a self wrought to splendor,
> brimmed with the Intellectual light, become that
> very light, pure, buoyant, unburdened, raised to
> Godhood.... When the soul begins again to mount
> it comes not to something alien but to its very self;
> thus detached, it is not in nothingness but in itself;
> self-gathered it is no longer in the order of being;
> it is in the Supreme. There is thus a converse in
> virtue of which the essential man outgrows Being,
> becomes identical with the Transcendent of Being.
> The self thus lifted, we are in the likeness of the
> Supreme.... This is the life of gods and of the god-
> like and blessed among men....[40]

**The goal for the Mormon is virtually identical with this. McConkie sums up the Mormon posi-
tion as follows:**

> Exaltation is eternal life, the kind of life which
> God lives.... They have eternal increase, a contin-
> uation of the lives, eternal lives ... They inherit in
> due course the fullness of the glory of the Father,
> meaning that they have all power in heaven and

> earth. (D. & C. 76:50-60; 93:1-40.) Then shall they
> be gods, because they shall have no end....[41]

There are fundamental differences between Plotinus and Mormonism that were not covered in Section Eleven. Mormonism holds to a radical materialistic view, while Plotinus came dangerously close to rejecting matter altogether. It is important to note, however, that both systems have schemes for accomplishing ultimate goals that parallel each other in an uncanny way.

12. Rejection of the Creator/creature distinction.

Mormon theology agrees completely with the Greek philosophers.

For example Pythagoras said that:

> Gods and men are akin....[42]

McConkie again shows the agreement with the ancient Greeks as follows:

All men and women are in the similitude of the universal Father and Mother, and are literally the sons and daughters of Deity.[43]

13. Plato taught an ethical dualism. He believed in two principles, the One or the good and the

> Indefinite Dyad the source of evil.[44] He also saw
> good and evil occurring in cycles.[45]

Specifically, Plato had this to say in his work *Theaetetus*:

> Socrates. Evils, Theodorus, can never pass away;
> for there must always remain something which is
> antagonistic to good.[46]

> The religion of Zoroastrianism also taught an eter-
> nal struggle between good and evil which is an eth-
> ical dualism.[47]

This same dualism appears in the *Book of Mormon*:

> For it must needs be, that there is an opposition in
> all things.[48]

In addition to these thirteen points, one can find an interesting parallel between the Greek gods coming from Mt. Olympus to visit men, and the Mormon gods coming from Kolob. In particular Zeus has sexual relations with a mortal woman to produce Hercules. In Mormonism, one of the Mormon deities comes to earth to have sexual relations with the mortal woman Mary to produce the Mormon version of Jesus. These thirteen points show the vast amount of Greek philosophy that has been absorbed by Mormonism concerning the nature of God, the nature of man, and the cosmos.

Some years ago, Mormon researchers were trying to show that elements of Mormon theology had survived among the Dead Sea Scrolls, the Nag Hammadi writings, and the Mandaean writings. Einar C. Erickson was a leader among this group of Mormon researchers. I would agree with them that you find Mormon theological parallels among the Gnostic sects. While parallels do exist, Erikson's use of the parallels with Gnosticism does not constitute historical validation of Mormonism. I reject that premise.

I believe, however, that Erickson's work inadvertently serves to confirm my thesis that Mormonism is in essential agreement with ancient pagan thought. Therefore, any similarities between Mormonism and Christianity would be only one of Mormonism using Christian terminology with substantial redefinitions.

When discussing Mormon dependence upon Greek philosophy we are not dealing with trivial points of similarity, but essential areas of agreement between the ancient Greek and Mormon worldviews. The following would be a fair description of the Mormon worldview:

EPISTEMOLOGY

William James describes empiricism as a:

> tough-minded materialistic epistemology.[49]

Mormon epistemology could be described as an Aristotelian based empirical system.

Mormon philosopher Sterling McMurrin appears to confirm this analysis of Mormon epistemology:

But it is possible to say that Mormonism in its philosophical inclinations participates strongly in the
empirical attitudes that are characteristic of recent
and contemporary thought. It [Mormon epistemol-
ogy] acknowledges the claims of scientific method
– [and] a combination of empiricism and qualified
rationalism and it even exhibits sensory empirical
leanings in its references to revelation....[50]

ONTOLOGY

Mormon ontology could be described as a Stoic, i.e., a materialistic, fundamentally monistic metaphysic.

McMurrin describes Mormon ontology as follows:

On the question of the qualitative nature of reality, the Mormon position is perhaps best described
as fundamentally monistic but with an important
dualistic facet....[51]

It should also be noted that, for Mormonism ultimate reality contains diversity, such as countless
corporeal finite gods scattered throughout the cosmos.

Again, McMurrin's analysis is informative:

Mormon philosophy is an unqualified commitment to metaphysical pluralism. The concept of
reality as a composition of independently real entities is established explicitly in certain statements
that have been accepted by Mormon writers as normative for doctrine, and it can be discerned as a
fundamental presupposition of popular Mormon
thought by inference from innumerable ideas and

attitudes that are commonplace with Mormon
people....[52]

How Mormonism attempts to escape this metaphysical monistic/pluralistic contradiction will be
of interest.

**McMurrin goes on to tell us about the temporal, spatial, and material aspect of the Mormon
god's being:**

> There are numerous important implications for
> religion resident in the doctrine that God is a spa-
> tial and temporal being. Among these in Mormon
> theology are the belief, contrary to the verdict of
> Christianity generally, that God is an embodied
> being with a spatially configured form, and the
> belief that not only is heaven located somewhere
> but that the eternal life of a heavenly being is tem-
> porally ordered....[53]

ETHICS

**Mormon ethics could be described simply as a type of pragmatic platonic humanism. McMur-
rin has described Mormon ethics in this very way:**

> Yet even though its moral philosophy has a pro-
> nounced platonic character, Mormonism in prac-
> tice has always exhibited marked pragmatic ten-
> dencies. Both William James and John Dewey
> evidenced an interest in the pragmatic facets of
> Mormonism, Dewey finding that Mormon group
> life expressed much that was central in his own
> instrumentalism.[54]

McMurrin goes on to say this about Mormonism:

It is the belief that though he is finite man nevertheless has necessary being, that constituted the philosophical justification of much that characterizes Mormon theology, supporting, for instance, its pelagian and arminian tendencies, and giving fundamental encouragement to its accent on the positive facets of human existence. Here is the philosophical ground for the paradoxical Mormon concept of the fall of man, the denial of original sin, the rejection of the traditional doctrine of grace, the intense preoccupation with the freedom of the will, the opposition to the dogmas of election and perseverance, the liberal estimate of human nature, and the affirmation of the radically unorthodox concepts of God and salvation.[55]

It should be noted that the Mormon is continually trying to interpret reality-utilizing methods of science, which are based upon man's finite reason and sensory experience, along with the revelations that the Mormon Kolobian deities give him. **This is the essence of humanistic ethics. Or again as McMurrin puts it:**

Indeed, it is not entirely inaccurate to describe Mormonism as a kind of naturalistic humanism within a general theistic context.[56]

TELEOLOGY

Mormon teleology could be described as cyclical. All pagan teleology was of this nature until Christianity introduced a linear view of history. Mormon history keeps repeating itself with new earths, and new saviors on to infinity. Again to quote McMurrin:

It is of major importance to Mormon doctrine that it is grounded in the idea that the universe is for the most part dynamic in the sense of there being

> a kind of cosmic evolution with the world moving
> endlessly in time toward goals which when reached
> inevitably propose others beyond....[57]

The ultimate goal for the faithful Mormon and their offspring is essentially the same and is best stated by Plotinus:

> In all this there is no sin--there is only matter of dis-
> cipline-but our concern is not merely to be sinless
> but to be God....[58]

It can be said, in summary, that the philosophical positions advanced by the Greeks influenced to such a large extent the areas of epistemology, ontology, ethics, and teleology that the Greek-influence argument is a sufficient explanation for positions that have been adopted by some western religions and philosophy. These same concepts have influenced present day Mormonism. While admitting that Mormonism may not be aware of the original source of some of its positions, it nevertheless is dependent upon Greek philosophical ideas at numerous points. Apostate thinking, down to the present day, has never escaped entirely from Greek thought. Mormon positions, along with other forms of paganism, are related also, and are the result of the superior philosophical thinking of the Greeks.

The Mormon worldview could be described as an empirical epistemology, working closely with a contradictory Stoic monistic/pluralistic metaphysic, along with a form of a pragmatic Platonic ethical dualism which incorporates a radical Pelagian/free-will view of man's nature, combined with a cyclical teleology. Or, more simply, you could describe this as the Greek-Mormon-Gnostic worldview.

BIBLICAL REFUTATIONS OF THE GREEK/MORMON POSITIONS

1. Knowledge comes through sensations, i.e., experience.
(Psalms 31:5; 136:6 John 1:9; 5:6; 17:3)

2. Finite (or limited gods). (Daniel 4:34-35; 5:21; Isaiah 43:10-13)

3. The rejection of a sinful heart or nature. (Job 15:15-16; Psalms 51:5; Ecclesiastes 7:20; 8:11; Jeremiah 17:9; Mark 7:21-23; Romans 3:9-18; 5:12)

4. Exceptional men becoming gods. (Isaiah 43:10; 44:6-8; 45:21)

5. The world or matter being eternal and not created by God or the gods. (Genesis 1:1)

6. Pre-existence of souls and men. (Genesis 2:7; Job 38:4; Romans 4:17)

7. Polytheism or believing that more than one God exists. (Isaiah 44:6-8; 45:21)

8. The corporeal or physical god concept.
(Numbers 23:19; Hosea 11:9; Luke 24:39; John 4:24)

9. All men are children of God. (John 8:44; Ephesians 2:3)

10. The concept of free agency or free will. (John 1:13; 5:40; Romans 3:11; 8:7) By rejecting free will or agency I am not saying that we do not make choices, but that we do not make undetermined choices.

11. A. The fall of man being necessary.
(Genesis 3:13; Job 34:10; 2 Corinthians 11:3; James 1:13)

When considering God's eternal plan, of course the fall is included in it. What I am objecting to is the Mormon view that the fall is necessary to continue advancing men to godhood. The Christian view is that the fall was permitted by divine decree. In the Mormon view however it is absolutely an essentially good thing that happened.

11. B. that souls come to this earth to learn good from evil. (Genesis 3:19; 6:5; Psalms 14:3; Romans 5:12; 7:18; Ephesians 2:1, 5, 12; 4:18) Man is not on probation or learning good from evil. The Scriptures declare mankind dead in sins and trespasses. Man is in bondage or a slave to sin.

11. C. then can return after meeting certain requirements and attain salvation, i.e., (Ephesians 2:8, 9). Man is not saved by meeting requirements or works but by grace. Grace is defined as God's undeserved love or unmerited favor.

11. D. becoming godlike. (Isaiah 43:10; 45:21)

12. Rejection of the Creator/creature distinction. (Numbers 23:19; Jeremiah 23:24; 2

Chronicles 6:18; Psalms 147:5)

13. An ethical dualism. (Exodus 7:13; 1 Samuel 16:14; 2 Samuel 17:14; 1 Kings 22:20-22, 34-38; Job 1:6-12; 2:1-6; Proverbs 16:9)

NOTES:
GREEK ORIGINS

1. David L. Paulsen, *Early Christian Belief in a Corporeal Deity: Origen and Augustine as Reluctant Witnesses* (Provo: unpublished manuscript 1988), p. 9.

2. Aristotle, De Anima, *The Basic Works of Aristotle* Trans. by J. A. Smith, (New York: Random House, 1941), [Bk.2.ch.12] 425a-428a p. 581.

3. Ibid., p. 587.

4. Diogenes Laertius, *Epicurus, Diogenes Laertius* 2 Trans. by R.D. Hicks, Loeb Classical Library (Campbridge: Harvard University Press, 1979), 10.40. p.569.

5. Joseph Smith,* the *Book Of Mormon* (Salt Lake City: The Church of Jesus Christ of Latter-day Saints, 1977), p. 520.

6. Joseph Smith, *Doctrine And Covenants* (Salt Lake City: The Church of Jesus Christ of Latter-day Saints, 1977), p. 13.

7. Plato, *Parmenides* Vol. 7 of Great Books of the Western World, Trans. by Benjamin Jowett, (Chicago: Encyclopedia Britannica, 1952), [134] p. 490.

8. Bruce R. McConkie, *Mormon Doctrine* (Salt Lake City: Bookcraft, 1989), p. 359.

9. James E. Talmage, *Articles Of Faith* (Salt Lake City: The Church of Jesus Christ of Latter-day Saints, 1988), p. 39.

10. Aristotle, *Nicomachean Ethics, The Basic Works of Aristotle* Trans. by W.D. Ross, (New York: Random House, 1941), [Bk.7:ch.2] 1145b p. 1038.

11. Emery & Brewster, *The New Century Dictionary* (New York: P. F. Collier & Son Corporation, 1927), p. 811.

12. LeGrand Richards, *A Marvelous Work And A Wonder* (Salt Lake City, Deseret Book Co. 1978), p. 345, 347.

13. Plato, *Gorgias, Vol. 7 of Great Books of the Western World* Trans. by Benjamin Jowett, (Chicago: Encyclopedia Britannica, 1952), [523, 524, 526] pp. 292, 293.

14. Plato, Apology, *Vol. 7 of Great Books of the Western World* Trans. by Benjamin Jowett, (Chicago: Encyclopedia Britannica, 1952), [41] p. 211.

15. Joseph Smith, *The Teachings of the Prophet Joseph Smith* Arranged by Joseph Fielding Smith; (Salt Lake City: Deseret Book Co., 1976), p. 346.

16. Milton Hunter, *The Gospel Thru The Ages* (Salt Lake City: Deseret Book Co., 1957), p. 115.

17. Diogenes Laertius, *Epicurus, Diogenes Laertius* 2 Trans. by R.D. Hicks, Loeb Classical Library (Cambridge: Harvard University Press, 1979), 10.39-46. pp. 569-575.

18. Smith, Arranged by J. F. Smith pp. 350-352.

19. Plato, *Phaedrus, The Works of Plato* Trans. by Benjamin Jowett, (New York: Random House, 1956), p. 289.

20. McConkie, p. 589.

21. Plato, *Laws, Vol. 7 of Great Books of the Western World* Trans. by Benjamin Jowett, (Chicago: Encyclopedia Britannica, 1952), [905] p. 768.

22. Smith, Arranged by J. F. Smith p. 349.

23. Plotinus, *The Six Enneads Vol. 17 of Great Books of the Western World*, Trans. by S. Mackenna and P.S. Page, (Chicago: Encyclopedia Britannica, 1952), 2.4,1; p. 50.

24. Joseph Smith, *Doctrine And Covenants* (Salt Lake City: The Church of Jesus Christ of Latter-day Saints, 1976), p. 238.

25. Talmage, p. 39.

26. Epictetus, *Discourses of Epictetus, Vol. 12 of Great Books of The Western World* Trans. By George Long, (Chicago: Encyclopedia Britannica, 1952), [Bk1:ch.9] p. 114.

27. Ibid., p. 115.

28. McConkie, p. 105.

29. Lucretius, *On the Nature of Things Vol. 12 of Great Books of the Western World*, Trans. by H. A. J. Munro, (Chicago: Encyclopedia Britannica, 1952), [1161,1194] pp. 76,77.

30. Plotinus, *The Six Enneads, Vol. 17 of Great Books of the Western World*, Trans. by S. Mackenna and P.S. Page, (Chicago: Encyclopedia Britannica, 1952), 2.9,15; p. 75.

31. McConkie, p. 26.

32. Plotinus, 2.3,8; p. 45.

33. Ibid., 4.8, 4; p. 203.

34. McConkie, pp. 268-269.

35. Plotinus, 4.8, 5&7; pp. 203-204.

36. Talmage, p. 52.

37. Plotinus, 1.2, 1; p. 6. 1.2, 3; p. 7. 1.2, 7; p. 10. 1.3; 1; p. 10.

38. McConkie, pp. 670-671.

39. Plotinus, 2.3, 9; p. 45.

40. Ibid., 6.9, 8; p. 358. 6.9, 9; p. 359. 6.9, 11; p. 360.

41. McConkie, p. 257.

42. Diogenes Laertius, Pythagoras, Diogenes Laertius 2 Trans. by R.D. Hicks, Loeb Classical Library Cambridge: Harvard University Press, 1979), 8.27. p. 343.

43. McConkie, p. 589.

44. A. H. Armstrong ed.. *The Cambridge History of Later Greek and Early Medieval Philosophy* (London: Cambridge University Press, 1967), p. 26.

45. A. H. Armstrong, *An Introduction to Ancient Philosophy* (Totowa: Rowman and Allan-held, 1977), pp. 58-59.

46. Plato, *Theaetetus, The Works of Plato* Trans. by Benjamin Jowett, (New York: Random House, 1956), p. 526.

47. Gordon H. Clark, *Thales To Dewey*, (Jefferson: Trinity, 1989), p. 192.

48. Joseph Smith, the *Book Of Mormon* (Salt Lake City: The Church of Jesus Christ of Latter-day Saints, 1977), 2 Nephi 2:11-27 pp. 53-55.

49. Clark, p. 504.

50. Sterling McMurrin, *The Theological Foundations of the Mormon Religion* (Salt Lake City: University of Utah Press, 1965), p. 11.

51. Sterling McMmurrin, *The Philosophical Foundations of Mormon Theology* (Salt Lake City: University of Utah Press, 1979), p. 17.

52. Ibid., p. 8.

53. Ibid., p. 14.

54. Ibid., p. 25.

55. Ibid., p. 29.

56. Ibid., p. 20.

57. Ibid., p. 21, 22.

58. Plotinus, 1.2, 6; p. 9.

PART 5

A CHALLENGE,
A RESPONSE,
AND A CONFESSION OF FAITH

CHAPTER 19
A THEOLOGICAL
AND PHILOSOPHICAL CHALLENGE

CHAPTER 20
A FOLLOW-UP LETTER TO CHALLENGE,
AND A RESPONSE FROM MORMON SCHOLARS

CHAPTER 21
A PERSONAL CONFESSION OF FAITH

Food for Thought:

"Why should we be indignant about slanders directed against a human friend, while at the same time we are patient about the basest slanders directed against our God?" - J. Gresham Machen, Christianity and Liberalism

CHAPTER 19

A Theological
and Philosophical
Challenge

To The President of the Mormon Church and The Twelve Apostles:
May 13, 1988

ver the years I have developed a very low view of the Mormon Church due in part to your official representatives called missionaries, or elders. After talking to many of them, I have noticed that all are unable to answer the questions I raised about your world view, and usually are unwilling to attempt to do so. Other members of your church have attempted to answer my questions, but without exception they say that their answers are their own personal opinions and do not represent the official position of their church. This is most frustrating. Who does represent your church? Does your church have something to hide? What accounts for the complete widespread ignorance of the official position of your church?

I'm interested in an official quotable position, even if it involves official speculation. That is why my letter is directed to you, the leaders of the Mormon religion. It is mind boggling to find a religious movement as large as yours in which its adherents are unable to articulate its official doctrine. In talking to members of your religion I have asked them if they would like me to adopt their Mormon beliefs. They answer in the affirmative. I then give them the opportunity to convince me with logical, biblical, reasons to surrender my beliefs and adopt their beliefs.

I now give you the same opportunity. For me to adopt your world view, you will have to show me that your world view can better answer the philosophical and theological questions that I will raise. The Christian Theistic world view has solid, biblical, and logical answers to these questions. The following questions represent a philosophical and theological challenge to your world view. If you provide no response to these questions, I will have no alternative but to conclude that you are unable to answer these questions, and Mormonism is therefore an idolatrous, subjective, emotional, and irrational system.

I will list the questions numerically under each of the basic elements of a world view.

Four philosophical areas will be covered.

Introduction:

1. Please offer me a definition of the Mormon world view. Do not give an answer like "read the *Book of Mormon*." I have already read this book and many other Mormon books.

2. Is your world view logically coherent?

A. Epistemology:

1. Are Mormons and your God, or gods, empiricists, rationalists, irrationalists, or do you hold to some other concept of gaining knowledge?

2. Sterling McMurrin on page eleven of his book, Theological Foundations of the Mormon Religion, states that Mormons and their Gods are basically empiricists. Is McMurrin correct in his perception of Mormon epistemology?

3. How would you respond to the arguments of Gordon Clark in *A Christian View of Men and Things* and *Religion, Reason, and Revelation* and of Cornelius Van Til in *Defense of the Faith* and *A Christian Theory of Knowledge* that neither empiricism nor rationalism can give certain knowledge?

4. How would Mormonism answer the objections to empiricism raised in writings by David Hume, Emmanuel Kant, and Jean-Paul Sartre? Hume was a skeptic despite his adherence to empiricism. Emmanuel Kant was reportedly awakened from his dogmatic slumbers when he saw the effects of Hume's skepticism on empirical epistemology.

5. Is empiricism a Christian epistemology?

6. Are the revelations of the Mormon God empirically based revelations?

7. Aristotle, John Locke, David Hume, George Berkeley, and Bertrand Russell were all empirical thinkers. They would all agree that knowledge comes through the senses in the following order: (a) sensations (b) perceptions (c) memory images, (d) development of

abstract ideas. Perceptions are inferences from sensations. How do you know valid from invalid inferences?

8. About five percent of the population does not have any memory images at all. How can these people be empiricists?

9. What about studies which deal in the areas of the threshold of sensations? These studies show unreliable the senses can be, especially sight (colors), and hearing (sound).

10. Can tiredness, drugs, and optical illusions deceive the senses?

11. What about sin? Demonic deception?

12. Will you defend empiricism by starting in the middle of, or at the end of the system? This is committing the logical fallacy of begging the question. Show me how the first part of your system works.

13. Empirical epistemology has its roots in the pagan philosopher Aristotle. Should a Christian incorporate pagan thinking into Christianity?

14. During the humanistic enlightenment, Locke, Hume, and Berkeley developed systematic empirical thought, or at least they thought they did. Does a Christian really want to be influenced by these enlightenment thinkers?

15. The main objection goes back to question number seven. Would it be more biblical to adopt a Christian theory of knowledge as stated by Cornelius Van Til in his book of the same title? See also Augustine's *De Magistro* for a historic study in the area of epistemology. This work refutes Aristotle's empiricism.

16. What do you mean by God?

17. Where did your God come from?

18. Are there other beings like your God?

19. If so, where did they come from?

20. What do you mean by "create?"

21. Can you present any conclusive lexical evidence that the Hebrew word for "create" (*bara*) means "to organize out of pre-existing matter?"

22. Let's summarize what I think Mormons are teaching, but correct me if I'm wrong. The Mormon God was once a man, had a beginning and organized pre-existent matter into a world and possibly other worlds. Who created or organized the world your God lived on when he was a boy before becoming God?

23. How can you use words like "omnipresent" (present everywhere), "omnipotent" (all powerful), and "omniscient" (all knowing) to describe a finite or limited God?

24. Does Mormon epistemology reject the use of logic?

25. How does your God travel? A space ship? Don't beg the question.

26. Does your God exist in time?

27. If he does exist in time, how can he know the future? Remember his body limits him to be in only one place at a time.

28. Existing in time prevents us from knowing the future, why not your God? Don't beg the question by saying "Because He's God." Being God doesn't seem to help him overcome the physical limitation of being at one place at a time.

29. How would it be logically possible for your God to control the future if He does not know the future?

30. How does the Mormon Church extricate itself from the logical contradiction between the doctrine of God's omnipresence and the fact that the Mormon god has a body, which by definition must be finite? By religious irrationalism? By Hegelian dialectical logic?

31. Mormon theology appears to accept the concept of God's omnipresence, but then holds to the antithesis of a God with a body. Is your belief that the Holy Spirit is like electricity and filling the universe, the synthesis? Is this Hegelian dialectics?

32. Inside the front cover of the *Book of Mormon* one finds the proposition that there is only one God. However, the Mormon religion seems to teach the antithesis of this proposition,

namely there are three separate Gods. Are your beliefs in the doctrine of three gods, but one in purpose, the synthesis? Is this another example of Hegelian logic?

33. What role does the law of non-contradiction have in Mormon theology?

34. What does the Mormon Church mean by "one?"

35. When Mormons declare that they believe in only one God, and at the same time really mean that they believe in three Gods, but one in purpose, is this the informal logical fallacy of equivocation?

36. Does your God submit to more senior Gods in the universe? If so, in what way?

37. How far does the dominion of your God extend? Just this solar system? The Milky Way Galaxy?

38. Where do the other Gods domains begin? Are their domains overlapping?

39. How does your God communicate with the other Gods? Intergalactic phone service, unknown radio frequency, mental telepathy, and celestial general conferences?

40. Is the universe bigger than your God is? Remember he has a body.

41. Is the universe endless?

42. Has your God been everywhere in the universe? When?

43. If answer to question 41 were yes, how would your God with a finite body ever finish exploring the universe?

44. When would he ever have time to be God over this world?

45. How does your God learn about the universe around him, i.e., the places he has not been yet? Can your God describe the physical characteristics of all the different planets, and stars he hasn't been to yet? If yes, how?

46. If not, is his knowledge limited?

47. Could your God be overthrown by more powerful Gods with a different agenda, from a region of the universe that he has not yet visited?

48. If not, how do you know? Don't beg the question.

49. If this is possible, why should I put my faith in him?

50. Could your God ever step down from being God? Or could his power disintegrate?

51. If this could happen, what would his followers do?

52. If your God is a junior God in the universe, and there are more senior Gods, why shouldn't I put my faith in a senior God?

53. Would it be logical to put my faith in a junior God who could be overthrown, step down, or who's power could disintegrate?

54. Would it be an expression of religious irrationalism to do so?

B. Ontology:

1. What is prime reality; i.e., the really real?

2. How does Mormonism try to solve "the one and the many" problem?

3. Is reality ultimately one (a unity), or many (a diversity)?

4. How do the universals relate to the particulars?

5. Is there a creator/creature distinction?

6. Does Mormonism teach valid principles of continuity and discontinuity? Please explain them.

7. Do men and the Gods exist in a realm of being in general?

8. Is God further up the scale of being than man?

9. Are there two types of being: created/uncreated?

10. Mormons in the past have told me that God and man share the same type of existence, and that there is no real distinction. God is only further along in the process of eternal progression than men. Is this true?

11. If this is true, how is Mormonism different metaphysically from ancient pagan concepts?

12. You may say "there is much truth in ancient religions." How do you know you believe the truth in the ancient religions and not falsehood? See Rushdoony's book *The One and the Many*.

13. Is chance, i.e., future contingency, part of the universe that your God lives in?

14. If so, could some kind of chance event start a chain reaction and thwart the plans of your God? Why not, if the answer is no?

15. Does the Mormon Church believe in the autonomy of human reason?

16. What about autonomy of the human will, i.e., free agency?

17. If so, how would the Mormon Church respond to the charge that they have uncritically accepted the position of the fifth century British monk Pelagius?

18. In 1523 A.D. a man named Erasmus tried to defend the doctrine of free will, i.e., free agency. In 1524 A.D. Martin Luther in his book, *The Bondage of the Will*, answered Erasmus's new semi-revised form of the Pelagian doctrine. Have the leaders of the Mormon Church ever responded to Luther's arguments? If not, will they in the future?

C. Ethics:

1. Where did evil come from?

2. Are there laws or a law structure higher than your God?

3. If so, where did these laws come from?

4. Can concepts such as good and evil exist in raw matter?

5. Or do they have to exist in a mind?

6. If concepts such as good and evil must exist in a mind, and many Gods exist in the universe, would not the definition of good and evil be very subjective, since there are many minds?

7. Do all the Gods in the universe interpret these laws the same? How do you know?

8. How do you know that your God is correctly interpreting these laws in the universe?

9. How do you know evil is not good?

10. Did evil exist when your God was boy on another planet?

11. Why should one prefer good over evil?

12. What assurance can be provided that the Mormon God is correctly interpreting the law structure above him?

13. Will your God ever defeat evil in the universe?

14. Why haven't the more senior Gods defeated it yet?

15. Are there evil Gods in the universe? If not, how do you know?

16. If so, could they destroy or defeat the good Gods?

17. Do you believe that the free will argument is a solution to save your God from being weak and responsible for evil, and its results?

18. How would you respond to Gordon Clark in his *Religion, Reason, and Revelation* that such a thing as free will can not save your God from being responsible? See also Antony Flew's *God and Philosophy*. Flew is a non-Christian.*

D. Teleology:

1. Is history linear or endless?

2. Is eternal progression a concept of history that involves endlessness?

3. Will time ever cease to exist in the part of the universe your God rules over? What about other parts of the universe?

4. Is there any real substantial difference between eternal progression and the Hindu teleological concept of history? What is the difference, if any?

5. How would you respond to the charge that the Mormon concept of teleology is in complete harmony with ancient pagan thought? See Rushdoony's *The One and the Many*.

6. Does your God control history? In what way? Partially? Completely?

7. What is the ultimate purpose of creation?

8. In what way does evolutionary theory differ from eternal progression? In what ways are they similar?

I will be looking forward to the official response to these questions, although I'm not sure a response will be forthcoming because of the apparent inability of the Mormon world view to answer these questions.

As I stated at the start, this theological and philosophical challenge is an attempt to force you to see the implications of your finite god concept. Your rejection of the God of Christian Theism, the ontological Trinity, has resulted in a chaotic world view. Your rejection of the self-attesting Christ of Scripture as your starting presupposition, or axiom, and your resulting commitment to independence, i.e., autonomy, has resulted in a false faith in a finite god.

When one's starting presupposition is human autonomy (see Genesis chap. 3), the only god that can be permitted to exist is a finite god, one that does not threaten the false delusion of human autonomy. When you do not allow God, the ontological Trinity, to be the ultimate standard for interpretation, confusion ensues. When man is the ultimate standard, all knowledge becomes futile, or hopeless. Take one look at the twentieth century and the popular humanistic existentialism that smothers the pursuit of true knowledge. Your rejection of the ontological Trinity as the interpretive principle has resulted in an un-biblical answer to the "one and the many problem."

Your resulting authoritarianism "when the leaders speak ..." and "listen to the prophet ..." cannot stop the collapse of what you believe is true and certain. Mormons cannot have absolute assurance of anything, especially assurance of their salvation. The questions, if honestly faced, show that the finite god of Mormonism is definitely not the God of Romans 8:28. Only a sovereign God who totally controls and predestinates all things can fulfill the promises contained in Romans 8:28.

The finite god of Mormonism is trapped in the space-time universe, and is surrounded by chance and mystery. Given enough time the plans of the finite god of Mormonism will be thwarted. The god of Mormonism can't save himself from the ultimate mystery and contingency the universe holds for him. How can he save you? Please do not react to this challenge the way that members of your religion do by committing several logical fallacies. Their first is to attack the historic Christian creeds, especially the Nicean creed. (See Rushdoony's *The Foundations of Social Order* for an intelligent explication of the creeds.)

All Mormons I have talked to reject the biblical doctrine of God summarized by the historic creeds because they can't comprehend or understand such a God. This is a ridiculous standard. If the average Mormon is consistent, he or she should reject microwave ovens, refrigerators, telephones, and cars because they can't comprehend how these everyday items work. Are you sure you have not committed the terrible sin of Romans 1:18-23 by making God into a man which you can comprehend and who will not threaten your human autonomy? The second fallacy I normally encounter is the attack upon the reliability of Scripture. Can you tell me the ordinary standards for evaluating historical documents? If you or members of your religion are unable to do so, why do you feel qualified to speak about the reliability of the Bible? A third fallacy is attacking motives, or character. God alone is the judge of these matters.

These fallacies are really nothing more than a smoke screen to hide the inability of Mormonism to deal with the objections raised against it. You may feel secure in Mormonism, but this is a sinful delusion. Your feeling of security is nothing more than emotions that come as result of the words of God borrowed from the Bible. Flee from your false assurance to Calvary. I will not cater to any false belief you hold in autonomy. The gospel of Jesus Christ is right in front of you. You are not invited, but rather the Scriptures command you to repent and believe the gospel.

Calvary is your only hope. The true saints will fall on their faces in the dust at Calvary and see their total inability and hopelessness. At Calvary there is a revelation of two things: grace and wrath. Because God is holy, sin will be punished. God is a jealous God and idolatry will not be tolerated. The Lord Jesus Christ suffered the wrath of God for His people, those who believe in him and have no confidence in themselves. Grace is revealed powerfully to those who put their trust totally in Jesus and His perfect complete work of redemption.

It is my prayer that you, the leaders of Mormonism, will consider the implications of your finite god concept and repent. If you continue to glory in and cherish human autonomy, the end result is death. The empirical god of Mormonism has given you unreliable revelations. The endless speculations and revisions in the writings of those who are within Mormonism, both official and non-official demonstrate this.

Any Mormon who happens to see this challenge to the Mormon world view is welcome to respond, but please indicate if your answers are the official position of your church. If they are not, what should I do with them? They may be interesting, but if they are not the official position, then they are nothing more than your own personal speculations, which cannot be cited as the official position. Surely the leaders of the Mormon Church are capable of providing official answers to these questions. Your own speculations would really be quite useless as far as quoting them is concerned. Is there something wrong with quoting an official church position?

Please consult the appendix for titles of books that present a Christian world view. If you expect to be taken seriously, you are obligated to answer the questions above and to interact with the books listed. Maybe it's not in your best interest to do so. As I mentioned at the beginning no response will be most revealing.

For Christ's Glory!

CHAPTER 20

A Follow-up Letter to Challenge and a Response from Mormon Scholars

*To The President of the Mormon Church
and the Twelve Apostles:*

November 14, 1988

Dear Sirs,

 ecently a Mormon scholar in Salt Lake City told me in a letter that the "Mormon god surrounds his body with light, and then can travel with the light at the speed of light." Rumor has it that the Mormon god had to travel to the region of *Alpha Centauri* to help his fellow gods put down a rebellion. *Alpha Centauri* is about 4.29 light-years away. A round trip would take 8.58 years at the speed of light. Assuming all goes well and the Mormon god is not put in some kind of intergalactic jail, we could be looking at close to nine years before the Mormon god can return.

Could this account for the delay in answering my letter of May 13, 1988? This same Mormon scholar told me that those who attain godhood cannot rebel or be overthrown. How does this scholar know this? Did he interview all the supposed gods in the universe including Satan? When did he do this? His statement appears to be nothing more than a bare assertion that was not proven epistemologically. Assertions of this nature are just not persuasive. Will you along with this scholar slip into subjectivism at this point to escape from your apparent inability to defend your beliefs, the "end all debate" Mormon testimony, which appears to be nothing more than subjective escapism. While I will admit that subjectivism is appealing and has arguments in its favor, there are numerous reasons to reject it. All organizations, whether religious, political, or whatever, can offer numerous testimonials in their favor.

For the sake of argument I have adopted your god concept, and then raised questions against it that you have not dealt with in any of the extensive Mormon literature that I've read. Could it be that you, the president of the Mormon Church and the twelve apostles, are really nothing more than a president of a large corporation with a counsel of twelve business men? Unless I am notified that an official response to my letter of May 13, 1988, is forthcoming, I really, have no choice but to make your inability to answer basic philosophical and theological questions public.

CLOSING COMMENTS

Now that you have read the questions that were sent to your leaders, please consider the following. Mormon attempts to convince me of Mormonism have failed for the following reasons. The first reason is my faith is rooted in historical reality. I have been to Jerusalem. I am unable to find any New World locations mentioned in the *Book of Mormon*. Mormon faith appears to be nothing more than a leap in the dark. The second reason is my God is infinite where the Mormon god is finite. A limited god is unworthy of my worship for reasons listed in this challenge. The third reason is being the Mormon inability to answer the epistemological questions.

Simply assuming empiricism to be true is not convincing. What kind of assurance do you have as a Mormon? I maintain that you have absolutely no assurance or certainty of anything - especially your eternal salvation. If you still think that you are secure within Mormonism, then either you have not understood the force of the questions or you have fled into religious irrationalism. The inability of Mormon leaders to answer questions of this nature demonstrates the logical absurdity of your finite god concept.

RESPONSES
FROM MORMON SCHOLARS

On September 1, 1988, Dr. Nibley, Mormon apologist promised to respond to three of my questions. Dr. Nibley said this, "Why the 98 questions? For a sensible person three could have done the job, which I intend to demonstrate in a forthcoming effusion."

After waiting one year for Dr. Nibley's forthcoming effusion, I began to wonder if Dr. Nibley had gotten stumped. On September 3, 1989 I wrote Dr. Nibley back and explained that my reason for the ninety-eight questions was due to vague answers I receive from Mormons when asking general philosophical questions. The ninety-eight questions would force any Mormon responding to be specific.

At this time, I also asked Dr. Nibley if his promised effusion would be coming anytime soon. Dr. Nibley wrote back on September 13, 1989 and said "Kind of soon maybe." At this point I can only speculate as to why Dr. Nibley has not responded yet. It is highly probable that Dr. Nibley got stuck on question number seven in the section on epistemology.* In fact, I again challenge any Mormon to answer this question. I simply do not believe any Mormon empiricist can defend the faulty epistemology of Mormonism.

Another scholar in Salt Lake City tried to respond to questions of this nature. See my follow up letter to your leaders November 14, 1988. This scholar's answers bordered on the bizarre. His answers were assertions that had no proof of any kind.

If Mormons have had the courage to face these questions with honesty, I am sure you agree that Mormonism is not all that you thought. In fact, epistemologically speaking, Mormonism is in shambles. The scholars at B.Y.U. cannot be of any help. They do not themselves grasp the epistemological weakness of Mormonism. To put it bluntly, your situation is perilous. There is a way out of the dark forest of empiricism. The answer is in the gospel of Jesus Christ. Mormonism is not the answer since, in reality it is nothing more than ancient pagan beliefs that have resurfaced. If you want to give up your faulty empirical epistemology, the books listed in the Bibliography Section Two will set forward a Christian Theistic epistemology. Regarding the questions that have been raised about your world view, please write.

* Dr. Nibley addresses my questions in "*The Terrible Questions*," from *Temple and Cosmos: Beyond This Ignorant Present*, volume 12 in *The Collected Works of Hugh Nibley*, Don E. Norton, Editor. (Salt Lake City: Deseret Book and F.A.R.M.S., 1992), pp. 336-378. In essence, Dr. Nibley says my questions are the wrong questions. He believes answers to questions of a theological and philosophical nature are such that they will never satisfy everyone. So what? Should students of theology and philosophy give up and become existentialists? Nibley asks "Why the thousands of volumes?" and "Why can't they come up with answers?" (339) "Theologians can talk about these things until the cows come home. It is inexhaustible; they keep themselves in work forever, talking about these things." (338) "In the hereafter, what difference will these questions make? The real question, of course, is, Is this all there is?" (339) Apparently, Dr. Nibley does believe that there is something to these types of questions because he refers me to a number of things he has published that deal

with "many of these questions." Dr. Nibley has kept himself employed over the years by dealing with questions concerning the truthfulness of Mormonism. Has Dr. Nibley's answers satisfied everyone? I ask Dr. Nibley have the cows come home yet?

Dr. Nibley concludes his comments on page 371 with his Mormon testimony. He believes that this inner feeling is more reliable than endless rationalistic wrangling. It should be noted that Dr. Nibley has done more than his share of rationalistic wrangling over the years. Some of Dr. Nibley's most incredible mental rationalistic gymnastics are found in his attempted defenses of the Book of Abraham. Please consult the book *...by his own hand upon papyrus* by Charles M. Larson, (Grand Rapids, Michigan: Institute for Religious Research, 1992). In this work, Larson interacts with some of Dr. Nibley's futile defenses of the *Book Of Abraham*.

In response to my theological and philosophical challenge to Mormonism, Dr. Nibley failed to justify his own presuppositions. This was the essence of my challenge, for he borrowed from Christian presuppositions in order to defend his Mormon beliefs. Dr. Nibley uses logically structured sentences in all his writings. Yet he neglects to inform his audience how his worldview can account for such things as the laws of logic, science, and ethics. Dr. Nibley simply begs the question and hopes that nobody will notice. It is only in terms of Christian presuppositions that answer the philosophical questions I raised can be found. Dr. Nibley believes in logic, science, and ethics. In the Mormon worldview, they are nothing more than arbitrary celestial social conventions.

The Mormon gods did not create the law structure of the universe. It is supposedly eternal. It is just there. The Mormon god is not free to break or change these laws or his power may disintegrate. (See *The First 2000 Years* by W. Cleon Skousen.) The Mormon concept of millions of gods in the universe guarantees no assurance that these laws will always be interpreted the same way by the gods. What evidence can Mormons provide these millions of gods interpret the law structure the same way? When remembering that the Mormon worldview incorporates time and chance into its universe, sooner or later some major changes will happen.

Mystery and contingency surround the Mormon gods. The Mormon gods may even become lost in space or overthrown by celestial revolutionaries. Their power may disintegrate if they violate the sensibilities of the intelligences (eternal life forms that exist prior to human existence). Dr. Nibley uses absolutist terminology at numerous places in his writings when referring to his god.

Many Mormons make use of words such as omniscience, omnipresence, and omnipotence. These words are meaningless when attributing them to finite deities. This is a smoke screen on Dr. Nibley's part to prop up his finite, limited god. It is contradictory and irrational to use absolutist terminology in defense of a finite deity. And furthermore, the use of absolutist terminology tends to give the average Mormon a false sense of security. Finite deities cannot control things so as to give absolute assurance.

By definition, a finite deity cannot do anything as an act of sovereignty. Finite deities cannot know the future. If the Mormon god cannot know the future how can he control the future? The Mormon god reacts to events as the future unfolds. As a result, Mormonism cannot give assurance of future security for the believer, although Mormons will appeal to the Bible to obtain assurance. In many Mormon writings, attempts have been made to prove the Bible unreliable. Why appeal to the Bible now? Has it suddenly become reliable?

The world is what God says it is in the Bible. The Christian God is the source of the universal laws that make life possible, as we know it. That is why the world is intelligible and science is possible. It is only when men reject biblical revelation as Dr. Nibley has done that the questions I have raised become terrible. Please consult the book titled *The Mormon Concept Of God* by Beckwith/Parrish, (Lampeter, Dyfed, Wales: Edwin Mellen Press, Ltd., 1991.) This work demonstrates that in terms of its own presuppositions, Mormonism is irrational, incoherent and false.

THE NONSENSE COLUMN,
ADDITIONAL RESPONSES
TO MORMON SCHOLARS

The purpose of the column is to interact with responses to my challenge of your leaders. This section will be continued as I receive attempts to defend the corporeal, empirical, finite god of the Mormon religion.

One philosophy professor at B.Y.U. tried to answer my questions about a finite corporeal god traveling around in an endless universe. The essence of his argument was that the Mormon god's influence and power is everywhere, so in effect the Mormon god is everywhere. This apparent irrationalist confusion of word definitions may be an evasion tactic. Influence and power are not the same as a person's being or physical presence. This is a violation of the law of contradiction, which says that a word has a definite meaning. It means something and it also does not mean other things. The word dog has a meaning as well as not meaning other things. Dog does not mean ice cream or lake. A boss at the office may be a mean, high-pressure manager who keeps his people in fear. He may be in one room and the employees in another. His influence and power may be exerted in the room where he is not. The fact remains that the boss is not there, and consequently the employees may be hiding many things from the powerful, influential boss.

The Mormon god may very well face a similar situation, such as a well-hidden rebellion in his corner of the universe. McConkie on page 359 of *Mormon Doctrine* and Talmage on page forty three of *Articles Of Faith* both taught that the Mormon god had a body that was limited to being in one place at a time. To be sure, Talmage amd McConkie believed that their God had a spiritual nature. But having a spiritual nature with great influence and power is still not the same as being there in person. Along with this, you have the Mormon concept of a plurality of gods in the universe. This means many influences and powers everywhere. In the Bible, God reveals Himself as the Sovereign One. By definition there can be only one Sovereign. The idea of many Sovereign Gods is a logical contradiction.

The attempt to answer questions about the Mormon god's inability to know things by postulating a theory of influence and power as being the same as his personal presence is a failure. The whole discussion when bringing in Mormon concepts such as many gods along with their influences and powers degenerates into total nonsense.

The same Salt Lake City scholar who somehow discovered how the Mormon god travels had some other interesting bits of knowledge. He informed me that, "This earth was once part of a much larger planet big enough to make a million earths like ours. This greater planet had such greater revolutions, that 1 day was a thousand years.

It was on this greater planet where the dinosaurs etc; existed and the part chosen to become this earth, where the garden was planted & Adam & Eve place along with the other living beings. When this chunk was hurled around the sun, its day became a 24 hour period and this earth, then became subject to the greater light, the sun & the lesser light the moon." I would respond to this in the same way that I did in my November 14, 1988, letter to your leaders. How does this scholar know these things?

The way this scholar talks makes you think he has been on a trip in outer space. With a planet the size that this scholar is talking about, imagine the gravitational force? This scholar did say that

"Every resurrected being, including the Gods, are no longer subject to the gravitational powers of this mortal earth." What about this large planet? The dinosaurs were not resurrected beings. They would have been smashed flat against the surface of a planet of that size. I would suggest this scholar try his hand at science fiction. Again I would say to this scholar, how do you know these things? Explain your epistemology to me. Are you getting special revelations? Do your views represent the official Mormon position? It sounds like so much religious mysticism.

MORE NONSENSE

Mormon scholar John Gee responded to my theological and philosophical challenge. Mr. Gee is associated with the Foundation for Ancient Research and Mormon Studies (F.A.R.M.S.). Elements of his response were seriously flawed. Gee provided some helpful but hardly conclusive lexicographical information on the Hebrew word *bara*.

This Hebrew word has to do with creation. Unfortunately, Gee did not deal with Isaiah 45:7 in which the Hebrew words *bara, asa* and *yasar* appear. This verse provides important context to the proper understanding of *bara*. Can Gee point out the pre-existing matter in this verse that his view of creation requires? The lexicographical information that Gee provided was restricted to a small portion of Scripture. He simply failed to take into account the overall context of Scripture when evaluating the lexicographical evidence. For example, on page six of his response the material he cited attempts to prove:

1. Genesis 1:1 is warmed over paganism; cf. *enuma elish*.

2. Use of Grimm's fairy tales make Gen. 1:1 like *enuma elish* or equal to fairy tales.

Gee also made unwarranted extensive use of foreign languages. A friend of mine (Dr. Leonard Coppes) who reads all of the languages contained in Mr. Gee's response does not believe that he is competent to handle some of the languages in his response. This is especially true of the Hebrew as the following reveals:

1. On page three of his response Gee's quotation of Jeremiah 31:29, 30 is garbled (sentence structure).

2. On page six there is a nonsensical grammatical error. He has a future becoming a past tense

when the two verbs refer to entirely different action.

3. On page seven, Gee confuses numbers. He has 80 written for what should be 20.

Gee's Mormon god organized the world out of pre-existing matter. This is a good Platonic belief. I'm sure that Gee would disagree with being accused of holding to Platonism.

Hostile Christian critic, Bertrand Russell, in his *A History of Western Philosophy*, in the section dealing with Plato's *Cosmogony*, (branch of metaphysics) has this to say:

Thus it appears that Plato's god, unlike the Jewish and Christian God, did not create the world out of nothing, but rearranged preexisting material. (144)

It appears that Russell, even though an avowed enemy of Christianity, was more honest in dealing with theological positions than Gee. Would Gee argue that Bertrand Russell was mistaken in his assessment of the Christian doctrine of creation being different from Platonism? Gee's position is the one that is substantially the same as Plato's. It could be that Gee cannot see that his own doctrine of creation is Platonic to the core.

In his response, Gee accused me of an historical anachronism. This is because of what I said about Socrates and his Pelagian like ideas. What I said was sufficiently qualified so that it was not an anachronism at all. Joseph Smith, in his *Book of Mormon* should have eliminated the following anachronisms:

1. In the *Book of Mormon* we find in Jacob 7:27 the French word *adieu*.

2. In Alma 11:7, barley is mentioned.

3. In 3 Nephi 14:16, grapes and figs are spoken of as if they existed in the New World at this time.

4. In Ether 9:18, 19, the following are mentioned: cattle, sheep, swine, goats, asses, and horses.

5. In Mosiah 9:9, wheat is mentioned.

6. 2 Nephi 5:15 describes steel, brass, iron, copper, and silver. In the above, Smith is guilty of a serious chronological misplacing of things in the *Book of Mormon*. It is interesting to note that Smith claimed he knew more than all the lawyers of his day combined and that "God was his right hand man."

Gee should pay heed to the wisdom of B. H. Roberts, a Mormon apostle. Roberts concludes that the *Book of Mormon* "is the product of one mind, and that, a very limited mind..." (Consult *Studies of The Book of Mormon* by B. H. Roberts and *New Approaches to the Book of Mormon* edited by Brent Lee Metcalfe).

There is one Mormon that Gee is not impressed with. His name is Sterling M. McMurrin. McMurrin was a professor at the University of Utah. I bring this up because Gee did not like my use of McMurrin to document Mormon philosophy. Gee says, "Furthermore, almost no good Mormons that I know believe (or even care about) McMurrin." This statement by Gee is non-sensible. Does Gee know all "good Mormons?" Has he interviewed all "good Mormons" to know what they believe about McMurrin? Contrary to Gee, McMurrin has some valuable insights into Mormonism. Sterling McMurrin admits a relationship between Mormonism and Greek philosophy. In his book *The Theological Foundations of the Mormon Religion* he openly acknowledges agreement with Greek philosophy at several points.

The following quotations by McMurrin establish a relationship between Mormonism and Greek philosophy in the area of creation:

> Now Mormonism has much in common with the naturalistic positions of the Greek. It holds, in the first place, that although the structure and configurations of the world are the product of God's creative act, that anything at all should exist is not due to God but is simply a given fact.... In the second place, the naturalistic disposition of Mormonism is found in the denial of the traditional conception of the supernatural. (2)

> An interesting and important facet of the Mormon conception of reality is the materialism that is defended so consistently and emphatically by Mormon writers.... The Greek atomists and the Hellenistic and Roman Epicureans were materialistic in their theories of reality. (5)

> The established Mormon doctrine is squarely opposed to the traditional concept of creation and is in principle reminiscent of the position common to the classical Greek naturalism. That position, which denies creation as an original beginning, was clearly enunciated in the fifth century before Christ by Parmenides of Elea. (24-25)

> As a constructor of artisan God, not entirely unlike Plato's demiurge of the Timaeus, the Mormon deity informs the continuing processes of reality and determines the world's configurations, but he is not the creator of the most ultimate constituents of the world, either the fundamental material entities or the space time that locate them. (29)

How are Gee and Mormonism substantially different from the Greek position concerning creation? What is wrong with McMurrin's analysis?

In his book *The Reformed Pastor and Modern Thought,* Dr. Van Till says the following concerning Greek philosophy:

> The ultimate concern of the Reformers was to bring the fullness of grace in its purity to men. They therefore sought to set it free from the encrustations of Greek metaphysics which are the metaphysics of fallen man. (171)

Van Til's use of the word encrustation shows how pervasive he believed Greek philosophy to be. The philosophical positions advanced by the Greeks influenced to such a large extent the areas of epistemology, ontology, ethics, and teleology that the Greek-influence argument is a sufficient explanation for positions that have been adopted by some western religions and philosophy. These same concepts have influenced present day Mormonism. While admitting that Mormonism may not be aware of the original source of some of its positions, it nevertheless is dependent upon Greek philosophical ideas at numerous points. Apostate thinking, down to the present day, has never escaped entirely from Greek thought. Mormon positions, along with other forms of paganism, are related also and are the result of the superior philosophical thinking of the Greeks.

The Mormon positions concerning God, man and the cosmos simply assume the validity of previous apostate thought. This is true of many Mormon positions. This is done because of the shared presuppositions with other forms of unbelief. If you strip away the veneer of Christian terminology, you are left with something that resembles Greek assumptions in a remarkable way. Thus, you could argue that Mormonism in its developmental stages had knowledge of certain positions developed by the Greeks, while not necessarily recognizing them as an original source. By embracing their positions rather than repudiating them, Mormon thought is shown ultimately to be dependent upon Greek thought.

Only Christianity has been able to break free from Greek reprobate thinking. This is true insofar as the Christian follows the Reformers in placing the self-attesting Christ, speaking authoritatively in the Scriptures of the Old and New Testaments, as paramount in all thought. One of the battle cries of the Reformation was "*sola scriptura*." Paul describes it this way: "Casting down imaginations, and every high thing that exalteth itself against the knowledge of God, and bringing into captivity every thought to the obedience of Christ" (2 Corinthians 10:5). Every other form of western philosophy has to a large extent resulted from the thinking of the Greeks. The religions of the west have also suffered to some extent from the same problem.

Some comments from Gordon Clark's *Thales To Dewey* may be helpful concerning Christianity and pagan influence. (This will be necessary to refute Mormon assertions of Christian dependence upon Greek philosophy.)

Clark makes the following summary in his section on paganism and Christianity:

> For such reasons as these it may be concluded that
> paganism and Christianity are radically distinct.
> Any points of similarity are superficial and trivial.
> To speak of them as alike is no better than identi-
> fying Epicureanism and Platonism on the ground
> that both were founded by men. This conclusion
> is not weakened by two cautions that should be
> observed. First, since the New Testament was

written in Greek, it uses words found in pagan writings. John even used the term Logos. But the point in question is not the use of words but the occurrence of ideas. Logos in John and hypostasis in Hebrews are not evidences of pagan ideas. Nor should one find Aristotle in the Nicene Creed because it says God is a substance or reality. One cannot forbid Christian writers to use common words on pain of becoming pagans. The second caution is that while Christianity and the Greek philosophies, as systems, have no element in common, the Christians, as people, often held pagan ideas. They had been converted from paganism and could not divest themselves of familiar modes of thought all at once. Therefore when they came to expound and defend Christianity, they inconsistently made use of Platonism or Stoicism. By a long and arduous struggle these inconsistent elements were gradually removed from a few fundamental areas, and thus a purely Christian Nicene Creed came into being. But on other topics, and especially in cases of individual authorship, the struggle was not so successful. Then, too, as time went on, the attempts to escape pagan ideas and to preserve the purity of New Testament thought grew weaker, and one might say, almost ceased. (195)

Unlike Joseph Smith, I have never claimed to be anything other than a layman. As a layman, it has been easy to identify numerous parallels between Greek philosophy and Mormon theology, just as Mormon writer Sterling McMurrin confirms the parallels that I have identified. In summary, it can be said that Mr. Gee's response did not rescue Mormonism from my charge that Greek reprobate thinking has influenced it. Gee's extensive use of foreign languages did not intimidate or impress me. Gee did point out some legitimate mistakes that I made due to the fact that I am a layman. However, none of these problems were significant enough to overthrow my thesis that

Mormonism has been influenced by various elements of Greek philosophy.

Mormon (BYU) scholar Louis Midgley, while not sending a formal response, did correspond with me over a six-month period concerning my challenge to Mormonism. His satirical questions were most gracious compared to Gee's response. Our correspondence consisted primarily of questions raised by Midgley. I responded by sending Midgley books by serious Reformed Christian scholars. This was an attempt to realize my goal of getting BYU faculty members to engage in serious interaction with conservative biblical scholarship. The following are some of the significant doctrines that Midgley questioned. Next to the Christian doctrine that Midgley questioned, I will list the material that was sent to him.

1. Presuppositions: Mr. Midgley received *By What Standard?* by R. J. Rushdoony, *Defense Of The Faith* by Van Til, and finally the book *Three Types of Religious Philosophy* by Gordon H. Clark.

2. Religious Liberalism: This topic arose because I questioned why Mormons interact with theological liberals and never serious Reformed scholarship. It appears as if Mormon scholars are more at home with theological liberalism. Mr. Midgley received *Christianity And Barthianism* by Van Til.

3. The Trinity: Mr. Midgley received an extensive article on the Trinity by B. B. Warfield in the book entitled *Calvin An Augustine*.

4. Original Sin: Mr. Midgley received *The Imputation of Adam's Sin* by John Murray.

5. The Authority of Scripture: Mr. Midgley received the work entitled *Scripture And Confession edited by John H. Skilton.*

Mr. Midgley offered no response to the above scholarly books. The titles all utilize what is known as the grammatical, historical, and exegetical method when interpreting Scripture. A response on Midgley's part would reveal the radical anti-Christian presuppositions that he is imposing on Scripture. Midgley's attack on the above positions, (three, four, and in particular, five) and his lack of response to the scholarly material he received, demonstrate that he is unable to refute historic Christian theology. Midgley did reveal that his presuppositions were anti-Christian in nature. Midgley did not want to give any credibility to my question about lack of interaction with conservative scholarship (point two). Yet the absence of interaction with Christianity's best defenders is most revealing.

NOTES

1. David L. Paulsen, *Must God Be Incorporeal?* (Provo: unpublished paper, 1988), pp. 8-9.

2. Alma Giggi**, (Salt Lake City: unpublished personal letter 1989).

Gordon Clark challenges the thinking of those who believe in finite gods and free will when he writes:

> On the road below, to the observer's left, a car is being driven west. To the observer's right a car is coming south. He can see and know that there will be a collision at the intersection immediately beneath him. But his foreknowledge, so the argument runs, does not cause [that is make necessary] the accident. Similarly, God is supposed to know the future without causing it.
>
> The similarity, however, is deceptive on several points. A human observer cannot really know that a collision will occur. Though it is unlikely, it is possible for both cars to have blowouts before reaching the intersection and swerve apart. It is also possible that the observer has misjudged speeds, in which case one car could slow down and other accelerate, so that they would not collide. The human observer, therefore, does not infallible foreknowledge.
>
> No such mistakes can be assumed for God. The human observer may make a probable guess that the accident will occur, and this guess does not make the accident unavoidable; but if God knows, there is no possibility of avoiding the accident. A hundred years before the drivers were born, there

was no possibility that either of them could have chosen to stay home that day, to have driven a different route, to have driven a different time, to have driven a different speed. They could not have chosen otherwise than as they did. This means either that they had no free will [understood as a liberty of indifference] or that God did not know.

Suppose it be granted, just for the moment, that divine foreknowledge, like human guesses, does not cause the foreknown event. Even so, if there is foreknowledge, in contrast with fallible guesses, free will is impossible. If man has free will, and things can be different, God cannot be omniscient. Some Arminians have admitted this and have denied omniscience [the open theists], but this puts them obviously at odds with Biblical Christianity. There is also another difficulty. If the Arminian . . . wishes to retain divine omniscience and at the same time assert that foreknowledge has no causal efficacy, he is put to explain how the collision was made certain a hundred years, an eternity, before the drivers were born. If God did not arrange the universe this way, who did?

If God did not arrange it this way, then there must be an independent factor in the universe. And if there is such, one consequence and perhaps two follow. First, the doctrine of creation must be abandoned. . . . Independent forces cannot be created forces, and created forces cannot be independent. Then, second, if the universe is not God's creation, his knowledge of it past and future cannot depend on what he intends to do, but on his observation of how it works. In such a case, how could we be sure that God's observations are accurate? How could we be sure that these independent forces will not later show us an unsuspected twist that will falsify God's predictions? And finally, on this view God's knowledge would be empirical, rather than an integral part of his essence, and thus he would be a dependent knower. These objections are insurmountable. We can consistently believe in creation, omnipotence, omniscience, and the divine decree. But we cannot retain sanity and combine any of these with free will.

Gordon Clark, From: *God and Evil* (Unicoi, TN: Trinity Foundation, 2004), 25 26. Cited in Reymond, What Is God? pp. 132, 133.

BIBLIOGRAPHY FOR
PAGAN INFLUENCE
UPON THE MORMON WORLD VIEW

SELECT BIBLIOGRAPHY ONE:
THE PLATONIC-GNOSTIC QUESTION

Armstrong, A. H. *An Introduction to Ancient Philosophy* (Boston: Beacon, 1963. Brown, Harold O. J., *Heresies*. New York: Doubleday, 1984.

Clark, Gordon H. *Thales To Dewey* (Jefferson: Trinity, reprinted [1989]. First printing Boston: Houghton Mifflin, 1957).

Selections from Hellenistic Philosophy (New York: F. S. Crofts & Co., 1940).

Machen, J. Gresham. *The Origin of Paul's Religion* (Grand Rapids: Eerdmans, reprinted [1978]. First printing, New York: Macmillan, 1925).

Metzger, Bruce M. *Methodology in the Study of the Mystery Religions and Early Christianity*. Chapter

1 in *Historical and Literary Studies: Pagan, Jewish, and Christian* (Grand Rapids: Eerdmans, 1968).

Morey, Robert A. *Battle of the Gods* (Southbridge: Crown Publications, 1989).

Nash, Ronald. *Christianity and The Hellenistic World* (Grand Rapids: Zondervan/Probe, 1984).

Yamauchi, Edwin. *Pre-Christian Gnosticism* (Grand Rapids: Eerdmans, 1973).

SELECT BIBLIOGRAPHY TWO:
A CHRISTIAN EPISTEMOLOGICAL CONSTRUCTION

Jerusalem and Athens, Critical Discussions on The Philosophy And Apologetics Of Cornelius Van Til. Edited by E. R. Geehan. Phillipsburg: Presbyterian and Reformed, 1971.

Clark, Gordon H. *God's Hammer The Bible and Its Critics* (Jefferson: Trinity, 1982).

A Christian Construction Chapter 8 in *Language And Theology* Phillipsburg: Presbyterian and Reformed, 1980.

hree Types of Religious Philosophy (Jefferson: Trinity, 1989).

The Philosophy of Gordon H. Clark Edited by Ronald Nash, (Philadelphia: Presbyterian and Reformed, 1969).

Nash, Ronald. *The Word of God and the Mind of Man* Grand Rapids: The Zondervan Corporation, 1982.

GENERAL PHILOSOPHICAL
BIBLIOGRAPHY

The Cambridge History of Later Greek and Early Medieval Philosophy Edited by A. H. Armstrong (Cambridge: Cambridge University Press, 1980).

Brown, Colin. *Christianity & Western Though* (Downers Grove: InterVarsity Press, 1990).

The Encyclopedia of Philosophy Edited by Paul Edwards (New York: Collier Macmillan Publishers, 1972).

Clark, Gordon H. *Thales To Dewey* (Jefferson: The Trinity Foundation, 1985).

Copleston, Frederick, *A History of Philosophy* Vol. 1-3, (New York: An Image Book Doubleday, 1963).

Fuller, B. A. G. *A History of Philosophy* (New York: Henry Holt and Company, 1945).

Hunney, Milton D. *Chronological and Thematic Charts of Philosophies and Philosophers* (Grand Rapids: Zondervan Publishing House, 1986).

Masterpieces of World Philosophy Editor, Frank N. Magill. (New York: Harper Collins Publishers, 1990).

Smith, T.V. *Philosophers Speak For Themselves* (Chicago: The University of Chicago Press, 1934).

A PERSONAL
CONFESSION OF FAITH

A TESTIMONY
OF AN EX-MORMON

 confess by the grace of God the truth of what the apostle Paul teaches in 1 Corinthians 15:1-4. In another place he declares the following concerning man's condition: "As it is written, There is none righteous, no, not one...that every mouth may be stopped, and all the world may become guilty before God" (Romans 3:10, 19). This was my condition. Paul goes on to say: "For the wages of sin is death, but the gift of God is eternal life through Jesus Christ our Lord" (Romans 6:23). I had earned the wages of death. God in his mercy gave me the gift of eternal life. The only thing that I earned and deserved was death. Eternal life came as a gift. One thing I am certain of , there was and is absolutely nothing in me that caused God to give me this gift. Jesus Christ gets all the glory and praise.

I attempt to do as the writer of Hebrews sets forth: "Looking unto Jesus the author and finisher of our faith" (Hebrews 12:2). I look to Jesus by giving him the glory. God gave me the gift of faith. I am saved by grace and even my faith is a gift. Ephesians 2:8 says: "and that not of yourselves". What is not of yourselves? Faith! Did I choose Christ and exercise faith? Yes, but why? Who gets the glory? Christ? Or me? Why did I choose to believe? Ephesians 1:4, 5 supplies us the answer. "According as he hath chosen us in him before the foundation of the world, that we should be holy and without blame before him in love: Having predestinated us unto the adoption of children by Jesus Christ to himself, according to the good pleasure of his will." Was this salvation in my hands to choose or reject? If this were the case, then could I not glory in and of myself? How can that be so? Because I would have done something others had not done. The following verse tells us that the predestination is: "according to the good pleasure of his will." "So then it is not of him that willeth, nor of him that runneth, but of God that showeth mercy" (Romans 9:16).

The doctrine of election, more than any other teaching of Scripture, takes salvation out of man's hands and places it in God's control. Men do not like God's control. The cause of God's choosing is found in Him. If we insist that we played a part in God's choice, then human merit is brought into the picture. Salvation then becomes synergistic rather than monergistic. Biblical salvation is monergistic. Christ alone, by his complete and finished work, saved me. Within a synergistic scheme, salvation becomes a cooperative effort. My work takes away from the work of Christ. How? I made a contribution. I played a part in my salvation. If I was not willing, then God could not save me. A synergistic scheme of salvation not only steals Christ's glory, it limits God's power. God can only do what I allow him to do within this type of system. Again, I confess by the grace of God that: "Not by works of righteousness which we have done, but according to his mercy he saved us, by the washing of regeneration, and renewing of the Holy Ghost" (Titus 3:5).

This is the close of my testimony. "To God only wise, be glory through Jesus Christ for ever. Amen". Romans 16:27. heirs according to the promise" (Galatians 3:28-29). Amen!

THE IMPORTANCE
AND NECESSITY
OF SPECIAL REVELATION

by Jack Kettler

his article is a reply that deals with certain criticisms concerning views expressed in my article titled *Pagan Philosophy, Unbelief, and Irrationalism.*[1] This article briefly exposed the bankruptcy of materialistic and empirical philosophy in particular and the worldview of non-belief in general. It was asserted: "Matter is silent; it does not speak. It does not say what is right or what is wrong. The definition between good and evil is found in the Bible. God is not silent." These assertions on my part were not original. Many Christian apologists have discussed these ideas when dealing with atheistic materialism.

The article was challenged regarding to the accuracy of these assertions and how assertions of this nature could be harmonized with the teaching of Scripture that shows matter does speak using passages such as Romans 1:19-20, dealing with creation's testimony, and is therefore not silent. To start with, the claim "matter is silent" must not be understood apart from the context of the article: to point out that the materialistic worldview is philosophically unable to arrive at truth from any source, particularly matter. Matter according to this view is ultimately just an accident and is therefore meaningless. As will be seen, the crux of the problem is with fallen man. The article in question did not deal with the broader subject of general revelation from a Christian perspective.

Also, when stated that "matter is silent" this assertion should be understood as meaning that matter does not speak in or with an audible sound like human speech and does not communicate or have any meaning at all within the framework of a non-believing worldview. This is especially true when dealing with specifics, notably in the areas of science, ethics, and logic. Considering the Christian worldview in contrast, it can be said that matter does have a testimony. Its testimony is imprinted in it by virtue of its creation. In this reply, there will be a brief account of general revelation (creation knowledge) and special revelation (biblical knowledge) along with additional challenges to materialistic philosophy, contrasted with biblical philosophy. However to clarify things, reformed Christians believe that God conveys truth through both of these avenues. There is no conflict between these two forms of revelation. I believe that all creation testifies that God exists e.g., Psalms 19:1-3, Romans 1:18-20 and that God has spoken authoritatively in the Holy Scriptures of the Old and New Testaments. As will be seen, the problem is with man and specifically fallen man.

The article in question points out that the non-believing worldview is unable to articulate in a credible way a theory of ethics. The transcendental argument, or as some might say a worldview apologetic, was briefly used to illustrate the deficiency in non-believing thought. The transcendental argument shows the Christian worldview to be true because of the impossibility of the contrary. A worldview must have a theory of knowledge that can account for certain things, such as ethics, logic and science. The non-believer has never shown how one can get from matter like rocks to a concrete argument of why Stalin's murder of millions of people, in particular the Ukrainians was wrong. The thrust of the aforementioned article is against atheistic materialistic philosophy, which produces death and destruction recorded repeatedly in history.

To start with, in light of the truth of Christianity and within the framework of the Christian worldview it can be said that creation has a testimony, albeit not audible like human speech. Creation does testify of God's existence. In contrast, within the framework of a materialistic worldview, matter is absolutely silent. This is a suppressed or imposed silence, the result of fallen man's ethical state reflected in his reprobate philosophy. Within the Christian worldview the testimony of creation or general revelation is absolutely true but limited in its scope. Being limited does not imply deficiency. God always intended to give special or biblical revelation. Jesus is God's fullest revelation to man and He is revealed to us in the Scriptures. General revelation does not tell us about Jesus' death on the cross and how men are to be saved. The book of Romans and the Gospels do.

Matter is not alive. God creates matter. Because of this, matter has God's imprint. Therefore, matter's testimony mirrors or is reflective. It reflects God's glory like the moon reflects the light of the sun. This testimony is general in scope. In the article it is said, "matter is silent" which is to point out the bankruptcy of materialistic philosophy and its inability to speak with intelligence concerning specifics in the area of ethics, since its worldview is deficient. The materialist starts with time and chance and matter. If non-believers start with matter, how do they get from A (matter) to B (ethics)? Matter does not logically lead to anything within the framework of materialism. There are obvious disagreements between Christians and non-Christians in the area of interpretation of matter. The reason for these disagreements can be accounted for by the way in which evidence is interpreted. In essence, fallen man rejects God's interpretation of creation and imposes his own autonomous interpretation on created things, thus suppressing the truth. As will be seen, the materialist has nowhere to turn except his own conflicting autonomous capricious subjective evaluations.

The Christian sees all of creation as testifying of God's existence. The Christian looks to God to find the true meaning of matter and the facts surrounding it. The non-believer, however, sees nothing except matter, which cannot mean anything nor have anything to say apart from man's imposed interpretation. From a Christian perspective, man is governed by presuppositions. These presuppositions are determined by his nature that is either fallen or redeemed. He interprets matter in a manner that is consistent with these presuppositions. Fallen man is still committed to the Satanic lie that "ye shall be as gods knowing good from evil" (Genesis 3:5). In the fall, mankind rejected God-given knowledge.

Many are not epistemologically self-conscious, including some Christians, and therefore are unaware that they have presuppositions which govern their interpretations. In particular, fallen man generally refuses to acknowledge that he has presuppositions and that his presuppositions govern interpretations of matter or anything else. To many, what is put forward as evidence and interpretation seems self-evident; but in reality it is nothing more than a subjective evaluation. Escaping from subjectivity is no easy task. Does non-believing philosophy enable man to get beyond his subjectivity? Can non-believing man's rationalism (reason alone using logic) save him? Can the laws of logic within the framework of a non-believing worldview accomplish this? How can they, since the laws of logic cannot even be explained or justified within the framework of this philosophy? For example, where did these laws come from? Are they universally interpreted in the same way? The laws of logic within the framework of non-belief are nothing more than a philosophical construct which ends up collapsing into irrationality.

Rational man, in other words, has no basis for his rationalism. The statement "matter is silent" should be understood in contrast to the statement that "God is not silent." This second assertion is the Christian solution to obtaining knowledge. God has spoken clearly to all men through the Scriptures. We have a biblical foundation for seeking knowledge and obtaining it. God given revelation is objective. Ungodly men reject biblical revelation, they suppress the truth that God has revealed to them through creation (Romans 1:18). God has clearly spoken in the Scriptures, i.e. special revelation to mankind concerning what is required by him. The suppression of God's revelation by fallen man is evidence of his epistemological rebellion.

In addition, regarding matter it can be said that whatever testimony general revelation has, it is because God is the author of it. In and of itself, matter has nothing to say. Someone may object and say, "We can learn many things from rocks." This type of assertion is naive. Evidence is interpreted within the framework of a worldview. The presuppositions that govern a worldview determine what may be learned. If the presuppositions are false, evidence will be misinterpreted or suppressed. The mind of man does not interpret raw data without the aid of controlling presuppositions. Some deny this. For example, empiricists, those who believe that man's mind is blank in the beginning of life and then knowledge comes through sensations, believe that man's mind is capable of assimilating and correctly interpreting raw data.

For example, empiricism historically argues that knowledge comes through sensations in the following order: (a) sensations, (b) perceptions, (c) memory images, (d) and the development of abstract ideas. In this system of interpretation, perceptions are inferences from sensations. How does the empiricist know valid from invalid inferences? Given this uncertainty, how can the empiricist be sure of anything, let alone what type of matter he has? In addition, studies have shown that some individuals do not have memory images. How can this group of people know things empirically? This is no small problem for empirical epistemology. Tiredness, drugs, and optical illusions can deceive the senses, particularly in the area of sight (color) and hearing (sound) causing further uncertainty. The Christian would also not rule out sin and demonic deception as factors leading to false conclusions. Assuming that empirical epistemology has resolved these difficulties is just that, an assumption.

Consistent empirical epistemology leads to skepticism, as in the case of Scottish philosopher David Hume. Allegedly, Emmanuel Kant was awakened from his dogmatic slumbers when he saw the effects Hume's skeptical consistencies were having on empirical epistemology. Kant tried to save empirical epistemology by positing that man's mind organized empirical data by *a priori* categories through which sensations could be understood. Whether he did or not is another issue. Another problem for the empiricist is that it is impossible to know the totality of empirical data on any subject with the endless complexities of inter-related details, which always leaves open the possibility that the empiricist is mistaken in more than just his perceptions. Moreover, empirically, how does the empiricist assimilate the numerous sensations such as sight and touch into a coherent basis for knowing what anything is? The empiricist needs to explain his process of abstraction and demonstrate that it is free from error. Assuming the system works without demonstrating the process is nothing more than begging the question. Empirical scientists are notorious for making unjustified metaphysical assertions. See Gordon H. Clark's *The Philosophy of Science and Belief in God*[2] and John W. Robbins, *The Sagan of Science*[3] for a number of instructive examples of this.

In addition to numerous philosophical problems relating to interpretation, it should be clear that matter has nothing to say within the framework of non-believing philosophy. What could it say? Within this framework, matter is ultimately an accident and therefore meaningless. In addition to this problem, all men have *a priori* commitments, which are at work and from which truth or falsity is deduced. The question is not does man have these commitments, but what are they? Do these commitments acknowledge God in the reasoning process? If one starts with non-Christian premises it is impossible to arrive at biblical truth. For a conclusion to be valid it cannot contain information not stated in the premises. The non-believer cannot have accurate knowledge because his presuppositions, starting premises, or axioms, which govern interpretations, are false.

When non-believers seem to arrive at conclusions consistent with biblical revelation, it is by accident, inconsistency, or theft. Many times the non-Christian worldview steals the ethical conclusions from the Christian worldview. This borrowing or more properly stealing from the Christian worldview is why non-believers at times seemingly speak the truth without having the necessary presuppositions to arrive at the truth. The non-believer, because of the bankruptcy of his position, is forced to live on stolen concepts. Thankfully, many non-believers rejected Nazism's "final solution." In other words, at times, by God's common grace, the non-believer sees the *reductio ad absurdum* and horror of where his own philosophical commitments lead.

Since God is the creator, He gives the true interpretation of all things. All true interpretation must come to grip with God's revelation, in which is found the meaning and interpretation of matter. When dealing with the difference between right and wrong one deals with specifics. Natural or general revelation is only good as far as it is intended. It is right and true as far as it goes. It is intended to show man that God exists and testifies of His eternal power and Godhead (Romans 1:18-20). General revelation testifies but its testimony is not intended to address specifics in the areas of science, logic and ethics. It is to special revelation in the Bible that we must turn.

Any theory of knowledge that attempts to build a philosophy without God's special revelation (the Scriptures) is doomed to failure. Reformed Christians believe that general revelation is sufficient to condemn man. Special revelation, i.e. biblical revelation, adds to man's culpability. God's purpose in general revelation is not to give man specific knowledge in many areas. To illustrate, matter does not give specifics concerning the difference between first degree murder and manslaughter nor adultery and fornication, or whether fornication (*pornea*) is a category under which adultery is defined. This is found in special revelation, e.g., in the case laws of the Old Testament.

THE RELIGION THAT STARTED IN A HAT

As has been seen, Christians have a solid basis for knowledge. All men have God's moral law stamped upon their conscience. The diligent reader should consult Ronald H. Nash's *The Word of God and the Mind of Man*[4] and his *The light of the mind: St. Augustine's theory of* knowledge.[5] These two books explain and develop for the modern reader elements of Augustine's philosophy in the area of epistemology that is found in his *De Magistro*.[6] These works deal with the mechanics of how the Christian receives knowledge into his mind. Man has a moral awareness of right from wrong, not learned from matter or uncertain sensations but from our mind being illuminated directly by God. We read: "That was the true Light which gives light to every man who comes into the world" in John 1:9; and, "For in Him we live and move and have our being..." in Acts 17:28a. God directly illuminates man's mind so he knows the difference between right and wrong. God's law is stamped upon our consciences. This knowledge gives man his moral awareness and is the result of man being created in the image of God.

In summary, to press non-belief further, it can be said that the anti-supernatural worldview man has erected is full of contradictions. Oftentimes, if consistent with this materialist worldview, he cannot know anything, since consistent empiricism leads to agnostic skepticism which he then uses as a smoke screen or cover to justify ignorance and hostility to God's law. If not consistent with the philosophical conclusions of a materialistic worldview derived from sensations, he then claims as an atheist to have certain knowledge of right and wrong using his reason alone, which is in defiance to biblical knowledge. Philosophically, unbelief vacillates between these two positions of knowing and not knowing. These two opposite poles of allegiance constitute a never-ending dilemma, thus revealing the futility of non-Christian epistemology. Does any of this consciously affect the non-believer? No, the philosophy of non-belief irrationally presses on, certain of its uncertainty, oblivious to the self-refuting contradictions being advanced. To illustrate, for example, some non-believers claim *absolutely* that there are no *absolutes*. The philosophy of non-belief contradicts itself when it claims *not to know* (uncertainty, agnosticism) *and to know* (certainty, atheism). Both atheism and agnosticism are two sides of the same coin. Fallen man's contradictory uncertainty and certainty are manifestations of his epistemological and ethical rebellion against God.

Also no less devastating, many examples could be given of non-believers asserting absolutes and omniscient statements within the framework of a system that does not allow absolutes. When finite man without biblical authority asserts absolute omniscient statements, it is indefensible. Also, it should be noted the absurdity of atheism's claim when asserting "There is no God." The absurdity is this: it is impossible to prove a universal negative. Furthermore, when the atheist asserts that "There is no God", the second question of the Socratic technique, "How do you know that?" reveals the failure of this unverifiable claim. So much for the non-believer's demand for verification. The agnostic claims ignorance for himself concerning the existence of God. It should be noted that this claim of ignorance is not an argument against the existence of God. Rather, it is a sign of epistemological bankruptcy, what could be described as a deficiency of knowledge, or a self-confessed mental condition.

In essence, fallen man has erected a closed system. His system is closed to God. He does not allow God to speak. Since man rejects the Creator, he has nothing within his closed system that he allows to speak with ethical certainty. He is left to himself. As long as fallen man excludes the biblical God from his system, he cannot know anything with certainty. Non-believing thought has no basis for absolutes. If there are no absolutes there can be no meaning attached to anything since everything could be said to be true and not true at the same time, which is unacceptable nonsense. Thus, fallen man is left with only endless matter, unintelligible sensations, or his naturalistic reason. This is the bankruptcy of atheistic materialistic humanism.

It is only the Christian that has a rational basis for knowledge. This is because we allow God to speak to us in creation and in Scripture. Our system is not closed like the non-Christian's. The Bible tells us about general revelation and man's requirement to worship the Creator. The Bible tells us the specifics of how to worship the Creator. It is only because we have special revelation that an intelligent conversation on these matters can be carried on. General and special revelation are biblical concepts. It would be impossible to have a discussion about these concepts without God's special revelation, the Bible, since biblical revelation is where the concepts appear. Clearly, without special revelation there would be no discussion of ethics, science, and logic with any certainty.

In conclusion, without the Bible, i.e. special revelation, we would not be able to talk about the concept of general revelation. This is because it is in Scripture that we learn the purpose of general or creation revelation. The objector to my previous article recognized the truth of Christian revelation, but gave away unnecessary ground to non-belief by not fully grasping the effects of the fall, and therefore missed the thrust of the argument, which was directed against non-believing philosophy. Our knowledge of general revelation is dependent upon special revelation. Therefore, special revelation is indispensable. The importance and necessity of special revelation is absolutely essential. Without special revelation we would be left in a swamp of autonomous, empirical subjectivity which is where the non-believer finds himself. The non-believer is left in the dark as long as they suppress the truth of God that has been revealed to them. God has spoken. This is certain: God speaks to us in the Scriptures (special revelation), with human language, utilizing logically structured sentences, in which He tells us the difference between right and wrong. Consequently, the strength of the Christian worldview is clearly seen by the impossibility of the contrary.

NOTES

1. Jack Kettler, *Pagan Philosophy, Unbelief, and Irrationalism* (Minneapolis: Contra Mundum, 1998). http://www.visi.com/~contra_m//cm/discuss2/cm98_jk_pagan.html

2. Gordon H. Clark, *The Philosophy of Science and Belief in God* (Jefferson, Maryland: Trinity, 1987).

3. John W. Robbins, *The Sagan of Science* (Jefferson, Maryland: Trinity, 1988).

4. Ronald H. Nash, *The Word of God and the Mind of Man* (Grand Rapids, Michigan: The Zondervan Corporation, 1982).

5. Ronald H. Nash, *The Light of the Mind: St. Augustine's Theory of Knowledge* (Lexington, Kentucky: The University Press of Kentucky, 1969).

6. Augustine, *De Magistro* in *Augustine: Earlier Writings* Editor, John H. S. Burleigh, (Philadelphia: The Westminster Press, MCMLIII).

SPECIAL NOTE

As in my previous article nothing in the above article should be understood as being original with me. I am indebted biblically and philosophically for the above comments to Francis A. Schaeffer, Gordon H. Clark, Ronald H. Nash, Cornelius Van Til, and Greg Bahnsen.

For though we walk in the flesh, we do not war after the flesh: (For the weapons of our warfare are not carnal, but mighty through God to the pulling down of strong holds;) Casting down imaginations, and every high thing that exalteth itself against the knowledge of God, and bringing into captivity every thought to the obedience of Christ. (2 Corinthians 10:3-5)

PAGAN PHILOSOPHY,
UNBELIEF, AND IRRATIONALISM
by Jack Kettler

iblically speaking, holding philosophical beliefs that contain internally self-refuting contradictions is an expression of irrationalism. It can also be a case of inexcusable ignorance. Ultimately, all non-Christian philosophy starts with bold rationalistic assertions about reality and ends up in irrationalism. The philosophy of logical positivism is one example. The positivist philosophy can be described as empiricism (all knowledge comes through sensations) with a vengeance. This positivist philosophy is a vengeance against all metaphysical statements. A popular contemporary form of empiricism that derives from John Locke is known as the theory that the mind at birth is a blank tablet (*tabula rasa*) and then assimilates knowledge through sensations. This theory could be called the "blank mind theory" of knowledge.

The Positivist School boldly asserted as its starting principle that they will only accept what can be verified empirically. The positivists would accept a statement like "Some cars are red," because this could be verified empirically. A color-blind person would have to take this statement by faith. A statement like "God exists" would be rejected since God cannot be brought into a science laboratory and inspected. Once upon a time, someone asked, "How does the positivist school verify its own starting principle empirically?" With that question, the empirical, positivist school collapsed. Yet there are still those who promote elements of this philosophically discredited theory, not realizing that in doing so they have become an irrationalist, or guilty of inexcusable ignorance. Positivism collapsed because, as in all non-Christian philosophy, it contains its own internally self-refuting contradiction. This positivist contradiction is in the same category as with those who assert, "There is no truth." Supposedly, this assertion is true.

Many non-Christians hold to a materialistic atheistic worldview. Adherents of this pagan worldview proclaim their belief in the laws of science, morality, and logic. It should be noted that adherents of this worldview have never shown how the laws of science, morality, and logic can ever arise in a materialistic universe. Non-Christians who hold this worldview continue to proclaim their belief in such things without showing how their system can account for them. This is philosophically called "begging the question." In the area of morality for example, the non-Christian is unable to define the difference between right and wrong in terms of his worldview or belief system. Today, many see this ignorance as a virtue. But if biblical absolutes are rejected, it is meaningless to even talk about right and wrong.

In a materialistic atheistic worldview, laws against evil, such as murder, are merely arbitrary social formalities. For example, in pagan democracies the laws change when a mere fifty-one percent of the population is swayed in a different direction. When it comes to knowing the difference between right and wrong many non-Christians act as though they have a blank mind. Pagan attempts to define right from wrong are arbitrary, or they borrow definitions from the Christian worldview in order to escape the utter bankruptcy of their own worldview.

Matter is silent; it does not speak. It does not say what is right or what is wrong. The distinction between good and evil is found in the Bible. God is not silent. For example, the definition of murder is found in the case laws of the Old Testament. The Bible even defines precisely the difference between premeditated murder and manslaughter. Only the Christian worldview can account for the laws of science, morality, and logic. This is because God is the creator of the world, and we understand all things as defined and interpreted by Him in Holy Scripture. Nothing exists apart from His definition. Since God governs the universe, we can under normal providential conditions use scientific procedures to help us systematically understand how elements of the world function. God speaks to us in Scripture with human language utilizing logically structured sentences in which He tells us the difference between right and wrong. Because God has spoken, the Christian has a biblical basis for the laws of science, morality, and logic. Only in Christ Jesus can one find answers to the questions of life. In Christ Jesus alone can one find the basis for truth and absolutes. All pagan philosophy suppresses the truth in unrighteousness and ends in internally self-refuting irrationalistic contradictions.

NOTE

Nothing in the above article should be understood as being original with me. I am indebted Biblically and philosophically for the above comments to Francis A. Schaeffer, Gordon H. Clark, Cornelius Van Til, and Greg Bahnsen.

CHAPTER I

OF THE HOLY SCRIPTURE
- Westminster Confession of Faith

I.

Although the light of nature, and the works of creation and providence, do so far manifest the goodness, wisdom, and power of God, as to leave men inexcusable; yet are they not sufficient to give that knowledge of God, and of his will, which is necessary unto salvation; therefore it pleased the Lord, at sundry times, and in divers manners, to reveal himself, and to declare that his will unto his Church; and afterwards for the better preserving and propagating of the truth, and for the more sure establishment and comfort of the Church against the corruption of the flesh, and the malice of Satan and of the world, to commit the same wholly unto writing; which maketh the holy Scripture to be most necessary; those former ways of God's revealing his will unto his people being now ceased.

II.

Under the name of holy Scripture, or the Word of God written, are now contained all the Books of the Old and New Testament, which are these:

OF THE OLD TESTAMENT

Genesis, Exodus, Leviticus, Numbers, Deuteronomy, Joshua, Judges, Ruth, I Samuel, 2 Samuel, I Kings, 2 Kings, I Chronicles, 2 Chronicles, Ezra, Nehemiah, Esther, Job, Psalms, Proverbs, Ecclesiastes, The Song of Songs, Isaiah, Jeremiah, Lamentations, Ezekiel, Daniel, Hosea, Joel, Amos, Obadiah, Jonah, Micah, Nahum, Habakkuk, Zephaniah, Haggai, Zechariah, Malachi

Of the New Testament

Matthew, Mark, Luke, John, Acts, Romans, 1 Corinthians, 2 Corinthians, Galatians, Ephesians, Philippians, Colossians, I Thessalonians, 2 Thessalonians, I Timothy, 2 Timothy, Titus, Philemon, Hebrews, James, I Peter, 2 Peter, First, Second, and Third Epistles of John, Jude, Revelation

All which are given by inspiration of God, to be the rule of faith and life.

III.

The books commonly called Apocrypha, not being of divine inspiration, are no part of the Canon of Scripture; and therefore are of no authority in the Church of God, nor to be any otherwise approved, or made use of, than other human writings.

IV.

The authority of the holy Scripture, for which it ought to be believed and obeyed, dependeth not upon the testimony of any man or Church, but wholly upon God (who is truth itself), the Author thereof; and therefore it is to be received, because it is the Word of God.

V.

We may be moved and induced by the testimony of the Church to an high and reverent esteem of the holy Scripture; and the heavenliness of the matter, the efficacy of the doctrine, the majesty of the style, the consent of all the parts, the scope of the whole (which is to give all glory to God), the full discovery it makes of the only way of man's salvation, the many other incomparable excellencies, and the entire perfection thereof, are arguments whereby it doth abundantly evidence itself to be the Word of God; yet, notwithstanding, our full persuasion and assurance of the infallible truth and divine authority thereof, is from the inward work of the Holy Spirit, bearing witness by and with the Word in our hearts.

VI.

The whole counsel of God, concerning all things necessary for his own glory, man's salvation, faith, and life, is either expressly set down in Scripture, or by good and necessary consequence may be deduced from Scripture: unto which nothing at any time is to be added, whether by new revelations of the Spirit, or traditions of men. Nevertheless we acknowledge the inward illumination of the Spirit of God to be necessary for the saving understanding of such things as are revealed in the Word; and that there are some circumstances concerning the worship of God, and the government of the Church, common to human actions and societies, which are to be ordered by the light of nature and Christian prudence, according to the general rules of the Word, which are always to be observed.

VII.

All things in Scripture are not alike plain in themselves, nor alike clear unto all; yet those things which are necessary to be known, believed, and observed, for salvation, are so clearly propounded and opened in some place of Scripture or other, that not only the learned, but the unlearned, in a due use of the ordinary means, may attain unto a sufficient understanding of them.

VIII.

The Old Testament in Hebrew (which was the native language of the people of God of old), and the New Testament in Greek (which at the time of the writing of it was most generally known to the nations), being immediately inspired by God, and by his singular care and providence kept pure in all ages, are therefore authentical; so as in all controversies of religion the Church is finally to appeal unto them. But because these original tongues are not known to all the people of God who have right unto, and interest in, the Scriptures, and are commanded, in the fear of God, to read and search them, therefore they are to be translated into the language of every people unto which they come, that the Word of God dwelling plentifully in all, they may worship him in an acceptable manner, and, through patience and comfort of the Scriptures, may have hope.

IX.

The infallible rule of interpretation of Scripture, is the Scripture itself; and therefore, when there is a question about the true and full sense of any scripture (which is not manifold, but one), it may be searched and known by other places that speak more clearly.

X.

The Supreme Judge, by which all controversies of religion are to be determined, and all decress of councils, opinions of ancient writers, doctrines of men, and private spirits, are to be examined, and in whose sentence we are to rest, can be no other but the Holy Spirit speaking in the Scripture.

—*Westminster Confession of Faith (1646)*

CHAPTER VI
OF THE FALL OF MAN, OF SIN, AND OF THE PUNISHMENT THEREOF
-Westminster Confession of Faith

I.

Our first parents, being seduced by the subtlety and temptation of Satan, sinned, in eating the forbidden fruit.[1] This their sin, God was pleased, according to his wise and holy counsel, to permit, having purposed to order it to his own glory.[2]

    1. Gen. 3:13; II Cor. 11:3

    2. See Chapter V, Section IV

II.

By this sin they fell from their original righteousness and communion with God,[3] and so became dead in sin,[4] and wholly defiled in all the parts and faculties of soul and body.[5]

    3. Gen. 3:6-8; Rom. 3:23

    4. Gen. 2:17; Eph. 2:1-3; see Rom. 5:12

    5. Gen. 6:5; Jer. 17:9; Titus 1:15; Rom. 3:10-19

III.

They being the root of all mankind, the guilt of this sin was imputed;[6] and the same death in sin, and corrupted nature, conveyed to all their posterity descending from them by ordinary generation.[7]

6. Acts. 17:26; Rom. 5:12, 15-19; I Cor. 15:21-22, 49

7. Psa. 51:5; John 3:6; Gen. 5:3; Job 15:14

IV.

From this original corruption, whereby we are utterly indisposed, disabled, and made opposite to all good,[8] and wholly inclined to all evil,[9] do proceed all actual transgressions.[10]

8. Rom. 5:6; 7:18; 8:7; Col. 1:21

9. Gen. 6:5; 8:21; Rom. 3:10-12

10. Matt. 15:19; James 1:14-15; Eph. 2:2-3

V.

This corruption of nature, during this life, doth remain in those that are regenerated;[11] and although it be, through Christ, pardoned, and mortified; yet both itself, and all the motions there-of, are truly and properly sin.[12]

11. Prov. 20:9; Eccl. 7:20; Rom. 7:14, 17-18, 21-23; I John 1:8, 10

12. Rom. 7:7-8, 25; Gal. 5:17

VI.

Every sin, both original and actual, being a transgression of the righteous law of God, and contrary thereunto,[13] doth, in its own nature, bring guilt upon the sinner,[14] whereby he is bound over to the wrath of God,[15] and curse of the law,[16] and so made subject to death,[17] with all miseries spiritual,[18] temporal,[19] and eternal.[20]

13. I John 3:4

14. Rom. 2:15; 3:9, 19

15. Eph. 2:3

16. Gal. 3:10

17. Rom. 6:23

18. Eph. 4:18

19. Rom. 8:20; Lam. 3:39

20. Matt. 25:41; II Thess. 1:9

FROM *THE SHORTER CATECHISM*
WITH THE SCRIPTURE PROOFS

Q. 13. Did our first parents continue in the estate wherein they were created?

A. Our first parents, being left to the freedom of their own will, fell from the estate wherein they were created, by sinning against God [a].

[a]. Gen. 3:6-8, 13; II Cor. 11:3

Q. 14. What is sin?

A. Sin is any want of conformity unto, or transgression of, the law of God [a].

[a]. Lev. 5:17; Jas. 4:17; I John 3:4

Q. 15. What was the sin whereby our first parents fell from the estate wherein they were created?

A. The sin whereby our first parents fell from the estate wherein thy were created, was their eating the forbidden fruit [a].

[a]. Gen. 3:6

Q. 16. Did all mankind fall in Adam's first transgression?

A. The covenant being made with Adam [a], not only for himself, but for his posterity; all mankind, descending from him by ordinary generation, sinned in him, and fell with him, in his first transgression [b].

    [a]. Gen. 2:16-17; Jas. 2:10

    [b]. Rom. 5:12-21; I Cor. 15:22

Q. 17. Into what estate did the fall bring mankind?

A. The fall brought mankind into an estate of sin and misery [a].

    [a]. Gen. 3:16-19, 23; Rom. 3:16; 5:12; Eph. 2:1

Q. 18. Wherein consists the sinfulness of that estate whereinto man fell?

A. The sinfulness of that estate whereinto man fell, consists in the guilt of Adam's first sin [a], the want of original righteousness [b], and the corruption of his whole nature [c], which is commonly called original sin; together with all actual transgressions which proceed from it [d].

    [a]. Rom. 5:12, 19

    [b]. Rom. 3:10; Col. 3:10; Eph. 4:24

    [c]. Ps. 51:5; John 3:6; Rom. 3:18; 8:7-8; Eph. 2:3

    [d]. Gen. 6:5; Ps. 53:1-3; Matt. 15:19; Rom. 3:10-18, 23; Gal. 5:19-21; Jas. 1:14-15

Q. 19. What is the misery of that estate whereinto man fell?

A. All mankind by their fall lost communion with God [a], are under his wrath [b] and curse [c], and so made liable to all miseries in this life [d], to death [e] itself, and to the pains of hell for ever [f].

    [a]. Gen. 3:8, 24; John 8:34, 42, 44; Eph. 2:12; 4:18

    [b]. John 3:36; Rom. 1:18; Eph. 2:3; 5:6

    [c]. Gal. 3:10; Rev. 22:3

[d]. Gen. 3:16-19; Job 5:7; Ecc. 2:22-23; Rom. 8:18-23

[e]. Ezek. 18:4; Rom. 5:12; 6:23

[f]. Matt. 25:41, 46; II Thess. 1:9; Rev. 14:9-11 The Westminster Shorter Catechism was completed in 1647

CHAPTER IX

OF FREE WILL

- Westminster Confession of Faith

I.

God hath endued the will of man with that natural liberty, that it is neither forced, nor, by any absolute necessity of nature, determined to good, or evil.[1]

    1. James 1:13-14; 4:7; Deut. 30:19; Isa. 7:11-12; Matt. 17:12; John 5:40

II.

Man, in his state of innocency, had freedom, and power to will and to do that which was good and well pleasing to God;[2] but yet, mutably, so that he might fall from it.[3]

    2. Eccl. 7:29; Gen. 1:26, 31; Col. 3:10

    3. Gen. 2:16-17; 3:6, 17

III.

Man, by his fall into a state of sin, hath wholly lost all ability of will to any spiritual good accompanying salvation:[4] so as, a natural man, being altogether averse from that good,[5] and dead in sin,[6] is not able, by his own strength, to convert himself, or to prepare himself thereunto.[7]

    4. Rom. 5:5; 8:7-8; John 6:44, 65; 15:5

    5. Rom. 3:9-10, 12, 23

6. Eph. 2:1, 5; Col 2:13

7. John 3:3, 5-6; 6:44, 65; I Cor. 2:14; Titus 3:3-5

IV.

When God converts a sinner, and translates him into the state of grace, he freeth him from his natural bondage under sin;[8] and, by his grace alone, enables him freely to will and to do that which is spiritually good;[9] yet so, as that by reason of his remaining corruption, he doth not perfectly, nor only, will that which is good, but doth also will that which is evil.[10]

8. Col. 1:13; John 8:34, 36; Rom. 6:6-7

9. Phil. 2:13; Rom. 6:14, 17-19, 22

10. Gal. 5:17; Rom. 7:14-25; I John 1:8, 10

V.

The will of man is made perfectly and immutably free to good alone, in the state of glory only.[11]

11. Heb. 12:23; I John 3:2; Jude 1:24; Rev. 21:27

CHAPTER XXXIII

OF THE LAST JUDGMENT

- Westminster Confession of Faith

I.

God hath appointed a day, wherein he will judge the world in righteousness by Jesus Christ, to whom all power and judgment is given of the Father. In which day, not only the apostate angels shall be judged; but likewise all persons, that have lived upon earth, shall appear before the tribunal of Christ, to give an account of their thoughts, words, and deeds; and to receive according to what they have done in the body, whether good or evil.

II.

The end of God's appointing this day, is for the manifestation of the glory of his mercy in the eternal salvation of the elect; and of his justice in the damnation of the reprobate, who are wicked and disobedient. For then shall the righteous go into everlasting life, and receive that fullness of joy and refreshing which shall come from the presence of the Lord: but the wicked, who know not God, and obey not the gospel of Jesus Christ, shall be cast into eternal torments, and punished with everlasting destruction from the presence of the Lord, and from the glory of his power.

III.

As Christ would have us to be certainly persuaded that there shall be a day of judgment, both to deter all men from sin, and for the greater consolation of the godly in their adversity: so will he have that day unknown to men, that they may shake off all carnal security, and be always watchful, because they know not at what hour the Lord will come; and may be ever prepared to say, Come, Lord Jesus, come quickly. Amen.

—Westminster Confession of Faith (1646)

BAPTISM
FOR THE DEAD

by Jack Kettler

lse what shall they do which are baptized for the dead, if the dead rise not at all? Why are they then baptized for the dead?" (1 Corinthians 15:29)

It has been a common interpretation of this passage to believe Paul is referring to some unknown group in the First-Century practicing baptism for dead people by proxy.

This passage is a favorite Mormon proof-text for one of their unique doctrines. Mormons are generally proud to point out that they still practice baptism for the dead, where Christendom has abandoned this Old Testament practice. In Mormonism, baptism by water is a necessary ordinance for salvation. Baptisms for the dead can only be performed in Mormon temples. Baptism for the dead in Mormon temples supposedly gives those who have died without embracing Christ the opportunity to do so after death.

How do we understand 1 Corinthians 15:29? And, to whom is Paul referring in this passage of Scripture?

The Bible teaches that Scripture is the best interpreter of Scripture. Using this scriptural approach, there is an Old Testament text to which Paul is referencing in 1 Corinthians 15:29. When Paul talks about "they," he is referring to the Old Testament practice in Numbers 19:11-22. This part of the law taught that an Israelite who touched a dead body became unclean and consequently unable to approach the Lord resulting in being cut off from covenant community. Contact with a dead body by an Israelite polluted him. In redemptive history, such contact served to demonstrate that the individual was under the biblical condemnation of death, the result of sin. No one but Jesus because of His sinless perfection, could come into contact with death and not be contaminated. Only Christ is able to vanquish the power of uncleanness and death.

How do we understand this baptism and its mode? This is crucial for a proper understanding of the passage.

As a necessary excursus, in Hebrews 9:10 we read: [ceremonies and offerings] "which stood only in meats and drinks, and divers washings, and carnal ordinances, imposed on them until the time of reformation." The writer of Hebrews is discussing how the ceremonies of the Old Testament pointed to the finished work of Christ. In Hebrews 9:10, the writer says that those Old Testament ordinances applied until the time of the New Covenant. Among those extraneous regulations of the Old Covenant, note how the writer refers to "divers washings." In the Greek, this passage mentioning "divers washings" is accurately translated "various baptisms." In addition to these First-Century Jewish "washings," i.e. baptisms, there were Old Covenant baptisms.

Were these ceremonial baptisms done by immersion? The "washings" referenced in Hebrews cannot be understood as immersions because of availability of water considerations. The Jews would not immerse furniture; "and, coming from the market-place, if they do not baptize themselves, they do not eat; and many other things there are that they received to hold, baptisms of cups, and pots, and brazen vessels, and couches" (Mark 7:4). If we understand that baptism can be done by sprinkling or pouring, then we find a satisfactory interpretation of Hebrews 9:10; Mark 7:4 and the Old Testament text to which Paul is referring to in Numbers 19 This sprinkling in Numbers 19:13 is equivalent to the washings, or "*baptismois*" (baptisms) in Hebrews 9:10 and is therefore, a baptism..

Paul is revealing to us that the Israelite who had been contaminated by contact with the dead was not only unable to approach the Lord's tabernacle in Numbers 19:13, he in fact would also be cut off from Israel because of his defilement. What was the Old Testament solution for this contamination resulting from defilement in touching a dead body? The remedy found in the law was that the unclean individual must be sprinkled or baptized with the water of purification on the third day, as is seen in verses 13 and 17. The unclean person would not be cleansed until the seventh day, as is seen in verse 19.

A Holy God could never have sin in His presence. The certainty of death exhibits that we are all spiritual rebels, debased and unclean in the sight of the Lord. Paul's assertion in 1 Corinthians 15:29 affirms that the water of purification in Numbers 19 is a ceremonially cleansing, which in reality is accomplished by Christ's resurrection.

By following the prescription of the law (the water of purification in Numbers 19) the power of death was broken. The unclean person could be made clean and able to approach the Lord, and restored to the covenant people. The water of purification in Numbers 19 was a shadow or type, like the blood of bulls and goats that in reality could never uproot or take away sin (Hebrews 10:4).

The water of purification in Numbers 19 also could never truly cleanse the pollution caused by sin. It was a type or shadow which finds fulfillment in Christ's atoning death and resurrection.

Paul's teaching in 1 Corinthians 15:29 now becomes clear; "they," or the Jewish practice based upon the law of God in Numbers 19, foreshadowed the resurrection of Christ. Today it would be wrong for Christians to practice the law of Numbers 19, and that is why Paul says "they" in Corinthians rather than "we." This Old Testament Jewish practice foreshadowed Christ's resurrection. To continue this Old Testament practice today would be to reproach the finished work of Christ by going back to a type or shadow of weak and beggarly elements (Galatians 4:9).

Paul, in 1 Corinthians 15:29 sets forth a splendid picture of the resurrection foreshadowed in Numbers 19. Paul was not referring to the practice of some unknown heretical group for proof of the resurrection; he was referring the Old Testament Jewish practice in Numbers 19, an incredible foreshadowing of Christ's atoning death and resurrection. When the apostle in 1 Corinthians 15:29 says "else what shall they do" he is referring to the Jews, the Old Testament covenant people of God.

The interpretation argued for in this article is not only consistent with types and shadows finding fulfillment in Christ, it does not depend on the purely speculative and unsatisfactory explanation of Paul referring to some unknown heretical practice in defending a key doctrine of the Christian Faith; namely, the resurrection of Christ. It refers to the Old Covenant Jewish practice now fulfilled in Christ.

I first heard of the connection between Corinthians and Numbers years ago from Rev. Steven M. Schlei from Loveland, CO.

What about the preposition "*huper*" in the translation of 1 Corinthians 15:29?

In 1 Corinthians 15:29, we find Greek preposition *huper*, which is translated in English as "for." What will those do who are baptized <u>for</u> the dead and if the dead are not raised at all, why then are they baptized <u>for</u> them? Normally, *huper* means "for the benefit of," or "on behalf of."

This is why translators and commentators have always believed the passage in 1 Corinthians 15:29 must be some type of vicarious baptism that some unknown esoteric aberrational group was practicing.

Can *huper* be translated differently?

In the New Testament, *huper* appears 160 times. Of these, *huper* is used a majority of times with words in the genitive case. Of particular interest for us is the text in question where it is translated "for" in 1 Corinthians 15:29, but it is also translated as "concerning" in Romans 9:27 and "because" in Philippians 1:7.

Consider what Joel R. White has written in his article titled: "Baptized On Account Of The Dead":

> As for the preposition υπέρ, it is to be understood in its causal sense and is best translated "because of" or, more precisely, "on account of." Standard grammars and lexicons give ample evidence for this usage in the NT usage in usage in the NT 63

> 63 See, in addition to BAGD, H. Riesenfeld, "υπέρ," *TDNT,* 8.514; J. H. Moulton, A *Grammar of New Testament Greek* (Edinburgh: Clark, 1963) 270-71; H. E. Dana and Julius R. Mantey, A *Manual Grammar of the Greek New Testament* (New York: Macmillan, 1927) 111. Υπέρ has an unambiguously causal sense when it describes the grounds for giving thanks or offering praise (Rom 15:9; 1 Cor 10:30; Eph 1:16; 5:20). It also seems to have a causal sense in many of the instances in which it is linked to suffering (Acts 5:41; 9:16; 15:26; 21:13; 2 Cor 12:10; Eph 3:13; 2 Thess 1:5). In Phil 1:29 this is undoubtedly so, for there we have two instances of υπέρ, the first, υπέρ Χριστού, giving the cause or ground of the Philippians' suffering; the second, υπέρ αυτού, stating its purpose. Additionally, a causal sense is possible, if not likely, in Rom 1:5; 15:8; 2 Cor 12:8; 1

James R. Rogers, in his article on "Baptism for the Dead" writes:

Nevertheless, this is not the only way to take huper. Indeed, the Scriptures also use the word to mean "on account of" or "because of." For example, huper appears in Romans 15:9, "the Gentiles...glorify God for His mercy." Quite obviously Gentiles do not give glory to God for the benefit of mercy—mercy does not benefit from the glory we give God. Rather, we glorify God on account of or because of His mercy. So, too, in 1 Corinthians 15:3, Paul writes that "Christ died for our sins." Now, Christ did not die for the benefit of our sins. Rather, he died on account of or because of our sins. This use of huper occurs often (see, e.g., 2 Cor. 12:8, Eph. 5:20, Heb. 5:1, 7:27, Acts 5:41, 15:26, and 21:13). I also consulted several of the best Greek lexicons, and pestered a couple of Greek scholars. All held that this is a permissible reading of the word. If so, then 1 Corinthians 15:29 can be properly translated or read as the following:

Otherwise, what will those do who are baptized because of the dead? If the dead are not raised at all, why then are they baptized because of the dead? 2

If White and Rogers are correct in their examples of the alternative translation and usage of *huper*, then the above interpretation holds up.

Significantly, A.T. Robertson M.A. D.D., L.I.D., regarding υπέρ notes:

A more general idea is that of 'about' or 'concerning.' Here υπέρ encroaches on the province of περί. Cf. 2 Cor. 8:23, υπέρ Τίτου, 2 Th. 2:1 υπὲρ τῆς παρουσίας τοῦ κυρίου. Perhaps 1 Cor. 15:29 comes in here also. Moulton1 finds commercial accounts in the papyri, scores of them with υπὲρ in the sense of 'to.' 3

In the Greek English Lexicon Of The New Testament and Other Early Christian Literature, we see other uses of ὑπὲρ under heading:

> d. because of to denote moving cause or the reason
> because of, for the sake of... and under f. about,
> concerning (about equivalent to περί). 4

In conclusion, as noted, the Greek preposition translated "for" in 1 Corinthians 15:29 is *huper*. It is possible to say that Paul is not writing about being baptized "in the place of," or "on behalf of," or "for" a dead person at all, as has been seen by the contrary evidence in how *huper* may be translated.

Since this is possible, then according to the context of 1 Corinthians 15:29, *huper* could be translated "because of " or "on account of." If *huper* can mean this, then the 1 Corinthians 15:29 text can be properly translated: "Else what shall they do which are baptized <u>because of</u> the dead, if the dead rise not at all? Why are they then baptized <u>because of</u> the dead?" or, "Else what shall they do which are baptized <u>on account of</u> the dead, if the dead rise not at all? Why are they then baptized <u>on account of</u> the dead?"

In light of the above and considerations that follow, based on exceptions to a general grammatical rule involving the Greek preposition *huper*, we could translate Paul in 1 Corinthians 15:29 to be saying: "else what do they, the Jews, mean by ceremonially washing or baptizing because of the dead? If the dead are not raised, why do the Jews ceremonially wash or baptize on account of the dead?"

In light of the differing usage and the adaptability of the preposition "*huper*", its use in 1 Corinthians 15:29 is by no means restricted to the translation conveying the idea of only proxy baptisms. In the matter of 1 Corinthians 15:29 we must let Scripture interpret Scripture. The connection between 1 Corinthians 15:29 and Numbers 19:11-22 is the most convincing interpretation.

Have there been in noted theologians in church history who have seen this connection?

Consider the leading 19th Century Southern Presbyterian theologian, Robert L. Dabney, and the connection between 1 Corinthians 15:29 and Numbers 19:11-13:

Baptism for the Dead by Robert L. Dabney (Appeared in the Christian Observer, February 3, 1897; vol. 84:5, pg. 10.)

The instructive and almost exhaustive treatise of Dr. Beattie upon 1 Cor. 15:29 suggests still another explanation which readers may compare with those recited by him. I first heard this from that devout, learned and judicious exegete, Rev. J. B. Ramsey, D. D., of Lynchburg, Va. He advocated it, not claiming originality for it. This explanation supposes that the holy apostle refers here to the Mosaic law of Num. 19:11-13, which required the Hebrew who had shared in the shrouding and burial of a human corpse to undergo a ceremonial uncleanness of seven days, and to deliver himself from it by two sprinklings with the water of purification containing the ashes of the burned heifer. This view is sustained by the following reasons:

I. We know from Mark 7:4, and Heb. 9:10 ("As the washing [baptisms] of cups and pots, brazen vessels and of tables." "And divers washings [baptisms] and carnal ordinances"), that both the evangelist and the Apostle Paul called the water purifications of the Mosaic law by the name of baptisms. Thus it is made perfectly clear that if the apostle designed in 1 Cor. 15:29 to refer to this purification of people recently engaged in a burial, he would use the word baptize.

II. This purification must have been well known, not only to all Jews and Jewish Christians, but to most gentile Christians in Corinth; because the converts from the Gentiles made in the apostles' days in a place like Corinth were chiefly from such pagans as were somewhat acquainted with the resident Jews and their synagogue worship. This explanation then has this great advantage, that it supposes the apostle to cite for argument (as is his wont everywhere) a familiar and biblical instance, rather than any usage rare, or partial or heretical, and so unknown to his readers and lacking in authority with them.

III. This view follows faithfully the exact syntax of the sentence. The apostle puts the verb in the present tense: "Which are baptized for the dead." For we suppose this law for purifying persons recently engaged in a burial was actually observed not only by Jews, but by Jewish Christians, and properly, at the time this epistle was written. We must remember that while the apostle firmly prohibited the imposition of the Mosaic ritual law upon gentile Christians according to the apostolic decree in Acts 15, he continued to observe it himself. He caused Timothy to be circumcised, while he sternly refused to impose circumcision upon gentile converts. He was at Jerusalem going through a Nazarite purification and preparing to keep the Jewish Passover, when he was captured by the Romans. His view of the substitution of the New Testament cultus in place of the Mosaic ritual seems to have been this: That, on the one hand, this ritual was no longer to be exacted of any Christian, Jew or Gentile, as necessary to righteousness, and that such exaction was a forfeiture of justification by grace; but on the other hand, it was proper and allowable for Jewish Christians to continue the observance of their fathers, such as the seventh day Sabbath, and the scriptural Mosaic ritual (not the mere rabbinical traditions) so long as the Temple was standing, provided their pious affections and associations inclined them to these observances.

IV. Dr. Ramsey's explanation is faithful to the idiomatic usage of the Greek words in the text. He correctly supposes that the apostle's term, "baptized," describes a religious water purification by sprinkling, founded on biblical authority; and here, perhaps, is the reason why expositors with immersionist tendencies have been blind to this very natural explanation; their minds refused to see a true baptism in a sprinkling, where the Apostle Paul saw it so plainly. Then, Dr. Ramsey uses the word "the dead" (nekron) in its most common, strict meaning of dead men; and that in the plural; not in the singular, as of the one corpse of Jesus. He also employs the preposition "for" (huper) in a fairly grammatical sense for its regimen of the genitive case; "on account of the dead."

V. Lastly, the meaning thus obtained for the apostle's instance coheres well with the line of his logic. If there be no resurrection what shall they do who receive this purification by water and the ashes of the heifer from the ceremonial uncleanness incurred on account of the corpses of their dead brethren and neighbors which they have aided to shroud and bury? If there be no resurrection, would there be any sense or reason in this scriptural requirement of a baptism? Wherein would these human corpses differ from the bodies of goats, sheep, and bullocks, dressed for food, without ceremonial uncleanness? Had Moses, inspired of God, not believed in the resurrection, he would not have ordained such a baptism as necessarily following the funeral of a human being. His doctrine is, that the guilt of sin is what pollutes a human being, the soul spiritually, and even the material body ceremonially; that bodily death is the beginning of the divine penalty for that guilt: that hence where that penalty strikes it makes its victim a polluted thing {herein). Hence even the man who touches it is vicariously polluted, as he would not be by the handling of any other material clod, and so needs purification. For all this points directly to man's immortality, with its future rewards and punishments; and these affecting not only the spirit but the body which is for a time laid away in the tomb, to be again reanimated and either to share the continued penalty of sin, or, through faith to be cleansed from it by the blood of Christ, and thus made to re-enter the New Jerusalem.

Robert Lewis Dabney (1829–1898) was one of the greatest Protestant theologians of the 19th century. A Southern Presbyterian, he was a teacher, statesman, writer, and social critic, as well as theologian, and taught at Union Seminary in Richmond, Virginia. In the American Civil War he once served as Chief of Staff to the Confederate general "Stonewall" Jackson. His work, especially his Systematic Theology, has been highly regarded by scholars from Benjamin Warfield to Karl Barth.

FOR FURTHER RESEARCH
ON BAPTISM, CONSULT

James W. Dale

Vol. 1-4; Classic Baptism; Judaic baptism; Johannic Baptism; Christic Baptism and Patristic Baptism (Presbyterian & Reformed Publishing Company, Phillipsburg, New Jersey).

NOTES

Baptized On Account Of The Dead: The Meaning Of 1 Corinthians 15:29 In Its Context

Joel R. White

Biblische Ausbildung am Ort, Vienna, Austria

Journal of Biblical Literature (JBL)116/3 (1997) 487-499

Biblical Horizons Newsletter

No. 76: Baptism for the Dead

by James R. Rogers

http://www.biblicalhorizons.com/biblical-horizons/no-76-baptism-for-the-dead/

A.T. Robertson M.A. D.D., L.I.D., *A Grammar Of The Greek New Testament In The Light Of Historical Research* (Broadman Press, Nashville, Tennessee), p. 632.

Walter Bauer, *Greek English Lexicon Of The New Testament and Other Early Christian Literature* (The University of Chicago Press, Printed in the United States of American) p. 839.

THE BOOK OF ABRAHAM IN THE *PEARL OF GREAT PRICE*

he Mormon Church is faced with an impossible task, namely defending the translation Joseph Smith made from some Egyptian papyri that he had acquired. The actual translation by modern Egyptologists reveal that Smith's translation of the papyri does not say what appears in Mormonism's *Book of Abraham in the Pearl of Great Price*.

The papyri Smith used were lost after his death in 1844. In 1967, the papyri were rediscovered by the Metropolitan Museum of Art in New York, which returned them to the Mormon Church, who subsequently confirmed them to be the originals and published them for others to see.

It is indisputable from Smith's own writing that he translated the Book of Abraham from the characters he found on the Egyptian papyri:

> The remainder of this month, I was continually engaged in translating an alphabet to the Book of Abraham, and arranging a grammar of the Egyptian language as practiced by the Ancients.
>
> Joseph Smith, *History of the Church* Vol. 2, p. 238.
>
> This afternoon I labored on the Egyptian alphabet... during the research, the principles of astronomy as understood by Father Abraham and the ancients unfolded to our understanding, the particulars of which will appear hereafter.
>
> Joseph Smith, *History of the Church* Vol. 2, p. 286.

As it turns out, Joseph Smith was mistaken in his translation of the Book of Abraham. This is no small matter to have mistranslated material that appears in Mormon Scripture. If Smith was wrong in his translation of the Book of Abraham, how can we trust Smith in his translation of the *Book of Mormon?* The evidence is overwhelming against Smith's erroneous translation.

The Lost Book of Abraham, a Documentary Film:

The Lost Book of Abraham is an award-winning documentary that investigates the remarkable claim that Mormon founder Joseph Smith translated a lost book of Scripture from an Egyptian papyrus scroll he obtained in 1835.

The Lost Book of Abraham: Investigating a Remarkable Mormon Claim: What scholars are saying:

"A fine documentary that from an Egyptological point of view is a sound assessment of the source of a most controversial piece of Mormon Scripture."
Marc Coenen, Ph.D.
Department of Oriental Studies, University of Leuven

"A balanced, professionally produced approach to a sensitive issue in Mormon history."
Stan Larson, Ph.D.
Marriott Library, University of Utah

"You are to be congratulated on a job well-done and on the tone you set in the over-all production. May your colleagues come to copy the thoroughness of research and method of presentation."
J. Gordon Melton, Ph.D.
Institute for the Study of American Religion

"This documentary must be seen by all those who are interested in the origins of the Book of Abraham. In an artful and educational manner, it sets forth in clarity the basic evidence that establishes Joseph Smith – not the biblical Abraham – as the author."
David P. Wright, Ph.D.
Brandeis University

"The Lost book of Abraham documentary not only gets the facts right with regard to this story, but tells this fascinating tale in an utterly captivating and professional way. The producers also obviously took tremendous care in writing the script so as not to unduly offend the LDS people. I just cannot recommend this documentary more highly."
Craig J. Hazen, Ph.D.
Biola University

The DVD presentation can be watched or purchase on line.

DNA VS.
THE *BOOK OF MORMON*

T he Church of Jesus Christ of Latter-Day Saints more commonly known as Mormons has promoted the idea that the Book *of Mormon* is a real, factual history. According to Joseph Smith:

> I told the brethren that the Book of Mormon was the most correct of any book on earth, and the keystone of our religion.

Joseph Smith, *History of the Church* Vol. 4, p. 461

The *Book of Mormon* sets forth the remarkable story of Israelites who migrated to America and eventually populated both North and South America. The *Book of Mormon* teaches that these Israelites are the actual ancestors of the modern-day indigenous peoples on both continents. If this important historical thesis of the book is not true, the credibility of the entire book is called into question.

The film, DNA vs. the *Book of Mormon* deals with impact of recent DNA testing proving that American indigenous people have no connection with the people of Israel. With the release of this film that makes a devastating scientific case for its primary thesis, that there is no connection between the indigenous people of the Americas. The film effectively challenges the historicity of the *Book of Mormon*. The film is literally rocking the foundations of Mormonism.

Simon Southerton is an Australian plant geneticist who is featured in the film. Mr. Southerton has published *Losing a Lost Tribe: Native Americans, DNA, and the Mormon Church*, a technical book. The book uses DNA evidence to examine the historical accuracy of the *Book of Mormon*. Southerton was a member of the LDS Church until he was excommunicated. Southerton, in an email sent to the Associated Press, stated that he was excommunicated for being too vocal regarding the results of the Genomics Project DNA.

See Simon G. Southerton's *Losing a Lost Tribe: Native Americans, DNA, and the Mormon Church* At:

http://signaturebooks.com/2010/02/losing-a-lost-tribe-native-americans-dna-and-the-mormon-church/

Documentation of bizarre Mormon teachings

Many converts to Mormonism have no idea what they are getting into. The material in this section should give any prospective convert a reason for pause before following through with the conversion process.

Brigham Young on Joseph Smith

Well, now, examine the character of the Savior, and examine the characters of those who have written the Old and New Testament; and then compare them with the character of Joseph Smith, the founder of this work . . . and you will find that his character stands as fair as that of any man's mentioned in the Bible. We can find no person who presents a better character to the world when the facts are known than Joseph Smith, Jun., the prophet, and his brother, Hyrum Smith, who was murdered with him.

Brigham Young, *Journal of Discourses* Vol. 14, p. 203.

I am an Apostle of Joseph Smith. . . . all who reject my testimony will go to hell, so sure as there is one, no matter whether it be hot or cold.

Brigham Young, *Journal of Discourses* Vol. 3, p. 212.

No man or woman in this dispensation will ever enter into the celestial kingdom of God without the consent of Joseph Smith. . . . Every man and woman must have the certificate of Joseph Smith, junior, as a passport to their entrance into the mansion where God and Christ are . . . I cannot go there without his consent. . . . He reigns there as supreme a being in his sphere, capacity, and calling, as God does in heaven.

Brigham Young, *Journal of Discourses* Vol. 7, p. 289.

I will now give my scripture—Whosoever confesseth that Joseph Smith was sent of God . . . that spirit is of God; and every spirit that does not confess that God has sent Joseph Smith, and revealed the everlasting Gospel to and through him, is of Anti-christ.

Brigham Young, *Journal of Discourses* Vol. 8, p. 176.

Brigham Young said his discourses are as good as Scripture:

I say now, when they [his sermons] are copied and approved by me they are as good Scripture as is couched in this Bible . . . .

Brigham Young, *Journal of Discourses* Vol. 13, p. 264.

Brigham Young said he had never given any counsel that was wrong:

I am here to answer. I shall be on hand to answer when I am called upon, for all the counsel and for all the instruction that I have given to this people. If there is an Elder here, or any member of this

Church, called the Church of Jesus Christ of Latter-day Saints, who can bring up the first idea, the first sentence that I have delivered to the people as counsel that is wrong, I really wish they would do it; but they cannot do it, for the simple reason that I have never given counsel that is wrong; this is the reason.

Brigham Young, *Journal of Discourses* Vol. 16, p. 161.

Brigham Young compared his sermons with Scripture:

I know just as well what to teach this people and just what to say to them and what to do in order to bring them into the celestial kingdom...I have never yet preached a sermon and sent it out to the children of men, that they may not call Scripture. Let me have the privilege of correcting a sermon, and it is as good Scripture as they deserve. The people have the oracles of God continually.

Brigham Young, *Journal of Discourses* Vol. 13, p. 95.

Brigham Young said you are damned if you deny polygamy:

Now if any of you will deny the plurality of wives, and continue to do so, I promise that you will be damned,

Brigham Young, *Journal of Discourses* Vol. 3, p. 266.

The only men who become Gods, even the Sons of God, are those who enter into polygamy.

Brigham Young, *Journal of Discourses* Vol. 11, p. 269.

Brigham Young commented about blacks:

You see some classes of the human family that are black, uncouth, uncomely, disagreeable and low in their habits, wild, and seemingly deprived of nearly all the blessings of the intelligence that is generally bestowed upon mankind....Cain slew his brother. Cain might have been killed, and that would have put a termination to that line of human beings. This was not to be, and the Lord put a mark upon him, which is the flat nose and black skin.

Brigham Young, *Journal of Discourses* Vol. 7, p. 290.

In our first settlement in Missouri, it was said by our enemies that we intended to tamper with the slaves, not that we had any idea of the kind, for such a thing never entered our minds. We knew that the children of Ham were to be the "servant of servants," and no power under heaven could hinder it, so long as the Lord would permit them to welter under the curse and those were known to be our religious views concerning them.

Brigham Young, *Journal of Discourses* Vol. 2, p. 172.

Shall I tell you the law of God in regard to the African race? If the white man who belongs to the chosen seed mixes his blood with the seed of Cain, the penalty, under the law of God, is death on the spot. This will always be so.

Brigham Young, *Journal of Discourses* Vol. 10, p. 110.

Brigham Young tells about gold and silver:

Gold and silver grow, and so does every other kind of metal, the same as the hair upon my head, or the wheat in the field; they do not grow as fast, but they are all the time composing or decomposing.

Brigham Young, *Journal of Discourses* Vol. 1, p. 219.

Have Mormons ever taught that Joseph Smith was a physical descendant of Christ? It is shocking but true; some Mormons have actually taught this. The material in this section will set forth the Mormon thinking on this:

For example, it is believed that *Doctrine & Covenants* 113:4, when speaking of a servant in the hands of Christ is partly a descendant of Jesse as well as of Ephraim. Believers in this theory say the rod-servant is Joseph Smith and that his bloodline extends back through the ages to both Jesse and Ephraim, to both the tribes of Judah and Joseph. They would then ask, "What proof do we have of this truth?"

Some Mormons ask, "Who is the root of Jesse spoken of in *Doctrine & Covenants* 113:5?"

It is believed that the root is a descendant of Jesse, as well as of Joseph, unto whom rightly belongs the priesthood, and the keys of the kingdom.

First, we must understand that according to Mormon theology, Jesus was married and fathered children. To establish this, we will consider some quotes.

Mormon Apostle Orson Hyde taught that the early Mormons were descended from Christ:

It will be borne in mind that once on a time, there was a marriage in Cana of Galilee; and...it will be discovered that no less a person than Jesus Christ was married on that occasion.... Did he multiply, and did he see his seed? Did he honour his Father's law by complying with it, or did he not? Orson Pratt, *Journal of Discourses* Vol. 4, p. 259.

At this doctrine the long-faced hypocrite and the sanctimonious bigot will probably cry, blasphemy!... How much so ever of holy horror this doctrine may excite in persons not impregnated with the blood of Christ, and whose minds are consequently dark and benighted, it may excite still more when they are told that if none of the natural blood of Christ flows in their veins, they are not the chosen or elect of God. Object not, therefore, too strongly against the marriage of Christ.

Orson Pratt, *Journal of Discourses* Vol. 4, p. 260.

Is there no way provided for those to come into this covenant relation who may not possess, in their veins, any of the blood of Abraham or of Christ? Yes! By doing the works of Abraham and of Christ.

Orson Pratt, *The Seer* pp.80-82; 172, 178.

Consider the following Mormon thoughts on this.

Doctrine and Covenants 113:4 refers to a servant in the hands of Christ, who is partly a descendant of Jesse as well as of Ephraim.

The rod-servant is Joseph Smith. His bloodline extends back through the ages to both Jesse and Ephraim, to both the tribes of Judah and Joseph. What proof do we have of this? The believers in this theory would say,the word of Isaiah and the latter-day prophets.

The Book of Mormon contains a prophecy about a descendant of the ancient Joseph who would also be named Joseph (Joseph Smith Jr.) and who would do a great work of salvation among the Israelites to bring them to the knowledge of God's covenants in the last days. (2 Ne. 3:6-11, 14-15) Joseph Smith, Jr., is this Joseph. His patriarchal blessing identifies him as the heir to the promises of Ephraim (son of the ancient Joseph), and he is called a pure Ephraimite by Brigham Young.

Joseph F. Smith, *Doctrines of Salvation* Vol. 3, pp. 250-254.

There were occasions in Mormon Church history when a number of the brethren, including Joseph Smith, claimed that they shared lineage with Jesus in the tribe of Judah.

Orson F. Whitney, *Life of Heber C. Kimball* (Salt Lake City: Bookcraft, 1973), p. 185; Heber C. Kimball, *Journal of Discourses*, Vol. 4, p. 248.

When a number of the brethren, including Joseph Smith, claimed that they shared lineage with Jesus in the tribe of Judah.

Victor L. Ludlow, *Isaiah: Prophet, Seer, & Poet* (Salt Lake City: Deseret Book Company, 1982), p. 375

What were Brigham Young's thoughts on this:

It was decreed in the counsels of eternity, long before the foundations of the earth were laid, that he, Joseph Smith, should be the man, in the last dispensation of this world, to bring forth the word of God to the people, and receive the fullness of the keys and power of the Priesthood of the Son of God. The Lord had his eyes upon him, and upon his father, and upon his father's father, and upon their progenitors clear back to Abraham, and from Abraham to the flood, from the flood to Enoch, and from Enoch to Adam. He has watched that family and that blood as it has circulated from its fountain to the birth of that man. He was fore-ordained in eternity to preside over this last dispensation.

> Brigham Young, *Discourses of Brigham Young* (Salt
> Lake City: Deseret Book Company, 1954), p. 108.

Mormon thinking on Isaiah 11:1 goes as follows:

> And there shall come forth a rod out of the stem
> of Jesse, and a Branch shall grow out of his roots.
> And there shall come forth a man named Joseph
> Smith as a servant in the hands of Christ, and the
> Messiah shall come through the his same lineage,
> or, the house of Jesse.

> See http://www.gospeldoctrine.com/content/sec-
> tion-113 for more on this.

Some Mormons would ask: Who fits this description better than the Prophet Joseph?

A summary of Mormon thinking as set forth above:

Doctrine and Covenants 113 says the stem (Joseph Smith) as well as the root (Joseph Smith) was a descendant of Jesse, as well as of Joseph. 2 Nephi 3:15 also identifies Joseph Smith as a descendant of Joseph.

This interpretation says that the "stem of Jesse" and "the Branch" both refer to Christ. And it demonstrates the common lineage of Joseph Smith and Jesus Christ, which is alluded to in *Doctrine and Covenants* 113:6.

Mormons would outline it like this:

The rod = servant in the hands of Christ = Joseph Smith

The stem of Jesse = Christ

The branch = Christ

His roots = Joseph Smith's roots through the lineage of Jesse

In Mormon thinking:

One would expect the root of Jesse to precede Jesse, perhaps the ancestor of Jesse. Yet, the explanation is that the root is a descendant of Jesse. The inverted parallelism device teaches us that this root is the same as the rod-servant, i.e., Joseph Smith.

A MODERN MORMON BOOK
DEFENDING THIS SHOCKINGLY
BIZARRE THESIS

The dust jacket flap states the following:

Throughout the ages, the ancients prophesied important events of the latter-days. The expectations of these future occurrences centered on a prophet who would be directly related to the Royal bloodline of the Kings of Israel! In fact, the ancients understood that this anticipated seer would not only be from the Royal bloodline of Ephraim through Joseph, but he would also be descended from the Royal bloodline of Judah! It is the same genealogical line of the Savior Himself.

Joseph Smith and His Royal Lineage: A Blood Descendant of Jesus Christ Vol. 1. R. Merle Fowler. by R. Merle Fowler (2006)

Another modern Mormon book arguing the same thing:

Dynasty of the Holy Grail: Mormonism's Sacred Bloodline Book Description Publication Date: June 30, 2006

Dr. Vern G. Swanson has produced a thought-provoking book on the topic of the Holy Grail and the bloodline of Jesus. His perspective on the subject has grown after reading nearly 400 books on the Holy Grail, and his 28 years of research on the topic. Going far beyond the mortally flawed best sellers, *Holy Blood, Holy Grail* and *The Da Vinci Code*, his epic book will be applicable to both Mormon and non-Mormon audiences. It is certainly the most significant scholarly tome on the Holy Grail and the bloodline yet.

What goes on inside the Mormon temples?

Many people have no idea what goes on inside the Mormon temples. Mormons are forbidden to talk about the temple ceremonies and when asked, say these ceremonies are too sacred to talk about. Saying that something is sacred and therefore cannot be talked about is baffling to say the least. There is no doctrine or practice in traditional Christianity that is hidden from the public by claiming sacredness.

The Mormon temple ceremony mocks Christian pastors:

Adam: Oh God, hear the words of my mouth!

Lucifer: I hear you. What is it you want?

Adam: Who are you?

Lucifer: I am the God of this world.

Adam: You, the God of this world?

Lucifer: Yes! What do you want?

Adam: I am looking for messengers.

Lucifer: Oh, you want someone to preach to you? You want religion do you? I will have preachers here presently.

(A preacher dressed in black, now enters the scene)

Lucifer: Good Morning Sir.

Preacher: Good morning. A fine congregation!

Lucifer: Yes, they are very good people. They are concerned about religion. Are you a preacher?

Preacher: I am. Lucifer: Have you been to college and received training for the ministry?

Preacher: Certainly! A man cannot preach unless he has been trained for the ministry!

Lucifer: Do you preach the orthodox religion?

Preacher: Yes, that is what I preach.

Lucifer: If you will preach your orthodox religion to these people and convert them, I will pay you well!

Preacher: I will do my best.

Lucifer: Here is a man who desires religion. He is very much exercised, and seems to be sincere.

(The action returns to "Adam")

Preacher: I understand you are inquiring after religion.

Adam: I was calling upon Father.

Preacher: I am glad to know that you were calling upon Father. Do you believe in a God who is without body, parts and passions, who sits on the top of topless throne, whose center is everywhere and whose circumference nowhere; who fills the universe, and yet is so small that he can dwell in your heart. Who is surrounded by myriads of beings who have been saved by Grace, not for any act of theirs, but by His good pleasure? Do you believe this great Being?

Adam: I do not? I cannot comprehend such a Being.

Preacher: That is the beauty of it!

Death Oaths Made by All Mormon Temple Patrons from the 1930's until April 1990:

MORMON TEMPLE DEATH OATH #1

Elohim: "All arise." (All patrons stand.)

Elohim: "Each of you make the sign of the First Token of the Aaronic Priesthood, by bringing your right arm to the square, the palm of the hand to the front, the fingers together, and the thumb extended. This is the sign. Now, repeat in your mind after me the words of the covenant, at the same time representing the execution of the penalty."

I _____, think of the new name, covenant before God, angels and these witnesses that I will never reveal the First Token of the Aaronic Priesthood, with its accompanying name and sign, and penalty. Rather than do so, I would suffer my life to be taken.

(Patrons perform the action as the Officiator guides them)

"That will do." (Patrons sit down)

MORMON DEATH OATH #2

Peter: The sign is made by bringing the right hand in front of you, with the hand in cupping shape, the right arm forming a square, and the left arm being raised to the square. This is the sign. (The officiator demonstrates.) The Execution of the Penalty is represented by placing the right hand on the left breast, drawing the hand quickly across the body, and dropping the hands to the sides. I will now explain the covenant and obligation of secrecy which are associated with this token, its name, and sign, and penalty, and which you will be required to take upon yourselves.

Peter: All arise. (All patrons stand) Each of you make the sign of the Second Token of the Aaronic priesthood by bringing the right hand in front of you, with the hand in cupping shape, the right arm forming a square, and the left arm being raised to the square. This is the sign.

Now, repeat in your mind after me the words of the covenant, at the same time representing the Executing of the Penalty.

I, _____, think of the first given name, solemnly covenant, before God, angels, and these witnesses that I will never reveal the second Token of the Aaronic Priesthood, with its accompanying name, and sign, and penalty. Rather than do so, I would suffer my life to be taken.

(Patrons perform the action as the Officiator guides them)

That will do. (All patrons sit down)

Mormon Temple Death Oath #3

Peter: All arise. (All patrons stand.) Each of you make the sign of the First Token of the Melchizedek Priesthood or Sign of the Nail by bringing the left hand in front of you with the hand in cupping shape, the left arm forming a square; also by bringing the right hand is also brought forward, the palm down, the fingers close together, the thumb extended, and by placing the thumb over the left hip. This is the sign.

Now repeat in your mind after me the words of the covenant, at the same time representing the Execution of the Penalty:

I solemnly covenant in the name of the Son that I will never reveal the First Token of the Melchizedek Priesthood or Sign of the Nail, with its accompanying name and sign and penalty. Rather than do so, I would suffer my life to be taken.

(Patrons perform the action as the Officiator guides them)

That will do. (All patrons sit down)

Even today, Mormon Temple patrons make the oaths of secrecy above, although without the death oaths transcribe above.

Today, Mormon temple patrons still make an oath to sacrifice their lives and all they possess for the church:

Temple narrator: (All patrons stand.) And as Jesus Christ has laid down his life for the redemption of mankind, so we should covenant to sacrifice all that we possess, even our own lives if necessary, in sustaining and defending the Kingdom of God.

All arise. Each of you bring your right arm to the square. You and each of you solemnly covenant and promise before God, angels, and these witnesses at this alter that you will observe and keep the

Law of Sacrifice, as contained in the Old and New Testament, as it has been explained to you. Each of you bow your head and say "yes."

Temple patrons: "Yes."

Elohim: That will do. (All patrons sit down)

Temple narrator: (All patrons stand.) Each of you bring your right arm to the square. You and each of you covenant and promise before God, angels, and these witnesses at this altar, that you do accept the Law of Consecration as contained in this, (the Officiator holds up a copy of the *Doctrine and Covenants* again), the *Book of Doctrine and Covenants*, in that you do consecrate yourselves, your time, talents, and everything with which the Lord has blessed you, or with which he may bless you, to the Church of Jesus Christ of Latter-day Saints, for the building up of the Kingdom of God on the earth and for the establishment of Zion.

Each of you bow your head and say "yes."

Temple patrons: "Yes."

Peter: "That will do." (All patrons sit down.)

Why would God require death oaths in the temple ceremony?

If these death oaths were necessary, then why were they removed from the ceremony after 1990?

A friend of mine recorded the above material in the Provo, Utah temple in 1984 after becoming convinced that the Mormon Church was not true and left his mission for the Church while in Idaho. Subsequently, copies of the temple ceremony were mailed to Tom Brokaw at NBC and other media outlets. As these tapes were copied and circulated the tapes, it became increasingly embarrassing for the Mormon Church. Subsequently portions of the temple ceremony were changed.

The above account was transcribed from the February, 1984 audio recordings from the Provo, Utah temple. I am in possession of the master copies of these tape recordings.

Mormons and their peculiar historical doctrines on the black race:

Joseph Smith's thoughts:

> Had I anything to do with the negro, I would con-fine them by strict law to their own species, and put them on a national equalization.
>
> Joseph Fielding Smith, *The Teachings of the Prophet Joseph Smith* p. 270.
>
> Thursday, 8 - Held Mayor's court and tried two negroes for attempting to marry two white women: fined one $25 and the other $5.
>
> Joseph Smith, *History of the Church* Vol. 6, p. 210.
>
> And the rebellious niggers in the slave states.
>
> Joseph Smith, *Millennial Star* Vol. 22, p. 602.

The Mormon's History of the Church now reads:

> and the rebellious negroes in the slave states. . .
>
> Joseph Smith, *History of the Church*, Vol. 6, p. 158.

Brigham Young's thoughts:

> You see some classes of the human family that are black, uncouth, uncomely, disagreeable and low in their habits, wild, and seemingly deprived of nearly all the blessings of the intelligence that is generally bestowed upon mankind....Cain slew his brother. Cain might have been killed, and that would have

put a termination to that line of human beings. This was not to be, and the Lord put a mark upon him, which is the flat nose and black skin.

Brigham Young, *Journal of Discourses* Vol. 7, p. 290.

In our first settlement in Missouri, it was said by our enemies that we intended to tamper with the slaves, not that we had any idea of the kind, for such a thing never entered our minds. We knew that the children of Ham were to be the "servant of servants," and no power under heaven could hinder it, so long as the Lord would permit them to welter under the curse and those were known to be our religious views concerning them.

Brigham Young, *Journal of Discourses* Vol. 2, p. 172.

Shall I tell you the law of God in regard to the African race? If the white man who belongs to the chosen seed mixes his blood with the seed of Cain, the penalty, under the law of God, is death on the spot.

Brigham Young, *Journal of Discourses* Vol. 10, p. 110.

Wilford Woodruff's thoughts:

What was that mark? It was a mark of blackness. That mark rested upon Cain, and descended upon his posterity from that time until the present. To day there are millions of the descendants of Cain, through the lineage of Ham, in the world, and that mark of darkness still rest upon them.

Wilford Woodruff, *Mormon Prophet, Millennial Star* 51:339.

Joseph Fielding Smith's thoughts:

> I would not want you to believe that we bear any animosity toward the Negro. "Darkies" are wonderful people, and they have their place in our church.
>
> Joseph Fielding Smith, *Look magazine* October 22, 1963, p.79.

Bruce R. McConkie's thoughts:

> Negroes in this life are denied the Priesthood; under no circumstances can they hold this delegation of authority from the Almighty... The gospel message of salvation is not carried affirmatively to them. Negroes are not equal with other races where the receipt of certain spiritual blessings are concerned.
>
> McConkie, *Mormon Doctrine* pp. 477, 527-28.

Thankfully, these racist teachings held by the Mormon Church were abandoned and changed after much political pressure was applied. On June 8, 1978, LDS President, Spencer W. Kimball, claimed that God had removed the curse. All worthy black men could now receive the Priesthood. While it is commendable that this unbiblical, long-standing racial prejudice was changed, it raises serious problems for the Mormon concept of god. The God of the Bible does not change, while the Mormon god does.

Do Mormons worship Joseph Smith? Singing hymns in a church service is an act of worship.

Consider two Mormon hymns:

PRAISE TO THE MAN (HYMN 282 STANZA 2)

2. Praise to his memory, he died as a martyr,
Honored and blest be his ever great name,
Long shall his blood which was shed by assassins,

Stain Illinois while the earth lauds his fame.

The Seer (Hymn 290)

1. The Seer, the Seer, Joseph the Seer!

I'll sing of the Prophet ever dear,

His equal now cannot be found,

By searching the wide world around,

With Gods he soared in the realms of day,

And men he taught the heavenly way.

The earthly Seer! The earthly Seer!

I love to dwell on his memory dear,

The chosen of God and the friend of man,

He brought the Priesthood back again,

He gazed on the past, and the present too,

And opened the heavenly world to view.

2. Of noble seed, of heavenly birth,

He came to bless the sons of earth

With keys by the Almighty given,

He opened the full rich stores of heaven,

O'er the world that was wrapped in sable night,

Like the sun, he spread his golden light;

He strove, O, how he strove to stay

The stream of crime in its reckless way!

With a mighty mind and a noble aim,

He urged the wayward to reclaim,

'Mid the foaming billows of angry strife,

He stood at the helm of the ship of life.

3. The Saints, the Saints, his only pride,

For them he lived, for them he died!

Their joys were his, their sorrows too,

He loved the Saints, he loved Nauvoo,

<u>Unchained in death, with a Savior's love</u>

<u>He pleads their cause in the courts above.</u>

<u>The Seer, the Seer! Joseph the Seer!</u>

O, how I love his memory dear!

The just and wise, the pure and free,

A father he was and is to me.

Let fiends now rage in their dark hour,

No matter, he is beyond their power. [Emphasis mine]

4. He's free! he's free! The Prophet's free!

He is where he ever will be,

Beyond the reach of mobs and strife,

He rests unharmed in endless life.

His home's in the sky, he dwells with the Gods,

Far from the furious rage of mobs.

He died! he died for those he loved,

He reigns, he reigns in the realms above.

He waits with the just who have gone before,

To welcome the Saints to Zion's shore.

Shout, shout, ye Saints; this boon is given,

We'll meet our martyr'd Seer in heaven.

Did Joseph Smith and Brigham Young believe that people lived on the moon?

Oliver B. Huntington, a faithful Mormon, said that as far back as 1837 Joseph Smith said the moon was inhabited:

> He described the men as averaging near six feet in height, and dressing quite uniformly in something near the Quaker style. In my patriarchal blessing, given by the father of Joseph the Prophet, in Kirtland, 1837, I was told that I should preach the gospel before I was 21 years of age; that I should preach the gospel to the inhabitants upon the islands of the sea, and - to the inhabitants of the moon, even the planet you can now behold with your eyes. The first two promises have been fulfilled, and the latter may be verified.

Oliver B. Huntington, *Young Woman's Journal* Vol. 3, (1892) p. 263-264.

Who can tell us of the inhabitants of this little planet that shines of an evening, called the moon? ...When you inquire about the inhabitants of that sphere you find that the most learned are as ignorant in regard to them as the most ignorant of their fellows. So it is with regard to the inhabitants of the sun. Do you think it is inhabited? I rather think it is. Do you think there is any life there? No question of it; it was not made in vain.

Brigham Young, *Journal of Discourses* Vol. 13, p. 271.

How many Gods there are, I do not know, But there never was a time when there were not Gods and worlds, and when men were not passing through the same ordeals that we are passing through. That course has been from all eternity, and it is and will be so to all eternity.

Brigham Young, *Journal of Discourses* Vol. 7, p. 333.

When the Virgin Mary conceived the child Jesus, the Father had begotten him in his own likeness. He was not begotten by the Holy Ghost. And who is the Father? He is the first of the human family; and when he took a tabernacle, it was begotten by his Father in heaven, after the same manner as the tabernacles of Cain, Abel, and the rest of the sons and daughters of Adam and Eve; from the fruits of the earth, the first earthly tabernacles were originated by the Father, and so on in succession.

Brigham Young, *Journal of Discourses* Vol. 1, p. 50.

What a learned idea! Jesus, our elder brother, was begotten in the flesh by the same character that was in the garden of Eden, and who is our Father in Heaven. Now, let all who may hear these doctrines, pause before they make light of them, or treat them with indifference, for they will prove their salvation or damnation.

Brigham Young, *Journal of Discourses* Vol. 1, p. 51.

The birth of the Saviour was as natural as are the births of our children; it was the result of natural action. He partook of flesh and blood - was begotten of his Father, as we were of our fathers.

Brigham Young, *Journal of Discourses* Vol. 8, p. 115.

From the day that the Priesthood was taken from the earth to the winding-up scene of all things, every man and woman must have the certificate of Joseph Smith, junior, as a passport to their entrance into the mansion where God and Christ are - I with you and you with me. I cannot go there without his consent.

Brigham Young, *Journal of Discourses* Vol. 7, p. 289.

Who can tell us of the inhabitants of this little planet that shines of an evening, called the moon?...when you inquire about the inhabitants of that sphere you find that the most learned are as ignorant in regard to them as the most ignorant of their fathers. So it is in regard to the inhabitants of the sun. Do you think it is inhabited? I rather think it is. Do you think there is any life there? No question of it; it was not made in vain. It was made to give light to those who dwell upon it, and to other planets; and so will this earth when it is celestialized.

Brigham Young, *Journal of Discourses* Vol. 13, p. 271.

When our leaders speak, the thinking has been done. When they propose a plan–it is God's plan. When they point the way, there is no other which is safe. When they give direction, it should mark the end of controversy. God works in no other way. To think otherwise, without immediate repentance, may cost one his faith, may destroy his testimony, and leave him a stranger to the kingdom of God.

The Church of Jesus Christ of Latter-day Saints, Improvement Era June 1945, p. 354.

The 14 Fundamentals in Following the Prophet, the President of The Church of Jesus Christ of Latter-Day Saints:

1. The prophet is the only man who speaks for the Lord in everything.
2. The living prophet is more vital to us than the standard works.
3. The living prophet is more important to us than a dead prophet.
4. The prophet will never lead the Church astray.
5. The prophet is not required to have any particular earthly training or credentials to speak on any subject or act on any matter at any time.
6. The prophet does not have to say "Thus saith the Lord" to give us scripture.
7. The prophet tells us what we need to know, not always what we want to know.

8. The prophet is not limited by men's reasoning.

9. The prophet can receive revelation on any matter, temporal or spiritual.

10. The prophet may be involved in civic matters.

11. The two groups who have the greatest difficulty in following the prophet are the proud who are learned and the proud who are rich.

12. The prophet will not necessarily be popular with the world or the worldly.

13. The prophet and his counselors make up the First Presidency - the highest quorum in the Church.

14. The prophet and the presidency - the living prophet and the First Presidency - follow them and be blessed; reject them and suffer.

Ezra Taft Benson, *Fourteen Fundamentals in Following the Prophet* 1980 Devotional Speeches of the Year: BYU Devotional Addresses (Provo, UT: Brigham Young University Press, 1981), 26-30

Does the earth conceive? It does and it brings forth. If it did not, why do you go and put your wheat into the ground? Does it not conceive it? . . . Where did the earth come from? From it's parent earths. Well, some of you may call that foolish philosophy. But if it is, I will throw out foolish things, that you may gather up wise things. The earth is alive. If it was not, it could not produce.

Heber C. Kimball, *Journal of Discourses* Vol. 6, p. 36.

And Christ was born into the world as the literal Son of this Holy Being; he was born in the same personal, real, and literal sense that any mortal son is born to a mortal father. There is nothing figurative about his paternity; he was begotten, conceived and born in the normal and natural course of events, Christ is the Son of Man, meaning that his Father (the Eternal God!) is a Holy Man.

McConkie, *Mormon Doctrine* p. 742

Now if any of you will deny the plurality of wives, and continue to do so, I promise that you will be damned.

Brigham Young, *Journal of Discourses* Vol. 3, p. 266.

The only men who become Gods, even the Sons of God, are those who enter into polygamy.

Brigham Young, *Journal of Discourses* Vol. 11, p. 269)

I say now, when they [his sermons] are copied and approved by me they are as good Scripture as is couched in this Bible . . .

Brigham Young, *Journal of Discourses* Vol. 13, p. 264.

Changes in the original 1830 edition of the *Book of Mormon* with modern editions:

Mormon prophet Joseph Fielding Smith stated in 1961 that:

...there was not one thing in the Book of Mormon or in the second edition or in any other edition since that in any way contradicts the first edition . . . there was no change of doctrine. Now, these sons of Belial who circulate these reports evidently know better.

I will not use the word that is in my mind.

The Improvement Era December 1961, pp. 924-925.

Is this true?

Original 1830 Edition, *Book of Mormon*

Joseph Smith, Jr. The author and proprietor of this work

20th Century Editions

Joseph Smith, Jr. the translator of this work

Original 1830 Edition, *Book of Mormon*

"The lamb of God is the Eternal Father."

1 Nephi 13:14

20th Century Editions

"The lamb of God is the son of the Eternal Father."

1 Nephi 13:14

Original 1830 Edition, *Book of Mormon*

"The Eternal Father" 1 Nephi 11:21

20th Century Editions

"Son of the Eternal Father" 1 Nephi 11:21

Original 1830 Edition, *Book Of Mormon*

"King Benjamin" Mosiah 21:28, Ether 4:1

20th Century Editions

"King Mosiah" Mosiah 21:28, Ether 4:1

A TALE OF TWO
FALSE PROPHETS

by Jack Kettler

THE AMERICAN MUHAMMAD: JOSEPH SMITH,
FOUNDER OF MORMONISM

Concordia Publishing House, 2013
By Alvin J. Schmidt, MDiv, PhD
A Review by Jack Kettler

he author, Alvin J. Schmidt, MDiv, PhD, is professor of sociology emeritus at Illinois College, Jacksonville, IL, and a fellow of the Society for the Scientific Study of Religion. He is the author of numerous books, including the award-winning *Fraternal Organizations* (1980); *The Menace of Multiculturalism* (1997); and *How Christianity Changed the World* (2004). Dr. Schmidt is professionally well prepared, in addition to being a Christian gentleman, to write this thought-provoking book on seventy parallels between Mormonism's founder, Joseph Smith and Muhammad, the founder of Islam.

Because those within the world of Mormonism cannot ever accept any criticism of their founder that would call into question his claims to be a prophet, it would be helpful to see what other objective individuals are saying about Dr. Schmidt's book:

"Dr. Alvin Schmidt is one of the foremost living specialists on the world's religions. ...No one is in a better position to identify the parallels between Islam and Mormonism and their radical differences as compared with creedal Christianity." - John Warwick Montgomery, PhD, DTheol, LLD; Distinguished Research Professor of Philosophy and Christian Thought, Patrick Henry College

"At a time when Christianity is under assault worldwide, this painstakingly researched and superbly written account of seventy parallels between the founders of two thriving socio-political faiths, Islam and Mormonism, should be compulsory reading for all." - Uwe Siemon-Netto, PhD, DLitt Director, Center for Lutheran Theology & Public Life

"A must-read for everyone who wants to understand Joseph Smith and Muhammad. It is extremely well researched and yet very readable. Schmidt reveals the dark side of both men in a logical, compelling way that will enlighten and equip the reader." -Ted Baehr, JD, LHD Founder and Publisher of MOVIEGUIDE®: The Family Guide to Movies and Entertainment

"The American Muhammad is a well-written and scholarly book - fascinating, well-researched, and eye-opening!" - Bill Federer, Author of What Every American Needs to Know about the Qur'an and a frequent guest on radio and TV programs.

"Alvin Schmidt in The American Muhammad did what no other Christian historian has ever done by gathering seventy valuable parallels between Joseph Smith, the founder of Mormonism and Muhammad, the founder of Islam....What history overlooked, Schmidt provided the missing links, proving that the two flowed out of the same dark fountain." - Walid Shoebat, Author of Why I Left Jihad (2005), nationally known speaker.

To start, we should consider the following quotes to see that Dr. Schmidt is not alone in seeing similarities between the founders of the religions in question:

> The Prophet inculcates the notion, and it is believed by every true Mormon, that Smith's prophecies are superior to the laws of the land. I have heard the Prophet say that he would yet tread down his enemies, and walk over their dead bodies; and if he was not let alone, he would be a second Mohammed to this generation, and that he would make it one gore of blood from the Rocky mountains to the Atlantic ocean; that like Mohammed, whose motto in treating for peace was, 'the Alcoran or the Sword.' So should it be eventually with us, 'Joseph Smith or the Sword.' These last statements were made during the last summer. The number of armed men at Adam-ondi-Ahman was between three and four hundred.
>
> Joseph Smith, *History of the Church* Vol. 3, p. 167.
>
> Modern Mohammedanism has its Mecca at Salt Lake.
>
> Clearly the Koran was Joseph Smith's model, so

closely followed as to exclude even the poor preten-
sion of originality in his foul "revelations."

Frances E. Willard, *The Women of Mormonism* 1882,
Introduction, p. xvi.

The student of Mormonism will be struck with
the similarity of experience and claims of Joseph
Smith and Mohammed.

T. B. H. Stenhouse, *The Rocky Mountain Saints*
1873, p 2.

Schmidt's book in a scholarly fashion, presents, discusses and analyzes seventy-some parallels between
Muhammad and Joseph Smith. Schmidt used as his source material for this book, the *Koran*, the
authoritative Hadiths, the *Book of Mormon, Doctrine and Covenants* and the *Pearl of Great Price*.

The following list is a brief overview of Schmidt's extensive analysis:

Both Muhammad and Smith claimed to be visited by angels.

Both claimed to have received visions.

Both were illiterate or uneducated.

Both were told in visions that no true religion existed on the earth anymore.

Both claimed the Bible was lost, altered, corrupted and unreliable.

Both had no knowledge of the original languages of the Bible.

Both set out to restore the lost faith as the one true religion.

Both wrote a book they claimed to have been inspired by God.

Both claimed their holy books were the most correct and perfect books on earth, even though
both religions had revelations that needed to be corrected.

Both claimed the source of their revelations, a perfect copy of the Koran and Smith's gold plates
are now stored in heaven.

Both claimed to be a final prophet of God.

Both seemed unaware or unconcerned with Jesus' warning of the coming of false prophets who
would lead people astray.

Both were narcissists and both had an individual who functioned as an alter-ego.

Both were polygamists.

Both committed adultery by violating the seventh commandment: "Do not commit adultery" with other men's wives and both showed no concern or knowledge that had God established the institution of marriage as being between one man and one woman in Genesis 2:24, which was repeated by Jesus in Matthew 19:5.

Both borrowed from paganism and polytheism.

Both were considered military generals by their followers.

Both had to flee for their safety.

Both were theocrats.

Both named no successor.

In conclusion, Schmidt writes:

> ...it is important to note that Smith's and Muhammad's many parallel activities have left an enduring legacy. That legacy has affected and continues to affect not only their followers but in different ways also non-followers. Only several, some of the more salient ones, are discussed below: (1) false revelations and false prophecies, (2) anti-biblical and anti-Christian teachings, (3) polygamy, (4) aggressive proselytizing, (5) theocracy, and (6) condemning the Christian church and rejecting the cross.
>
> Alvin Schmidt, *The American Muhammad: Joseph Smith, Founder of Mormonism* (Saint Louis, Concordia Publishing House, 2013), p. 248.

And finally, all that needs to be said is best stated by the Apostle Paul:

> But though we, or an angel from heaven, preach any other gospel unto you than that which we have preached unto you, let him be accursed. As we said before, so say I now again, if any man preach any other gospel unto you than that ye have received, let him be accursed (Galatians 1:8-9).

MINISTRY TO MORMONS: RESOURCES

List of sects in the Latter Day Saint movement

http://en.wikipedia.org/wiki/List_of_sects_in_the_Latter_Day_Saint_movement

Recovery from Mormonism

A ministry that examines Mormonism from a Christian viewpoint.
http://exmormon.org/d6/drupal/

Mormonism Research Ministry

Located in the San Diego CA. area, MRM has been challenging the claims of the LDS Church since 1979. The MRM Home Page offers numerous articles that will both inform the Christian and challenge the Latter-day Saints. http://www.mrm.org/

Alpha and Omega

This site includes debates and excellent articles such as: "A Test Case Of Scholarship" See the glaring errors in the "scholarship" of F.A.R.M.S." Alpha and Omega Ministries responds to: 17 Points of the True Church" Do they stand up to examination? - "Temples Made With Hands" - Where does God dwell? "Joseph Smith the Translator" "Verses Relevant to Sharing the Gospel with Mormons" http://vintage.aomin.org/Mormonism.html

Utah Lighthouse Ministry, founded by Jerald and Sandra Tanner

The purpose of this site is to document problems with the claims of Mormonism and compare LDS doctrines with Christianity. http://www.utlm.org/

Mormons in Transition

Resources for researching and evaluating the claims, doctrines and Scriptures of the Church of Jesus Christ of Latter-day Saints in light of history and the Bible.
http://www.irr.org/mit/default.html

Answers for Mormons

http://www.mscbc.org/mormonism/index.htm

Bible Study Resources

http://www.undergroundnotes.com/Resourses.html

CARM Christian Apologetics & Research Ministry: with Matt Slick M. Div.
https://carm.org/

An Earnest Plea to Latter-day-Saints at:

http://www.undergroundnotes.com/Plea.html

DOCUMENTATION OF MY CORRESPONDENCES IN DEALING WITH MORMONISM:

1. A letter signed by a large number of denominational priests and pastors supporting Ex-Mormons for Jesus is seen in the first picture.

2. My statement to a Mormon publication as president of Ex-Mormons for Jesus is seen in the second picture.

My correspondence with Mormon scholar Hugh Nibley is seen in three pages.

Dr. Nibley addresses my questions in "The Terrible Questions," from Temple and Cosmos: Beyond This Ignorant Present, volume 12 in The Collected Works of Hugh Nibley, Don E. Norton, Editor. (Salt Lake City: Deseret Book and F.A.R.M.S., 1992), pp. 336-378.

My correspondence with Dr. Nibley correspondence is seen in three pages.

See Joseph Smith's Jupiter Talisman and His court record conviction for hunting for buried treasure for money issued by Judge Albert Neely in 1826 called glass looking (inside back cover).

AN URGENT LETTER TO ALL CHRISTIAN CLERGY

Shepherd of the Hills
Lutheran Church

Greetings in the name of Jesus Christ.

Did you know that every hour of every day YOU are mocked and ridiculed in
every Mormon Temple in their secret temple ceremonies? I, and those signing
this letter with me, ask you to read this carefully so that you will not
unwittingly help the Mormons in their attack on all of Christianity.

The Mormons are soon to open their new Temple in Littleton. Mormon Bishops
and missionaries have been visiting Christian clergy in the area to tell
them they will receive invitations to the dedication ceremonies.

These are the same people who, in this very Temple, in their secret ceremonies, will portray ALL Christian clergy as hirelings of Satan. In these
ceremonies you are also ridiculed for taking pay for your religious work and
for going to school to learn how to do your job. They mock the God we know
and believe. (They believe God was once a man and has a body.) In the
ceremony Lucifer is portrayed defending orthodox Christian belief.

These are the same people whose entire faith is founded on Joseph Smith's
report of his first vision. Joseph said he went to the woods to ask God
which church he should join. He claims that two personages, God and Jesus,
appeared to him. Joseph said, "I asked the personages who stood above me in
the light, which of all the sects was right... I was answered that I must
join none of them, for they were all wrong, and the personage who addressed
me said that all their creeds were an abomination in his sight; that those
professors [that's you] were all corrupt."

The Mormons say they are Christian because they believe in Christ. BUT the
Christ they believe in is not the same Jesus Christ who is our Lord and
Saviour. Their Jesus is but one of many gods. They totally reject the
doctrine of the Trinity. They believe salvation is gained solely by obedience to Mormonism, that it is in no way dependent on the Grace of God, and
that there is NO SALVATION possible outside The Church of Jesus Christ of
Latter Day Saints.

The Mormons, nonetheless, want you to come sit in a special VIP section at
the Temple dedication to give them Christian credibility in the community.
Then their missionaries, going after your flock, can claim to be Christian,
citing all the Christian clergy who attended their dedication.

If you need more information, or if you want to alert your congregation to
the dangers of Mormonism, there is a dedicated group in our community called
Ex-Mormons for Jesus who are knowledgeable and wonderfully helpful. (Phone:
449-0455.) They are ex-Mormons and concerned Christians who are truly
loving in their ministry even though the Mormons have made accusations to
the contrary. We all recommend their presentation.

In the name of Christ, the Lord of the Church,

Henry F. Fingerlin

Julius B. Clausen
Pastor Julius Clausen
Christ Lutheran Church, Denver

Fr. Roger W. Mollison
Father Roger W. Mollison, Pastor
Columbine Catholic Church, Littleton

John H. Wengrovious
Father John H. Wengrovious
St. Gregory's Episcopal Church, Littleton

Kenneth G. Summers
Kenneth Summers, Pastor
Strasburg Assembly Of God Church

Lester W. Turner
Lester W. Turner, Jr., Pastor
South Broadway Church Of The Nazarine, Boulder

† James O. Mote
Bishop James O. Mote
St. Mary's Anglican Catholic Church, Denver

Rev. Duane K. Kelderman
Rev. Duane K. Kelderman
Ridgeview Hills Christian Reformed Church, Littleton

Pastor Clyde B. McDowell
Pastor Clyde B. McDowell
Mission Hills Baptist Church, Littleton

Calvin Gray
Calvin Gray, Pastor
Bear Creek Evangelical Presbyterian Church, Denver

Fr. Alexy Young
Father Alexy Young
All Saints Russian Orthodox Church, Denver

Pastor L. A. Smith
Pastor L. A. Smith, Jr.
Open Bible Christian Center, Littleton

Fr. Richard Kautz
Father Richard Kautz
St. Aidan's Episcopal Church, Boulder

Henry F. Fingerlin and C. Eric Morgenthaler, pastors
7691 South University Blvd. ● Littleton, Colorado 80122 ● 303 / 798-0711 ● 303 / 798-0703

THE mormon TRAIL

NBC special wasn't what was promised

by Stephen W. Gibson

The long awaited NBC special was finally televised to about nine million people nationwide Oct. 24th Comments from those who sae the Tom Brokow segment were varied.

Originally the idea was presented to local Church leaders as a special on the phenomenal growth of the Church in Denver. What the special turned out to be was a report on a five-month-old controversy.

JoAnn Wandry, from Southglenn First Ward, whose family was featured in the clip was unhappy with the final production.

"We were assured by the New York producer that there would be very little controversy and that the end result would not be a negative piece. As it ended up, even the title, 'Latter Day Conflict' was negative.

"Roger O'Neil, who is the local NBC person," Sister Wandry continued, "wrote the script. He quoted us as saying that 17 years ago we embraced a new religion, because we felt it would bring us closer together as a family.

"We were never interviewed by Roger O'Neil. When we joined the Church we only had one child, a two-year old. We felt we were already a close family.

"In a word, I think we were deceived," Sister Wandry said.

Jack Kettler, local president of Ex-Mormons for Jesus, refused to make a comment about the NBC special without clearing it with his board members, citing general distrust of the news media based on past experience.

Rev. Henry Fingerlin, who led the controversy some months ago and who was the central figure in the special, said he was disappointed in the final product.

"When the media takes things out of context, a false impression can be created. It did, however, show that there was disagreement in the Christian community."

Malin Jacobs, a defender of the faith from Littleton Second Ward, felt the special was balanced. "It clearly showed the negativism of the critics while the Mormons weren't mad at anyone. They just wanted to practice their religion without being hassled.

"I feel," he continued, "that to someone familiar with the teaching of Jesus, the special clearly showed the Mormons with a more Christian attitude than their detractors."

Perhaps Pres. Hinckley's comments were most appropriate. "Nothing is as old as yesterday's news," he said, inferring that in the big picture a two-minute and 53 second special has little, if any consequence.

Brigham Young University

Ancient Studies

September 1, 1988

Jack Kettler
P.O. Box 29753
Thornton, CO 80229

Dear Mr. Kettler:

Your book-length letter deserves a book-length reply. Fortunately for me,
I have anticipated your questions in a number of writings among which I would
recommend <u>The World of The Prophets</u> and <u>Mormonism and Early Christianity</u> (both
Salt Lake City, Deseret Book Co., 1987). There is much more, for as a certain
primitive Christian remarked during the preliminaries of the glorious Nicene
Council, it is a question which is the more miraculous--to make a stone speak
or a theologian shut up.

How would we respond to the arguments of this philospher? How would we
answer the objections of that one? We would dismiss their arguments as
irrelevant, as Dr. Faustus does in the first act. Nothing could be plainer
than that we will never get from the schoolmen a clear answer to the only
questions that really count. You challenge the Mormons on various specific
heads: "Espistemology, Ontology, Ethics, Teleology." You will find those
problems discussed in first year courses in philosphy where the student always
comes "out by the same door wherein he went." After an exhibition of
sophmoronic intellectualism, you fall back on the old revivalist rhetoric
admonishing us to "flee to Calvary" in the rhetorical style of what Idris Bell
called "the gush and slobber of St. Augustine." You can have it; in this age of
hyperbole evangelistic fervor will not cut it.

Your whole letter is an attack on "motives or character," a weakness of
which you accuse the Mormons. Sometime ago in a cabin high in the local
mountains I met with some of the eminent people who visit us from time to time.
On this occasion James Charlesworth, Frank Cross, Jacob Milgrom, Jacob Kaplan,
Kristen Stendahl, and others were present and we talked for hours. What
disturbed the great Stendahl was a statement of Joseph Smith's that "no man was
ever damned from believing too much." But if anyone is damned for that, say I,
we are all damned, for we all believe many things that are simply not true. In
proof of which Stendahl himself the next day abandoned the speech he was
prepared to give in Provo after a talk with one of our people correcting him on
certain factual matters, and instead on very short notice gave a moving address
on the Book of 3 Nephi in the Book of Mormon. The point of this is that we

4012 Harold B. Lee Library   Brigham Young University   Provo, Utah 84602

4 9 1

have no business censuring other people's beliefs. We may question them, but
to fly into a 5-star screaming rage as you do is pointless. We have Mormons as
self-righteous as any Presbyterian, and we tolerate even them.

                    Yours truly,

                    Hugh Nibley
                    Hugh Nibley

PS: Why the 98 questions? For a sensible person three could have done the
     job, which I intend to demonstrate in a forthcoming effusion.

                    HN.

September 3, 1989

Hugh Nibley
Brigham Young University
Provo, Utah 84602

Dear Dr. Nibley,

You asked why the ninety eight questions. I've found that if you ask

Mormons general questions you get extremely vague answers. It has been one

year since your short reply. Will your promised effusion be coming soon? I

have been looking forward to receiving it.

                              Sincerely,

                              Jack Kettler

September 13, 1989

Jack Kettler
P.O. Box 29753
Thornton, CO 80229

Dear Brother Kettler,

    Kind of soon, maybe.

                Yours intensely,

                Hugh Nibley

HN/pw

ANCIENT STUDIES
4012 HAROLD B. LEE LIBRARY
BRIGHAM YOUNG UNIVERSITY
PROVO, UTAH 84602

MORMON CONFESSION IN ARTICLES OF FAITH, ONE AND EIGHT, COMPARED WITH THE WESTMINSTER CONFESSION OF FAITH AND CATECHISMS

he Mormon confession has a total of 13 articles of faith. In this comparison with the Westminster Confession of Faith, we will look at just two of the Mormons articles of faith. The first and eighth Mormon articles get to the heart of matter, namely, who is God, and the authority of His Word. It is immediately apparent that Mormons provide no authority for these assertions in their confession. Hence, why should anyone believe these two articles or assertions? In contrast with the Westminster Confession of Faith, the first and second chapters of the confession deal with Scripture, and the definition of God's nature and existence.

THE FIRST MORMON
ARTICLE OF FAITH

1. We believe in God, the Eternal Father, and in His Son, Jesus Christ, and in the Holy Ghost.

In this first Mormon article of faith, the student of Scripture will notice that none of the terms listed are defined. Without defining these terms, no one really has any idea of what is meant. For example, what does the article mean when it says Eternal?

In contrast:

WESTMINSTER CONFESSION OF FAITH CHAPTER II

Of God, and of the Holy Trinity

I

There is but one only,[1] living, and true God,[2] who is infinite in being and perfection,[3] a most pure spirit,[4] invisible,[5] without body, parts,[6] or passions;[7] immutable,[8] immense,[9] eternal,[10] incomprehensible,[11] almighty,[12] most wise,[13] most holy,[14] most free,[15] most absolute;[16] working all things according to the counsel of His own immutable and most righteous will,[17] for His own glory;[18] most loving,[19] gracious, merciful, long-suffering, abundant in goodness and truth, forgiving iniquity, transgression, and sin;[20] the rewarder of them that diligently seek Him;[21] and withal, most just, and terrible in His judgments,[22] hating all sin,[23] and who will by no means clear the guilty.[24]

II

God has all life,[25] glory,[26] goodness,[27] blessedness,[28] in and of Himself; and is alone in and unto Himself all-sufficient, not standing in need of any creatures which He has made,[29] nor deriving any glory from them,[30] but only manifesting His own glory in, by, unto, and upon them. He is the alone fountain of all being, of whom, through whom, and to whom are all things;[31] and has most sovereign dominion over them, to do by them, for them, or upon them whatsoever Himself pleases.[32] In His sight all things are open and manifest,[33] His knowledge is infinite, infallible, and independent upon the creature,[34] so as nothing is to Him contingent, or uncertain.[35] He is most holy in all His counsels, in all His works, and in all His commands. [36] To Him is due from angels and men, and every other creature, whatsoever worship, service, or obedience He is pleased to require of them.[37]

III

In the unity of the Godhead there be three Persons of one substance, power, and eternity: God the Father, God the Son, and God the Holy Ghost.[38] The Father is of none, neither begotten nor proceeding; the Son is eternally begotten of the Father; [39] the Holy Ghost eternally proceeding from the Father and the Son. [40]

Scriptural
proofs texts 1-40:

[1] DEU 6:4 Hear, O Israel; The Lord our God is one Lord. 1CO 8:4 As concerning therefore the eating of those things that are offered in sacrifice unto idols, we know that an idol is noth-

ing in the world, and that there is none other God by one. 6 But to us there is but one God, the Father, of whom are all things, and we in him; and one Lord Jesus Christ, by whom are all things, and we by him.

[2] 1TH 1:9 For they themselves shew of us what manner of entering in we had unto you, and how ye turned to God from idols, to serve the living and true God. JER 10:10 But the Lord is the true God, he is the living God, and an everlasting King.

[3] JOB 11:7 Canst thou by searching find out God? canst thou find out the Almighty unto perfection? 8 It is as high as heaven; what canst thou do? deeper than hell; what canst thou know? 9 The measure thereof is longer than the earth, and broader than the sea. 26:14 Lo, these are parts of his ways; but how little a portion is heard of him? but the thunder of his power who can understand?

[4] JOH 4:24 God is a Spirit: and they that worship him must worship him in spirit and in truth.

[5] 1TI 1:17 Now unto the King eternal, immortal, invisible, the only wise God, be honour and glory for ever and ever. Amen.

[6] DEU 4:15 Take ye therefore good heed unto yourselves; for ye saw no manner of similitude on the day that the Lord spake unto you in Horeb out of the midst of the fire: 16 Lest ye corrupt yourselves, and make you a graven image, the similitude of any figure, the likeness of male or female. JOH 4:24 God is a Spirit: and they that worship him must worship him in spirit and in truth. LUK 24:39 Behold my hands and my feet, that it is I myself: handle me, and see; for a spirit hath not flesh and bones, as ye see me have.

[7] ACT 14:11 And when the people saw what Paul had done, they lifted up their voices, saying in the speech of Lycaonia, The gods are come down to us in the likeness of men. 15 And saying, Sirs, why do ye these things? We also are men of like passions with you, and preach unto you that ye should turn from these vanities unto the living God, which made heaven, and earth, and the sea, and all things that are therein.

[8] JAM 1:17 Every good gift and every perfect gift is from above, and cometh down from the Father of lights, with whom is no variableness, neither shadow of turning. MAL 3:6 For I am the Lord, I change not; therefore ye sons of Jacob are not consumed.

[9] 1KI 8:27 But will God indeed dwell on the earth? behold, the heaven and heaven of heavens

cannot contain thee; how much less this house that I have builded? JER 23:23 Am I a God at hand, saith the Lord, and not a God afar off? 24 Can any hide himself in secret places that I shall not see him? saith the Lord. Do not I fill heaven and earth? saith the Lord.

[10] PSA 90:2 Before the mountains were brought forth, or ever thou hadst formed the earth and the world, even from everlasting to everlasting, thou art God. 1TI 1:17 Now unto the King eternal, immortal, invisible, the only wise God, be honour and glory for ever and ever. Amen.

[11] PSA 145:3 Great is the Lord, and greatly to be praised; and his greatness is unsearchable.

[12] GEN 17:1 And when Abram was ninety years old and nine, the Lord appeared to Abram, and said unto him, I am the Almighty God; walk before me, and be thou perfect. REV 4:8 And the four beasts had each of them six wings about him; and they were full of eyes within: and they rest not day and night, saying, Holy, holy, holy, Lord God Almighty, which was, and is, and is to come.

[13] ROM 16:27 To God only wise, be glory through Jesus Christ for ever. Amen.

[14] ISA 6:3 And one cried unto another, and said, Holy, holy, holy, is the Lord of hosts: the whole earth is full of his glory. REV 4:8 And the four beasts had each of them six wings about him; and they were full of eyes within: and they rest not day and night, saying, Holy, holy, holy, Lord God Almighty, which was, and is, and is to come.

[15] PSA 115:3 But our God is in the heavens: he hath done whatsoever he hath pleased.

[16] EXO 3:14 And God said unto Moses, I Am That I Am: and he said, Thus shalt thou say unto the children of Israel, I Am hath sent me unto you.

[17] EPH 1:11 In whom also we have obtained an inheritance, being predestinated according to the purpose of him who worketh all things after the counsel of his own will.

[18] PRO 16:4 The Lord hath made all things for himself: yea, even the wicked for the day of evil. ROM 11:36 For of him, and through him, and to him, are all things: to whom be glory for ever. Amen.

[19] 1JO 4:8 He that loveth not knoweth not God; for God is love. 16 And we have known and believed the love that God hath to us. God is love; and he that dwelleth in love dwelleth in God, and God in him.

[20] EXO 34:6 And the Lord passed by before him, and proclaimed, The Lord, The Lord God, merciful and gracious, longsuffering, and abundant in goodness and truth, 7 Keeping mercy for thousands, forgiving iniquity and transgression and sin, and that will by no means clear the guilty; visiting the iniquity of the fathers upon the children, and upon the children's children, unto the third and to the fourth generation.

[21] HEB 11:6 But without faith it is impossible to please him: for he that cometh to God must believe that he is, and that he is a rewarder of them that diligently seek him.

[22] NEH 9:32 Now therefore, our God, the great, the mighty, and the terrible God, who keepest covenant and mercy, let not all the trouble seem little before thee, that hath come upon us, on our kings, on our princes, and on our priests, and on our prophets, and on our fathers, and on all thy people, since the time of the kings of Assyria unto this day. 33 Howbeit thou art just in all that is brought upon us; for thou hast done right, but we have done wickedly.

[23] PSA 5:5 The foolish shall not stand in thy sight: thou hatest all workers of iniquity. 6 Thou shalt destroy them that speak leasing: the Lord will abhor the bloody and deceitful man.

[24] NAH 1:2 God is jealous, and the Lord revengeth; the Lord revengeth, and is furious; the Lord will take vengeance on his adversaries, and he reserveth wrath for his enemies. 3 The Lord is slow to anger, and great in power, and will not at all acquit the wicked: the Lord hath his way in the whirlwind and in the storm, and the clouds are the dust of his feet. EXO 34:7 Keeping mercy for thousands, forgiving iniquity and transgression and sin, and that will by no means clear the guilty; visiting the iniquity of the fathers upon the children, and upon the children's children, unto the third and to the fourth generation.

[25] JOH 5:26 For as the Father hath life in himself; so hath he given to the Son to have life in himself.

[26] ACT 7:2 And he said, Men, brethren, and fathers, hearken; The God of glory appeared unto our father Abraham, when he was in Mesopotamia, before he dwelt in Charran.

[27] PSA 119:68 Thou art good, and doest good; teach me thy statutes.

[28] 1TI 6:15 Which in his times he shall shew, who is the blessed and only Potentate, the King of kings, and Lord of lords. ROM 9:5 Whose are the fathers, and of whom as concerning the flesh

Christ came, who is over all, God blessed for ever. Amen.

[29] ACT 17:24 God that made the world and all things therein, seeing that he is Lord of heaven and earth, dwelleth not in temples made with hands; 25 Neither is worshipped with men's hands, as though he needed any thing, seeing he giveth to all life, and breath, and all things.

[30] JOB 22:2 Can a man be profitable unto God, as he that is wise may be profitable unto himself? 3 Is it any pleasure to the Almighty, that thou art righteous? or is it gain to him that thou makest thy ways perfect?

[31] ROM 11:36 For of him, and through him, and to him, are all things: to whom be glory for ever. Amen.

[32] REV 4:11 Thou art worthy, O Lord, to receive glory and honour and power: for thou hast created all things, and for thy pleasure they are and were created. 1TI 6:15 Which in his times he shall shew, who is the blessed and only Potentate, the King of kings, and Lord of lords. DAN 4:25 That they shall drive thee from men, and thy dwelling shall be with the beasts of the field, and they shall make thee to eat grass as oxen, and they shall wet thee with the dew of heaven, and seven times shall pass over thee, till thou know that the most High ruleth in the kingdom of men, and giveth it to whomsoever he will. 35 And all the inhabitants of the earth are reputed as nothing: and he doeth according to his will in the army of heaven, and among the inhabitants of the earth: and none can stay his hand, or say unto him, What doest thou?

[33] HEB 4:13 Neither is there any creature that is not manifest in his sight: but all things are naked and opened unto the eyes of him with whom we have to do.

[34] ROM 11:33 O the depth of the riches both of the wisdom and knowledge of God! how unsearchable are his judgments, and his ways past finding out! 34 For who hath known the mind of the Lord? or who hath been his counsellor? PSA 147:5 Great is our Lord, and of great power: his understanding is infinite.

[35] ACT 15:18 Known unto God are all his works from the beginning of the world. EZE 11:5 And the Spirit of the Lord fell upon me, and said unto me, Speak; Thus saith the Lord; Thus have ye said, O house of Israel: for I know the things that come into your mind, every one of them.

[36] PSA 145:17 The Lord is righteous in all his ways, and holy in all his works. ROM 7:12 Wherefore the law is holy, and the commandment holy, and just, and good.

[37] REV 5:12 Saying with a loud voice, Worthy is the Lamb that was slain to receive power, and riches, and wisdom, and strength, and honour, and glory, and blessing. 13 And every creature which is in heaven, and on the earth, and under the earth, and such as are in the sea, and all that are in them, heard I saying, Blessing, and honour, and glory, and power, be unto him that sitteth upon the throne, and unto the Lamb for ever and ever. 14 And the four beasts said, Amen. And the four and twenty elders fell down and worshipped him that liveth for ever and ever.

[38] (Traditionally, I John 5:7 is placed here, but we have, for obvious reasons, omitted it in our online edition) MATT 3:16-17 And Jesus, when he was baptized, went up straightway out of the water: and, lo, the heavens were opened unto him, and he saw the Spirit of God descending like a dove, and lighting upon him: And lo a voice from heaven, saying, This is my beloved Son, in whom I am well pleased. MATT 28:19 Go ye therefore, and teach all nations, baptizing them in the name of the Father, and of the Son, and of the Holy Ghost. II COR 13:14 The grace of the Lord Jesus Christ, and the love of God, and the communion of the Holy Ghost, be with you all. Amen.

[39] JOHN 1:14,18 And the Word was made flesh, and dwelt among us, (and we beheld his glory, the glory as of the only begotten of the Father,) full of grace and truth. No man hath seen God at any time; the only begotten Son, which is in the bosom of the Father, he hath declared him.

[40] JOHN 15:26 But when the Comforter is come, whom I will send unto you from the Father, even the Spirit of truth, which proceedeth from the Father, He shall testify of me. GAL 4:6 And Because ye are sons, God hath sent forth the Spirit of his Son into your hearts, crying, Abba, Father.

WESTMINSTER LARGER
CATECHISM, QUESTIONS 7-11

Q. 7. What is God?

A. God is a Spirit,[18] in and of himself infinite in being,[19] glory,[20] blessedness,[21] and perfection;[22] all-sufficient,[23] eternal,[24] unchangeable,[25] incomprehensible,[26] every where present,[27] almighty,[28] knowing all things,[29] most wise,[30] most holy,[31] most just,[32] most merciful and gracious, long-suffering, and abundant in goodness and truth.[33]

Q. 8. Are there more Gods than one?

A. There is but one only, the living and true God.[34]

Q. 9. How many persons are there in the Godhead?

A. There be three persons in the Godhead, the Father, the Son, and the Holy Ghost; and these three are one true, eternal God, the same in substance, equal in power and glory; although distinguished by their personal properties.[35]

Q. 10. What are the personal properties of the three persons in the Godhead?

A. It is proper to the Father to beget the Son,[36] and to the Son to be begotten of the Father,[37] and to the Holy Ghost to proceed from the Father and the Son from all eternity.[38]

Q. 11. How doth it appear that the Son and the Holy Ghost are God equal with the Father?

A. The Scriptures manifest that the Son and the Holy Ghost are God equal with the Father, ascribing unto them such names,[39] attributes,[40] works,[41] and worship,[42] as are proper to God only.

CATECHISM
SCRIPTURAL PROOFS, 18-42:

[18] John 4:24. God is a Spirit: and they that worship him must worship him in spirit and in truth.

[19] Exodus 3:14. And God said unto Moses, I AM THAT I AM: and he said, Thus shalt thou say unto the children of Israel, I AM hath sent me unto you. Job 11:7-9. Canst thou by searching find out God? canst thou find out the Almighty unto perfection? It is as high as heaven; what canst thou do? deeper than hell; what canst thou know? The measure thereof is longer than the earth, and broader than the sea.

[20] Acts 7:2. And he said, Men, brethren, and fathers, hearken; The God of glory appeared unto our father Abraham, when he was in Mesopotamia, before he dwelt in Charran.

[21] 1 Timothy 6:15. Which in his times he shall show, who is the blessed and only Potentate, the King of kings, and Lord of lords.

[22] Matthew 5:48. Be ye therefore perfect, even as your Father which is in heaven is perfect.

[23] Genesis 17:1. And when Abram was ninety years old and nine, the LORD appeared to Abram, and said unto him, I am the Almighty God; walk before me, and be thou perfect.

[24] Psalm 90:2. Before the mountains were brought forth, or ever thou hadst formed the earth and the world, even from everlasting to everlasting, thou art God.

[25] Malachi 3:6. For I am the LORD, I change not; therefore ye sons of Jacob are not consumed.

[26] 1 Kings 8:27. But will God indeed dwell on the earth? behold, the heaven and heaven of heavens cannot contain thee; how much less this house that I have builded?

[27] Psalm 139:1-13. O LORD, thou hast searched me, and known me. Thou knowest my down-sitting and mine uprising, thou understandest my thought afar off. Thou compassest my path and my lying down, and art acquainted with all my ways. For there is not a word in my tongue, but, lo, O LORD, thou knowest it altogether. Thou hast beset me behind and before, and laid thine hand upon me. Such knowledge is too wonderful for me; it is high, I cannot attain unto it. Whither shall I go from thy spirit? or whither shall I flee from thy presence? If I ascend up into heaven, thou art there: if I make my bed in hell, behold, thou art there. If I take the wings of the morning, and dwell in the uttermost parts of the sea; Even there shall thy hand lead me, and thy right hand shall hold me. If I say, Surely the darkness shall cover me; even the night shall be light about me. Yea, the darkness hideth not from thee; but the night shineth as the day: the darkness and the light are both alike to thee. For thou hast possessed my reins: thou hast covered me in my mother's womb.

[28] Revelation 4:8. And the four beasts had each of them six wings about him; and they were full of eyes within: and they rest not day and night, saying, Holy, holy, holy, Lord God Almighty, which was, and is, and is to come.

[29] Hebrews 4:13. Neither is there any creature that is not manifest in his sight: but all things are naked and opened unto the eyes of him with whom we have to do. Psalm 147:5. Great is our Lord, and of great power: his understanding is infinite.

[30] Romans 16:27. To God only wise, be glory through Jesus Christ for ever. Amen.

[31] Isaiah 6:3. And one cried unto another, and said, Holy, holy, holy, is the LORD of hosts: the whole earth is full of his glory. Revelation 15:4. Who shall not fear thee, O Lord, and glorify

thy name? for thou only art holy: for all nations shall come and worship before thee; for thy judgments are made manifest.

[32] Deuteronomy 32:4. He is the Rock, his work is perfect: for all his ways are judgment: a God of truth and without iniquity, just and right is he.

[33] Exodus 34:6. And the LORD passed by before him, and proclaimed, The LORD, The LORD God, merciful and gracious, longsuffering, and abundant in goodness and truth.

[34] Deuteronomy 6:4. Hear, O Israel: The LORD our God is one LORD. 1 Corinthians 8:4, 6. As concerning therefore the eating of those things that are offered in sacrifice unto idols, we know that an idol is nothing in the world, and that there is none other God but one.... But to us there is but one God, the Father, of whom are all things, and we in him; and one Lord Jesus Christ, by whom are all things, and we by him. Jeremiah 10:10. But the LORD is the true God, he is the living God, and an everlasting king: at his wrath the earth shall tremble, and the nations shall not be able to abide his indignation.

[35] 1 John 5:7. For there are three that bear record in heaven, the Father, the Word, and the Holy Ghost: and these three are one. Matthew 3:16-17. And Jesus, when he was baptized, went up straightway out of the water: and, lo, the heavens were opened unto him, and he saw the Spirit of God descending like a dove, and lighting upon him: And lo a voice from heaven, saying, This is my beloved Son, in whom I am well pleased. Matthew 28:19. Go ye therefore, and teach all nations, baptizing them in the name of the Father, and of the Son, and of the Holy Ghost. 2 Corinthians 13:14. The grace of the Lord Jesus Christ, and the love of God, and the communion of the Holy Ghost, be with you all. Amen. John 10:30. I and my Father are one.

[36] Hebrews 1:5-6, 8. For unto which of the angels said he at any time, Thou art my Son, this day have I begotten thee? And again, I will be to him a Father, and he shall be to me a Son? And again, when he bringeth in the firstbegotten into the world, he saith, And let all the angels of God worship him.... But unto the Son he saith, Thy throne, O God, is for ever and ever: a sceptre of righteousness is the sceptre of thy kingdom.

[37] John 1:14, 18. And the Word was made flesh, and dwelt among us, (and we beheld his glory, the glory as of the only begotten of the Father,) full of grace and truth.... No man hath seen God at any time; the only begotten Son, which is in the bosom of the Father, he hath declared him.

[38] John 15:26. But when the Comforter is come, whom I will send unto you from the Father, even the Spirit of truth, which proceedeth from the Father, he shall testify of me. Galatians 4:6. And because ye are sons, God hath sent forth the Spirit of his Son into your hearts, crying, Abba, Father.

[39] Isaiah 6:3, 5, 8. And one cried unto another, and said, Holy, holy, holy, is the LORD of hosts: the whole earth is full of his glory.... Then said I, Woe is me! for I am undone; because I am a man of unclean lips, and I dwell in the midst of a people of unclean lips: for mine eyes have seen the King, the LORD of hosts.... Also I heard the voice of the Lord, saying, Whom shall I send, and who will go for us? Then said I, Here am I; send me. John 12:41. These things said Esaias, when he saw his glory, and spake of him. Acts 28:25. And when they agreed not among themselves, they departed, after that Paul had spoken one word, Well spake the Holy Ghost by Esaias the prophet unto our fathers. 1 John 5:20. And we know that the Son of God is come, and hath given us an understanding, that we may know him that is true, and we are in him that is true, even in his Son Jesus Christ. This is the true God, and eternal life. Acts 5:3-4. But Peter said, Ananias, why hath Satan filled thine heart to lie to the Holy Ghost, and to keep back part of the price of the land? Whiles it remained, was it not thine own? and after it was sold, was it not in thine own power? why hast thou conceived this thing in thine heart? thou hast not lied unto men, but unto God.

[40] John 1:1. In the beginning was the Word, and the Word was with God, and the Word was God. Isaiah 9:6. For unto us a child is born, unto us a son is given: and the government shall be upon his shoulder: and his name shall be called Wonderful, Counsellor, The mighty God, The everlasting Father, The Prince of Peace. John 2:24-25. But Jesus did not commit himself unto them, because he knew all men, And needed not that any should testify of man: for he knew what was in man. 1 Corinthians 2:10-11. But God hath revealed them unto us by his Spirit: for the Spirit searcheth all things, yea, the deep things of God. For what man knoweth the things of a man, save the spirit of man which is in him? even so the things of God knoweth no man, but the Spirit of God.

[41] Colossians 1:16. For by him were all things created, that are in heaven, and that are in earth, visible and invisible, whether they be thrones, or dominions, or principalities, or powers: all things were created by him, and for him. Genesis 1:2. And the earth was without form, and void; and darkness was upon the face of the deep. And the Spirit of God moved upon the face of the waters.

[42] Matthew 28:19. Go ye therefore, and teach all nations, baptizing them in the name of the Father, and of the Son, and of the Holy Ghost. 2 Corinthians 13:14. The grace of the Lord Jesus

Christ, and the love of God, and the communion of the Holy Spirit be with you all. Amen.

THE 8TH MORMON
ARTICLE OF FAITH

We believe the Bible to be the word of God as far as it is translated correctly; we also believe the *Book of Mormon* to be the word of God.

I would say that the first part of the article or assertion casts doubt upon the Bible. The second part of the article accepts the *Book of Mormon* without reservation. It is interesting to note that a search of Mormon literature will provide no examples of where the Bible has been shown to have been mistranslated by Mormon leaders utilizing original languages and rules of grammar. When witnessing to Mormons, Christians should never let the Mormon make an assertion about the Bible being mistranslated without a response. The response should be to ask the Mormon for specific examples of where the Bible has been mistranslated and by whom. Specify that you expect them to show examples of the mistranslation of original languages and the rules of grammar being violated. Never let assertions of biblical mistranslation go unchallenged.

In contrast:

WESTMINSTER CONFESSION
OF FAITH CHAPTER I

Of the Holy Scripture

I

Although the light of nature, and the works of creation and providence do so far manifest the goodness, wisdom, and power of God, as to leave men unexcusable;[1] yet are they not sufficient to give that knowledge of God, and of His will, which is necessary unto salvation.[2] Therefore it pleased the Lord, at sundry times, and in divers manners, to reveal Himself, and to declare that His will unto His Church;[3] and afterwards for the better preserving and propagating of the truth, and for the more sure establishment and comfort of the Church against the corruption of the flesh, and the malice of Satan and of the world, to commit the same wholly unto writing;[4] which

makes the Holy Scripture to be most necessary;[5] those former ways of God's revealing His will
unto His people being now ceased.[6]

II

Under the name of Holy Scripture, or the Word of God written, are now contained all the books
of the Old and New Testament, which are these: Of the Old Testament: Genesis, Exodus, Levit-
icus, Numbers, Deuteronomy, Joshua, Judges, Ruth, I Samuel, II Samuel, I Kings, II Kings, I
Chronicles, II Chronicles, Ezra, Nehemiah, Esther, Job, Psalms, Proverbs, Ecclesiastes, The Song
of Songs, Isaiah, Jeremiah, Lamentations, Ezekiel, Daniel, Hosea, Joel, Amos, Obadiah, Jonah,
Micah, Nahum, Habakkuk, Zephaniah, Haggai, Zechariah, Malachi. Of the New Testament: The
Gospels according to Matthew, Mark, Luke, John, The Acts of the Apostles, Paul's Epistles to the
Romans, Corinthians I, Corinthians II, Galatians, Ephesians, Philippians, Colossians, Thessalonians I , Thessalonians II , To Timothy I , To Timothy II, To Titus, To Philemon, The Epistle to
the Hebrews, The Epistle of James, The first and second Epistles of Peter, The first, second, and
third Epistles of John, The Epistle of Jude, The Revelation of John. All which are given by inspiration of God to be the rule of faith and life.[7]

III

The books commonly called Apocrypha, not being of divine inspiration, are no part of the canon
of the Scripture, and therefore are of no authority in the Church of God, nor to be any otherwise
approved, or made use of, than other human writings.[8]

IV. The authority of the Holy Scripture, for which it ought to be believed, and obeyed, depends
not upon the testimony of any man, or Church; but wholly upon God (who is truth itself) the
author thereof: and therefore it is to be received, because it is the Word of God.[9]

V. We may be moved and induced by the testimony of the Church to an high and reverent esteem
of the Holy Scripture.[10] And the heavenliness of the matter, the efficacy of the doctrine, the
majesty of the style, the consent of all the parts, the scope of the whole (which is, to give all glory
to God), the full discovery it makes of the only way of man's salvation, the many other incompa-

rable excellencies, and the entire perfection thereof, are arguments whereby it does abundantly evidence itself to be the Word of God: yet notwithstanding, our full persuasion and assurance of the infallible truth and divine authority thereof, is from the inward work of the Holy Spirit bearing witness by and with the Word in our hearts.[11]

VI

The whole counsel of God concerning all things necessary for His own glory, man's salvation, faith and life, is either expressly set down in Scripture, or by good and necessary consequence may be deduced from Scripture: unto which nothing at any time is to be added, whether by new revelations of the Spirit, or traditions of men.[12] Nevertheless, we acknowledge the inward illumination of the Spirit of God to be necessary for the saving understanding of such things as are revealed in the Word:[13] and that there are some circumstances concerning the worship of God, and government of the Church, common to human actions and societies, which are to be ordered by the light of nature, and Christian prudence, according to the general rules of the Word, which are always to be observed.[14]

VII

All things in Scripture are not alike plain in themselves, nor alike clear unto all:[15] yet those things which are necessary to be known, believed, and observed for salvation are so clearly propounded, and opened in some place of Scripture or other, that not only the learned, but the unlearned, in a due use of the ordinary means, may attain unto a sufficient understanding of them.[16]

VIII.

The Old Testament in Hebrew (which was the native language of the people of God of old), and the New Testament in Greek (which, at the time of the writing of it, was most generally known to the nations), being immediately inspired by God, and, by His singular care and providence, kept pure in all ages, are therefore authentical;[17] so as, in all controversies of religion, the Church is finally to appeal unto them.[18] But, because these original tongues are not known to all the people of God, who have right unto, and interest in the Scriptures, and are commanded, in the fear of God, to read and search them,[19] therefore they are to be translated in to the vulgar language of every nation unto which they come,[20] that, the Word of God dwelling plentifully in all, they may worship Him in an acceptable manner;[21] and, through patience and comfort of the Scriptures, may have hope.[22]

IX

The infallible rule of interpretation of Scripture is the Scripture itself: and therefore, when there is a question about the true and full sense of any Scripture (which is not manifold, but one), it must be searched and known by other places that speak more clearly.[23]

X

The supreme judge by which all controversies of religion are to be determined, and all decrees of councils, opinions of ancient writers, doctrines of men, and private spirits, are to be examined, and in whose sentence we are to rest, can be no other but the Holy Spirit speaking in the Scripture.[24]

SCRIPTURAL
PROOFS TEXTS

[1] ROM 2:14 For when the Gentiles, which have not the law, do by nature the things contained in the law, these, having not the law, are a law unto themselves: 15 Which shew the work of the law written in their hearts, their conscience also bearing witness, and their thoughts the mean while accusing or else excusing one another; 1:19 Because that which may be known of God is manifest in them; for God hath shewed it unto them. 20 For the invisible things of him from the creation of the world are clearly seen, being understood by the things that are made, even his eternal power and Godhead; so that they are without excuse. PSA 19:1 The heavens declare the glory of God; and the firmament sheweth his handiwork. 2 Day unto day uttereth speech, and night unto night sheweth knowledge. 3 There is no speech nor language, where their voice is not heard. ROM 1:32 Who knowing the judgment of God, that they which commit such things are worthy of death, not

only do the same, but have pleasure in them that do them. 2:1 Therefore thou art inexcusable, O man, whosoever thou art that judgest: for wherein thou judgest another, thou condemnest thyself; for thou that judgest doest the same things.

[2] 1CO 1:21 For after that in the wisdom of God the world by wisdom knew not God, it pleased God by the foolishness of preaching to save them that believe. 2:13 Which things also we speak, not in the words which man's wisdom teacheth, but which the Holy Ghost teacheth; comparing spiritual things with spiritual. 14 But the natural man receiveth not the things of the Spirit of God: for they are foolishness unto him: neither can he know them, because they are spiritually discerned.

[3] HEB 1:1 God, who at sundry times and in divers manners spake in time past unto the fathers by the prophets.

[4] PRO 22:19 That thy trust may be in the Lord, I have made known to thee this day, even to thee. 20 Have not I written to thee excellent things in counsels and knowledge, 21 That I might make thee know the certainty of the words of truth; that thou mightest answer the words of truth to them that send unto thee? LUK 1:3 It seemed good to me also, having had perfect understanding of all things from the very first, to write unto thee in order, most excellent Theophilus, 4 That thou mightest know the certainty of those things, wherein thou hast been instructed. ROM 15:4 For whatsoever things were written aforetime were written for our learning, that we through patience and comfort of the scriptures might have hope. MAT 4:4 But he answered and said, It is written, Man shall not live by bread alone, but by every word that proceedeth out of the mouth of God. 7 Jesus said unto him, It is written again, Thou shalt not tempt the Lord thy God. 10 Then saith Jesus unto him, Get thee hence, Satan: for it is written, Thou shalt worship the Lord thy God, and him only shalt thou serve. ISA 8:19 And when they shall say unto you, Seek unto them that have familiar spirits, and unto wizards that peep, and that mutter: should not a people seek unto their God? for the living to the dead? 20 To the law and to the testimony: if they speak not according to this word, it is because there is no light in them.

[5] 2TI 3:15 And that from a child thou hast known the holy scriptures, which are able to make thee wise unto salvation through faith which is in Christ Jesus. 2PE 1:19 We have also a more sure word of prophecy; whereunto ye do well that ye take heed, as unto a light that shineth in a dark place, until the day dawn, and the day star arise in your hearts.

[6] HEB 1:1 God, who at sundry times and in divers manners spake in time past unto the fathers by the prophets, 2 Hath in these last days spoken unto us by his Son, whom he hath appointed heir of all things, by whom also he made the worlds.

[7] LUK 16:29 Abraham saith unto him, They have Moses and the prophets; let them hear them. 31 And he said unto him, If they hear not Moses and the prophets, neither will they be persuaded, though one rose from the dead. EPH 2:20 And are built upon the foundation of the apostles and prophets, Jesus Christ himself being the chief corner stone. REV 22:18 For I testify unto every man that heareth the words of the prophecy of this book, If any man shall add unto these things, God shall add unto him the plagues that are written in this book: 19 And if any man shall take away from the words of the book of this prophecy, God shall take away his part out of the book of life, and out of the holy city, and from the things which are written in this book. 2TI 3:16 All scripture is given by inspiration of God, and is profitable for doctrine, for reproof, for correction, for instruction in righteousness.

[8] LUK 24:27 And beginning at Moses and all the prophets, he expounded unto them in all the scriptures the things concerning himself. 44 And he said unto them, These are the words which I spake unto you, while I was yet with you, that all things must be fulfilled, which were written in the law of Moses, and in the prophets, and in the psalms, concerning me. ROM 3:2 Much every way: chiefly, because that unto them were committed the oracles of God. 2PE 1:21 For the prophecy came not in old time by the will of man: but holy men of God spake as they were moved by the Holy Ghost.

[9] 2PE 1:19 We have also a more sure word of prophecy; whereunto ye do well that ye take heed, as unto a light that shineth in a dark place, until the day dawn, and the day star arise in your hearts. 21 For the prophecy came not in old time by the will of man: but holy men of God spake as they were moved by the Holy Ghost. 2TI 3:16 All scripture is given by inspiration of God, and is profitable for doctrine, for reproof, for correction, for instruction in righteousness. 1JO 5:9 If we receive the witness of men, the witness of God is greater: for this is the witness of God which he hath testified of his Son. 1 TH 2:13 For this cause also thank we God without ceasing, because, when ye received the word of God which ye heard of us, ye received it not as the word of men, but as it is in truth, the word of God, which effectually worketh also in you that believe.

[10] 1TI 3:15 But if I tarry long, that thou mayest know how thou oughtest to behave thyself in the house of God, which is the church of the living God, the pillar and ground of the truth.

[11] 1JO 2:20 But ye have an unction from the Holy One, and ye know all things. 27 But the anointing which ye have received of him abideth in you, and ye need not that any man teach you: but as the same anointing teacheth you of all things, and is truth, and is no lie, and even as it hath taught you, ye shall abide in him. JOH 16:13 Howbeit when he, the Spirit of truth, is come, he will guide you into all truth: for he shall not speak of himself; but whatsoever he shall hear, that shall he speak: and he will shew you things to come. 14 He shall glorify me: for he shall receive of mine, and shall shew it unto you. 1CO 2:10 But God hath revealed them unto us by his Spirit: for the Spirit searcheth all things, yea, the deep things of God. 11 For what man knoweth the things of a man, save the spirit of man which is in him? even so the things of God knoweth no man, but the Spirit of God. 12 Now we have received, not the spirit of the world, but the spirit which is of God; that we might know the things that are freely given to us of God. ISA 59:21 As for me, this is my covenant with them, saith the Lord; My spirit that is upon thee, and my words which I have put in thy mouth, shall not depart out of thy mouth, nor out of the mouth of thy seed, nor out of the mouth of thy seed's seed, saith the Lord, from henceforth and for ever.

[12] 2TI 3:15 And that from a child thou hast known the holy scriptures, which are able to make thee wise unto salvation through faith which is in Christ Jesus. 16 All scripture is given by inspiration of God, and is profitable for doctrine, for reproof, for correction, for instruction in righteousness: 17 That the man of God may be perfect, throughly furnished unto all good works. GAL 1:8 But though we, or an angel from heaven, preach any other gospel unto you than that which we have preached unto you, let him be accursed. 9 As we said before, so say I now again, if any man preach any other gospel unto you than that ye have received, let him be accursed. 2TH 2:2 That ye be not soon shaken in mind, or be troubled, neither by spirit, nor by word, nor by letter as from us, as that the day of Christ is at hand.

[13] JOH 6:45 It is written in the prophets, And they shall be all taught of God. Every man therefore that hath heard, and hath learned of the Father, cometh unto me. 1CO 2:9 But as it is written, Eye hath not seen, nor ear heard, neither have entered into the heart of man, the things which God hath prepared for them that love him. 10 But God hath revealed them unto us by his Spirit: for the Spirit searcheth all things, yea, the deep things of God. 11 For what man knoweth the things of a man, save the spirit of man which is in him? even so the things of God knoweth no man, but the Spirit of God. 12 Now we have received, not the spirit of the world, but the spirit which is of God; that we might know the things that are freely given to us of God.

[14] 1CO 11:13 Judge in yourselves: is it comely that a woman pray unto God uncovered? 14 Doth

not even nature itself teach you, that, if a man have long hair, it is a shame unto him? 14:26 How is it then, brethren? when ye come together, every one of you hath a psalm, hath a doctrine, hath a tongue, hath a revelation, hath an interpretation. Let all things be done unto edifying. 40 Let all things be done decently and in order.

[15] 2PE 3:16 As also in all his epistles, speaking in them of these things: in which are some things hard to be understood, which they that are unlearned and unstable wrest, as they do also the other scriptures, unto their own destruction.

[16] PSA 119:105 Thy word is a lamp unto my feet, and a light unto my path. 130 The entrance of thy words giveth light; it giveth understanding unto the simple.

[17] MAT 5:18 For verily I say unto you, Till heaven and earth pass, one jot or one tittle shall in no wise pass from the law, till all be fulfilled.

[18] ISA 8:20 To the law and to the testimony: if they speak not according to this word, it is because there is no light in them. ACT 15:15 And to this agree the words of the prophets; as it is written. JOH 5:39 Search the scriptures; for in them ye think ye have eternal life: and they are they which testify of me. 46 For had ye believed Moses, ye would have believed me: for he wrote of me.

[19] JOH 5:39 Search the scriptures; for in them ye think ye have eternal life: and they are they which testify of me.

[20] 1CO 14:6 Now, brethren, if I come undo you speaking with tongues, what shall I profit you, except I shall speak to you either by revelation, or by knowledge, of by prophesying, or by doctrine? 9 So likewise ye, except ye utter by the tongue words easy to be understood, how shall it be known what is spoken? for ye shall speak into the air. 11 Therefore if I know not the meaning of the voice, I shall be unto him that speaketh a barbarian, and he that speaketh shall be a barbarian unto me. 12 Even so ye, forasmuch as ye are zealous of spiritual gifts, seek that ye may excel to the edifying of the church. 24 But if all prophecy, and there come in one that believeth not, or one unlearned, he is convinced of all, he is judged of all: 27 If any man speak in an unknown tongue, let it be by two, or at the most three, and that by course; and let one interpret. 28 But if there be no interpreter, let him keep silence in the church; and let him speak to himself, and to God.

[21] COL 3:16 Let the word of Christ dwell in you richly in all wisdom; teaching and admonishing one another in psalms, and hymns, and spiritual songs, singing with grace in your hearts to the Lord.

[22] ROM 15:4 For whatsoever things were written aforetime, were written for our learning; that we, through patience and comfort of the scriptures, might have hope.

[23] 2PE 1:20 Knowing this first, that no prophecy of the scripture is of any private interpretation. 21 For the prophecy came not in old time by the will of man; but holy men of God spake as they were moved by the Holy Ghost. ACT 15:15 And to this agree the words of the prophets; as it is written, 16 After this I will return, and will build again the tabernacle of David, which is fallen down; and I will build again the ruins thereof, and I will set it up. [24] MATT. 22:29,31. Jesus answered and said unto them, Ye do err, not knowing the scriptures, nor the power of God. But as touching the resurrection of the dead, have ye not read that which was spoken unto you by God, saying. EPH. 2:20. And are built upon the foundation of the apostles and prophets, Jesus Christ himself being the chief corner-stone. With ACTS 28:25. And when they agreed not among themselves, they departed, after that Paul had spoken one word, Well spake the Holy Ghost by Isaiah the prophet unto our fathers.

WESTMINSTER LARGER
CATECHISM, QUESTIONS 3-5

Q. What is the Word of God?

A. The holy Scriptures of the Old and New Testament are the Word of God,[5] the only rule of faith and obedience.[6]

Q. 4. How doth it appear that the Scriptures are of the Word of God?

A. The Scriptures manifest themselves to be the Word of God, by their majesty[7] and purity;[8] by the consent of all the parts,[9] and the scope of the whole, which is to give all glory to God;[10] by their light and power to convince and convert sinners, to comfort and build up believers unto salvation:[11] but the Spirit of God bearing witness by and with the Scriptures in the heart of man, is alone able fully to persuade it that they are the very word of God.[12]

Q. 5. What do the Scriptures principally teach?

A. The Scriptures principally teach, what man is to believe concerning God, and what duty God requires of man.[13]

CATECHISM
PROOFS TEXTS, 6-13

[6] Ephesians 2:20. And are built upon the foundation of the apostles and prophets, Jesus Christ himself being the chief corner stone. Revelation 22:18-19. For I testify unto every man that heareth the words of the prophecy of this book, If any man shall add unto these things, God shall add unto him the plagues that are written in this book: And if any man shall take away from the words of the book of this prophecy, God shall take away his part out of the book of life, and out of the holy city, and from the things which are written in this book. Isaiah 8:20. To the law and to the testimony: if they speak not according to this word, it is because there is no light in them. Luke 16:29, 31. Abraham saith unto him, They have Moses and the prophets; let them hear them.... And he said unto him, If they hear not Moses and the prophets, neither will they be persuaded, though one rose from the dead. Galatians 1:8-9. But though we, or an angel from heaven, preach any other gospel unto you than that which we have preached unto you, let him be accursed. As we said before, so say I now again, If any man preach any other gospel unto you than that ye have received, let him be accursed. 2 Timothy 3:15-16. And that from a child thou hast known the holy scriptures, which are able to make thee wise unto salvation through faith which is in Christ Jesus. All scripture is given by inspiration of God, and is profitable for doctrine, for reproof, for correction, for instruction in righteousness.

[7] Hosea 8:12. I have written to him the great things of my law, but they were counted as a strange thing. 1 Corinthians 2:6-7, 13. Howbeit we speak wisdom among them that are perfect: yet not the wisdom of this world, nor of the princes of this world, that come to nought: But we speak the wisdom of God in a mystery, even the hidden wisdom, which God ordained before the world unto our glory:... Which things also we speak, not in the words which man's wisdom teacheth, but which the Holy Ghost teacheth; comparing spiritual things with spiritual. Psalm 119:18, 129. Open thou mine eyes, that I may behold wondrous things out of thy law.... Thy testimonies are wonderful: therefore doth my soul keep them.

[8] Psalm 12:6. The words of the LORD are pure words: as silver tried in a furnace of earth, purified seven times. Psalm 119:140. Thy word is very pure: therefore thy servant loveth it.

[9] Acts 10:43. To him give all the prophets witness, that through his name whosoever believeth in him shall receive remission of sins. Acts 26:22. Having therefore obtained help of God, I continue unto this day, witnessing both to small and great, saying none other things than those which the

prophets and Moses did say should come.

[10] Romans 3:19, 27. Now we know that what things soever the law saith, it saith to them who are under the law: that every mouth may be stopped, and all the world may become guilty before God…. Where is boasting then? It is excluded. By what law? of works? Nay: but by the law of faith.

[11] Acts 18:28. For he mightily convinced the Jews, and that publicly, showing by the scriptures that Jesus was Christ. Hebrews 4:12. For the word of God is quick, and powerful, and sharper than any twoedged sword, piercing even to the dividing asunder of soul and spirit, and of the joints and marrow, and is a discerner of the thoughts and intents of the heart. James 1:18. Of his own will begat he us with the word of truth, that we should be a kind of firstfruits of his creatures. Psalm 19:7-9. The law of the LORD is perfect, converting the soul: the testimony of the LORD is sure, making wise the simple. The statutes of the LORD are right, rejoicing the heart: the commandment of the LORD is pure, enlightening the eyes. The fear of the LORD is clean, enduring for ever: the judgments of the LORD are true and righteous altogether. Romans 15:4. For whatsoever things were written aforetime were written for our learning, that we through patience and comfort of the scriptures might have hope. Acts 20:32. And now, brethren, I commend you to God, and to the word of his grace, which is able to build you up, and to give you an inheritance among all them which are sanctified.

[12] John 16:13-14. Howbeit when he, the Spirit of truth, is come, he will guide you into all truth: for he shall not speak of himself; but whatsoever he shall hear, that shall he speak: and he will show you things to come. He shall glorify me: for he shall receive of mine, and shall show it unto you. 1 John 2:20, 27. But ye have an unction from the Holy One, and ye know all things…. But the anointing which ye have received of him abideth in you, and ye need not that any man teach you: but as the same anointing teacheth you of all things, and is truth, and is no lie, and even as it hath taught you, ye shall abide in him. John 20:31. But these are written, that ye might believe that Jesus is the Christ, the Son of God; and that believing ye might have life through his name.

[13] 2 Timothy 1:13. Hold fast the form of sound words, which thou hast heard of me, in faith and love which is in Christ Jesus.

FOOD FOR THOUGHT

The 1647 Westminster Confession of Faith is the most precise and theologically rich confession produced by the Christian Church. The Westminster Confession of Faith is a summary of the Bible's teaching on The Holy Scriptures, The Trinity, Creation, The Fall of Man, Free will, Election, The Law of God, God's Eternal Decree, Assurance of Grace and Salvation, Good Works, and many other doctrines. The Westminster Confession has its foundation in the unchanging truth of Scripture as seen in its copious references from the Bible which are printed on each page. Because of its faithfulness to Scripture, the Confession has permanent worth and abiding relevance.

FINAL THOUGHTS

In conclusion, consider the following Mormon leaders and their opposition to Christianity:

Those Who Reject the Gospel to Be Damned [Observe]...Christendom at the present day, and where are they, with all their boasted religion, piety, and sacredness while at the same time they are crying out against prophets, apostles, angels, revelations, prophesying and visions, etc. Why, they are just ripening for the damnation of hell. They will be damned...Yes, I say, such will be damned, with all their professed godliness.

Joseph Smith, *History of the Church* Vol. 5, p. 389.

What! Are Christians ignorant? Yes, as ignorant of the things of God as the brute beast.

John Taylor, *Journal of Discourses* Vol. 6, p. 25.

We talk about Christianity, but it is a perfect pack of nonsense.... Myself and hundreds of the Elders around me have seen its pomp, parade, and glory; and what is it? It is a sounding brass and a tinkling symbol; it is as corrupt as hell; and the Devil could not invent a better engine to spread his work than the Christianity of the nineteenth century.

John Taylor, *Journal of Discourses* Vol. 6, p. 167.

The Christian world, so called, are heathens as to their knowledge of the salvation of God. If those nations that we call heathen were civilized as we are, intelligent as we are, we would not call them heathen... With regard to true theology, a more ignorant people never lived than the present so-called Christian world.

Brigham Young, *Journal of Discourses* Vol. 8, pp. 171, 199.

Both Catholics and Protestants are nothing less than the 'whore of Babylon' whom the Lord denounces ...as having corrupted all the earth by their fornications and wickedness. And any person who shall be so wicked as to receive a holy ordinance of the gospel from the ministers of any of these apostate churches will be sent down to hell with them, unless they repent of the unholy and impious act.

Orson Pratt, *The Seer* p. 255.

In the next four verses we see that: (1) the Word of God comes to His servants, (2) He will not acquit the wicked, and (3) He will most certainly bring down false leaders by giving them their just reward.

The word of the LORD which came unto Zephaniah the son of Cushi, the son of Gedaliah, the son of Amariah, the son of Hizkiah, in the days of Josiah the son of Amon, king of Judah. (Zephaniah 1:1)

The LORD is slow to anger, and great in power, and will not at all acquit the wicked: the LORD has his way in the whirlwind and in the storm, and the clouds are the dust of his feet. (Nahum 1:3)

> For the day of the LORD is near upon all the
> heathen: as thou hast done, it shall be done unto
> thee: thy reward shall return upon thine own head.
> (Obadiah 1:15)

> So they hanged Haman on the gallows that he had
> prepared for Mordecai. Then was the king's wrath
> pacified. (Esther 7:10)

God will always protect His Church and will turn all evil plans upon the heads of those conspiring against the advance of His kingdom.

The most unbiblical sin that Mormons need to repent of is their belief and hope to progress into exalted men, or become as gods and getting their own planet to rule over.

> Then will they <u>become Gods</u>...they will never cease
> to increase and to multiply, worlds without end.
> When they receive their crowns, their dominions,
> <u>they then will be prepared to frame earths like</u>
> <u>unto ours and to people them</u> in the same manner
> as we have been brought forth by our parents, by
> our Father and God. (emphasis mine)

> Brigham Young, *Journal of Discourses* Vol. 17, p. 143.

Contrary to Mormon doctrine, this belief about becoming god is the ultimate Satanic lie as seen from Genesis:

> For God doth know that in the day ye eat thereof,
> then your eyes shall be opened, and ye shall be as
> gods, knowing good and evil. (Genesis 3:5)

Francis A. Schaeffer explains the implications of the fall and man's rebellion:

> The basic position of man in rebellion against God
> is that man is at the centre of the universe, that he is
> autonomous, here lies his rebellion. Man will keep

his rationalism and his rebellion, his insistence on
total autonomy or partially autonomous areas, even
if it means he must give up his rationality.

Francis A. Schaeffer, *Escape From Reason* (Downers
Grove: IVP, 1968), p. 42.

Why fallen rebellious man cannot find the truth on his own:

The intellect of fallen man may, as such, be keen
enough. It may be compared to a buzz-saw that is
sharp and shining, ready to cut the boards that
come to it. Let us say that a carpenter wishes to
cut fifty boards for the purpose of laying the floor
of a house. He has marked his boards. He has set
his saw. He begins at one end of the mark on the
boards. But he does not know that his seven year
old son has tampered with the saw and changed
its set. The result is that every board he saws is
cut slantwise and thus unusable because [it is] too
short except at the point where the saw first made
its contact with the wood. So also whenever the
teachings of Christianity are presented to the natural man they will be cut according to the set of sinful human personality. The result is they may have
formal understanding of the truth, mere cognition
[mental perception] but no true knowledge of God.

Cornelius Van Til, *Defense of the Faith* (New Jersey:
Presbyterian & Reformed Publishing Company), p.74.

As we can see from Van Til, the result of man attempting to be as God is that man sees himself as
the ultimate reference point for interpreting all of life. He attempts to interpret and gives meaning to all facts and to what is true and untrue. This is what Genesis is saying "ye shall be as gods,
knowing good and evil" (Genesis 3:5). This is great idolatry!

If Mormons repent of this great evil of desiring to be their own god, there is hope in Christ. Christ will receive and show great love to sinners who acknowledge their sins and repent by the grace of God. King Solomon wrote under the influence of the Holy Spirit of the great love that reconciled sinners have with Christ.

> The song of songs, which is Solomon's. Let him kiss me with the kisses of his mouth: for your love is better than wine. Because of the smell of your good ointments your name is as ointment poured forth, therefore do the virgins love you. Draw me, we will run after thee: the king hath brought me into his chambers: we will be glad and rejoice in thee, we will remember thy love more than wine: the upright love thee. (Song of Solomon 1:1-4)

J.D. Davies comments on this beautiful section of Scripture explaining God's love in Songs 1:1-4:

> Love's native language is poetry. When strong and happy feeling dominates the soul, it soon bursts into a song. As young life in a fruit tree breaks out into leaf and blossom, so the spiritual force of love unfolds in metaphor and music. Among the lyrics composed by King David, those which celebrate the Messiah-Prince have the richest glory of fervour, blossom most into Oriental imagery; and inasmuch as Solomon inherited somewhat the poetic genius of his father, it was natural that he should pour out in mystic song the heart throb of a nation's hopes. The deep and inseparable union between Christ and his saints is by no one set forth so clearly as by Jesus the Christ; hence love is strong and tender, because love's Object is noble, winsome, kingly, Divine.
>
> *The Pulpit Commentary* (Electronic Database).

Paul, writing to Onesimus concerning Philemon, also provides the grounds that Mormons can be recipients of God's grace:

> For perhaps he therefore departed for a season, that you should receive him for ever; Not now as a servant, but above a servant, a brother beloved, specially to me, but how much more unto thee, both in the flesh, and in the Lord? (Philemon 1:15-16)

The great Puritan Scholar John Gill notes this certainty:

> Thou shouldest receive him for ever; or during life, referring to the law in Exodus 21:6 or to all eternity, since they were in the same spiritual relation, partakers of the same grace, and had a right to the same heavenly inheritance, and should be together with Christ for evermore.
>
> John Gill, *Exposition of the Old and New Testaments, Philemon* (Grace Works, Multi-Media Labs, 2011), p. 14.

My final plea to the Mormon people is best said by Matthew Henry, commenting on 3rd John 1:9-12:

> Both the heart and mouth must be watched. The temper and spirit of Diotrephes was full of pride and ambition. It is bad not to do good ourselves; but it is worse to hinder those who would do good. Those cautions and counsels are most likely to be accepted, which are seasoned with love. Follow that which is good, for he that doeth good, as delighting therein, is born of God. Evil-workers vainly pretend or boast acquaintance with God. Let us not follow that which is proud, selfish, and of bad design, though the example may be given by persons of rank and power; but let us be followers of God, and walk in love, after the example of our Lord.

Matthew Henry's *Concise Commentary, 3 John* pp. 2075, 2076

And we agree with the apostle John when he says:

> Beloved, follow not that which is evil, but that which is good. He that doeth good is of God: but he that doeth evil hath not seen God. (3 John 1:11)

Consider the following explosive sexual-logistical math problem for Mormon theology's celestial-corporeal finite gods:

A r*eductio ad absurdum:*

According to Mormon theology, every person on this earth lived as spirit children prior to coming to this earth and were the product of the Mormon corporeal-finite god and his wives through sexual procreation. The Mormon god and his wives must have had lots of heavenly, celestial sex in order to produce the billions of spirit children who eventually come to live on this earth.

The Mormon god is an exalted man with a body that can only be in one place at a time. The Mormon god exists in the space-time continuum. The time clock turns for the Mormon god like it does for all humans. This means the Mormon god is governed by a 24-hour day. How does the Mormon god have sex to produce children? From the following quote by a Mormon apostle, the process appears to be no different than regular human sexual relations.

Mormon apostle Bruce R. McConkie gives us this information on Christ's birth:

> Christ was begotten by an immortal Father in the same way that mortal men are begotten by mortal fathers.

> McConkie, *Mormon Doctrine* p. 547.

For the sake of argument, let's assume counting the current population of the earth and all persons who have ever lived would total around 10 billion. Let's assume the Mormon god has 1000 wives and the sexual procreation process from inception to birth of the spirit child would just take one day instead of nine months. How much time would the Mormon god have to visit his 1000 wives individually within a 24 period to procreate spirit children? Unfortunately for the Mormon god, he would only have 1 minute and 26 seconds per visit with each of his goddess wives.

The Mormon god would be very busy in order to procreate 1000 spirit babies per day. How long would it take the Mormon god to produce 10 billion spirit babies? With the Mormon god working overtime, it would take billions of years. At any rate, the term 'sexually active' takes on a whole new meaning for Mormonism's sexually active, procreating gods. The celestial kingdom for Mormonism would literally have to be non-stop sex. "Move over *HIMEROS*, there is a new god in town."

Jesus said:

> For in the resurrection they neither marry, nor are given in marriage, but are as the angels of God in heaven. (Matthew 22:30)

When men reject the God of Scripture, they often end up believing all kinds of fantastical absurdities like the above math problems illustrates.

RECOMMENDED
READING

CRITICAL ANALYSIS
OF MORMONISM

Jerald and Sandra Tanner
Mormonism Shadow or Reality
Utah Lighthouse Ministry, Salt Lake City

Richard Abanes
One Nation Under Gods: A History of the Mormon Church
Basic Books, New York/ London

Alvin Schmidt
Joseph Smith, Founder of Mormonism
Concordia Publishing House, St. Louis, MO

Charles M. Larson
...by his own hand upon papyrus
Institute for Religious Research, Grand Rapids, MI

Stan Larson
Quest For The Gold Plates
Freethinker Press, Salt Lake City

John L. Brooke
The Refiner's Fire: The Making of Mormon Cosmology
Cambridge University Press, Cambridge

Beckwith, Mosser, Owen
The New Mormon Challenge
Zondervan, Grand Rapids, MI

Simon G. Southerton
Losing a Lost Tribe: Native Americans, DNA, and the Mormon Church
Signature Books, Salt Lake City

Brent Lee Metcalfe, editor
New Approaches to the Book of Mormon
Signature Books, Salt Lake City

David Whitmer
An Address To All Believers In Christ
Richmond, Missouri: 1887, reprinted by Pacific Publishing Company

H. Michael Marquardt & Wesley P. Walters
Inventing Mormonism
Smith Research Associates, Salt Lake City

LaMar Petersen
The Creation Of The Book Of Mormon: A Historical Inquiry
Freethinker Press, Salt Lake City

David A. Reed and John R. Farkas
Mormons Answered Verse by Verse
Baker Book House, Grand Rapids, MI

James R. White
Is The Mormon My Brother?
Bethany House Publishers, Minneapolis, MN

CHRISTIAN
THEOLOGY

J. Gresham Machen
The Virgin Birth of Christ
Attic Press, Greenwood, S.C.

Gordon H. Clark
The Bible and Its Critics
Trinity, Jefferson, Maryland

Keith A. Mathison
The Shape Of Sola Scriptura
Canon Press, Moscow, Idaho

David T. King
Holy Scripture: The Ground and Pillar of Our Faith, Vol. 1
Christian Resources Inc., Battle Ground, WA

William Webster
Holy Scripture: The Ground and Pillar of Our Faith, Vol. 2
Christian Resources Inc., Battle Ground, WA

David T. King and William Webster
Scripture: The Ground and Pillar of Our Faith, Vol. 3
Christian Resources Inc., Battle Ground, WA,

Benjamin B. Warfield
The Inspiration And Authority Of The Bible
Presbyterian and Reformed Publishing Company, Phillipsburg, New Jersey

Benjamin B. Warfield

The Person And Work Of Christ

Presbyterian and Reformed Publishing Company, Phillipsburg, New Jersey

John Calvin

Institutes of the Christian Religion Vol. 1-2

Westminster Press, Philadelphia, PA

Francis Turretin

Institutes of Elenctic Theology Vol. 1-3

Presbyterian & Reformed Publishing Company, Phillipsburg, New Jersey

James Bannerman

The Church Of Christ Vol. 1-2

Still Waters Revival Books, St. Edmonton, AB Canada

William Symington

Messiah the Prince

Still Waters Revival Books, St. Edmonton, AB Canada

Harold O.J. Brown

Heresies: The Image of Christ in the Mirror of Heresy and Orthodoxy from the Apostles to the Present Doubleday, & Company, Garden City, New York

Louis Berkhof

Systematic Theology

Eerdmans, Grand Rapids, MI

Charles Hodge

Systematic Theology Vol. 1-3

Eerdmans, Grand Rapids, MI

Douglas F. Kelly
Systematic Theology Volume One
The God Who Is: The Holy Trinity
Systematic Theology Volume Two
The Beauty Of Christ: A Trinitarian Vision
Christian Focus Publications, Scotland, Great Britain

G.K. Beale and D. A. Carson
Commentary on the New Testament Use of the Old Testament
Baker Academic, Grand Rapids Michigan
Christian Eschatology

Kenneth L. Gentry, Jr.
Before Jerusalem Fell: Dating the Book of Revelation
Institute for Christian Economics, Tyler, TX

Kenneth L. Gentry, Jr.
He Shall Have Dominion
Institute for Christian Economics, Tyler, TX

Charles E. Hill
Regnum Caelorum: Patterns of Future Hope in Early Christianity
Clarendon Press, Clarendon Press, Oxford

Oswald T. Allis
Prophecy And The Church
Presbyterian & Reformed Publishing Company, Phillipsburg, New Jersey

Gary DeMar
Last Days Madness
American Vision, Powder Springs, Georgia

Keith A. Mathison
Postmillennialism An eschatology of Hope
Presbyterian and Reformed Publishing Company, Phillipsburg, New Jersey

R. C. Sproul
The Last Days According To Jesus
Baker Books, Grand Rapids, MI

Greg L. Bahnsen
Victory In Jesus: The Bright Hope of Postmillennialism
Covenant Media Press, Tyler, TX

CHRISTIAN
SOERIOLOGY

Martin Luther
The Bondage of the Will
Fleming H. Revell Company, Old Tappan, New Jersey

Loraine Boettner
The Reformed Doctrine of Predestination
Presbyterian and Reformed Publishing Company, Phillipsburg, New Jersey

Thomas R. Schreiner and Bruce A. Ware, Editors
The Grace of God and The Bondage of the Will Vol. 1-2
Baker Books, Grand Rapids, MI

John Gill
The Cause Of God & Truth
Baker Books, Grand Rapids, MI

D.N. Steele, C.C. Thomas & S.L. Quinn
The Five Points of Calvinism
Presbyterian & Reformed Publishing Company, Phillipsburg, New Jersey

Abraham Kuyper
Lectures on Calvinism
Eerdmans, Grand Rapids, MI

John Calvin
The Bondage and Liberation of the Will
Baker Books, Grand Rapids, MI

Saint Augustine
Answer to the Pelagians III
New City Press, Hyde Park, New York

MORMON SOURCES

D. Michael Quinn (Excommunicated Mormon)
Early Mormonism and the Magic World View
Signature Books, Salt Lake City

B. H. Roberts
Studies of the Book of Mormon
University of Illinois Press, Urbana and Chicago

R. Merle Fowler
Joseph Smith and his Royal Lineage: a Blood Descendant of Jesus Christ
Fowler and Advance Press

Editor, Daniel H. Ludlow
Encyclopedia Of Mormonism, Vol. 1-4
Macmillan Publishing, Company, New York

MAJOR MORMON QUOTES SOURCE

Joseph Smith, the *Book of Mormon* (Salt Lake City: The Church of Jesus Christ of Latter-Day Saints, 1977).

Joseph Smith, *Doctrine And Covenants* (Salt Lake City: The Church of Jesus Christ of Latter-Day Saints, 1977).

Joseph Smith, *Pearl Of Great Price* (Salt Lake City: The Church of Jesus Christ of Latter-Day-Saints, 1977).

Joseph Smith, *History of the Church* Volumes 1-6, (Salt Lake City: Deseret Book Company 1978).

Joseph Smith, *The Teachings of the Prophet Joseph Smith* Arranged by Joseph F. Smith, (Salt Lake City: Deseret Book Company, 1976).

James E. Talmage, *Articles Of Faith* (Salt Lake City, Deseret Book Co. 1988).

Joseph Fielding Smith, *Doctrines of Salvation* Vol. 1-3, (Salt Lake City: Bookcraft, 1990).

LeGrand Richards, *A Marvelous Work And A Wonder* (Salt Lake City, Deseret Book Co. 1978).

Milton R. Hunter, *The Gospel Thru The Ages* (Salt Lake City: Deseret Book Company, 1957).

Bruce R. McConkie, *Mormon Doctrine* (Salt Lake City: Bookcraft, 1979).

Joseph Smith, Brigham Young, Orson Pratt, Wilford Woodruff, *Journal of Discourses* Vol. 1-26, (Liverpool, England: Asa Calkin, 1854-1886).

Orson Pratt, *The Seer* (Salt Lake City: Eborn Books, 1990).

W. Cleon Skousen, *The First 2000 Years* (Salt Lake City, Bookcraft, 1991).

TOPICAL INDEX

SCRIPTURE INDEX BY BOOK

Mark 15:38 - 250

Personal Notes

Q: What is the chief end of man?

A: Man's chief end is to glorify God, (1)http://www.shortercatechism.com/resources/wsc/wsc_001.html - 1 **and to enjoy him forever. (2)**

(1) 1st Corinthians 10:31 - Whether therefore ye eat, or drink, or whatsoever ye do, do all to the glory of God. Romans 11:36 - For of him, and through him, and to him, are all things: to whom be glory for ever. Amen.

(2) Psalm 73:24-26 - Thou shalt guide me with thy counsel, and afterward receive me to glory. Whom have I in heaven but thee? and there is none upon earth that I desire beside thee. My flesh and my heart faileth: but God isthe strength of my heart, and my portion for ever. John 17:22, 24. And the glory which thou gavest me I have given them; that they may be one, even as we are one... Father, I will that they also, whom thou hast given me, be with me where I am; that they may behold my glory, which thou hast given me: for thou lovedst me before the foundation of the world.

Personal Notes

Question 24. How doth Christ execute the office of a prophet?

Answer 24. Christ executeth the office of a prophet, in revealing to us, by his word and Spirit, the will of God for our salvation. (1)

(1) John 1:18; I Peter 1:10-12; John 15:15; 20:31.

Personal Notes

Q. 25. How doth Christ execute the office of a priest?

A. Christ executeth the office of a priest, in his once offering up of himself a sacrifice to satisfy divine justice, (68) and reconcile us to God, (69) and in making continual intercession for us. (70)

(68) Isaiah 53; Acts 8:32-35; Hebrews 9:26-28; Hebrews 10:12

(69) Romans 5:10-11; 2 Corinthians 5:18; Colossians 1:21-2

(70) Romans 8:34; Hebrews 7:25; Hebrews 9:24

Personal Notes

Question 26. How doth Christ execute the office of a king?

Answer 26. Christ executeth the office of a king, in subduing us to himself, (1) in ruling (2) and defending us, (3) and in restraining and conquering all his and our enemies. (4)

(1) Acts 15:14-16. (2) Isa. 33:22. (3) Isa. 32:1-2. (4) I Cor. 15:25, Ps. 110.

ACKNOWLEDGMENTS

To my lovely wife Marea who put with me during this project and has never complained about my ever growing home library of over five thousand volumes.

I'm indebted to my proof reading editors, Jeremiah Wood, John Greene, Jude Barton, Nathan Martin and Eva Kettler.

Front and Back Cover Art work by Ron Adair at http://www.RonAdair.com

Special encouragement and ideas from Francis X Gumerlock at http://francisgumerlock.com/

Many thanks to Mike Kluherz who help me start on my Reformed theological journey. If anyone is responsible for my library, it is Mike.

To my dear friends Richard and Zandra Lee who have been the dearest friends. Richard helped me learn the basics of witnessing to Mormons. Richard was trained by Kurt Van Gordon at the time, founder of Practical, Apologetics, and Christian Evangelism (PACE)

To the pastor and ruling elders at Westminster Presbyterian Church (RPCNA) for their prayers and support http://www.westminsterrpchurch.org/

"To God only wise, be glory through Jesus Christ for ever. Amen" (Romans 16:27). "heirs according to the promise" (Galatians 3:28-29). Amen!

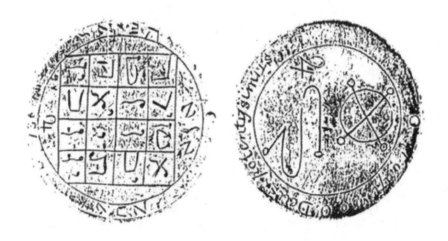

Photo of Joseph Smith's Jupiter talisman (both sides) from *Mormonism, Magic and Masonry.* D. Michael Quinn's book, *Early Mormonism and the Magic World View* also contains photos of Joseph Smith's Jupiter talisman.